SHILOH
1862

Also by Winston Groom

Nonfiction

Shrouds of Glory (1995)

The Crimson Tide (2002)

A Storm in Flanders (2002)

1942 (2004)

Patriotic Fire (2006)

Vicksburg, 1863 (2009)

Kearny's March (2011)

Novels

Better Times Than These (1978)

As Summers Die (1980)

Conversations with the Enemy (1982, with Duncan Spencer)

Only (1984, novel)

Forrest Gump (1986)

Gone the Sun (1988)

Gump and Co. (1995)

Such a Pretty, Pretty Girl (1998)

SHILOH
1862

Winston Groom

NATIONAL GEOGRAPHIC

WASHINGTON, D.C.

Published by the National Geographic Society
1145 17th Street N.W., Washington, D.C. 20036

ISBN: 978-1-4262-0874-4
ISBN: 978-1-4262-0982-6 (deluxe edition)

The National Geographic Society is one of the world's largest nonprofit scientific and
educational organizations. Founded in 1888 to "increase and diffuse geographic knowledge,"
the Society's mission is to inspire people to care about the planet. It reaches more than 400
million people worldwide each month through its official journal, *National Geographic,* and
other magazines; National Geographic Channel; television documentaries; music; radio;
films; books; DVDs; maps; exhibitions; live events; school publishing programs; interac-
tive media; and merchandise. National Geographic has funded more than 9,600 scientific
research, conservation and exploration projects and supports an education program promot-
ing geographic literacy.

For more information, visit www.nationalgeographic.com

National Geographic Society
1145 17th Street N.W.
Washington, D.C. 20036-4688 U.S.A.

For information about special discounts for bulk purchases, please contact
National Geographic Books Special Sales: ngspecsales@ngs.org

For rights or permissions inquiries, please contact National Geographic Books
Subsidiary Rights: ngbookrights@ngs.org

Interior design: Cameron Zotter

Printed in the United States of America

12/RRDC-CML/1

*To Len Riedel, without whom the
Civil War would never be the same.*

For Romans, in Rome's Quarrel,
Spared neither land nor gold.
Nor son nor wife, nor limb nor life,
In the brave old days of old.

—THOMAS BABINGTON MACAULAY
from "Horatius" (1842), on civil war

CONTENTS

Author's Note

T HE BATTLE OF SHILOH, ALSO KNOWN AS PITTSBURG Landing, has intrigued me since my first encounters with Civil War history, but for years I viewed it mostly as some great chunk of pandemonium obscured within the fog of war. More recently, as I began to engross myself in the literature of the battle, what struck me hard was its enormity, its ferocity, and most of all its disorder. As I suspected, it was not an easy story to tell.

My first book of Civil War history sixteen years ago was *Shrouds of Glory*, about the fateful Battle of Nashville toward the end of the war, which grew, of course, out of the Battle of Atlanta, with Shiloh hovering in the background. After that I wrote about World War I, World War II, and the Battle of New Orleans during the War of 1812 before returning to the Civil War in an account of the Battle of Vicksburg. Many of the same characters who began their Civil War combat careers at Shiloh fought on against one another at Vicksburg,

Atlanta, Franklin, and Nashville. For a writer or historian it is both fascinating and astonishing to watch as these reappearing notables are fired, promoted, killed off, celebrated, or removed. The Rebel generals Hardee, Forrest, Wheeler, A. P. Stewart, and Govan come to mind, and Sherman, Grant, and McClernand on the Union side. A. S. Johnston, Polk, Cleburne, and McPherson died on the field. The names drift past, familiar faces and personalities who from time to time inhabited my stories. Each got his start at Shiloh.

Shiloh was different from most large Civil War conflicts in that once the soldiers entered the chaotic terrain of Pittsburg Landing, control became nearly impossible and the battle largely broke down into individual fights between regiments, of which there were some 170 involved.

Some very good historians have attempted to chronicle the battle at this level, and several, noted in my acknowledgments at the end of this book, have been successful. They detail the fighting almost moment to moment on all parts of the field, during all times of the day, quoting manifold sources to frame their narrative. I chose not to try to unravel it that way—first, because it had been done, and second, because I thought I saw a different way to present the essence of the Battle of Shiloh to readers who are not necessarily the kind of Civil War buffs who dote on every minute detail and technical aspect.

There were more than 100,000 soldiers fighting in the 12 square miles that constituted Pittsburg Landing, and every one of them who survived had a story to tell. A great many told it—in books, memoirs, diaries, letters, and other mediums of the day. There are thousands of accounts available through many venues, and I probably went through most of these.

Afterward, it became my thought to tell a good part of this story through the eyes of just a score or so of these participants. I tried to pick sophisticated observers as they endured the battle and the repercussions from it. Foremost, I chose the good writers, and I weighed heavily on what seemed to be the honesty of their accounts. Ambrose Bierce, for instance, who fought for the Union, became one of America's most well read authors. Henry Morton Stanley, a Confederate soldier, was later celebrated worldwide for his accounts of exploits in Africa and elsewhere. Others became popular journalists, and still others were simply good diarists or memoirists.

I hope the reader likes this approach. I did, as I wrote it, because it seemed that these observers worked their way at length into the inner seams of the story of Shiloh and propelled it along as the drama unfolded.

In all my previous histories—from the War of 1812 to World War II—I have noted the presence of a direct relative involved in the action. My great-great-great-grandfather, for example, fought in the Battle of New Orleans in 1815 and was promoted from captain to major by Andrew Jackson himself. My grandfather fought in World War I, and my father served in World War II, and blood relatives also served in the Confederate cavalry during the Civil War. It almost sounds as though we are a family of military people, but we are not; America's wars just fell at the right (or wrong) age for the men, including me, who had just graduated from college with a second lieutenant's commission in 1965 when Vietnam broke out in earnest.

Alas, neither the 56th Alabama Cavalry of my maternal great-grandfather Fremont Sterling Thrower nor the Fourth Mississippi

Cavalry of my great-great-grandfather James Wright Groom were at the Shiloh battle. Apparently these units had not yet been organized in April of 1862, when the fighting broke out, though they were present at Vicksburg, Atlanta, and other campaigns. It always lent a sense of immediacy and distinction to the story to know that I had a relative in the action, and after a while it began to bother me that one day I'd likely write a book of military history with no ancestral connections. Well, here it is, and here I am, and so far as I can tell I don't think it has hurt the telling of the tale. Besides, I'll bet those grandfathers at least *knew* people who were at Shiloh.

Point Clear, Alabama
November 1, 2011

Prologue

⊰◆⊱

THE BATTLE OF SHILOH ON APRIL 6 AND 7, 1862, was the first great and terrible battle of the Civil War and the one that set the stage for those to come. It was so bloody and destructive that in many cases soldiers writing home simply could not find words to describe it. "I cannot bring myself to tell you of the things I saw upon yesterday," wrote one man, or, another, "The scenes of the past few days beggar description." Anyone who has seen the violence and death of battle, who has experienced the horrors of war, will understand a person's reluctance to revisit it, to reengage their feelings in it, but Shiloh elicited a particularly strong response.

One of the early chroniclers of the battle, the historian Otto Eisenschiml, wrote, "I consider Shiloh the most dramatic battle ever fought on American soil; if not the most dramatic battle ever fought anywhere. True, Gettysburg was bigger; Vicksburg was more decisive; Antietam even more bloody, but no other battle was interwoven with so many momentous *ifs*. If any of these *ifs* had gone the other way, it would have had incalculable consequences."

Since the beginning of the war, everyone knew that a big battle in the West was inevitable, even if they did not know where or when. But in early 1862 when Ulysses Grant took an army up the Tennessee River it was apparent that the Confederates could not tolerate this intrusion, and as the months passed by both armies began to build strength. The stakes were enormous—control of the Mississippi River Valley, the heart of the Confederacy.

By the time the Civil War broke out, great advances in weaponry had been made in both artillery and small arms, but both complex strategies and, more important, the field tactics used to carry them out remained Napoleonic, meaning they were outmoded by nearly 50 years. Thus large columns of infantry again and again were needlessly and recklessly exposed to the worst kind of close-on slaughter (there is no other word for it). Nor had medicine made any appreciable inroads other than the invention of crude anesthesia that was often unavailable. The result was a ruthless battlefield butchery almost unimaginable at that day and time. Americans, for instance, suffered more casualties in the daylong fight at Shiloh than all of the casualties during the American Revolution, the War of 1812, and the Mexican War *combined*.

The battle was fought on some of the worst imaginable terrain, at least for those on the attack, a site chosen almost by accident— thick, brushy oak and other hardwood forests cut up with ridges, deep ravines, and miry swamps that made control of troops problematical if not impossible. In this small, mean patch of ground in the far southwest corner of Tennessee near the Mississippi border, the Tennessee River hemmed in the battlefield to the east, while the deep, moccasin-infested morass of Owl and Snake Creeks defined the western boundary. There were few cleared areas—farm fields of perhaps 40 acres, or clearings carved out by Indians in earlier times, or natural-made openings created in the past by the violent tornadoes that often tore through that section of the country. Confederate troops on the attack would have to cross these open fields, while Union defenders often had an advantage of being able to hide in the wooded edges, clumped around artillery pieces, the mobility of which, for both sides, presented stern battlefield challenges.

And what of the troops of these two great armies soon to form and fight here? At Shiloh, so early in the war, the vast majority of the soldiers were completely green. Some had never fired their rifles; some had never even been taught to load their rifles; some in fact had no rifles at all. A day before the battle, a Texas regiment unpacked the trunks containing its clothing and discovered, to its horror, that the quartermaster had given them uniforms that were completely white. "It was like wearing your own shroud!" one of the Texans complained. An outfit of Louisiana Confederates went into the battle wearing their prewar state-issue militia uniforms, which were blue, and consequently they were shot down by their own side.

The officers were likewise untested. With the exception of Ulysses Grant and several of his brigades that had recently stood some combat downriver, few on either side had heard a shot fired in anger except some of the older men during the war with Mexico in 1846. With the Civil War still young, even many regimental officers on both sides offered themselves up as unmistakable targets by riding their horses into battle within clear range of enemy fire. There were West Point graduates in both armies, but most of the senior and practically all of the junior officers were, until recently, civilians, whose only experience was with their hometown guard or militia. A considerable number of these turned out to be lawyers, who tended to insist that everything be put down in writing.

Grant himself was an enigmatic study, as we shall see, undistinguished, accused of dereliction, and certainly at that point an unlikely candidate for command of such an important army in such an important battle, which was viewed far and wide in the North as a great showdown, the battle that would end the war. There was some justification for this notion, since if the Rebel army was destroyed at Shiloh there would be nothing between the South and ruin. Federal forces so deep in Confederate territory would have had their choice of which Southern cities and capitals to capture or destroy before marching east to converge on Richmond, then in the early stages of a siege by George McClellan's Army of the Potomac.

Apart from the horror, "confusion" might be the most accurate description applied to the battle itself. The Confederates were confused simply getting to the battlefield, struggling in violent rainstorms along roads that were barely ruts in the ground, and wondering once they arrived if the enemy was not alerted and waiting for them, as in a trap. The Yankees, for the most part, were blissfully unaware that a great Rebel army had come out of its lair seeking a war of annihilation. In the case of commander Grant, it was the first and, essentially, the last time he was ever surprised in battle.

Many of the soldiers, on both sides, had come "to see the elephant," a quaint expression of the times that implied confronting something novel, huge, and terrible—something few if any of them had seen before. It was a lively turn of phrase with grave implications.

All battles are tragic. The larger the battle, the greater the tragedy. And Shiloh ranks high on the list of the largest Civil War
engagements. In human suffering it left many widows and orphans
and mothers to weep. It almost on its own account changed the
mind-set of the military, the politicians, and the American people—
North and South—regarding what they had unleashed in creating a
civil war.

In the months before war came, many in Congress and elsewhere had predicted a future "drenched in blood." Yet few, it
seemed, had actually believed or fully understood their rhetoric.
Most Americans thought that if it came to blows, a relatively small
fight or two would settle the thing, and life would return to normal. They simply could not comprehend a European-style conflict
here in America, complete with "terrible armies with banners."

But that is precisely what they got. Twenty years of unabated
name-calling and hatred building had created a generation of young
men who could be turned into raw killers—a recipe for tragedy. Shiloh was an early, stark, and frightening symbol of it, and rather than
a finale that finished the war quickly the battle ended in cataclysmic
failure on both sides. True, the North still held the ground, but only
by an eyelash, and everyone knew it. Even Grant now conceded that
the only way to restore the Union was by the total subjugation of the
South—a colossal undertaking.

For their part, the Southern fire-eaters were forced to admit that
one Confederate soldier could not, in fact, lick ten Yankees and,
more ominously, that those selfsame Yankees remained deep in
Dixieland, a new and undeniable menace.

As for the men—not just the soldiers, but the ranking officers,
and the politicians, and the editors and stump speakers, the pulpit

preachers, and the eggers-on from all over the land—when the results of Shiloh were in they, too, had at last "seen the elephant" and were alarmed by what they saw, because their neat, easy plans now lay askew. Far from being over, the Civil War, it seemed, had barely gotten under way.

A Note on Weapons, Tactics, Units, and Military Customs—1862

———◆◆———

A RMIES OF THE MID-19TH CENTURY WERE GENERALLY organized on the Napoleonic model, and for purposes of command and control were broken down into the following units, with many variations, depending on manpower, including absences from illness, casualties, and other causes, details, and the like.

Company 100 men composed of squads and platoons, commanded by a captain

Regiment (ten companies) 1,000 men, commanded by a colonel

Brigade (four to six regiments) 4,000 men, commanded by a brigadier general

Division (three or four brigades) 12,000 men, commanded by a major general

Army Corps (three to six divisions) 36,000 to 72,000 men, commanded by a lieutenant general

Army several corps 100,000 men and more, commanded by a full general*

Rarely, if ever, did either army in the Civil War reach the full manpower of this table of organization, often lucky to have half the numbers shown here when going into battle.

On the battlefield, the regiment was the basic unit of maneuver. It had its own colors (distinctive flag) and, in many Northern units, badges or other insignia that were worn on caps.

At the Shiloh stage of the war most men were volunteers. Many had had training in their hometown militia but most had not. Later in the war both sides conscripted men, with dubious results.

Artillery was broken down into batteries of four to six guns each; in Confederate armies it was usually assigned at the brigade level, but Union armies assigned it to divisions. Artillery was rated by the weight of the iron shot that each piece fired (i.e., 6-pounder gun, 12-pounder gun, 32-pounder gun, etc.) or by the diameter of its barrel (i.e., 6-inch gun, 8-inch gun, 10-inch gun, etc.). The most popular weapon during the first two years of the war was the 6-pounder smoothbore (served by a five-man crew), which was later replaced by the 12-pounder bronze "Napoleon" (served by a nine-man crew), with an effective range of more than a mile. At Shiloh the two armies had 235 cannons of various sizes divided about equally between them.

Infantry drill was not merely the quaint parade field formality that it has become in the military today but a dead-earnest part of

---

* Occasionally, there would be separate battalion-size units of 400 or 500 men, about half as large as regiments, usually connected to state or local militia.

19th-century warfare. When troops weren't marching, fighting, or performing other duties they were drilling—half steps, step and a halfs, right wheels, obliques, close file, about-face, left flank, right flank, left wheel, right wheel, at ease, at rest, and dozens more commands all orchestrated and anticipated to be executed dainty as a French minuet. In major army movements, such as at Shiloh where thousands of men marched shoulder to shoulder to mass their fire on an enemy, they were expected to arrive at a precise point at a precise moment in order to produce the desired effect. The slightest variation in terrain—such as we shall see at Shiloh: a swamp or stream, bramble thicket, hidden gully, even a fallen tree—could throw the plan out of whack, so attention to marching orders was paramount.

At Shiloh and elsewhere, the firepower of an assault could be stunning. The principal infantry weapon of the Union army was the .58-caliber Springfield with an effective rage of 500 yards (at 200 yards—twice the length of a football field—it could drill a hold through an 11-inch pine plank).

Confederate infantry were usually equipped with the .577-caliber British Enfield rifle, with similar characteristics. During battle infantry soldiers had an effective aimed firing rate of three rounds per minute, so that in the full fury of an assault, such as at Shiloh, it would not be inconceivable that during any given minute on the battlefield some 50,000 to 100,000 deadly projectiles would be ripping through the air toward flesh and bone. The weight and size of the bullet, even as it hit a hand or foot, was sufficient to disable a man.

Medicine had progressed very slowly from the days of the American Revolution. Antibiotics were in the future, and the raw power of a bullet striking a limb invariably brought on gas gangrene, an infection usually caused by germs and filth on the clothing being driven into the wound. This could be deadly within a few days, and it was common medical practice to amputate limbs that had been struck to spare a patient's life.

Artillery pieces had developed considerably since Napoleonic days. Ammunition was divided into *shot,* a large, spherical solid iron ball, and *shell,* a hollow iron ball filled with gunpowder and fused to explode in front of, or above, an enemy formation, flinging deadly pieces of metal shrapnel as it burst into pieces. For "close range work" cannons could be loaded with *case, canister,* or *grape-shot,* all of which sprayed out lethal iron balls, and sometimes the guns were loaded with whatever else was available, including nails, nuts, bolts, pieces of chain—even rocks. Artillery was especially feared by the troops because of its shock value and ghastly effects.

The bayonet, which in many Civil War rifles was attached to the barrel, was then considered an extraordinary weapon, supposed to put a singular type of fear and loathing into the hearts of the enemy for it carried with it the likely prospect of hand-to-hand combat, with all of its dreadful implications.

Among all the noises of the battlefield, the drum stands out as one of the most peculiar and alarming. Drummers, or drummer boys, were attached to each rifle company, and were principally employed to keep cadence while marching. But the drums were also used for signaling such things as "assembly" (the "long roll"), "attack," "retreat," "chow," "officers' call," and similar messages in camp or on the battlefield.* Drummer boys, some as young as ten years old but most in their teens, were often on the field during a

---

* The cavalry used the bugle for these signaling messages.

fight, and sometimes as an inevitable result were wounded or killed. The sound of the drum on the battlefield had been used for several hundred years to disturb and unnerve the enemy, similar to the hair-raising buzz of the rattlesnake's tail.

"Colors," consisting of national, state, divisional, and regimental flags, were a military tradition that inspired profound and intense feeling among the soldiers. From the beginning of their training the men were taught that these symbols were sacred and to be protected at all costs. The flags were made of the best silks, embroidered with delicate braids of real gold by the ladies of the various towns or counties where regiments were raised. To lose one's colors in battle was to lose one's pride and, as we soon shall see, many a soldier in the Civil War fell guarding them with his life.

Quite a few Civil War generals experienced the Mexican War and, in theory, idealized the military tactics set forth by the French military philosopher Antoine-Henri Jomini, which stressed maneuver rather than frontal attacks. But at Shiloh, as elsewhere, this proved to be mostly lip service, at least by the Confederate leaders who, because the terrain was so dense and uneven, quickly adopted the famous advice of Napoleon's grand marshal Étienne Maurice Gérard at the Battle of Waterloo and "marched to the sound of the guns."

Maps

—◆—

The
UNITED STATES
in 1862

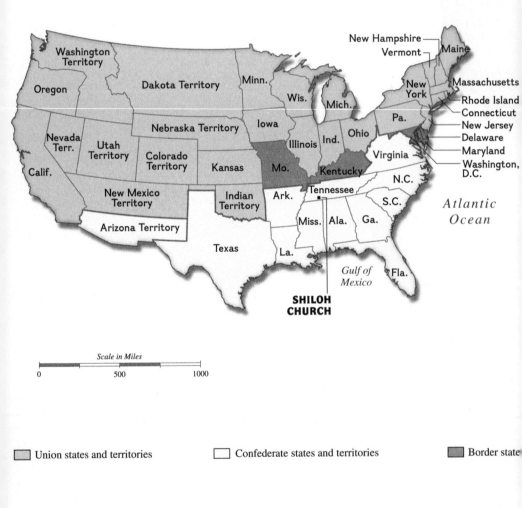

New Hampshire
Vermont
Maine
Washington Territory
Oregon
Dakota Territory
Minn.
Wis.
Mich.
New York
Massachusetts
Rhode Island
Connecticut
Pa.
New Jersey
Nevada Terr.
Utah Territory
Colorado Territory
Nebraska Territory
Iowa
Illinois
Ind.
Ohio
Delaware
Maryland
Washington, D.C.
Calif.
Kansas
Mo.
Kentucky
Virginia
New Mexico Territory
Indian Territory
Ark.
Tennessee
N.C.
S.C.
Arizona Territory
Miss.
Ala.
Ga.
Atlantic Ocean
Texas
La.
Fla.
Gulf of Mexico
SHILOH CHURCH

Scale in Miles

0   500   1000

☐ Union states and territories   ☐ Confederate states and territories   ▨ Border state

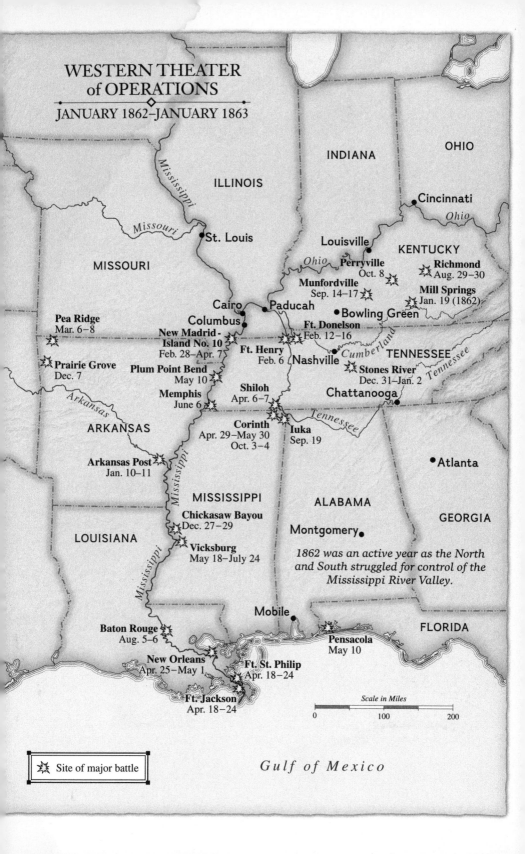

WESTERN THEATER
of OPERATIONS
◇
JANUARY 1862–JANUARY 1863

OHIO

INDIANA

ILLINOIS

Cincinnati

Ohio

Louisville

KENTUCKY

Ohio Perryville
Oct. 8

Richmond
Aug. 29–30

Munfordville
Sep. 14–17

Mill Springs
Jan. 19 (1862)

St. Louis

Missouri

Mississippi

MISSOURI

Cairo

Paducah

Bowling Green

Pea Ridge
Mar. 6–8

Columbus

New Madrid -
Island No. 10
Feb. 28–Apr. 7

Ft. Henry
Feb. 6

Ft. Donelson
Feb. 12–16

Cumberland

Nashville

TENNESSEE

Tennessee

Prairie Grove
Dec. 7

Plum Point Bend
May 10

Stones River
Dec. 31–Jan. 2

Arkansas

Memphis
June 6

Shiloh
Apr. 6–7

Chattanooga

ARKANSAS

Corinth
Apr. 29–May 30
Oct. 3–4

Iuka
Sep. 19

Tennessee

Atlanta

Arkansas Post
Jan. 10–11

Mississippi

MISSISSIPPI

ALABAMA

GEORGIA

Chickasaw Bayou
Dec. 27–29

Montgomery

LOUISIANA

Vicksburg
May 18–July 24

*1862 was an active year as the North
and South struggled for control of the
Mississippi River Valley.*

Mississippi

Mobile

FLORIDA

Baton Rouge
Aug. 5–6

Pensacola
May 10

New Orleans
Apr. 25–May 1

Ft. St. Philip
Apr. 18–24

Ft. Jackson
Apr. 18–24

Scale in Miles

0   100   200

※ Site of major battle

Gulf of Mexico

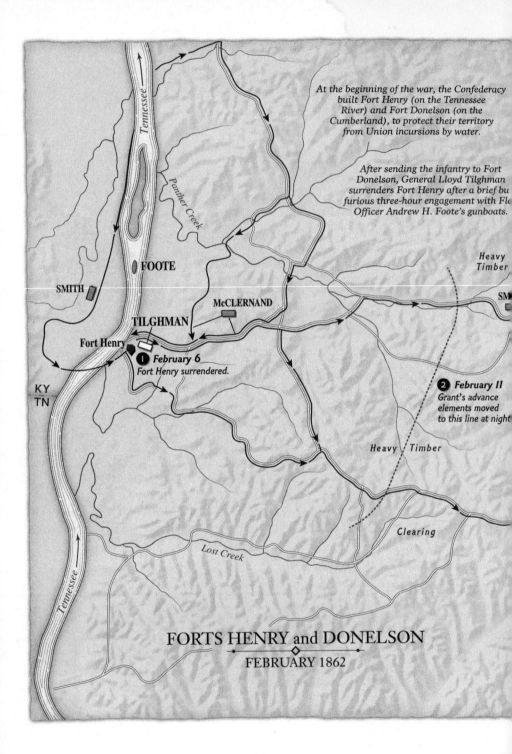

At the beginning of the war, the Confederacy built Fort Henry (on the Tennessee River) and Fort Donelson (on the Cumberland), to protect their territory from Union incursions by water.

After sending the infantry to Fort Donelson, General Lloyd Tilghman surrenders Fort Henry after a brief bu furious three-hour engagement with Flo Officer Andrew H. Foote's gunboats.

Tennessee

Panther Creek

Heavy Timber

FOOTE

SMITH

SM

McCLERNAND

TILGHMAN

Fort Henry

1 *February 6*
Fort Henry surrendered.

KY
TN

2 *February 11*
Grant's advance elements moved to this line at night

Heavy Timber

Clearing

Lost Creek

Tennessee

FORTS HENRY and DONELSON
◆
FEBRUARY 1862

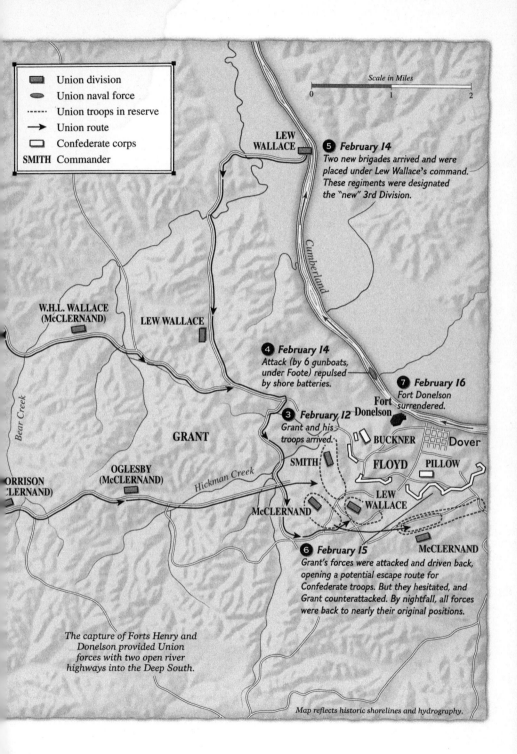

Union division

Union naval force

Union troops in reserve

Union route

Confederate corps

SMITH Commander

Scale in Miles

0   1   2

LEW WALLACE

5 *February 14*
Two new brigades arrived and were placed under Lew Wallace's command. These regiments were designated the "new" 3rd Division.

Cumberland

W.H.L. WALLACE (McCLERNAND)

LEW WALLACE

4 *February 14*
Attack (by 6 gunboats, under Foote) repulsed by shore batteries.

7 *February 16*
Fort Donelson surrendered.

Fort Donelson

3 *February 12*
Grant and his troops arrived.

GRANT

BUCKNER

Dover

SMITH

FLOYD   PILLOW

OGLESBY (McCLERNAND)

Bear Creek

Hickman Creek

ORRISON LERNAND)

LEW WALLACE

McCLERNAND

McCLERNAND

6 *February 15*
Grant's forces were attacked and driven back, opening a potential escape route for Confederate troops. But they hesitated, and Grant counterattacked. By nightfall, all forces were back to nearly their original positions.

The capture of Forts Henry and Donelson provided Union forces with two open river highways into the Deep South.

Map reflects historic shorelines and hydrography.

31

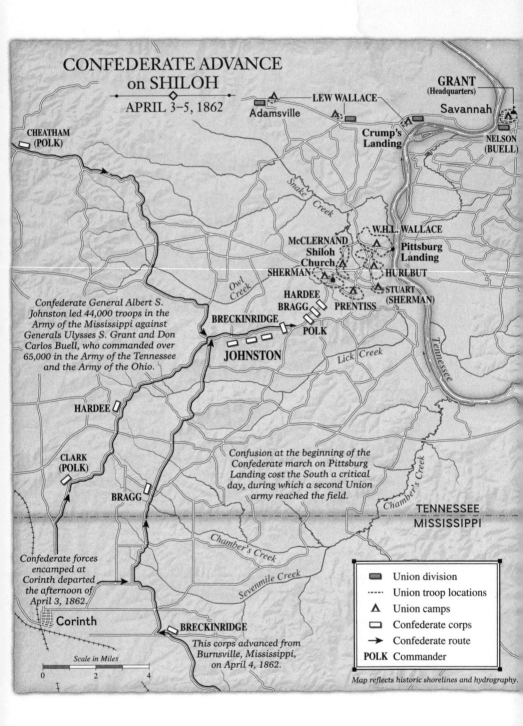

CONFEDERATE ADVANCE
on SHILOH
APRIL 3–5, 1862

LEW WALLACE

Adamsville

GRANT
(Headquarters)

Savannah

Crump's
Landing

CHEATHAM
(POLK)

NELSON
(BUELL)

Snake Creek

W.H.L. WALLACE

McCLERNAND
Shiloh
Church

Pittsburg
Landing

SHERMAN

HURLBUT

Owl Creek

HARDEE
BRAGG

STUART
(SHERMAN)

PRENTISS

Confederate General Albert S. Johnston led 44,000 troops in the Army of the Mississippi against Generals Ulysses S. Grant and Don Carlos Buell, who commanded over 65,000 in the Army of the Tennessee and the Army of the Ohio.

BRECKINRIDGE

POLK

JOHNSTON

Lick Creek

Tennessee

HARDEE

CLARK
(POLK)

Confusion at the beginning of the Confederate march on Pittsburg Landing cost the South a critical day, during which a second Union army reached the field.

Chamber's Creek

BRAGG

TENNESSEE
MISSISSIPPI

Confederate forces encamped at Corinth departed the afternoon of April 3, 1862.

Chamber's Creek

Sevenmile Creek

Corinth

BRECKINRIDGE

This corps advanced from Burnsville, Mississippi, on April 4, 1862.

🔲	Union division
-----	Union troop locations
▲	Union camps
▭	Confederate corps
→	Confederate route
POLK	Commander

Scale in Miles

0   2   4

Map reflects historic shorelines and hydrography.

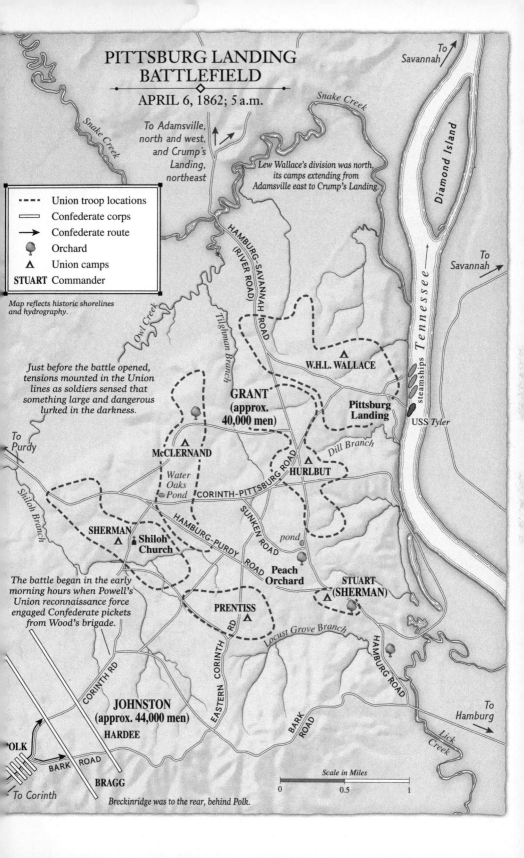

PITTSBURG LANDING
BATTLEFIELD

◆ APRIL 6, 1862; 5 a.m. ◆

To
Savannah

Snake Creek

To Adamsville,
north and west,
and Crump's
Landing,
northeast

*Lew Wallace's division was north,
its camps extending from
Adamsville east to Crump's Landing.*

Snake Creek

Diamond Island

- - - - Union troop locations
▭ Confederate corps
→ Confederate route
🌳 Orchard
△ Union camps
STUART Commander

*Map reflects historic shorelines
and hydrography.*

Owl Creek

HAMBURG-SAVANNAH ROAD
(RIVER ROAD)

Tilghman Branch

To
Savannah

*Just before the battle opened,
tensions mounted in the Union
lines as soldiers sensed that
something large and dangerous
lurked in the darkness.*

W.H.L. WALLACE

GRANT
(approx.
40,000 men)

**Pittsburg
Landing**

To
Purdy

△
McCLERNAND

Water
Oaks
🌳 Pond

Dill Branch

steamships Tennessee

USS *Tyler*

CORINTH-PITTSBURG ROAD

△
HURLBUT

HAMBURG-PURDY ROAD

SUNKEN ROAD

Shiloh Branch

SHERMAN
△ ⛪ **Shiloh
Church**

pond

🌳
**Peach
Orchard**

**STUART
(SHERMAN)**
△

*The battle began in the early
morning hours when Powell's
Union reconnaissance force
engaged Confederate pickets
from Wood's brigade.*

PRENTISS
△

CORINTH RD

EASTERN CORINTH ROAD

Locust Grove Branch

HAMBURG ROAD

🌳

To
Hamburg

JOHNSTON
(approx. 44,000 men)

HARDEE

BARK ROAD

*Lick
Creek*

OLK

BARK ROAD

BRAGG

To Corinth

Breckinridge was to the rear, behind Polk.

Scale in Miles

0   0.5   1

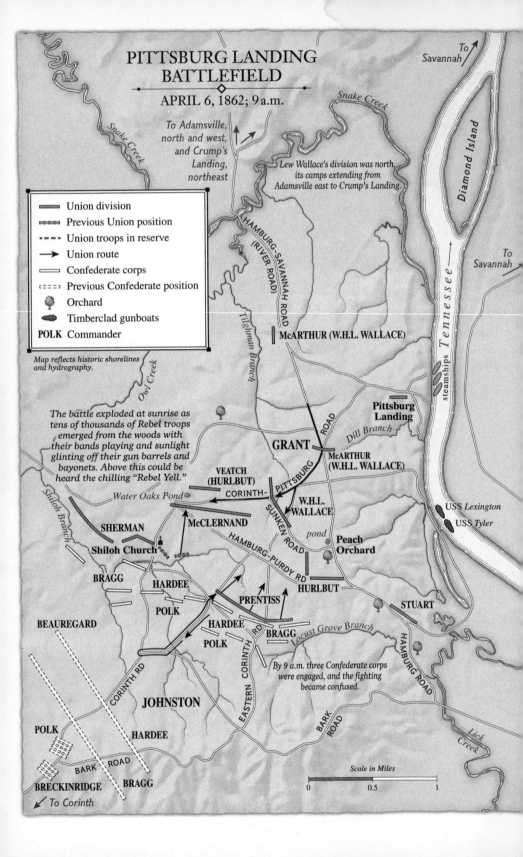

PITTSBURG LANDING
BATTLEFIELD
◆
APRIL 6, 1862; 9 a.m.

Legend:
- Union division
- Previous Union position
- Union troops in reserve
- Union route
- Confederate corps
- Previous Confederate position
- Orchard
- Timberclad gunboats
- **POLK** Commander

Map reflects historic shorelines and hydrography.

To Adamsville, north and west, and Crump's Landing, northeast

Lew Wallace's division was north, its camps extending from Adamsville east to Crump's Landing.

Snake Creek

Snake Creek

To Savannah

To Savannah

Diamond Island

Tennessee

steamships

HAMBURG-SAVANNAH ROAD (RIVER ROAD)

Tilghman Branch

Owl Creek

McARTHUR (W.H.L. WALLACE)

Pittsburg Landing

PITTSBURG ROAD

Dill Branch

GRANT

McARTHUR (W.H.L. WALLACE)

The battle exploded at sunrise as tens of thousands of Rebel troops emerged from the woods with their bands playing and sunlight glinting off their gun barrels and bayonets. Above this could be heard the chilling "Rebel Yell."

VEATCH (HURLBUT)

Water Oaks Pond

CORINTH-

SUNKEN ROAD

W.H.L. WALLACE

pond

USS *Lexington*

USS *Tyler*

Shiloh Branch

SHERMAN

McCLERNAND

Shiloh Church

HAMBURG-PURDY RD

Peach Orchard

BRAGG

HARDEE

PRENTISS

HURLBUT

POLK

STUART

BEAUREGARD

HARDEE

POLK

BRAGG

Locust Grove Branch

EASTERN CORINTH RD

CORINTH RD

HAMBURG ROAD

By 9 a.m. three Confederate corps were engaged, and the fighting became confused.

JOHNSTON

POLK

HARDEE

BARK ROAD

Lick Creek

BRECKINRIDGE

BRAGG

BARK ROAD

Scale in Miles

0   0.5   1

↙ To Corinth

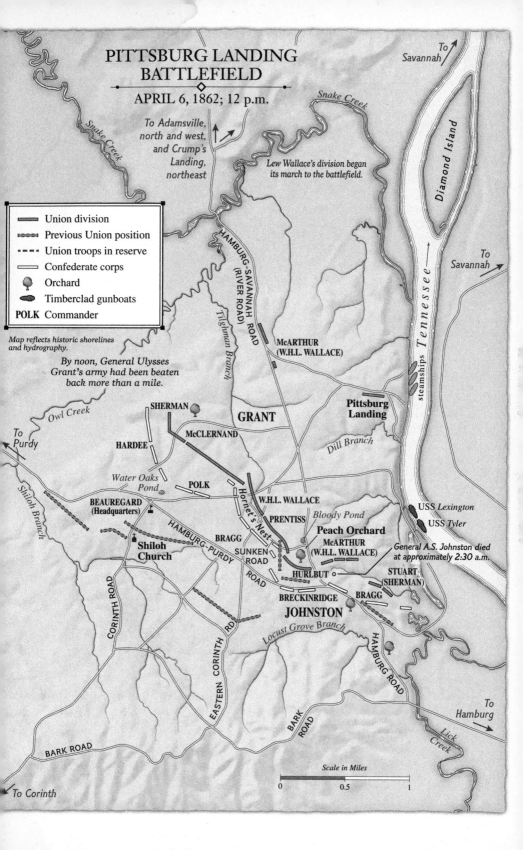

PITTSBURG LANDING BATTLEFIELD

◇ APRIL 6, 1862; 12 p.m. ◇

To Savannah

Snake Creek

To Adamsville, north and west, and Crump's Landing, northeast

Lew Wallace's division began its march to the battlefield.

Diamond Island

Snake Creek

Legend

— Union division
⬛ Previous Union position
- - - Union troops in reserve
☐ Confederate corps
🌳 Orchard
🛥 Timberclad gunboats
POLK Commander

Map reflects historic shorelines and hydrography.

By noon, General Ulysses Grant's army had been beaten back more than a mile.

HAMBURG-SAVANNAH ROAD (RIVER ROAD)

Tilghman Branch

McARTHUR (W.H.L. WALLACE)

Pittsburg Landing

steamships Tennessee

To Savannah

Owl Creek

To Purdy

SHERMAN 🌳

GRANT

Dill Branch

McCLERNAND

HARDEE

Water Oaks Pond

POLK

BEAUREGARD (Headquarters)

Shiloh Branch

W.H.L. WALLACE

PRENTISS

Bloody Pond

Peach Orchard 🌳

McARTHUR (W.H.L. WALLACE)

USS *Lexington*
USS *Tyler*

General A.S. Johnston died at approximately 2:30 a.m.

HAMBURG-PURDY ROAD

Shiloh Church

BRAGG

SUNKEN ROAD

Hornet's Nest

HURLBUT

STUART (SHERMAN)

BRECKINRIDGE

BRAGG

JOHNSTON

CORINTH ROAD

EASTERN CORINTH RD.

Locust Grove Branch

HAMBURG ROAD

To Hamburg

BARK ROAD

Lick Creek

BARK ROAD

To Corinth

Scale in Miles

0   0.5   1

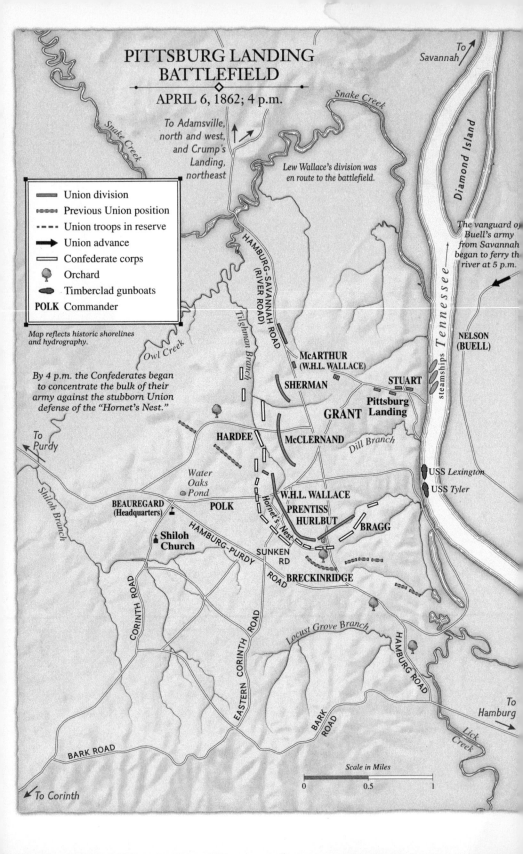

PITTSBURG LANDING
BATTLEFIELD
◇
APRIL 6, 1862; 4 p.m.

To Savannah

To Adamsville,
north and west,
and Crump's
Landing,
northeast

Snake Creek

Lew Wallace's division was
en route to the battlefield.

Legend
- Union division
- Previous Union position
- Union troops in reserve
- Union advance
- Confederate corps
- Orchard
- Timberclad gunboats
- **POLK** Commander

Map reflects historic shorelines
and hydrography.

Snake Creek

Owl Creek

Diamond Island

The vanguard of
Buell's army
from Savannah
began to ferry the
river at 5 p.m.

HAMBURG-SAVANNAH ROAD
(RIVER ROAD)

Tilghman Branch

NELSON
(BUELL)

By 4 p.m. the Confederates began
to concentrate the bulk of their
army against the stubborn Union
defense of the "Hornet's Nest."

To
Purdy

McARTHUR
(W.H.L. WALLACE)

SHERMAN

STUART

HARDEE

McCLERNAND

GRANT

Pittsburg
Landing

Dill Branch

Water
Oaks
Pond

Hornet's Nest

W.H.L. WALLACE
PRENTISS
HURLBUT

POLK

BEAUREGARD
(Headquarters)

Shiloh
Church

BRAGG

USS Lexington

USS Tyler

steamships Tennessee

Shiloh Branch

HAMBURG-PURDY ROAD

SUNKEN
RD

BRECKINRIDGE

CORINTH ROAD

EASTERN CORINTH ROAD

Locust Grove Branch

HAMBURG ROAD

To
Hamburg

Lick
Creek

BARK
ROAD

BARK ROAD

Scale in Miles

0   0.5   1

To Corinth

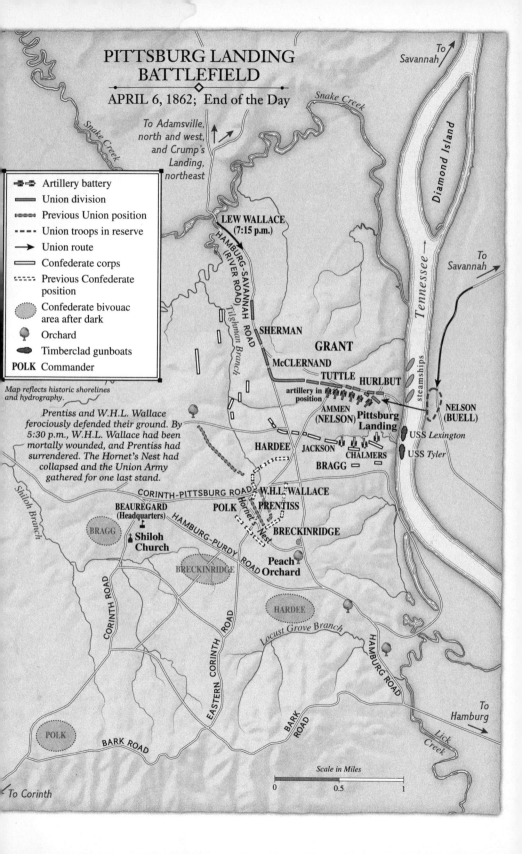

PITTSBURG LANDING BATTLEFIELD

APRIL 6, 1862; End of the Day

To Savannah

Snake Creek

To Adamsville, north and west, and Crump's Landing, northeast

Legend:
- Artillery battery
- Union division
- Previous Union position
- Union troops in reserve
- Union route
- Confederate corps
- Previous Confederate position
- Confederate bivouac area after dark
- Orchard
- Timberclad gunboats
- **POLK** Commander

Map reflects historic shorelines and hydrography.

Prentiss and W.H.L. Wallace ferociously defended their ground. By 5:30 p.m., W.H.L. Wallace had been mortally wounded, and Prentiss had surrendered. The Hornet's Nest had collapsed and the Union Army gathered for one last stand.

LEW WALLACE (7:15 p.m.)

HAMBURG-SAVANNAH ROAD (RIVER ROAD)

Tilghman Branch

SHERMAN

GRANT

McCLERNAND

TUTTLE   **HURLBUT**

artillery in position

AMMEN (NELSON)   **Pittsburg Landing**

HARDEE   **JACKSON**

CHALMERS

BRAGG

W.H.L. WALLACE

POLK   **PRENTISS**

Hornet's Nest

BRECKINRIDGE

Corinth-Pittsburg Road

BEAUREGARD (Headquarters)

BRAGG

Shiloh Church

BRECKINRIDGE

HAMBURG-PURDY ROAD

Peach Orchard

HARDEE

Locust Grove Branch

CORINTH ROAD

EASTERN CORINTH ROAD

BARK ROAD

POLK

BARK ROAD

Shiloh Branch

To Corinth

Snake Creek

Diamond Island

Tennessee

To Savannah

steamships

NELSON (BUELL)

USS *Lexington*

USS *Tyler*

HAMBURG ROAD

Lick Creek

To Hamburg

Scale in Miles
0   0.5   1

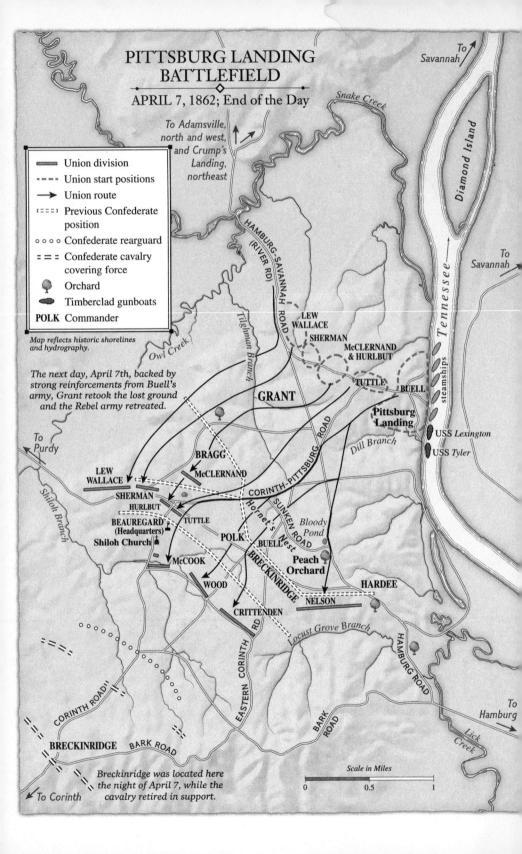

PITTSBURG LANDING BATTLEFIELD

APRIL 7, 1862; End of the Day

To Savannah

Snake Creek

To Adamsville, north and west, and Crump's Landing, northeast

Diamond Island

HAMBURG-SAVANNAH ROAD (RIVER RD)

Legend

- ▬▬ Union division
- ▬ ▬ ▬ Union start positions
- ➝ Union route
- ⊏▭▭⊐ Previous Confederate position
- ∘ ∘ ∘ ∘ Confederate rearguard
- = = = Confederate cavalry covering force
- 🌳 Orchard
- 🚢 Timberclad gunboats
- **POLK** Commander

Map reflects historic shorelines and hydrography.

The next day, April 7th, backed by strong reinforcements from Buell's army, Grant retook the lost ground and the Rebel army retreated.

Owl Creek

Tilghman Branch

To Savannah

Tennessee

steamships

LEW WALLACE
SHERMAN
McCLERNAND & HURLBUT
TUTTLE
BUELL

GRANT

Pittsburg Landing

USS *Lexington*
USS *Tyler*

To Purdy

Shiloh Branch

BRAGG
McCLERNAND

Dill Branch

CORINTH-PITTSBURG ROAD

PITTSBURG ROAD

LEW WALLACE
SHERMAN
HURLBUT
BEAUREGARD (Headquarters)
Shiloh Church
TUTTLE

Hornet's Nest

SUNKEN ROAD

Bloody Pond

POLK
BUELL

Peach Orchard

HARDEE

McCOOK

BRECKINRIDGE

WOOD

NELSON

CRITTENDEN

EASTERN CORINTH RD

BRECKINRIDGE RD

Locust Grove Branch

HAMBURG ROAD

BARK ROAD

To Hamburg

Lick Creek

CORINTH ROAD

BRECKINRIDGE BARK ROAD

To Corinth

Breckinridge was located here the night of April 7, while the cavalry retired in support.

Scale in Miles

0   0.5   1

CHAPTER I

APRIL IS THE CRUELEST MONTH

⫸◆⫷

B Y EARLY APRIL 1862 THE SPRING STORM SEASON HAD already begun in Tennessee. The thunderheads made up on the southern plains, then tore across the South with lightning and killer tornadoes. Terrifying as this was, it paled before the violent thing then gathering along the Mississippi River Valley.

From Illinois, Ohio, and Iowa, Indiana, Michigan, Wisconsin, and Minnesota, Northern men had begun to converge. They marched in turn by squads, platoons, companies, regiments, brigades, and finally whole infantry divisions. As the cold Dixie weather receded and they tramped farther south, before them loomed a great battle they were told would bring an end to the war.

Up from the South likewise they came, from Alabama, Mississippi, Louisiana, Texas, Georgia, Florida, and Arkansas; Tennessee, of course, was represented in full. And from the border states Kentucky and Missouri came men of both sides who fought as friend against friend, sometimes brother against brother. There were more than a hundred thousand in all—whose average age was not yet 20.

———◆———

Down in the far southwestern corner of the state the winding Tennessee River straightens out for twenty or so miles after changing its course northward toward the wide Ohio. Halfway along that stretch is a bight on the western bank, occupied long ago by a tribe of mound builders, now called Pittsburg Landing, a nondescript hog-and-cotton loading station perched before tall oak-strewn bluffs where steamboats put in from time to time. There they took on cargo and traded with the residents, who were fairly low on the scale of Southern sophistication in the era of King Cotton and the fanciful aura of moonlight and magnolias. These Pittsburg Landing people might have had plenty of the latter, but it was about all they had. The curse of slavery was barely a whisper in the scratched-out fields among the shocking thickets where they eked a living and went to Sunday meetings at an ax-hewn chink-and-mortar Methodist church named Shiloh chapel. The church itself was hardly better than a respectable Missouri corncrib in its design and architectural aspect, but it was a house of God and gave its name to one of the bloodiest battles of the Civil War.

On Sunday morning, April 6, the fateful day, Elsie Duncan, then age nine, told of being in the garden of her family's home about a mile west of Pittsburg Landing. The place was peaceful "as paradise" itself, she remembered, surrounded as it was "by a beautiful forest with every kind of oak, maple and birch," plus "fruit trees and berry bushes and a spring-fed pond with water lilies blooming white." Her father, Joseph, was one of the few substantial citizens of the area, owning a farm of 200 acres called Pleasant Land as well as being a circuit-riding preacher of the Gospel. Everybody had been on edge for several weeks, ever since the Duncans' black nurse Margie had come back from a visit to the landing to report that there were "strange steamboats on the river, and Yankees camped in the hills."

Hardin County, where Pittsburg Landing was located, was fairly typical of rural Tennessee outside the state's main cotton belt. In the 1861 referendum on secession, the residents voted to stay with the Union, and there was still strong Union sentiment on the east side of the river. But on the west side, where Elsie Duncan lived, the young men had been formed to fight for the Confederacy, and had been drilling regularly, led by her own father, whom she described as a "drill master" in addition to his duties as a Rebel chaplain. It was at one of these drill sessions, or parades, that she spent her final time in "that dear old Shiloh church." It had been appropriated for a Rebel celebration, she recalled, complete with Confederate flags and a chorus of little girls "dressed in red, white, and blue, and singing 'Dixie.'"

The suddenness with which war had come to Hardin County alarmed everyone. Citizens began to plan for some sort of cataclysm as the blue-clad Federals arrived by the hundreds, and then the thousands, at Pittsburg and other landings along the river. Reverend Duncan had a cave on his property, "at the edge of the woods, just above the spring which was under a bluff just back of the orchard." It was "about the size of a large room," she said, and her father reinforced the roof with heavy planks and laid a floor, then "sealed the entrance off with brush and made a trap door with a ladder to go down." It would prove to be a safe harbor when fighting broke out.

The people in that part of the country, she said, "did not know how long the war was going to last," and so in a small cabin far back in the woods her father also hid "eight barrels of home-raised flour upstairs, buried a large box of home-raised hams in the garden and put a sweet potato bed on top of them." The men, she recalled, "left everything as secure and safe as they could to protect their homes and families, and then left them in the care of the Lord" to join the Confederate army.

Thus, Elsie, her mother, Harriet, and her five children ranging in age from 7 to 15, as well as their nurse Margie, were home alone on Sunday morning, April 6, 1862, when from somewhere beyond the deep woods came the rough, guttural muttering of artillery like distant thunder. Elsie had not had breakfast and was out in the garden playing.

"It was a beautiful Sunday morning. The sun was shining, birds were singing, and the air was soft and sweet," she said. "I sat down under a holly-hock bush which was full of pink blossoms and watched the bees gathering honey."

Elsie Duncan hadn't the faintest idea at that point—nor had many of the 40,000-strong Yankee host nearby—that something dreadful was brewing in the tangled forests to the south and descending upon them as swift and merciless as a cyclone from the southern plains.

———◆◆———

The war was still one week shy of a year old, and the issues that had brought it on were not yet fully absorbed by the armies of young men who had signed on to fight it. For the sturdy, traditional midwesterners in the Federal service it was mainly about saving the Union that their forefathers created; for the majority of young men under the Confederate banner it was mostly about the invading Yankee army, which they saw as a clear and present danger to their homes and loved ones. The Emancipation Proclamation was long months into the future. The war was young; the men were inexperienced; some of the Northern soldiers learned to shoot their weapons by firing at things along the banks of the river, including people's homes or barns, and a sizable number of Rebels were armed only with shotguns or squirrel rifles. It was a mean pity that less than three generations after the creation of the first authentic democracy the world had ever known, such a wretched schism had broken out among nominally peace-loving peoples. It is worth a side trip to understand why.

At the time of the Revolution, the U.S. population had reached 2.5 million, including 500,000 slaves. By the War of 1812 three decades later, it had grown to some 8 million, and just a half century later, on the eve of the Civil War, it had exploded to more than 30 million, including about 4 million slaves.

By the election year of 1860 the United States had grown into a huge but unwieldy economic giant, selling commodities and foodstuffs throughout the world. During the 250 years since the first settlers landed on American shores, their rude paths and huts had given way to homes, many of them substantial. Highly developed roadways and waterways connected great cities north and south. In 40 years, steamboats had advanced from rudimentary vessels to floating palaces while railroads linked all important places, and the invention of the Morse telegraph and code 20 years earlier had spawned a nationwide web of timely communications.

In the Northeast great manufactories arose; New England embraced the shipbuilding, textile, and armaments industries, while around the shores of the Great Lakes and in Pittsburgh iron foundries produced railroad engines, cars, and track. Elsewhere plants and shops large and small turned out everything from leather goods to buggies and buggy whips, shoes and tools and rubber goods and all things in between. In the Midwest (then still known as the "West") was the "breadbasket of America"; farmers in the Great Plains, many of them German and Scandinavian immigrants, raised corn, wheat, and grain for the vast flourmills of Minnesota and Michigan. Farther west were beef cattle and hogs, this last the staple meat of rural life.

The American South, ignoring the advice of some of its wisest citizens, produced few if any of these goods and commodities, but instead purchased what it needed from above the Mason-Dixon Line or from abroad. In the meantime it raised cotton. A visitor to the region in the 1840s made this analysis of southerners' misapplication of capital: "To raise more cotton, to buy more slaves, to raise more cotton, to buy more slaves—ad infinitum."

Indeed, until the turn of the 19th century the South grew very little cotton, save for the long-staple variety, which flourished along the Georgia seacoast and had few seeds, pods, or other entanglements to be combed (or ginned) out. The other kind of cotton, short staple, could grow in abundance almost anywhere in the South, but the manpower it took to hand-comb out the detritus wasn't worth the effort. Then, in 1793, Eli Whitney invented his cotton gin and the entire Southern agricultural dynamic changed dramatically.

Go-getters began farming large upland tracts with short-staple cotton. In a few short years they wore out the soil and soon moved from Georgia and the Carolinas into the wilds of Tennessee, Alabama, and Mississippi, then jumped the river into Louisiana and

Arkansas; it wasn't long before the whole sunny South seemed to have turned into an ocean of white cotton bolls waving toward Texas and the promise of the West. That was where some said the trouble started. With all the riches embodied in the American system, one would have thought that an abiding harmony should have existed among the sections of the country, but beneath its great prosperity America seethed.

The trouble in fact had started 250 years earlier, when a Dutch ship's captain offloaded 62 miserable Africans at Jamestown, Virginia, introducing slavery to North America. They were the first of some 640,000 brought over before importation of slaves was officially ended in 1808. But the trade had spread throughout the Caribbean Basin, and in America to all the colonies, which became the states. Before the turn of the century slavery in the United States had appeared to be dying out of its own accord as "inefficient, wasteful, and increasingly morally repugnant."

Then Whitney invented his gin and slavery was back in vogue in the South. Raising cotton was a highly labor-intensive business, with immense profits, and slaves seemed to be the only answer, even though the institution remained just as "morally repugnant" as before.

By the eve of the Civil War cotton accounted for two-thirds of America's exports and in time cotton and slavery became almost inextricably bound together with every facet of Southern life. The larger plantations were like small cities, with their own gardeners, blacksmiths, carpenters, bricklayers, horse handlers, and, of course, field hands. Architects made their living designing mansions and offices for cotton agents (called "factors"). Steamboat companies hauled cotton from the landings and to the planters delivered European furniture, fine carpets, china, and so on. Engineers and draftsmen thrived by surveying cotton land. Southern lawyers represented the cotton interests and Southern doctors tended their ailments. Bankers, gin operators, railroad companies, warehouse owners, hoteliers, hardware salesmen, longshoremen, farriers, druggists, houses of worship, and houses of prostitution— all of these, and more, were in one way or another interdependent on the cotton trade. Even the myriad small "subsistence farmers," who owned no slaves, tried to put in a few acres of the crop to earn a little cash.

Thus the South viewed it with alarm when, in the 1820s, Northern abolition parties first made themselves known. Initially the abolitionists had declared slavery to be a social evil and lobbied to ship freed slaves back to Liberia, on the west coast of Africa. They would later change this tactic, but first, in 1828, during the presidency of John Quincy Adams—and against the strenuous objections of its Southern members—Congress passed a revenue tariff that caused the prices of goods that southerners typically purchased to soar by 50 percent.

It was quickly dubbed the "tariff of abominations" by enraged southerners, and in South Carolina the notion of secession first reared its head when the legislature passed a law asserting that no state was bound to enforce a federal law that it found obnoxious. This produced the so-called Nullification Crisis, which pitted the power of an individual state against the power of the federal government, and *Marbury* v. *Madison* be damned.*

---

* This was the 1803 case in which the U.S. Supreme Court established the precedence of federal law over state law.

Outright rebellion was diffused after President Andrew Jackson inherited the controversy and threatened to enforce the law, with military action if necessary, but it left a bitter taste in the minds of most southerners, who saw the legislation as a slap in the face against the South.* At times, Southern historians have tried to argue that the tariff was the root cause of the Civil War, but that is untrue. It is fair to say, however, that it was a critical ingredient in the onset of Southern mistrust of the North and also seemed to have created a mazy kind of dividing line in which the South began to think of itself as a separate entity with the right to withdraw, or secede, from the Union if given just cause.

The tariff, which had become abominable for everybody, thus set the stage for the states' rights dispute, which pitted states' laws against the notion of federal sovereignty, an argument that continued into the next century, and the next. States' rights political parties sprang up across the South during the 1830s. A noteworthy example of just how crucial the issue had become was embodied in the decision in 1831 by Mr. and Mrs. Nathaniel Gist (ironically from Union, South Carolina) to name their firstborn son States Rights Gist, which he bore proudly until November 30, 1864, when, as a Confederate brigadier general, he was shot dead leading his men at the Battle of Franklin, Tennessee.

The squabble naturally spilled over into politics. The North, with its millions of immigrants pouring in, hopelessly outnumbered the South in population and thus controlled the House of Representatives. But by a sort of gentlemen's agreement the Senate had effectively remained fifty-fifty, because whenever a territory

---

* The historian Robert Remini, biographer of Adams and Jackson, described the tariff as both "ghastly" and "lopsided."

was admitted to the Union as a free state the South was "allowed" to add a corresponding slave state—and vice versa.*

But in 1820, when Missouri applied for statehood and antislavery forces insisted it must be free, there were no other slaveholding territories to offset the addition. Ultimately, this resulted in the Missouri Compromise (brokered by Senator Henry Clay of Kentucky), which decreed that Missouri could come in as a slave state but that any other state created north of Missouri's southern border would have to be free. That held the thing together for 30 years—longer than it deserved.

By the 1840s abolitionism had become a full-fledged movement, with preaching from pulpits, stumps, and lecture halls across the North; the abetting of runaway slaves via the Underground Railway; and the distribution of pamphlets and other antislavery literature in the Southern mails. Not only that, the abolitionists had modified their position that slavery was merely a "social evil," condemning it now as a "moral wrong," and began to agitate on that basis.

This shocked and angered many churchgoing southerners, who were distressed at being called scandalous names by northerners they did not even know. In turn, that inspired religious schisms that caused the Baptist and Methodist churches to split into Northern and Southern denominations. The Presbyterians hung together, but it was a strain, while the Episcopal Church remained a Southern stronghold and firebrand bastion among the wealthy and planter classes. Catholics also maintained their unity, prompting cynics to suggest it was only because they owed their allegiance

---

*   For instance, when Texas was admitted to the Union in 1845 as a slave state, so also was Iowa, which came in as a free state in the following year.

to the pope of Rome rather than to any state, country, or ideal.

Meantime, the cotton revolution had caused the southerners to evolve their notion of slavery as well, from a "necessary evil," which is how Thomas Jefferson once characterized it, to a "positive good," according to John C. Calhoun, South Carolina's prominent U.S. senator, a generation later. This naturally infuriated the abolitionists, who redoubled their efforts, prompting southerners to assert that the North was agitating for a murderous slave rebellion. Slave revolt was a horror that remained high on most southerners' anxiety list. Bloody slave uprisings had occurred in Haiti, Jamaica, and Louisiana, and more recently resulted in the killing of 60 whites during the Nat Turner revolt in Virginia in 1831.

<hr />

During the Mexican War of 1846–48 the United States acquired vast territories in the West, which southerners sought to colonize as slave states. It was not so much that they believed slavery would be successful in the West—because of the climate and terrain most people in fact did not think so—but rather for purely political reasons having to do with control of the Senate.

Early in that conflict, a near crisis arose when an obscure congressman from Pennsylvania placed an amendment onto the war funding bill of 1846 that would have banned slavery in any territory the United States acquired from Mexico, which became known, after its author, as the Wilmot Proviso. It did not pass into law, but the mere act became a cause célèbre for southerners, who offered it as further evidence that the North was out to destroy not only slavery but the South's political power as well.

The 1850s brought new levels of anger fueled by "fire-eaters" in the South and "black radicals" in the North, backed by their newspapers and journals. By then the arguments of national politics had become almost completely sectional and adversarial. In 1850, when California sought to join the Union, it was admitted as a free state, prompting South Carolina's Calhoun, then nearly on his deathbed, to declare that the move had "upset the equilibrium of the nation and [would] lead to Civil War."

To assuage the furious South, Congress passed the Fugitive Slave Act, a law that made northerners personally responsible for the return of runaway slaves. Where before many in the North had little or no opinions or feelings on slavery, this law seemed to demand their direct assent to the practice of human bondage, and it galvanized Northern sentiments against slavery.

Another polarizing incident between the two sections occurred upon the 1852 publication of Harriet Beecher Stowe's bestselling novel *Uncle Tom's Cabin,* which depicted the slave's life as a relentless nightmare of sorrow and cruelty. Northern passions were incensed and inflamed, while southerners dismissed the tale as outrageously skewed, overdramatized, and unfair.*

In 1854 agitation by both sides over the future of the Kansas Territory resulted in the Kansas-Nebraska Act, sponsored by future presidential candidate and Lincoln debater Stephen A. Douglas. This new law overturned the Missouri Compromise and authorized settlers in the Kansas Territory to decide for themselves whether they wanted their state to be slave or free. This was known as "popular sovereignty."

---

* After the conflict began it was said that Abraham Lincoln, upon meeting Mrs. Stowe, remarked, "So you are the little lady who started this great war."

Outraged abolitionists began raising funds to send antislavery settlers to Kansas, prompting equally outraged southerners to fund their own settlers, and a brutish group from slaveholding Missouri known as Border Ruffians went into Kansas to make trouble for the abolitionists. Into this ill-fated mix rode an abolitionist fanatic named John Brown with his three sons, and as the murders and massacres began to pile up, newspapers throughout the land began to carry headlines of "Bleeding Kansas."

Other changes were in store for the political class, especially in the Senate, where southerners had dominated, if not always in numbers, at least in oratory style. For every Yankee Daniel Webster, it seemed, there was a Henry Clay, or a Calhoun, or a Thomas Hart Benton to speak the part of the South. But in 1851 two new Northern senators—then Democrats but soon to be Radical Republicans—entered the chamber. Together, they brought great political weight and bearing to what was otherwise a notoriously staid and compromising body politic.

Judge Ben Wade of Ohio was one of them and 40-year-old Charles Sumner of Massachusetts was the other. Sumner was tall, statesmanlike, and had the looks of "an Apollo," a sharply honed, speechified Boston lawyer who was vehemently opposed to slavery. Wade, on the other hand—and this according to an admirer—was a "self-made, untutored yokel, heavy, old, glum and square," who not only opposed slavery but had the brass to silence those who weren't. Once seated in the formally genteel Senate chambers Wade was just uncouth enough to shout "You're a liar" at gentlemen from the Cotton Kingdom who were trying to defend their "peculiar institution," as slavery had come to be known. And when the Southern gentlemen objected to his behavior, Wade was just bold enough to retort "Well, what are you going to do about it?"

Those words were far more weighty than they are now, for while the practice of dueling over insulted honor was banned in many states and the District of Columbia, it was still very much alive as means of settling personal disputes, including those in Congress. In Ben Wade's case, his reputation had preceded him. He was vouched to be an expert shot with a squirrel rifle from his days as a back-woodsman, and the advantage Wade had—and he knew it—was that, if challenged, the choice of weapons would be his. And South-ern gentlemen, while they may have been many things, were rarely accomplished squirrel hunters.

Wade's tactics soon cast a pall over the Southern senators, who at least had better judgment than to face Wade's squirrel rifle on the field of honor, even as they seethed furiously at the embarrassment of their situation. For its part, the Southern press held up Wade as an indelible symbol of that bullying kind of Yankee, the abolitionist tyrant.

Senator Sumner, on the other hand, owned no squirrel rifle, or weapon of any kind, so far as it was known, but relied on logic, a higher sense of morality, and advanced oratory skills to overwhelm opponents in the slavery debates. Southerners, already careful, lest they provoke Ben Wade, generally chose their words cautiously, but nevertheless managed to drive home the point that so far as old Dixie was concerned slavery wasn't going away and in fact was des-tined to spread to the far-flung outlands of the nation.

One day in 1856 Senator Sumner startled even his fellow radi-cals during a lofty, three-hour disquisition against slavery by sin-gling out his colleague Andrew Butler for a severe personal ridicule. Among other things, Sumner declared that Senator Butler kept "a mistress who, though ugly to others, is lovely to him . . . I mean the harlot, slavery"; moreover, he further proceeded to mock the 59-year-old South Carolinian, who had suffered a stroke, for his posture and manner of speech.

This so infuriated Butler's nephew, a congressman named Preston Brooks, that two days later he accosted Sumner at his desk in the Senate chamber and caned him nearly to death with a gold-headed gutta-percha walking stick.

The incident triggered profound indignation throughout the North and helped give rise to the formation of the Republican Party, which had a firm antislavery platform.* Later that year the Republicans' candidate for President was the western explorer John C. Frémont, the famed "pathfinder" of the 1840s, and even though Frémont was defeated his candidacy established the Republicans as a force to be reckoned with.

By this time the country had been lurching from political crisis to crisis for more than a decade, and secession talk increasingly inflamed the South and was seriously taken. In 1857 the Supreme Court delivered its infamous *Dred Scott* decision, which elated southerners and enraged northerners. It was the opinion of the court that a slave was neither a "citizen" nor, for that matter, even a "person," and "so far inferior that [slaves] have no rights which the white man [is] bound to respect." The immediate effect of the ruling was that southerners could now move their slaves into and out of free states and territories without losing them; for northerners the decision drove more people into the antislavery camp.

In 1859 John Brown, of "Bleeding Kansas" notoriety, staged a

---

* Many southerners, on the other hand, reacted by sending Brooks replacements for the cane, which he had broken during the fracas.

murderous raid on the U.S. arsenal at Harpers Ferry, Virginia, in hopes of inspiring a general slave uprising. The raid was thwarted by U.S. troops, and Brown was tried for treason and hanged, but when it came out that he was being financed by wealthy Northern abolitionists, Southern anger was profuse—especially after the Northern press elevated Brown to the status of hero and martyr.

As the election year of 1860 approached it seemed the nation was consumed in a furor as political parties dissolved or split into factions. Influential Southern fire-eaters insisted that Northern "fanatics" intended to free the slaves "by law if possible, by force as necessary," and hectoring Northern newspapers and orators (known as "black" or Radical Republicans) provided ample fodder for that conclusion.

When the Republicans nominated Abraham Lincoln as their candidate, the Southern press whipped up its populace to such a pitch of fury it seemed as if John Brown himself had been put on the ticket. Lincoln was lampooned in words and cartoons as an archetypal abolitionist—a kind of Antichrist who would turn loose the slaves to rape, murder, and pillage. This goes a long way in explaining why fewer than one in three Confederate soldiers came from slaveholding families. To them, it wasn't to keep slaves that they joined the army, it was rather to save their homes and families against the notion of slaves gone wild.*

Meantime, the Northern press was pouring fuel on the fire by

---

* Interestingly, many of the wealthiest southerners were opposed to secession for the simple reason that they had the most to lose if it came to war and the war went badly. But in the end they, like almost everyone else, were swept along on the tide.

damning southerners as brutal lash-wielding torturers and heartless family separators. By the time hostilities broke out, neither side had much use for the other. One elderly Tennessean later penned this sentiment: "I wish there was a river of fire a mile wide between the North and South, that would burn with unquenchable fury forevermore, and that it could never be passable to the endless ages of eternity by any living creature." With talk like that it's a wonder the war didn't start earlier.

The new alignment of political parties ultimately ensured a 40 percent plurality victory for Lincoln.* With the inclusion of Minnesota (1858) and Oregon (1859) as free states, the southerners' worst fears were about to be realized—complete control of both Houses of Congress and the White House by free-state, antislavery politicians.

Much of the Southern apprehension that Lincoln would free the slaves was misplaced. No matter how distasteful he found the practice, the overarching philosophy that drove Lincoln was a hard pragmatism that did not include forcible abolition by the federal government, probably for the simple reason that he could not envision any political way of accomplishing it at the time. By then, though, southerners' mistrust had degenerated into such a caustic fog of hatred, recrimination, and outrageous statements that most in the South simply did not believe Lincoln when he promised he had no interest in abolishing slavery where it already existed.

However, like a considerable number of Northern people, Lincoln was decidedly against allowing slavery to spread into new states

---

* Neither Ulysses Grant nor William Tecumseh Sherman, who would be so instrumental in the Shiloh Campaign, voted for Lincoln, for fear that his election would lead to war.

and territories. By denying slaveholders the right to extend their boundaries he not only would have weakened the slave power in Washington, but over time it would have almost inevitably resulted in the voluntary abolition of slavery, since sooner or later the Southern land would have worn out from overfarming with cotton.

The southerners weren't sticking around to find out. In short order, pugnacious South Carolina voted to secede from the Union, followed by eight other Deep South states that were heavily invested in cotton. After South Carolina drove Federal forces from Fort Sumter in the Charleston harbor, Lincoln called for the other states to produce 75,000 volunteers to put down the rebellion, which resulted in further secession. Virginia, North Carolina, Tennessee, and Arkansas joined the Confederacy rather than fight against their fellow southerners.

A Southern woman was heard to lament at the time that "Because of incompatibility of temper . . . we have hated each other so. If we could only separate, a *separation a l'agreable,'* as the French say it, and not have a horrid fight for divorce."

That was not to be. During the early months of 1861 Lincoln was able to quell secession in several of the so-called border states— including Missouri, Kentucky, and Maryland—by a combination of politics and force, including suspension of the Bill of Rights. But by the spring of 1862 it was painfully apparent that the "horrid fight for divorce" could not be avoided. To be sure, there had been fighting and killing in 1861, but with the exception of Bull Run and a few others most of those actions were in the nature of skirmishes that did not rise to the dignity of a "battle."

That was the reason why on Sunday morning, April 6, 1862, tens of thousands of boys in blue were encamped at Pittsburg

Landing, and tens of thousands more dressed in gray or butternut were stealthily marching toward them through the deep Tennessee woods. Everyone knew that a big battle had to be fought; battles were what settled things. The armies had gathered; the line had been drawn. It is impossible to guess how much of the foregoing history these soldiers apprehended, but most of them by then understood they were destined to be part of something very great, and very awful, and that sooner rather than later they were going to see that elephant.

CHAPTER 2

YOU MUST BE BADLY SCARED

—◦—◆—◦—

B Y THE TIME HE REACHED PITTSBURG LANDING Gen. William Tecumseh Sherman was a changed man. That is to say he wasn't "insane" any more, or a "nervous Nellie," or "flighty," which was how the press had portrayed him six months earlier when he lost command at Louisville for expressing fear he was going to be attacked and then having the gall to tell Washington that 200,000 Federal troops would be needed to subdue Rebels in the Mississippi River Valley. Instead, after a period of recuperation, Sherman ("Cump," to his friends since West Point days) regained his confidence: A sharp, bristling personality, he began to channel the staunch singularity of purpose he would demonstrate for the remainder of the war.

For now, though, Sherman seemed to be overcompensating for the Louisville disgrace. From the time of his arrival at Pittsburg Landing he refused even to entertain the possibility of an attack by the large Rebel army known to be converging just twenty miles south at Corinth, Mississippi.

As the senior regular army officer he should have known better. As commander of one of the six Yankee infantry divisions recently arrived at the landing, Brigadier General Sherman was also, nominally, in charge of the day-to-day operations at the encampment, while Ulysses ("Sam" to his West Point classmates) Grant exercised overall control from his headquarters at Savannah, Tennessee, a town located nine miles downstream on the Tennessee River, in an opulent mansion offered to him by William H. Cherry, a wealthy slaveholding planter and Union sympathizer.

Owing to the riparian topography, the Union position at Pittsburg resembled a giant cornucopia of roughly 12 square miles, with its stem, north of the landing, less than a mile wide, and its mouth opening nearly 3 miles wide to the south between the Tennessee River and Owl Creek. By some amazing blunder, the most inexperienced divisions—those of Sherman and Brig. Gen. Benjamin M. Prentiss*—were placed in the outer lines at the maw of the cornucopia, close to the Rebel army at Corinth. It was later explained, quite unsatisfactorily, that the encampments were arranged by engineers with regard to sanitation, nearness of water and firewood, and similar conveniences and without concern for their ability to defend the field—in other words, disposed the way a peacetime army might be. The various camps to the south along the cornucopia's mouth were not even set in a continuous line but placed helter-skelter with huge, heavily forested gaps in between. The whole of the Pittsburg

---

* In fact, these were brand-new units, filled with raw, untrained, undisciplined recruits.

Landing area had become a virtual tent city, with more than 5,000 of the big, conical eight-man Sibley tents occupying the five division encampment areas.

William Camm, lieutenant colonel of the 14th Illinois, had located for himself a swimming hole in Owl Creek where he liked to bathe. One day while he was enjoying his ablutions, two soldiers appeared, carrying squirrels they had shot for dinner. He inquired if they had seen any pickets protecting the outer edges of the encampment. They had not, they said, and neither had he. "We must have some queer generals," Camm remarked that night to his diary, "with the enemy in force only eighteen miles away."

Even worse, although the Federal army had begun arriving at Pittsburg Landing more than two weeks earlier, neither Sherman, Grant, nor anyone else had made the slightest attempt to entrench or erect fortifications, which in all probability would have deterred a Confederate attack. Instead, they spent their days teaching the men drill formations in the farm fields and holding spit-and-polish dress parades.

What has never been satisfactorily explained is the role of Grant's engineering officer, Lt. Col. James Birdseye McPherson, first in his West Point class of 1853 and destined to become a major general and commander of the Army of the Tennessee before his untimely death during the Battle of Atlanta.* It remains unknown whether McPherson protested the placement of the campsites in

---

* McPherson was so highly thought of that Grant once prophesied to Sherman that McPherson would probably "go all the way," meaning he would rise to command the entire army. "Yes—if he lives," was Sherman's solemn reply.

such indefensible and unfortified positions, but in any case Grant, as Maj. Gen. Charles F. Smith's successor, must have approved the arrangement, even tacitly. For his part, Sherman seemed to rely on his original assessment of the area on March 18, not long after his arrival, when he wrote to Grant, "Magnificent plain for camping and drilling, and a military point of great strength."

And it might have been, if advantage of the military opportunities had been taken. Since the position was protected on both flanks by water, if either Grant or Sherman had told the engineers that the mouth of the cornucopia must be strongly fortified with embrasures, protected batteries, head logs, abatis,* with cleared fields of fire and other expedient military architecture, the encampment would have been nearly impregnable. But this was not done, and to Grant, and to a lesser extent Sherman, great blame attaches; their later excuses that it was more desirable for the soldiers to train and learn how to drill than it was for them to fortify seem lame and self-serving, especially in light of what happened. Sherman even went to the point of excusing himself "because [building fortifications] would have made our raw men timid," as though fortifying would have somehow suggested that the Yankee soldiers were scared of their Rebel adversaries. Equally cavalier was the notion that the Confederate army would never come out from behind its own fortifications at Corinth. In fact, what Sherman and Grant

---

* A head log was a large tree limb or trunk placed along and atop a dirt fortification with room to shoot beneath it, while offering some protection to the shooter's head. An abatis was a device of sharpened stakes that slowed or repelled enemy infantry and functioned similar to the way barbed wire did in the next century.

took for a "military point of great strength," with its flanks protected by water, was viewed by the Rebel generals as a trap for the Yankee army, if they could catch them napping.

It so happened that among Grant's orders from higher headquarters in St. Louis was a directive from his superior Maj. Gen. Henry Wager Halleck ordering him not to bring on a general engagement with the enemy until the arrival of the imposingly named general Don Carlos Buell and the 25,000-man army he was marching overland from Nashville. Buell had set his men in motion on March 15 and was supposed to reach Grant at Savannah by April 6. But Grant and Sherman's determination to wait for Buell led them to ignore any possibility that the enemy might be so obliging, and this seemed to create a kind of blindness even as the evidence of danger mounted.

There were ample warnings, the first of which should have been that the Rebel army was under Gen. Albert Sidney Johnston, whom Winfield Scott, general in chief of the Union armies, had declared to be "the finest soldier I have ever commanded." All knowledgeable Union officers should have at least calculated that Johnston might not keep his army idling in Corinth like a bunch of cardboard dummies waiting to be attacked or besieged.

On April 4—two days before the storm—a Yankee lieutenant and half a dozen men on picket duty were captured by Rebel cavalry. When a detachment of the volunteer Fifth Ohio Cavalry went out looking for them, its commander, Maj. Elbridge G. Ricker, rushed back to report encountering a whole Confederate line of battle, complete with artillery, just two miles from Sherman's headquarters near the little Shiloh church. To prove his point, Major Ricker had brought back ten Confederate prisoners and the splendid saddle of a Rebel cavalry colonel they had killed. Sherman's response was dismissive: "Oh, tut-tut. You militia officers get scared too easy," and he chided Ricker for running the risk of drawing the army into a fight before it was ready.

That same morning, a captain and two sergeants from the 77th Ohio strolled away from their camp to visit a nearby cotton plantation about a quarter mile to the south. As they reached a line of trees they beheld, across a field, "the enemy in force, and to all appearances they were getting breakfast. We saw infantry, cavalry and artillery very plainly."

The captain sent one of the sergeants dashing to Sherman's headquarters, but by this time Sherman was so annoyed that he ordered the sergeant *arrested* for sounding a false alarm!

The next day Col. Jesse Appler, commanding the 53rd Ohio, sent Sherman a report of gray-clad infantry in woods to his front. Appler had already called his soldiers to arms when Sherman responded by having a messenger tell Appler, in front of his men, "Take your damned regiment back to Ohio. There is no enemy nearer than Corinth!"

Major Ricker's Rebel prisoners, who had been confined in the Shiloh church, presently became talkative with their guards and boasted that there was a great Confederate army poised to attack next day. In response to a guard's inquiry as to whether there were enough "greybacks" in the woods to make "interesting hunting," a resentful Rebel private told him, "Yes, and there's more than you'uns have ever seen, and if you ain't mighty careful, they'll run you into hell or into the river before tomorrow night."

None of these things seemed to faze Cump Sherman or Sam Grant. From the time the Union forces began arriving at Pittsburg Landing, Confederate cavalry had kept a close eye on them, and skirmishes were inevitable, some of them deadly. But even as the reports began to pile up ominously in the early days of April there was little or no alarm that something besides enemy cavalry or an infantry company or two might be lurking in the deep woods.

Sherman seemed more determined than ever to put the lie to scaredy-cats. "For weeks," he scoffed, "old women reported that [the Rebel army] was coming, sometimes with 100,000, sometimes with 300,000." He brushed off these worried reports by saying that at worst the Confederates were conducting a "reconnaissance in force." He even estimated its strength as being "two regiments of infantry and an artillery battery."

On April 5, the very eve of battle, Sherman sent a note to Grant in response to an inquiry about enemy activity in the army's front: "I have no doubt that nothing will occur today other than some picket firing. The enemy is saucy, but got the worst of it yesterday and will not press our pickets far. I do not apprehend anything like an attack on our position."

That evening, secure in his mansion downriver, Grant doubtless relied on Sherman's appraisal when he sent a telegram to Major General Halleck, his superior in St. Louis, "The main force of the enemy is at Corinth and points east. I have scarcely the faintest idea of an attack (general one) being made upon us, but will be prepared should such a thing take place." As he wrote those lines, the advance regiments of a 40,000-man Rebel army were not a mile away from the Union encampment at Pittsburg Landing.

All that Saturday, April 5, there was a growing "uneasiness" among the officers and men in the southernmost camps—the men of Sherman's and Prentiss's divisions—for it was they who had either seen for themselves or heard animated reports and rumors that the Rebels were in great strength in the woods to their front.

They were accustomed to seeing Confederate cavalry watching them at discreet distances from the fringes of the forest, but lately the news was more menacing.

That afternoon Prentiss, a dour-faced Virginia-born, Missouri-bred ropemaker, failed Republican politician, Mexican War veteran, and direct *Mayflower* descendant with dazzling blue eyes and an Amish-style beard, held a review of his division in Spain Field, during which Maj. James. E. Powell, an experienced soldier of the 25th Missouri, spotted a large body of enemy cavalry hovering on the edges of the woods, taking in the proceedings. He notified Prentiss, who decided to investigate with a reconnaissance at 4 p.m. of five companies, commanded by Col. David Moore. This patrol marched about a mile to the southwest where, in Seay Field, they came upon several black slaves who said they had seen about 200 Confederate cavalry a while earlier. By then it was nearly twilight and the men "could hear the enemy moving in every direction," according to one of the soldiers; that was enough for Moore, and he withdrew the patrol and reported seeing no Rebels.

After dark, Capt. Gilbert D. Johnson, a company commander in the 12th Michigan who had been sent to reinforce the regiment's picket lines, reported there was definitely suspicious movement in the woods to his front. He took his story to General Prentiss, who, like Sherman before him, replied, in effect, that there was nothing to worry about.

No one in high command, it seemed, wanted to upset the applecart and suggest that the Union encampment was in danger, but that did not satisfy Captain Johnson, who, along with the habitually suspicious Major Powell, went to see General Prentiss's First Brigade commander, Col. Everett Peabody, a six-foot-one, 240-pound bear of a man, with a disposition to match. Peabody was a Massachusetts-born, Harvard-educated engineer who had moved to St. Joseph 11 years earlier and became one of the most prominent rail builders in the West. With his wary New England upbringing and engineer's practicality Peabody was just skeptical enough to risk the wrath of his superiors. After hearing out Johnson and Powell, Peabody ordered them to muster five companies—some 400 men—from Powell's 25th Missouri and Johnson's 12th Michigan and find out just what in hell was going on in the misty dews and damps beyond their encampment.

It was well past the midnight hour on Sunday, April 6, when Major Powell's patrol filed out toward the forbidding line of trees to the south. He marched them again toward Seay Field, where earlier they had encountered the slaves. Cautiously feeling their way in the darkness, with the sickle moon just a pale sliver hanging low in the western sky, they reached another clearing.

Suddenly shots rang out, then the sound of horses' hooves: Rebel cavalry. Powell ordered the patrol to form a skirmish line and pressed forward. If he had known what he was headed for, he would have been horrified—as any sane man would—for he was marching nearly straight into the 10,000-man corps of the Rebel general William J. Hardee, who in the Old Army had written the standard West Point textbook *Rifle and Light Infantry Tactics* and was now waiting patiently for daylight to launch his attack.

Joseph Ruff was a 20-year-old German immigrant who had hired himself out to Michigan farmers for $16 a month* before he joined the army and landed as a private in the 12th Michigan Volunteer Infantry. He had just been detailed as cook for the week, but when Captain Johnson commenced rounding up men for the reconnaissance patrol Ruff decided to join up. Now he was fumbling along in the false dawn past deserted log cabins disturbed only by "the crowing of fowls," until they came to that 40-acre open spot in the timber beyond Seay Field, which turned out to be farmer Fraley's field.

"When we halted the first streak of daylight had appeared," Ruff remembered. "As we watched, we noticed something white moving through the brush and in another moment we spied a horseman whose movements we made out to be those of an enemy," he said. Then, suddenly, came "the crack of several muskets, and bullets were soon whizzing after us."

Ruff and the others began forming in line and advancing, firing at the unseen Rebels as the sky first paled gray, then pink, and the landscape revealed "a rise of ground which seemed to be covered with thick underbrush," from which they could see "the flashes of Rebel guns." Several of the Michiganders were wounded, one mortally as the fire became thicker and faster. Ruff took cover, only to have "several enemy bullets driven into the tree about the line of my head. One just clipped by my right ear," he said. Around him, men began to fall in irregular ways; some uttered peculiar noises. The

---

* In the slave states, slaves could be rented for about eight dollars to ten dollars per month. Thus the term "slave wages." Ruff didn't do much better, but it was a living, at least, and an impetus for the Free Soil Party and others to oppose the spread of slavery, which would have reduced wages for everyone else—especially poor immigrants like Ruff—in any state where it came into existence.

world was suddenly out of kilter, as though the beauty of the bright Tennessee sunrise was merely a prelude to death, and that nature, with all her morning splendor, was mocking mankind's folly.

Major Powell's patrol had disturbed a picket outpost of Mississippians from Hardee's corps, and their compatriots responded like an angry swarm of bees. As daylight finally came streaming through the woods, this savage little fight at last touched off what was to be thus far the bloodiest battle in American military history. It would be remembered as the most brutal battle in the West during the entire Civil War.

As the weight of the Confederate force began to tell, Powell sent a note with a messenger telling Colonel Peabody that they had encountered a Rebel force of 3,000 and were being driven back. Just as the New Englander was digesting this news, his division commander, General Prentiss, who had heard the shooting in the woods, rode into camp wondering what all the racket was about. When he learned that Peabody had sent out a reconnaissance, Prentiss became irate, accusing him of starting a battle without permission. Peabody retorted, "You'll soon see that I am not mistaken." Prentiss then ordered Colonel Moore, who had led yesterday's patrol, to take another five infantry companies out to reinforce Powell, who was clearly involved in some kind of fight. Prentiss then moved on.

It seemed to several observers on the scene that Moore and his force had barely disappeared across the field and into the woods before the racket of the skirmishing quickly "doubled in intensity." Men listened and glanced at one other in alarm. Peabody then ordered his drummer to beat the long roll. He was taking no chances.

As the soldiers began to fall in and Peabody called for his horse,

Prentiss reappeared in a cloud of dust and high dudgeon, confronting him from the height of his mount. "Colonel Peabody," he cried, "I will hold you personally responsible for bringing on this engagement." No doubt Prentiss was infuriated that he, himself, would be held responsible by Grant and the others. Peabody replied with a defiant salute and an unmistakable air of disgust—"If I brought on the fight, I am to lead the van"—and without further adieu he cantered away toward the sound of the firing.

Back at Fraley Field Major Powell's patrol had taken a serious fright. As they stubbornly withdrew into the forest away from the mounting Confederate opposition, those men who looked back were stunned to behold an entire Rebel line of battle emerge from the woods and fields—21 regiments—nearly 10,000 men, many flags flying, officers on horseback, swords drawn, gun barrels glinting, sergeants shouting orders. Their breaths caught tight as they watched this Rebel line come crashing toward them.

At just this juncture Colonel Moore's relief column collided with the head of Powell's withdrawal. Before noticing the Rebel battle line, Moore began to rebuke Powell's men for running away. "He rated us cowards for retreating," said Private Ruff. "We warned him not to be too bold or he would get into trouble." Moore rejected this perfectly sound advice, and pressed on—dragooning Powell's unwounded men to accompany him until he, too, encountered the Confederate attack in motion.

Moore quickly sized up the situation and became intent on buying time for the unsuspecting Union ranks back in the camps. After sending for reinforcements, he and the remnants of Major Powell's command fought a tooth-and-nail delaying action that cost Moore his leg and Major Powell his life and saw most of their force "nearly annihilated or put to rout." But the 25 minutes that their lopsided little battle lasted was worth a thousand times the effort in blood and tears, because Moore and Powell had bought enough time to prevent the Rebel attack from falling on Prentiss's division completely unexpected.

———◆◆◆———

Over in his own camp Sherman had heard the commotion and decided to investigate. A few minutes earlier, a messenger sent by Moore had warned Sherman that Rebel units were marching toward his front. Barely an hour earlier he had discounted a similar alarm sent by the ever anxious Colonel Appler, but all these reports had finally spurred the nervous-natured Sherman to action despite his best efforts to remain calm in the face of whatever was causing everybody else to be so jumpy.

In most of his sector it had been, thus far, a typical Sunday morning on the "plain of Pittsburg Landing," as Sherman had dubbed it. Soldiers had finished their breakfast and were attending to routine tasks such as washing clothes or writing letters or simply lounging around; some were engaged in playing cards or other games of chance, while still others attended services conducted by brigade chaplains on the lovely Sabbath day. It was cool, bright, clear, and too early in the year for bugs. The orchards were in full blossom, oaks were tasseling, dogwoods and redbuds were blooming, and an inordinate number of those on hand recorded in diaries and memoirs how many birds were singing in the trees; some singled out robins, some bluebirds or mourning doves. Others noted the disharmony of the sounds of the birds and the distant spatter of gunfire.

Accompanied by his staff, Sherman shortly after 7 a.m. rode out into farmer Rhea's open field in front of the 53rd Ohio, Colonel Appler's bothersome regiment. Appler himself had been fretting half the night as he listened to the sporadic firing somewhere out in the darkness. About six, one of Major Powell's men came staggering wild-eyed and bloody into his camp shouting, "Get into line, the Rebels are coming!" Appler once more ordered the long roll drumbeat and sent his quartermaster to alert Sherman. As the 53rd Ohio's bedraggled officers and men began falling into line, the quartermaster returned with a sarcastic message that he delivered to Appler confidentially: "General Sherman says you must be badly scared over there."

There was barely time to process this deflating reply when one of two companies Appler had sent out earlier to check on the picket line returned with a report that "the Rebels out there are thicker than fleas on a dog's back." Appler ordered his men to load up and form in a line of battle. It was about this time that Sherman's party appeared in Rhea's field in front of Appler's position and the general halted to take out his spyglass and begin studying what appeared to be a large body of enemy troops marching diagonally across the south end of the field half a mile away.

Someone in Appler's regiment suddenly glimpsed a line of Rebel skirmishers* emerge from the brush close by on Sherman's right, opposite from the direction he was looking; they halted and raised their weapons to aim. A warning was shouted out but not in time. Sherman started and threw up his hands before his face,

---

* On the attack or march, each regiment would throw a company in advance as "skirmishers" to make first contact with the enemy and report on his strength.

exclaiming, "My God, we are attacked!" An instant later the flash and crash of fire from the Rebel volley killed Sherman's orderly right next to him—blew him off his horse and onto his back on the ground spouting blood. Sherman himself was struck in the hand, apparently from buckshot, then wheeled his horse with the rest of his staff, dashing away from the field, yelling to Appler as he passed by, "Hold your position, I will support you."

———————◆◆◆———————

At the Cherry mansion in Savannah, nine miles downriver, Ulysses S. Grant was just sitting down to breakfast when an ill-omened boom reverberated from somewhere upstream on the Tennessee River. Perhaps the most lucid description of Grant at this weighty juncture in his career was given 31 years later when Mrs. W. H. Cherry, mistress of the house where Grant was staying, replied to a question posed by one T. M. Hurst, assistant postmaster of Nashville; their exchange was ultimately published in the February 1893 issue of the *Confederate Veteran*.

"Dear Sir—Your letter of inquiry concerning 'Gen. Grant's physical condition on the morning the battle of Shiloh began,' is received. You will please accept my assurance, gladly given, that on the date mentioned I believe Gen. Grant was thoroughly sober. He was at my breakfast table when he heard the report from a cannon. Holding, untasted, a cup of coffee, he paused in conversation to listen a moment at the report of another cannon. He hastily arose, saying to his staff officers, 'Gentlemen, the ball is in motion; let's be off.' His flagship (as he called his special steamboat) was lying at the wharf, and in fifteen minutes he, staff officers, orderlies, clerks, and horses had embarked."

While her husband remained loyal to the Union, Mrs. Cherry (née Annie Irwin) was a staunch supporter of the rebellion, and in fact had a brother in the Confederate cavalry. While she evidently loathed the notion of Yankee officers in her home, she was much taken, even then, with Grant's character and his "magnanimity," as she put it. The question of Grant's sobriety, at Shiloh and elsewhere, dogged him even to the grave—and beyond it—as evinced by the inquiry Mrs. Cherry received. It has also dogged historians from that day to this, especially those who do not wish to admit their idols might have feet of clay. But this day in southwest Tennessee was shaping up to be the most trying ever of Grant's long and illustrious military career, and one thing for certain is that a drunkard could never have made his way through it.

CHAPTER 3

FROM FAILURE
TO FORTUNE

———◆———

Ulysses Grant is a captivating military study, if for no other reason than he had earned a reputation as the most unmilitary-looking officer in the army. He often dressed in a plain blue suit and a gray felt hat, prompting one wag to suggest that he looked like a streetcar conductor. On those occasions when he wore a uniform he usually put on a plain private's tunic unadorned except for his insignia of rank—the gold braid, sashes, and epaulettes he left to French admirals and the like—and sometimes he was even mistaken for a man of the ranks. He was 39 years old when the war started, of medium height and slender build, and his manner was taciturn and unpretentious. In fact there was little in his bearing or his upbringing to suggest that he was destined for greatness, except perhaps for the piercing gaze in his blue eyes, which, only later, was interpreted as a determination to succeed. He was an American of his day, with both the strengths and weakness of the American character. Low-keyed, enigmatic, he often frustrated his staff by not communicating his intentions before issuing major battle orders. He was an unusual man, a gifted man, sometimes he was mysterious; perhaps he was a puzzle even to himself.

To those who knew him young, it was a wonder that he accomplished anything at all; to a nation that ultimately worshipped him it remained a wonder how, in the space of a decade, he rose from failed soldier, unsuccessful farmer, hardscrabble wood peddler, lackluster store clerk, and notorious drunkard to the most celebrated military hero of the age and President of the United States. In fact, the most remarkable thing about Grant was that, by all accounts, he was so *unremarkable.*

Grant's father, Jesse, was a tannery worker in Point Pleasant, Ohio, when Grant was born on April 27, 1822. Over time, Jesse worked his way up to start his own tannery and slaughterhouse, and in later years he owned a leather goods store and haberdashery. In the meantime he dabbled in local politics and was acknowledged about town as a kind of self-educated know-it-all, widely read in everything from the classics to contemporary politics. He frequently bombarded local newspapers with abolitionist-style editorial letters, though such sentiments never rubbed off on Grant. What *did* rub off on him from those early years, however, was a lifelong revulsion at the sight of blood, in consequence of frequent exposure to his father's tanning operations. In fact, he was unable to eat even a rare-cooked piece of meat and always ordered his "charred gray."

As a baby, Grant went unnamed for a month before the family selected as a middle name Ulysses—after the fabulous Greek hero who conquered Troy by hiding his soldiers inside a giant wooden horse—by drawing choices out of a hat. In homage to Grant's mother, Hannah, they selected as a first name Hiram, after the biblical king who built the temple of Solomon, which made Grant's initials H.U.G. and set him up for a bit of consternation down the road.

During the languid years of the 1830s about the only thing Grant seemed interested in were horses, with which he appeared to share some kind of hidden understanding. His equestrianship led people to remark that in the saddle Grant seemed "as one" with his horse. At the age of six he earned money using his father's horses to haul brush for his neighbors and by his teens he was breaking and training horses for sale and had set up carriage teams to take passengers to nearby towns.

When Grant reached his teens his father began trying to secure for him a West Point education on grounds that the young man was beginning to show an aptitude for mathematics—about the only thing that interested him aside from horses—but more important, because it was free. A congressional appointment came in due time, and Grant entered the United States Military Academy in 1839 at the age of 17. Before he left, Grant's cousins carved his initials into his luggage, but for some reason Grant decided he had had enough of H.U.G. He promptly reversed his first and second names to become Ulysses Hiram Grant, which lasted only until he arrived at "the gray castle" on the Hudson, whereupon an adjutant supervising admissions noted that he had been nominated as Ulysses *Simpson* Grant—Simpson being his mother's maiden name. In typical army fashion it was put to Grant that he would either become Ulysses Simpson Grant or board a steamer back downriver, never to see West Point again. Thus the legend of U. S. Grant was born, and in time his friends began calling him Sam, after "Uncle Sam."

From the beginning, Grant was an indifferent student. He nearly flunked French and languished in the library reading romantic fiction, at one point writing home, "I do love the place, it seems as though I could live here forever if my friends would only come too." He did make one friend, Fred Dent of Missouri, who would have a lasting impact on his life, but he excelled only in math and drawing, barely getting by in other subjects. He could not have known it then, of course—none of them could—but the acquaintances and friendship of those days would furnish the cream of the officer corps of the Civil War, including Union generals William Tecumseh Sherman, George B. McClellan, Don Carlos Buell, John Pope, George Thomas, and William Rosecrans, as well as the Confederate generals James Longstreet, George Pickett, and Thomas ("Stonewall") Jackson.

Despite Grant's lackadaisical academic performance, as a West Point equestrian he was peerless. To see him riding, said one student, was "to watch a circus," and he set a record for the equestrian high jump at West Point that would stand for the next 25 years.

————◆————

In 1843 Grant graduated in the bottom half of his class and was stuck in the infantry because the elite Corps of Engineers would not have him and there was no room in the cavalry. He received a further humiliation when he went home to Ohio on leave before reporting to his first post. He had put on his fancy new uniform only to learn that people were making fun of him because of his clothes. It seems to have been a seminal moment for him with regard to military dress. As his biographer Brooks Simpson put it, "The new brevet second lieutenant never liked wearing a full-dress uniform. The memory of being laughed at . . . never quite faded away."

That autumn Grant reported to the Fourth U.S. Infantry Regiment at Jefferson Barracks, which was near St. Louis and the home of his West Point roommate Fred Dent, who happened to have a sister, Julia, just returned from boarding school, who "was possessed of a lively and pleasing countenance," according to one observer. Grant promptly became fascinated with her. The Dents were well-to-do slaveholders who kept a large plantation in the country in addition to their fashionable town house in St. Louis. Before long, Grant and Julia were riding together over the 1,200 acres of White Haven, which had been built by her father, "Colonel" Fredrick Dent—after which the young lieutenant and the old "colonel" would often engage in spirited though affable conversations over what had now become the overarching topic of the day: the future of African slavery.

The calls that handsome Lieutenant Grant paid to the Dents must have been refreshing interludes from the drudgery of Jefferson Barracks, and he made the most of them, riding with Julia through meadows "knee deep in bluegrass and clover" and along the banks of sparkling, pebbly Gravois Creek. And before that winter of 1846 faded into spring, Grant's fancy had turned to love. But just as quickly fate snatched him away to the wilds of western Louisiana, right on the Texas border, where his regiment had been ordered to join a new "U.S. Army of Observation" that would remain as a deterrent force in the ongoing disputes between Texas and Mexico. Less than a decade earlier Texas had gained its independence from Mexico—though Mexico refused to admit it—and was currently in the process of becoming a U.S. state, though the Mexicans promised war if that occurred.

Grant had been on leave with his family in Illinois when news of his assignment reached him, and he rushed back to ask Julia to marry him. He did this in a way that Julia characterized as "awkward," and she demurred, mainly because old Colonel Dent had sensed what was going on and had spoken with his daughter of the vicissitudes of marrying an ill-paid, low-ranking military officer, whose very career demanded that upon any whim of the War Department he could be seized up and posted hundreds or even thousands of miles away. So Julia did not say yes, but neither did she say no, and there things stood for the next two years while Grant stewed in Louisiana until the long-expected war with Mexico became reality.

Grant was afforded a brief leave and he immediately caught a steamer back to St. Louis. Old man Dent was still against a marriage, but he softened somewhat when Grant informed him that once the war was over he planned to resign from the army and take up teaching, preferably at West Point, where he believed his skills in mathematics would be put to good and profitable use. Colonel Dent relented to the extent that Grant was now permitted to write "courting letters" to Julia.

* ◆ *

With that arrangement behind him, Grant returned to the army, only to be informed he had been assigned as quartermaster for his regiment, which was basically a noncombat position. His West Point training, of course, would have made Grant aware that the duties of quartermasters included such critical responsibilities as providing food, ammunition, transportation, living accommodations, pay, and other services fundamental to keeping troops in the field. Grant, however, received the news of his assignment with mixed feelings, since promotion in the army was almost always tied to experience under fire. On the other hand, Grant—like any sane person—had a fear of combat, a shortcoming that he shared in a letter to Julia.

Be that as it may, Grant somehow managed to find his way into nearly every big fight of the Mexican War. His friend James Longstreet recalled, "You could not keep him out of battle . . . [He] was everywhere on the field." During the bloody house-to-house fighting at the Battle of Monterrey, Grant's regiment was running out of ammunition and a trip to the rear where the supply dumps were located meant riding a lethal gauntlet of Mexican gunfire from every roof and window. Afterward it became the talk of the regiment how young Lieutenant Grant had leapt upon his horse and, clinging Indian-style to the neck and one side, galloped up one street and down the other, dodging bullets until he reached the rear. In his memoirs he modestly recalled going so fast that "generally, I was past and under the cover of the next block before the enemy fired."

Despite the early American victories, the Mexican War dragged on for 16 more bloody months, during which Grant lost a number of friends and grew disenchanted with the conflict. Nevertheless, in the last days of the final Battle of Mexico City, he managed to drag a small cannon to the bell tower of a church, where he and a squad of men placed fire into the rear of a Mexican column, breaking up their formation.

For this he was made a brevet captain,* but even with the fall of the Mexican capital the war had persisted, and Grant agonized

---

* Brevet was a temporary rank given for bravery or meritorious service. It is not permanent for purposes of pay or promotion.

over not being able to be with Julia. When at last the fighting concluded, Grant and other regulars were kept on as an Army of Occupation, while the volunteers were sent home and details of the peace were worked out. Soon he became dismayed by the masses of peons, those "poor and starving subjects," he wrote to Julia, "who are willing to work more than any country in the world," and yet "the rich keep down the poor with a hardness of heart that is almost incredible." If Grant made any correlation between this and the slaves of the South he never said so, perhaps out of deference to Julia's slaveholding family.

Grant found occupation duty in peacetime dreary, which seems to have led to dissolution on his part, if a superior officer's letter to his family can be believed: "[Grant] drinks too much, but don't you say a word about it," wrote the officer, who was from Grant's hometown. His time in Mexico City also reinforced Grant's aversion toward the pomp and circumstance of military life. In the first battles, including Monterrey, Grant had served under Gen. Zachary Taylor, whom he greatly admired and who usually dressed in an old leather duster and slouch straw hat. In the later stages of the war, however, Grant's commanding general had been Winfield Scott, "Old Fuss and Feathers" himself, who Grant said, somewhat derisively, wore "all the uniform prescribed or allowed by law."

It was also during this period that he found time for further reflection upon the Mexican War, which he decided had been trumped up by President Polk, a Tennessean, as a way of acquiring new U.S. territories from Mexico in order to create new slave states. Years afterward, Grant famously wrote in his memoirs that the conflict was "one of the most unjust wars every waged by a stronger nation against a weaker one."

In August 1848 Grant returned to St. Louis and, with her father's blessing, at last married Julia Dent. Among the army officers present were Longstreet, who was still recovering from battle wounds, and Cadmus Wilcox, who one day would face Grant as a Confederate major general commanding a division.

He was soon assigned to a quartermaster post in Detroit where Julia dutifully tried to fill the roll of army wife, but with no cooking or housekeeping experience, and no slaves to assist her, it was a trial. Two years later, Frederick Dent Grant was born and Julia began dividing her time between the army post and her more agreeable family home in St. Louis, which evidently added to Grant's boredom and the attendant temptations. This, in turn, possibly led to his joining, at one point, the Sons of Temperance, with a pledge to stop drinking.

In 1852, with Julia pregnant again, and young Fred only two, the Fourth Infantry was ordered to the Pacific coast, and there was no question of Julia going with him. Instead, Grant set out from New York on a steamship with several companies of the regiment and their dependents, bound for the Isthmus of Panama and thence overland to the Pacific. The journey across Panama was risky and abominable under the best of conditions, but in Grant's case it was nightmarish from the beginning.

Mules that the army had requisitioned to carry everyone through the fetid and pestilent swamps did not arrive, and Grant had to hire dugout boats operated by drunken knife fighters who spoke no English. People came down with tropical fevers, including malaria, and an epidemic of cholera broke out. By journey's end more than a third of Grant's party—a hundred soldiers, their wives, and their children— had perished in Panama. By all the participants' accounts Grant was an angel of mercy to the sick and dying and worked tirelessly throughout the ordeal to save lives, but he soon got a taste of the capriciousness of the press after an English newspaper blamed him for the disaster.

When what remained of the party reached California, Grant was sent to Fort Vancouver at the mouth of the Columbia River in the wilds of the Washington-Oregon borderlands. Presently word arrived that Julia had given birth to a boy, Ulysses S. Grant, Jr. In an attempt to enhance his poor army pay Grant bought a piece of land and in his spare time planted a crop of potatoes and chopped wood to sell to steamships. Floods drowned the potato fields and washed away the wood. An endeavor to raise poultry and livestock likewise failed, as did Grant's attempts to collect money he lent to fellow officers.

All this, and more, were reflected in melancholy letters to Julia, in which his gloominess and ennui were palpable. Not surprisingly, perhaps, Grant returned to drinking. It was commonly agreed that even a small amount of liquor had a disproportionate effect on him. After only a glass or two his speech would slur, and any more would "make him stupid." By varying accounts he either became a "consistent" drinker or indulged in "sprees" that could last for days. On a certain occasion in the officers' mess it was said that his conduct was taken account of by his fellow West Pointer George McClellan, whose surveying party Grant had been detailed to outfit.

After two years at Fort Vancouver Grant was reassigned to the even more remote outpost of Fort Humboldt, 250 miles north of San Francisco. There, with wife and family half a world away, he began to think of resigning from the army, but before that developed an unhappy incident occurred that haunted Grant for the rest of his army career. There are several accounts, but the gist of it was that Grant was discovered to be drunk while on duty as quartermaster on payday and was given the choice of facing court-martial or resigning from the service. Later, some of his friends defended Grant, saying that the commander "had it in for him," but the end result was that in May of 1854 Grant wrote Julia that he was coming home.

———◆———

Even before his hasty resignation from the army Grant had begun to picture himself as a gentleman Missouri farmer, but he had no savings and in fact had to borrow money from his West Point classmate Simon Bolivar Buckner just to get home. As a wedding present Colonel Dent had given him and Julia 60 acres of White Haven, which Grant planned to farm and expand until he could make a respectable living from the land, but this did not work out. Despite his toiling in the fields alongside Julia's slaves, fluctuating crop prices, droughts, and other farming perils all conspired to undo farmer Grant. Barely able to make ends meet, Grant was finally reduced to cutting and hauling wood up to St. Louis, just as he had done as a boy back in Illinois.

During the panic and subsequent depression of '57, Grant was so poor he had to pawn his gold pocket watch to buy Christmas presents for the family. Finally he gave up. A cousin of Julia's helped him find a job at a St. Louis real estate concern, but Grant failed at that too. He hated collecting rents and despised the idea of evicting anyone. Instead he sought a position as county engineer, for which his West Point training had made him eminently qualified, but partisan politics cost him the job. At last he swallowed his pride and accepted a clerkship at his father's leather-goods store in Galena, Illinois, near the Wisconsin border.

While Ulysses endured more than a decade of abject failures, his father Jesse Grant had become quite prosperous and owned leathermaking enterprises in several midwestern states. He had also become an insufferable windbag, inserting himself into local politics and vilifying Julia's family as "that tribe of slaveholders."

In the spring of 1860 Grant rented out the family slaves in Missouri and made his way north to Galena, which was across the Mississippi River and a little southeast of Dubuque, Iowa. Customers at his father's store there remembered him as an indifferent salesman, and that when the leaves began to fall he walked to and from work wearing his old army greatcoat and a dark slouch hat. That same autumn Abraham Lincoln was elected President, and talk of Southern secession electrified the air. It had been twenty years since Grant had entered West Point, and his career since then had gone in a downward way. But it was there, on the banks of the northern Mississippi River, that war found him.

Grant was not surprised by the firing on Charleston's Fort Sumter by the new Confederate States of America. He had spent too much time with Julia's family in Missouri and among his Southern West Point classmates and officers in the Mexican War to think that the South would not fight. Grant's own feelings were ambivalent; he detested the notion of disunion and in fact had voted against the Republican ticket in the election of 1856 because he believed its success would cause the South to secede. He did not vote in the election of 1860.* He also disliked slavery yet kept his wife's slaves within his own household and in fact even acquired a

---

* Much later, in his memoirs, Grant wrote somewhat peculiarly that if he had in fact voted in 1860 it would have been for the Democrat, Stephen A. Douglas, adding, however, that he would have preferred to vote for Lincoln.

slave of his own, one William Jones, whom he freed in 1859 when Jones was 35.*

Matters had boiled over and a fight was quickly becoming the only thing that would settle it. Grant understood this, and, being a military man, he felt honor-bound to offer his services to the Union. As he saw it, if Washington allowed the South to secede, nothing would prevent other states from doing the same, until in the end the first and only true experiment in democracy the world had ever known would dissolve itself into a disastrous and irretrievable collection of petty states squabbling among themselves.

He had also concluded that despite the Confederacy's seizure of enormous Federal stores, munitions, and military equipment in Southern forts and armories, and the defection of so many West Point–educated officers, the war nevertheless would be a short one. The Northern population was nearly twice that of the South, and its industrial superiority would soon take the starch out of the rebellion. Once that had occurred, Grant wrote in a letter to his father, with the abolitionist Republicans in control of the government, the market for slaves would bottom out until "the nigger will never disturb this country again." So reasoned Ulysses S. Grant.

After the attack on Fort Sumter in April 1861, Lincoln called for the various states to raise 75,000 volunteers to put down the rebellion. This resulted in an overwhelming response in most Northern states, including Illinois, where Grant helped to muster in troops. It also resulted in the secession of four more Southern states. On

---

*   The document of manumission states that Grant had bought Jones, but others, including historian Brooks Simpson, suggest that Jones might have come as a gift.

May 4, 1861, Grant wrote a letter to the adjutant general of the U.S. Army offering his services. It was never answered. Puzzled, he went to Cincinnati to see his old West Point acquaintance George B. McClellan, who had just been made a major general. He waited for three days but McClellan wouldn't see him.*

Grant was about to return to Galena, 39 years old and washed up, with the war passing him by, when a message came that the Illinois governor Richard Yates wished to see him. He went to Springfield, where the governor was waiting with an offer. There was a new regiment of volunteers, the governor said, who had revealed themselves as little more than a mob of chicken thieves led by a drunkard. Would Grant take charge of these people and try to straighten them out? He would have the rank of colonel. It was a stroke of fate that would change Grant's life forever.

In a month of hard work, patience, and liberal doses of the guardhouse, Grant had whipped these miscreants into such fine shape that Governor Yates turned over to him three other errant regiments. The number of troops under Grant now constituted a brigade, and technically the rank of brigadier general was his due. Still, Grant was stunned to read in the St. Louis newspapers that he had just been promoted, with some unexpected help from an acquaintance from Galena, Republican congressman Elihu Washburne. In two months Sam Grant had gone from a has-been former captain, failed farmer, and second-rate businessman to the command of several thousand men and induction into the most exclusive club the U.S. Army had to offer.

---

* It has been surmised that Grant's drunken episode in McClellan's presence at the officers' mess at Fort Vancouver may have had something to do with this obvious snub.

Not long after news of the North's disaster at the Battle of Bull Run in Virginia had reached the western command, Grant was put in charge of the District of Southeast Missouri, with headquarters at Cairo, Illinois, at the confluence of the Mississippi and Ohio Rivers. At that point Missouri and Kentucky were hanging in the Union by the slenderest political thread. As slave states, their loyalties were decidedly mixed and in the outlying areas Rebel detachments, abetted by Southern sympathizers, were recruiting, reconnoitering, burning bridges, and shooting at Yankee patrols. It was Grant's job to suppress these activities, and he was given considerable latitude to accomplish it.

The first thing Grant decided to do after he reached Cairo was seize the nearby city of Paducah, Kentucky, whose citizens were merrily anticipating the arrival of the Rebel general Gideon Pillow and his band of Confederates. This, Grant said, he had learned "from a scout belonging to General [John. C.] Frémont," who commanded the department. Control of Paducah, located about 40 miles east of Cairo at the confluence of the Ohio and the Tennessee Rivers, was critical if the Union planned to use the rivers as highways into the heart of the Confederacy.

One of the most brilliant ideas that the Union came up with during the war was the concept of the armed river gunboat as a strategic weapon. Rivers were, and had been, main arteries of travel, but until Robert Fulton's development of the steamboat in 1807 it was nearly impossible for a military operation to go against the current of a river. Now the Union snatched up a number of large river vessels, reinforced their superstructures with heavy oak, and armed them with big guns. These became the so-called timberclads, two of which played such a large role at the Battle of Shiloh. At

89

the same time, the Yankees were developing an even more powerful river warship—the ironclad. These were shoal draft vessels up
to 200 feet in length carrying crews of 150 or more. Their armament consisted of 2½-inch-thick iron plate over heavy oak blocking from 12 to 24 inches deep. The ship's main batteries consisted
of 32-pounder cannons, as well as big 42- and 64-pounder Dahl-
gren guns. By comparison, the typical army field gun was a mere
6-pounder or 12-pounder Napoleon gun. The ironclads were self-
sustaining, except for coal tenders that supplied their fuel, and their
firepower could flatten an average-size town within half a day. Eight
of these enormous craft were produced in less than four months in
1861–62.

Acting upon the information provided by Frémont's scout,
Grant telegraphed Frémont for permission to depart that night on
riverboats for Paducah and occupy it with two regiments and a battery. When he received no reply from the department commander,
Grant again telegraphed his plans to Frémont. Again no reply was
forthcoming, so Grant went ahead, and imagine the surprise on
the faces of the dumbfounded Paducahans when instead of the
Confederate army they had anticipated they were met by a blue-
coated regimental band playing "Hail Columbia" as it marched to
the town square. Once there, however, the citizens seemed relieved
when Grant delivered a proclamation that began, "I have come
among you as your friend and fellow citizen" and went on to pledge
to respect their "rights and property," which both parties understood to include slaves.

Grant's bloodless occupation of Paducah was just the sort of
thing Abraham Lincoln liked to see, and he certainly had not seen
much of it since the war began. Only last month there had been the

awful humiliation of the Battle of Balls Bluff right outside Washington, and now the British were threatening to intercede on behalf of the South because of the notorious Trent Affair.* With things looking down in the East, Lincoln had cast an eye to the war in the West, not least because of political concerns, including the upcoming congressional elections of 1862.

With the Mississippi River closed to Northern traffic since the war started, the midwestern states were suffering badly from lack of an outlet to sell their products to the South or ship them abroad. The result was steamboats rotting at the wharfs, crops rotting in the fields, timber and manufactured goods piling up in sheds, and no market for hogs, cattle, and dairy products. Almost since war broke out Lincoln had been pressing for a Union advance downriver but to no avail.

Part of the problem seemed to be finding a Union general willing to risk his reputation in battle against the Confederates. The only one who had tried, Nathaniel Lyon, was killed and his army defeated at the Battle of Wilson's Creek several months earlier. But the greatest problem of all seemed to lie with famed general "Pathfinder" Frémont, mastermind of the California conquest a decade and a half past.

Once disgraced by court-martial for insubordination and sentenced to dismissal from the service, Frémont had political connections (he was married to the daughter of Thomas Hart Benton, an influential Democratic senator for 30 years) that had brought him

---

* A Union warship captain intercepted the British steamship *Trent* in the Atlantic and removed and arrested two Confederate emissaries en route to London. The incident nearly brought England into the war.

out of mothballs and installed him in this important job. A series of published accounts of his western exploits had made Frémont a national hero, but he was trained as a topographical engineer and had no formal military education, nor any experience in handling large bodies of troops. The results ranged from disorder to chaos.

Like a self-imposed Prisoner of Zenda, Frémont established himself in a palatial St. Louis mansion surrounded by a ridiculous coterie of pompously dressed guards, and he received almost no one in his headquarters, including his own generals. Inquiries went into the headquarters and remained there, mysteriously ignored. His logistics were hopelessly plagued by extravagant government contracts with unscrupulous dealers, while Frémont's attention seemed focused on freeing slaves wherever and whenever he could—a policy that, for political reasons, was the last thing Lincoln wanted.

It was under these stressful circumstances that Grant set out to do battle with the Confederates who had recently established themselves near the small settlement of Belmont, Missouri, about 25 miles downriver from Cairo. After his peaceful occupation of Paducah, Grant had looked for some new task and decided that the concentration of Rebels at Belmont was not only a menace to navigation but offered an opportunity for his troops to get some real battle experience.

Even that early in the war, Grant seemed to grasp that the overarching Union strategy in the West should focus on clearing the Mississippi River—as opposed to merely capturing cities—and restoring Federal commerce from the Midwest to the Gulf of Mexico, while at the same time cleaving the Confederacy in two. Accordingly, he applied to the navy for steamship transportation and gunboat protection, and early on the morning of November 1, 1861, he shoved off downriver with five infantry regiments, six artillery batteries, and two companies of cavalry—about 3,100 men in all—accompanied by the "timberclad" gunboats *Tyler* and *Lexington*.

The expedition was in the nature of a raid rather than conquest and occupation. The Confederates under Gen. Sterling Price were using Belmont for an induction and training center and reinforcement channel both to and from their powerful new fortifications at Columbus, Kentucky, on the opposite shore.

Columbus had become a hot potato as the war intensified. At the beginning of the conflict Kentucky, a slave state divided almost evenly in sentiment between North and South, tried to remain neutral, which was to say that its legislature voted not to take sides in the contest and declared that neither Federal nor Rebel troops were welcome on its soil. It was a notion that would have been almost laughable had the stakes not been so high, for neither the Union nor the Confederacy was going to leave Kentucky be.

However, its fragile neutrality lasted through the spring and summer of 1861, with neither Lincoln—who was born there—nor Jefferson Davis—who also was born in the state and attended college there—wishing to disturb the equipoise. Pressure continued to build, however, and Kentucky's internal politics seethed with volatile and rancid hatreds. At the end of the summer the Union general William "Bull" Nelson, a bombastic former Annapolis graduate and naval officer and native Kentuckian, could stand it no longer. He established a Union recruiting camp right in the middle of the state and defied the legislature to remove it. This "violation" of Kentucky's neutrality by the Yankees prompted the Rebel general Leonidas Polk, formerly the Episcopal bishop of Louisiana, and a West Point classmate of Jefferson Davis's, to order troops to take

Columbus, which was both a tactical and strategic strongpoint on the Mississippi.

Located on a curve in the river, Columbus's most commanding feature were the imposing bluffs that reared nearly 180 feet straight up from the banks almost like the ramparts of a medieval castle. (In one of his many decisions-never-made, Frémont had nearly ordered Grant to take the place, but the Rebel Polk beat him to it on September 2, 1861.) The Confederates set out to make Columbus impregnable by land or sea, installing 140 large guns, underwater mines, and a gigantic anchor chain with links eight inches thick that spanned a solid mile and was connected to a capstan across the river at Belmont, from where it could be lifted from the bottom and wound tight to block Northern shipping. The fortifications were manned by a small army of 17,000 troops served by a line of the Mobile and Ohio Railroad to Memphis and points south. Thus Columbus became the end of the end of the line so far as Yankee navigation of the Mississippi was concerned. Leonidas Polk made the installation so formidable-looking that Union intelligence estimated some 80,000 Rebels inhabited the place.

＊ ＊ ＊

Initially, Grant's intention had been to annihilate both Columbus and Belmont, but Frémont had not given him enough troops to do the job, so now the best he could hope for was to disrupt the Rebel encampment at Belmont and perhaps forestall its expansion. Union strategy in the West at this point seemed more bent on securing places than invading the Confederate South, which Grant clearly saw as the way to victory, and the sooner the better. He had a vision of amphibious operations that other officers seemed to lack.

He saw the rivers as an easy way to get to the Rebel heartland, deep into Tennessee to places like Corinth, Nashville, and even Shiloh, which at that point he'd never heard of.

Military bureaucracy continued to block his way, but at Belmont Grant got off to a good enough start, landing without opposition about two miles north of the Confederates and marching in line of battle through a landscape of woods and cornfields. The Rebels had been forewarned by their lookouts across the river at Columbus, but Grant's attack still took them more or less by surprise. Quickly the brisk fire from Grant's Yankees had the Confederates scrambling down six-foot-tall bluffs along the riverbanks. It looked as though an easy victory had been obtained, but there then occurred an evil that dogged commanders on both sides all through the conflict.

As Grant lamented afterward, if his men had pressed the attack, the Rebels would have been either driven into the river or forced to surrender. Instead, his soldiers began looting the Confederate tents. "The moment the enemy camp was reached," Grant bitterly complained, "our men laid down their arms and commenced rummaging the tents to pick up trophies.* Some of the higher officers were little better than the privates. They galloped about from one cluster of men to the other, and at every halt delivered a short eulogy upon the Union cause and the achievements of the command."

Not only that, but while the looting progressed the Confederates managed to reorganize themselves and began working upriver, out of sight beneath the bank, so as to get between Grant and his troop

---

* Pillaging has been the bane of armies since time immemorial; it was certainly a factor at Shiloh.

transports. Even worse, Union soldiers suddenly saw coming full steam across the river from the fort at Columbus Rebel troopships crammed "from boiler deck to roof" with enemy reinforcements.

It was all Grant could do to escape. He began organizing his men to retreat back to the ships and detailed others to burn the Rebel camp, but then the Confederate artillery on the opposite shore—until now unsure of who was where—opened up on them. As if that wasn't bad enough, the Rebels along the riverbank began to emerge and form into a battle line, and some of Grant's men began to shout, "We are surrounded!"

As Grant told it later, "When I announced that we had cut our way in, and could cut our way out just as well, it seemed a new revelation." Somehow Grant's people managed to get on the boats and away before a catastrophe befell them, but it was a narrowly run operation. It was said that the general himself had to leap his horse from the bank and scramble onto the deck of a departing steamer. According to Grant, the battle proved two things: His troops would fight and the Confederates now knew they could not operate in Missouri with impunity.

The press did not see it that way, however, characterizing the Battle of Belmont as a retreat that was "wholly unnecessary and barren of results, nor the possibility of them from the beginning." Four hundred eighty-five Union soldiers were killed, wounded, or captured; Rebel losses were put at about the same. Never mind that the newspapers lampooned him, Grant had taken his first major steps down what would be a long, bloody road.

The question now became: What next? His inclination remained to attack the big Rebel installations at Columbus, Kentucky, which had supplied those last-minute reinforcements at the Belmont fight.

But Frémont still would not give him the troops. Then a stroke of luck: Grant was hardly returned from the Belmont raid when Lincoln fired Frémont for issuing his own, premature "emancipation proclamation" and replaced him with the nervous-natured, bug-eyed Maj. Gen. Henry Halleck, who had written several military textbooks but never fought a battle.

Known as "Old Brains," the 47-year-old Halleck had been ranked number three in his West Point class of '39, and he was married to the granddaughter of Alexander Hamilton. During the Mexican War he was assigned to the West Coast, where he soon resigned his commission and became a wealthy lawyer and land speculator, but he returned to the army when war broke out. Not as cautious as Frémont, perhaps, Halleck nevertheless was hesitant to fight battles unless he had complete military superiority, which was difficult enough, given that Union intelligence estimates routinely doubled, or even tripled, the numbers of the Confederate enemy.

To Grant the departure of the ineffectual and aloof Frémont must have seemed a godsend, but Halleck was a different character entirely. An ambitious martinet who tended to connive and micromanage, Halleck was particularly overbearing where his generals were concerned, and Grant was singled out for special oversight because of rumors Halleck had picked up about his drinking. In a subterfuge drenched in irony, Halleck sent to Grant the young, energetic colonel James McPherson, who had finished first in his class at the Academy in 1853. Ostensibly, McPherson—who had once been on Halleck's staff—was to be Grant's chief engineering officer, but in fact he was meant also to serve as Halleck's spy. McPherson, however, turned out to be utterly loyal to Grant and soon became one of his most trusted officers.

Then, in an almost classic example of "what the right hand giveth, the left hand taketh away," Halleck also sent to Grant Col. John A. McClernand, a lawyer with no previous military experience who was soon to join the class of "political generals" that so vexed the Federal Army of the West. A Democrat and something of a gasbag, McClernand was responsible for at least some of the rumors of Grant's drunkenness, but he had also formed a political friendship with Lincoln that the President found indispensable. Though personally brave, McClernand proved to be an opportunist who sought to glorify himself at every turn and, unlike the steadfast McPherson, caused Grant much trouble as the war wore on.

It was McPherson who came up with the idea to attack Fort Henry, the maneuver that launched Grant's meteoric rise. Knowing they lacked the manpower to overcome Columbus, McPherson studied the maps and the scouting reports—with Grant "looking over his shoulder and puffing relentlessly on his pipe"—and contemplated the scheme to bypass Columbus entirely and end the Union logjam in the West.

Fifty miles east of Columbus, near the Kentucky-Tennessee border, the Tennessee and Cumberland Rivers come within ten miles of each other (each flowing north) before they empty into the Ohio, which in turn flows into the Mississippi. The Confederates had installed fortresses on each of these rivers, blocking the Federal armies from their heartland by waterway. Near the confluence of the Tennessee and the Ohio stood the Rebel Fort Henry; if it fell, the South would be open to invasion all the way into northern Alabama—an inviting prospect for the Union. But Grant took it even further. If Fort Henry fell, then Fort Donelson, on the Cumberland less than a dozen miles away, would also become vulnerable. And the Cumberland was the key to the grand prize of the mid-South: Nashville.

Grant and McPherson carefully formulated an amphibious attack integrating the navy and its powerful new ironclads, with which they felt they could cleave the Confederacy in two east of the Mississippi River all the way down to the Alabama-Mississippi border. On January 6, 1862, Grant carried this proposal to his new boss, Major General Halleck, in St. Louis, where both he and it were received with "such little cordiality" that, Grant said later, "I was cut short as if my plan was preposterous."

CHAPTER 4

NOTHING
CAN BE DONE

H ALLECK'S ODD AND DISCOURTEOUS BEHAVIOR is a perfect illustration of the kind of paralysis that gripped the Union in the early years of the war. Although the account in Grant's memoirs was much abbreviated, an expanded version of the encounter from one of Grant's staff members, Col. John Wesley Emerson, is even more surprising.

According to Emerson, who said he had spoken with an officer who was present at the meeting, Halleck "shook hands with Grant rather stiffly, then sat at his desk shuffling papers, and told Grant to 'state briefly the nature of the business connected with your command which brought you to headquarters.' Grant took out a map, unfolded it, and began to explain the situation at Fort Henry and Fort Donelson, saying that with an army of twenty-five thousand men, aided by the gunboats, he could take both forts in ten days.

"Halleck stopped him by asking coldly, 'Is there anything connected with the good of your command that you would wish to discuss?'

"Grant tried to trace the projected movement on his map, but Halleck stood up, waved the map aside, and said, 'All of this, General Grant, relates to the business of the general commanding the department. When he wishes to consult you on the subject, he will notify you.'

"Having said this, Halleck stalked out, leaving Grant to pocket his map and go back to Cairo."*

The historian Bruce Catton sums up Halleck this way—and no one could say it better—"What Halleck knew about war came out of books, and when the time came for action he would make war in a bookish manner. He was, in addition, waspish, petulant, gossipy, often rather pompous, and afflicted with the habit of passing the buck."

What Ulysses Grant made of Halleck's treatment is anybody's guess; in Emerson's version, the snub was so blatant that it would have been hard not to find it highly offensive, but all Grant would say in his memoirs was that he returned to Cairo "very much crestfallen." Yet in his letters to Julia around this time Grant somehow seemed to believe that Halleck was a great man and, more than that, a good friend. It was only much later, after the war was over and all the papers were revealed, that Grant discovered what a chameleon Henry Halleck could be.

---

* Emerson's version of the story is contained in his work *Grant's Life in the West and His Mississippi Valley Campaigns,* first serialized in the *Midland Monthly,* 1896–98.

Indeed, Halleck had been considering strategy along the same lines that Grant had been trying to propose, which makes his refusal to share that information with Grant all the more odd, and his abrupt behavior toward him almost inexplicable. The only logical explanation could have been if Halleck believed that such a move was so delicate as to be kept top secret even from Grant. Yet that calls into question why any department commander would keep in his employ a senior general who could not be trusted—especially when it was his men who were going to do the fighting.

Recently Halleck had telegraphed McClellan—who had become the new commander in chief of the army after old Winfield Scott was forced into retirement—that Grant's plan, an attack up the rivers, was exactly the right strategy in his department. Responding to McClellan's suggestion that Halleck move straight down the Mississippi and take Columbus, "Old Brains" countered that "a much more feasible plan is to move up the Cumberland and the Tennessee, making Nashville the first objective point. Columbus," he continued, "cannot be taken without a terrible loss of life. However, it can be turned, and forced to surrender, but the plan should not be attempted without a large force, not less than 60,000 men."

The only difference between Grant's plan and Halleck's was that Grant proposed to do it with 25,000 troops (of which he already had 20,000 on hand). But Halleck required more than *twice* that many men, which he didn't have, and the only source for them would be to borrow from General Buell's force at Louisville, which was beyond his authority.

Buell, in turn, was being pressured by McClellan to launch an all-out assault into eastern Tennessee and break up the Confederate rail lines there. That was because McClellan was planning his own movement to capture Richmond and end the war—or so he said. Instead of marching his army straight south to the Rebel capital—an approach that had ended so disastrously the previous summer at the Battle of Bull Run—"Little Mac" intended to move his 100,000-man host by steamship to the tip of the Virginia peninsula and attack Richmond from the east. In order to do so, he insisted that Buell clear and hold eastern Tennessee and its rail lines so that the Confederates could not reinforce their Virginia army before he captured Richmond. This was truly "long range" strategy.

Buell complained that he could not move into eastern Tennessee because the Confederates would reinforce the army there with men from their base in Columbus, and possibly defeat him (he also believed in the inflated 60,000-man figure). And when, in turn, McClellan prodded Halleck about attacking and destroying Columbus he got nowhere. Even Halleck's counterproposal to attack up the Cumberland and the Tennessee would require him to borrow twenty or thirty thousand soldiers from Buell, who claimed he was already short of men for the Tennessee operation. The result was military deadlock both east and west—precisely the kind of self-inflicted stalemate that Lincoln abhorred and yet seemed helpless to prevent.

In early January the President sent a telegram to each of his senior commanders expressing his desire that Federal armies begin moving south to crush the rebellion. He even set a timetable for the kickoff: no later than February 22, 1862, which happened to be George Washington's birthday. When Lincoln approached Halleck about attacking Columbus to break the logjam, "Old Brains" brought to bear all of his considerable military scholarship and appended this final appraisal for the President's edification: "To operate on exterior lines against an enemy occupying a central position will fail, as it has always failed in ninety-nine cases out of a hundred. It is condemned by every military authority I have ever read."

To this Lincoln dejectedly appended a note of his own on the envelope, apparently for posterity's sake: "Within is a copy of a letter just received from General Halleck. It is exceedingly discouraging. As everywhere else, nothing can be done."

Thus Halleck fiddled while the Confederates fortified and built their schemes to retake Kentucky and bring the war back to the banks of the Ohio. There was another issue, too, which shed considerable light on the military differences between Halleck and Grant. When the subject of Columbus had come up, Halleck pulled out his maps and books and concluded, rightly so, that if his Federal army captured the river forts and took Nashville, Columbus would be turned and the Confederates would likely abandon it, because their southern lines of communication and supply would have been severed. Thus Columbus would fall into Union hands.

Here is how Grant approached the same situation. During a discussion with some of his senior officers about capturing Fort Henry and Fort Donelson, someone brought up the question of whether that would cause the Confederates to abandon Columbus—to which Grant countered that it was "better [to] attack and capture their entire force where they are. Why allow them to withdraw and [have to] follow and fight them in the interior of Mississippi or Alabama under greater disadvantages?" Grant was having none of Halleck's Jomini–like "grand turning movements." He wanted to get at the enemy and wipe him out, wherever and whenever he was found.

Lincoln's sorrowful conclusion that "nothing can be done" was about to change, however. For some reason it suddenly dawned on Henry Halleck that, no matter how gloomily he saw his military situation, the commander who first made a move to placate the President at this tense stage of affairs could possibly find himself in high standing upon the slippery ladder to military power, while those who continued to procrastinate (such as Buell) would likely slide down out of sight, rung by greasy rung.

Also playing a part in his decision was a report—more like a warning—from McClellan that the infamous but highly regarded Rebel general P.G.T. Beauregard was on his way to Kentucky, along with 15,000 reinforcements. Even though the last part was false, to the Union high command—Halleck included—the notion of Beauregard himself coming west was enough to sound the fire bell in the night.

Thus on January 30, 1862, Grant received from Halleck these terse instructions: "You will immediately prepare to send forward to Fort Henry, on the Tennessee River, all your available forces."

This was music to Grant's ears. Halleck's directive could not have come at a better time, for Grant had been currying an exemplary military friendship with the commanding officer of the new Federal ironclad fleet, Commodore Andrew H. Foote, and the two had cooked up detailed plans for a joint amphibious operation to take Fort Henry *and* Fort Donelson. It would become one of the first such operations in U.S. military history.

Foote was truly a sailor of the seven seas. He had fought from China to the South Atlantic, had apprehended slavers, and at one point purchased and transported a regiment of camels—including their drivers—from the khedive of Egypt, pursuant to an order from

Jefferson Davis, then U.S. secretary of war, who wanted them for army topographical engineers to use as they surveyed routes for a continental railroad across the deserts of the American Southwest.*

Foote was a puritanical antislavery New Englander who held Sunday school classes for his sailors, abolished the rum ration aboard his vessels, and was an ardent believer in amphibious warfare—or at least joint army-navy operations, once telling his brother that the two services "were like blades of shears: united they were powerful—separated they were almost useless." In this he held something very much in common with Grant; in fact, it may have been the only thing he held in common with him, given that Grant's attitudes on drinking, slavery, and religion were ambiguous, at best.

Both men realized that merely taking the two Confederate forts would not be of much consequence in the long run, but opening the streams into the Southern heartland would be an immense blow to the rebellion. First off, when the water was high—as it was now—Foote's powerful gunboats could maraud all the way down to Mississippi and northern Alabama, blasting Confederate railway bridges into toothpicks and otherwise disrupting the economy and communications in the enemy's rear. Then transports of soldiers would follow on a hundred river steamers and assemble to fight and win a major battle that would decide the fate of the West. And with it, likely, the fate of the war itself, for if the rebellion was put down in the West the war in Virginia and the East Coast could not be sustained, or so the theory went.

---

* The camels performed as advertised but were abandoned during the Civil War. Sightings of them and their progeny out in the deserts persisted until the late 1920s.

These were thrilling concepts, almost too large to grasp for the crusty old sailor and the ill-dressed Union general sitting in the captain's cabin on the ironclad *Cincinnati*. Then word came that a part of Buell's army under Gen. George "Pap" Thomas, had whipped a small Rebel army at Mill Springs, in the southern part of Kentucky 150 miles to the east, and was now moving to confront the large Confederate force at Bowling Green. Grant's attack on Fort Henry would thus constitute a general Union movement southward all across the Confederate front from the Cumberland Gap to the Tennessee—nearly 250 miles. No one dreaded this more than the Rebel general Albert Sidney Johnston, who commanded the Confederacy's Department of the West.

———◆◆◆———

Things had been more or less going the Confederates' way until the reverse at Mill Springs, a dreary, agonizing affair characterized by misfortune (the Rebel commander Gen. Felix Zollicoffer, who was nearsighted, was shot and killed after he inadvertently rode into the Yankee lines) and insobriety (Zollicoffer's superior Gen. George Crittenden, of the famed Kentucky family, was rumored to have been drunk during the battle).

General Johnston, after surveying his assignment and the state of his army, despaired over the status of Fort Henry on the Tennessee River. Hastily erected by the state right after war broke out, it was in wretched shape to begin with, unfinished, and now half flooded by high water in the river. (The fort was located improperly in the first place, and without consideration for the possibility that the Yankees would come with huge ironclad vessels of war capable of carrying large-caliber, long-range cannons.) Johnston received many messages conveying the sorry state of affairs at Fort Henry. Gen. Lloyd Tilgh-man, a West Pointer, wrote that it was placed in a location "without one redeeming feature," and, he concluded in abject disgust, "The history of military engineering records no parallel in this case."

All through the autumn of 1861 Johnston served up orders to various officers concerning the river forts. On October 17, for instance, the bishop general Polk was warned to "Keep a vigilant eye on the Tennessee River . . . Fortify opposite to Fort Henry. No time should be lost." Again on October 31 he warned that the riv-ers "require incessant watching . . . The Cumberland and Tennes-see Rivers afford lines of transportation by which an [enemy] army may turn your right with ease and rapidity." To Tilghman, who had been assigned command of Fort Henry on November 17, Johnston wrote, "The utmost vigilance is enjoined, as there has been gross neg-ligence in this respect . . . You will push forward the completion of the works and armament with the utmost activity." And on January 18: "Occupy and *intrench* the heights opposite Fort Henry. Do not lose a moment. Work all night." But in the end it came to no avail.

However much he realized it, Johnston had taken on a stupen-dous assignment. Certainly he must have begun to appreciate the gravity of it when he reached his headquarters and compared the scope of what he was supposed to accomplish with the personnel and materials on hand. His army was outnumbered by the Federal forces more than two to one, and many of his troops carried only their personal shotguns or hunting rifles—or else they had been armed with old flintlock weapons left over from the War of 1812. Uniforms, in many units, were a matter of personal taste, but as a general rule soldiers in the ranks wore an outfit of homespun cloth in a brown shade known as butternut.

Worse, the strategy that Jefferson Davis had decreed for the defense of the West was fatally flawed. He had drawn an imaginary line—below which no Yankee was to set foot—from the Cumberland Gap in the Appalachians all the way through Tennessee and across the Mississippi River into Arkansas and Oklahoma until, after more than a thousand miles, it "trickled out somewhere in the desert sands of Arizona." In other words, Davis intended to fight for every inch of Southern soil, a notion that was attributed to his forlorn hope for European intervention.* It might have worked in a small area, such as Virginia, but strategically, in the vastness of the West, it became a practical impossibility.

Furthermore, the Confederacy was monstrously unprepared at this stage of the war. Soon after he had arrived in Kentucky, Johnston sent a subordinate to Richmond to protest that he desperately needed arms and men. "My God!" Davis told the startled emissary. "Why did General Johnston send you to me for arms and reinforcements, when he must know that I have neither?"

When this unpleasant news reached Johnston's ears he was ensconced with his army of about 27,000 at Bowling Green, Kentucky, keeping a sharp eye on the Yankee general Buell at Louisville, who was beginning to inch toward him with an army of his own. And that was not to mention Ulysses Grant, who had his eye on Bowling Green as well.

---

* Davis's logic here was that in order for the Confederacy to be recognized by other nations it had to demonstrate that it was powerful enough to control its borders. Subsequently it has become a military maxim that in a major war to defend equally all of one's territory is to defend none of it well.

It's worth lingering a few moments to focus on the terrible and conflicting civilian drama spawned by the war. Nowhere, perhaps, is it exposed so nakedly as in the diary of Josie Underwood, a 20-year-old daughter of a wealthy family of Kentucky slaveholders who were also staunch Unionists. Until the threat of secession sheared their lives, the Underwoods had led a nearly idyllic life in Bowling Green. Then came the storm of war, and General Johnston marched his army into town.

Bowling Green was a tranquil southern Kentucky city of about 2,500 souls, whose population likely shared a greater cultural and political affinity with the Tennesseans right across the border than, say, the citizens of Louisville in the north, who were just downriver from Yankee Cincinnati, Ohio. Josie Underwood's family was among the most prominent in town. Her father was a successful planter and lawyer and had been a state representative as well as a U.S. congressman until 1859, and he was the principal leader of the community until the question of secession broke out. Like most Unionists in that part of the state, he reviled Lincoln and his policies and had supported the conciliatory ticket of John Bell, yet he abhorred the notion of secession. The family lived at Mount Air, a thousand-acre cotton plantation on the outskirts of town, in a palatial two-story brick manor house surrounded by orchards and with a ballroom upstairs.* The 1860 census valued their land and personal property (including the 28 slaves who worked the place) at $105,000—some $2.8 million in today's money.

---

* The property had originally been named Mount Ayre, but Underwood thought that pretentious.

In mid-December of that year, a month after Lincoln's election and a mere week before South Carolina would vote to secede from the Union, Josie and her friend Jane Grider took the train to Memphis to spend the winter with Josie's sister Jupe, and her husband, William Western, a prosperous lawyer and ardent secessionist, who owned a mansion in the Memphis Garden District. It was Josie's first time away from home since she became, in her own words, "a full fledged 'Young lady.' " But had it not been for Western's "general good-naturedness," her arrival might have invited a level of unwanted tension since, like her father, she remained a Unionist.

This general good nature did not necessarily extend to Memphis's social circles, however, as Josie would soon discover. She was an attractive young woman and highly sought after by the town's leading bachelors, especially a 28-year-old lawyer named Thomas Grafton. Josie soon felt herself as much drawn to the wealthy, witty, and handsome Grafton as she was repelled by his political views. He took her to a play, and instead of watching it he watched her; he brought her flowers.

As their relation blossomed it is evident from Josie's diary how the most basic emotions became cramped, twisted, and too often torn apart by the prospect of secession. As weeks passed during the early winter of 1861, and more Southern states seceded, discussions often turned to arguments—or worse—as became the case with Tom Grafton.

Will Webb, another young lawyer in Memphis, the brother-in-law of William Western's legal partner, was outspoken in his strong Unionist sentiments and less than circumspect in the way he expressed them. As Josie remarked to her diary, "The subject of secession like Banquo's ghost *will not die down* but will come up—no matter what the place or time—especially if Will Webb and Tom Grafton meet."

The occasion this time and place was the Grand New Year's Eve Ball at Memphis's famed Gayosa Hotel,* at which all of Memphis society turned out. In Josie's estimation, it was "the most splendid affair I ever attended—my first big *full grown* ball!" With Tom Grafton as her escort, they encountered Will Webb, "whose bad taste started the subject," she wrote, adding, "I as bad as any of them." What infuriated her most was that whenever the secession issue came up Tom Grafton—in his most lawyerly fashion—would invariably link her to Lincoln and the abolitionists, who were despised in those parts, referring jokingly to "*your friend* Lincoln."

Still, of all the young men, "Tom Grafton interests me most," she admitted. "I don't know just why."

It was a scene playing out all over the state. Josie's cousin, for example, a West Point graduate, was on the verge of becoming engaged to a girl who insisted that he resign his U.S. Army commission and join the Confederacy. Lifelong friends suddenly found themselves not just in opposite political camps but divided by hatreds that transcended politics.

Josie continued her conflicted relationship with Tom Grafton, often at the same time trying to talk herself out of it. "For truly I do not know whether I love him or not," she wrote in her diary. "I know I don't feel as I want to feel towards the man I would marry

---

* In August 1864 Nathan Bedford Forrest staged a midnight cavalry raid into Memphis during which he rode his horse up the steps, through the lobby, and into the offices of the Gayosa Hotel in search of the Yankee general Hurlbut, who had fled from his room in his underclothes.

but maybe there is no such exalted love as I imagine," she said. "Yet I would not be satisfied with less, and his secessionism is a great barrier between us."

One day word came that Grafton and Will Webb had become embroiled in a "personal altercation" inside the law offices during which Webb had called Grafton a "traitor" and a "liar," and Grafton "jerked up a chair and would have killed Mr. Webb" but another of Josie's cousins, Jack Henry, "sprang forward and caught the chair" and got the matter settled down. Grafton then "marched out glaring at Webb saying, 'this is not the end. Sir—insignificant as you are, pistols make us even.'"

Next day Grafton sent his challenge to Webb, and for the rest of that day and the next the seconds were busy arranging for the duel across the river in Arkansas where such things were routinely conducted. The night before the affair was to take place, Grafton appeared at the Westerns' residence, where Josie was, by chance, alone. As was the custom, a cloak of silence had descended over the matter of the duel, so neither the authorities nor the ladies, Josie included, were aware of it. There in the parlor Grafton professed his love.

He was an orphan, he said. Both mother and father died when he "was too young to remember," and there were no siblings, and thus "there was no one to love him, even if he should die."

He said to her, "Miss Underwood, I generally take life as it comes to me, and waste no time on self pity, but tonight I felt so unutterably lonely . . . [and] in my loneliness my heart turned to you." He was leaving town next day, he said, "and then he told me—in words I can't write—that he loved me—also that it was wrong for him to tell me—as he had already offered himself to his state as a soldier, . . . and he could not ask any bright young life to be tied to his, but he found he could not leave me without trying for the happiness of winning a little word of love from me."

She tried to soothe him but in the end could not bring herself to honor his request. "I don't know just what to think of myself—whether I am capable of love or not," she told her diary. "I tried to explain to him that I liked him more than any man I knew, . . . I don't feel as he feels toward me—for he seems to be everything a girl might love except, alas! his desire to break up our country."

He kissed her hand and said goodbye, then asked her "in a solemn sort of way 'Pray for me tonight—for I have no mother to do it.' " And then he was gone.

Next day when Josie went in to breakfast she found that William Western had left early. She "couldn't help but feel uneasy, just why I couldn't say." Her cousin Warner came in and informed everyone that Grafton had challenged Webb to a duel at sunup that morning, and suddenly she realized what all the talk of dying and going away had been about the night before. Her friend Miss Jane asked, "Are they dead?" When Western replied, "No, neither," Josie's "heart gave a great throb of joy!" He further explained that "they had gone across the river but with so many interested parties it leaked out and the [law] officers got wind of it and got there just in time to stop the awful murder and suicide, for that is just what a duel is."

Josie saw Grafton a few times after that. Her stay in Memphis was cut short by the dramatic events surrounding secession and the forming of the Confederacy. "There is so much excitement and nobody knows from one day to another—what will happen next—that I think I must bring my visit to an end soon," she wrote in the early days of 1861. "The young men here have organized a company called the Shelby Grays, and all our Secession friends are in it." That included Tom Grafton, whom she saw for a final time on January 31, 1861. There was a gathering at the Westerns' "for the girls and gentlemen we have known best—about 30—to spend the evening." When the evening came to an end Josie noticed Tom Grafton walking out the door and wondered why he had not said goodbye. Suddenly her cousin Jack Henry tugged on her sash from outside one of the tall, open French windows and asked if she "had a pin." She thought that "he had met with some accident," and stepped onto the wide veranda. "What can I do?" she asked, to which he replied, "Give it to Grafton."

Tom Grafton stepped from the shadows. "I could not say good-bye to you in there," he told her. Then, "with broken sentences, with feeling, repeated what he had before told me and taking my hand— lifted it quickly to his lips and was gone." Again he'd confided his worry—that there'd be no one to grieve for him if he were killed. She lingered awhile on the veranda, her cheeks flushed, then her cousin came out. "That's a fine fellow—don't be too hard on him," he told her. Josie's world was quickly falling apart, and her story is intertwined with this tale. We will revisit her as it goes along.

At last, in early February 1862, with Halleck's approval, Grant got his invasion of the South under way.

The Rebel general Tilghman was in Fort Henry on the Tennessee River with 3,400 Confederates on February 4 when Commodore Foote's gunboats appeared several miles downstream, followed by a score of Ulysses Grant's troop transports, whose smoke painted the northern horizon with dark, warlike clouds "as far as the eye could see." The men were in awe as they entered the enemy's lair. They were mystified to see odd bunches of green leaves growing in trees that were supposed to be leafless in February—until someone informed them it was a plant called mistletoe. The body of a dead soldier floated by, whether Northern or Southern they could not tell. Sometimes they shot at people along the banks whom they feared might be Confederates. As they steamed deeper into Rebel territory, one Iowa soldier remarked ominously—if not ironically—to his companions, "The further we go, the larger the elephant gets."

The transports put in to the bank about three miles below the fort, out of artillery range, and began debarking the troops under the firing cover of Foote's four ironclads—the *Essex, Carondelet, St. Louis,* and the commodore's flagship, *Cincinnati*—then returned to Paducah, 50 miles downstream, for more soldiers.

By the morning of February 6 all was in place. While Grant's 15,000 soldiers floundered through the miry marshes toward Fort Henry, Foote's big black ironclads steamed upriver in line of battle, four abreast. The firing commenced at a range of about one mile.

Inside Fort Henry there was an air of "unwonted animation," according to Capt. Jesse Taylor of the Confederate States Navy— late of the U.S. Naval Academy at Annapolis—who had been tapped to train the artillerists within Fort Henry in the management of large, anti-warship cannons. Artillery for the Confederacy was a major problem at that stage of the war. The Rebels had only what they had seized from Federal arsenals located in the South, which consisted mainly of field guns and the larger caliber cannons from shore batteries along the Atlantic and Gulf coasts. When war broke out there were no cannon foundries in the South, and it would be some time before the Confederates got these up and running.

Just before the Yankee onslaught General Tilghman had called together his senior commanders, including the enigmatic cavalry commander Nathan Bedford Forrest, and all agreed that their 3,500 or so men, "armed with shot-guns and hunting rifles," would be no match for Grant's thousands. The sensible plan, then, was to evacuate the men to Fort Donelson and combine with its 12,000 troops to make a stand on the Cumberland. In the meantime, "recognizing the difficulty of withdrawing undisciplined troops from the front of an active and superior opponent," Tilghman turned to Captain Taylor with a question: "Can you hold out for one hour against a determined attack?" When the reply was affirmative, Tilghman began preparing his men for the 12-mile march to Fort Donelson, leaving Taylor and his 54 artillerists to their fate.

When he first arrived at the fort Taylor had felt an ill-omened shiver of fear after noticing "a high water mark that the river had left on a tree which convinced me that we had a more dangerous foe to contend with than the Federals—namely, the river itself." When he began directing his gunners toward Foote's attack, the river was running 14 feet higher than normal. It had risen nearly to the mouths of the cannons and was threatening the ammunition magazine itself. Many of the gunners were up to their knees in water while they waited for the range to close.

As the gunboats "slowly passed up this narrow stream" the tension aboard the Yankee warships was acute. In the wheelhouse of *Carondelet*, her captain, Henry Walke, recorded that "not a sound could be heard or a moving object seen in the dense woods which overhung the dark and swollen river." The gun crews of *Caronde-let* stood silent at their posts. "About noon," Walke said, "the fort and the Confederate flag came suddenly into view, the barracks, the new earthworks, and the great guns well-manned." *Cincinnati*, Foote's flagship, fired the first shot, which was a signal for all to commence firing.

Watching from the ramparts of Fort Henry, where he had taken personal charge of a powerful 6-inch Whitworth rifle, Captain Taylor later wrote: "As [the ironclads] swung into the main channel they showed one broad and leaping sheet of flame. The command was given to commence firing from the fort. The action now became general, and for the next twenty or thirty minutes was, on both sides, as deliberate, rapid, and accurate as a heart could wish, and apparently inclined in favor of the fort."

Aboard the hard-fighting but luckless *Essex* the steering apparatus had been shot away and she turned broadside in the river. Seventy shots had been fired from her 9-inch guns when calamity struck. A shell from the fort pierced the iron casemate—which was thinner amidships—decapitated the master's mate, and went on to strike the middle boiler, releasing a horrible cloud of scalding steam. The captain, who had been standing nearby, was fearfully burned and leaped out a porthole. A number of officers and crew were killed outright at their posts, while many others were "writhing in their last agony." In the pilothouse the steersman was found scalded to death, "standing erect, his left hand holding the spoke and his right hand grasping the signal-bell rope." Everyone else in the wheelhouse was scalded to death, including an ammunition bearer who was found still on his knees, "in the act of taking a shell from the box to hand to the loader. The escaping steam had struck him square in the face, and he met death in that position."*

Thirty-two of *Essex*'s officers and crew were killed, wounded, or missing in this mishap, and the vessel itself fell out of the action and began twisting helplessly downstream. A number of her scalded crew had jumped into the water and many of these presumably drowned, as they were never heard from again.

Foote's flagship *Cincinnati* received 32 hits from the fort. "Her chimneys, after-cabin, and boats were completely riddled," Walke said. "I happened to be looking at the flag-steamer when one of the enemy's heavy shot struck her. It had the effect of a thunder-bolt, ripping her side timbers and scattering the splinters over the vessel."

Foote did not slacken speed but instead brought the three remaining ironclads nearer to the fort, and nearer yet, until he was standing within the almost unheard of distance of 200 yards, where he defiantly exchanged shot and shell with the Rebel artillery.

Inside the fort the Rebel captain Taylor was almost at the end of his rope. He had started the fight with eight 32-pounder cannons, two 42-pounders, and one 128-pounder, known as a Columbiad.† He also had five 18-pounder siege guns as well as the dangerous rifled Whitworth gun that could crack a level shot a mile and more with terrifying accuracy. Its conical projectile was said to make an

---

* The account is by James Laning, second master of *Essex,* in a letter to Captain Walke of the *Carondelet,* later printed in *Battles and Leaders of the Civil War,* serialized by the Century Publishing Company, New York, 1884–87.

† The Columbiad was a 15,000-pound bottle-shaped cannon on recoil tracks that fired ten-inch shot weighing 128 pounds and an effective range of more than a mile.

eerie noise, which caused Captain Walke on the *Carondelet* to note, "The wild whistle of their rifle-shells was heard on every side of us."

Taylor had promised to give Tilghman an hour for his men to get a head start on Grant's army; he had been fighting now for two hours, and against all odds. The rising river was nearly upon him and the protective earthen ramparts of Fort Henry had been torn to pieces by the relentless cannon fire of Foote's ironclads.

Taylor had been directing the fire of the rifled gun when a messenger arrived asking that he go with him to the Columbiad to confer with General Tilghman who, to everyone's surprise, had returned to the fort to share in its fate. Lucky for Taylor, because no sooner had he departed than the rifled cannon burst, killing all those serving it and severely injuring others in the immediate vicinity. What is more, just as Taylor reached General Tilghman "a sudden exclamation" was uttered by someone serving the Columbiad, which, upon Taylor's investigation, proved to have been evoked by the accidental spiking of the fort's most effective weapon by an inexperienced cannoneer. With both the Whitworth rifle and the Columbiad now out of action, Commodore Foote pressed his attack, and Yankee shells and shot quickly struck two of the 32-pounders, killing or wounding all the men around them.

After a short consultation, Tilghman decided that further resistance "would only result in a useless loss of life," and he ordered the Confederate flag hauled down. After the surrender a number of Foote's officers visited the fort—most of them "friends, messmates," or at least "known" to Captain Taylor from the old navy. General Tilghman and the other Rebel officers, himself included, "were treated with every courtesy," Taylor reported. Presently, Grant arrived for a look-see. "At the time," Taylor wrote, "he impressed me as a modest, amiable, kind-hearted but resolute man."

After the victory at Fort Henry, Foote withdrew his ironclads from the Tennessee and went back to Cairo—flying the huge Rebel flag from the fort upside down from his halyard mast—to deal with the battle damage. Meanwhile, the three wooden gunboats, *Lexington, Tyler,* and *Conestoga* embarked on a spectacular joyride on the Tennessee, steaming all the way into northern Alabama and Mississippi, blowing up bridges, trestles, and any Southern steamboat unlucky enough to get in their way. This caused a wild panic among the population, which had been assured that the abominable Yankees would never come that far south.

CHAPTER 5

"UNCONDITIONAL SURRENDER" GRANT

———◆———

N<small>OW</small> F<small>ORT</small> D<small>ONELSON'S</small> <small>HOUR HAD COME, BUT</small> it would prove a far tougher nut to crack than Fort Henry, which had been reduced by naval gunfire alone. Nevertheless, Fort Donelson's capture represented one of the great strategic errors made by the Confederates during the Civil War.

On February 6, the same day that Fort Henry fell, Grant sent a telegram to Halleck apprising him of the victory and informing him that "I shall take and destroy Fort Donelson on the 8th." As always there were delays, owing to the late arrival of additional troops and material—and most especially because Commodore Foote's gunboats were not yet repaired—but by February 12 Grant felt ready enough to tell Halleck that his army was getting on the move. With reinforcements pouring down the river Grant's force would soon total 27,000. The temperature had turned balmy, and the mood of the men matched the weather. However, Southern winters can be deceiving, as anyone familiar with them knows—the weather is, in fact, subject to sudden, violent changes—but as the day wore warmly on Grant's men began to shed their heavy overcoats and even their blankets along the roadside. The officers, who should have known better, did not stop them from abandoning valuable clothing.

On Wednesday, February 12, Grant and his staff rode ahead of the army to get a close-up look at the ground. Little was known about Fort Donelson, and the engineers and cartographers had only the vaguest rumors and notions of what was there; however, it was generally thought to be inferior to Fort Henry, which proved to be a miscalculation. Word had come down that the Rebel general Gideon Pillow was in command at Fort Donelson. Grant knew this controversial officer from his Mexican War days and had little regard for him. A verbose, pinch-faced, 56-year-old Tennessee lawyer with an Eastern-looking goatee, Pillow in 1846 had received a high military appointment from his friend the President James K. Polk, and although he showed bravery in battle during the Mexican War—being wounded twice—he became embroiled in a disgraceful public quarrel with the commanding general, Winfield Scott, which did his reputation little credit.

As it turned out, however, Pillow was not in charge at Fort Donelson, as rumor had it. He was there as second in command, having been superseded by Maj. Gen. John B. Floyd, another cantankerous lawyer who had once been governor of Virginia and the U.S. secretary of war before secession. A portly, hook-nosed man with scant military experience, Floyd had been relieved of command in the Shenandoah Valley at the insistence of Robert E. Lee and was currently under indictment in Washington for shady manipulations with Indian Trust Bonds. He was also widely suspected in the North as having used his position as secretary of war to arrange the transfer of large numbers of weapons and munitions to Southern arsenals on the eve of war. How he came to command at Fort Donelson has been something of a mystery from that day to this.

Third in command was Brig. Gen. Simon Bolivar Buckner, a 39-year-old Kentuckian who was, ironically, the West Point classmate of Grant's who lent him the money to get back to St. Louis after he resigned from the army in California. Buckner had been cited for bravery in the Mexican War, and with his military education was probably better suited to the command of Fort Donelson than either of the other two generals.

The loss of Fort Henry had disordered General Johnston's entire defensive strategy for the West. After conferring with Beauregard and Hardee at Bowling Green, it was concluded that the Confederate army's position at Columbus was no longer tenable, and those troops would have to be evacuated by train to Memphis, along with the smaller artillery pieces. The larger ones would probably be lost. Bowling Green as well was no longer defensible, since the Union army at Fort Henry was squarely between Columbus and themselves. Making the best of a bad situation, Johnston ordered the troops to fall back to southern Tennessee, then try to reunite with the units from Columbus to form an army to defeat Grant. In the meanwhile, however, Johnston felt duty-bound to send a force to defend Fort Donelson, since if that position fell the important hub and manufacturing center of Nashville would be left exposed and unprotected.

Perhaps Johnston chose Floyd to defend Donelson because he had arrived from across the mountains bringing with him a number of Virginia regiments; it certainly could not have had anything to do with Floyd's military acumen. Whatever the reason, Johnston ordered Floyd's force to join Pillow's and Buckner's men who were currently occupying Fort Donelson, which—when added to the 3,300 that Tilghman had sent out of Fort Henry—would compose an army of 17,200 Rebel soldiers. As an additional safeguard, Johnston included in the Fort Donelson contingent the thousand-man cavalry command of 40-year-old Nathan Bedford Forrest, a Tennessee cotton planter, former slave trader, and one of the richest men in the South. Known for his "great energy and brute courage," Forrest was already living up to his well-known reputation as the "wizard of the saddle."

General Pillow, who had been sent by General Johnston, had barely arrived at Fort Donelson when information from scouts and spies reported that Grant's army had grown significantly in size since the Fort Henry operation, and now appeared to outnumber him at least two to one. That was not quite so—nor did Grant have anywhere near the number of three to one, which military science of the day considered the desired ratio when attacking fortified positions. Nevertheless, the news seemed to have rattled Pillow, and as Grant's people filed into position in a semicircle around the fort, rather than roaring out and attacking the Yankee force before it deployed and threw up defenses he instead drew in, turtle-like, until Grant's investment was complete.

As positions went, Pillow's wasn't a bad one, and certainly much more favorable than at Fort Henry, which was underwater. Fort Donelson was sited on a 130-foot bluff and was not a fort in the popular image, which is often thought of as a castle-like structure with high parapets, moat, etc. Like Fort Henry, it was of earthen construction, with soil having been thrown up to protect the large gun batteries on the river, and defensive strongpoints on the land-ward side, a roughly three-mile arc anchored on the Cumberland to the south and Hickman's Creek to the north. This defensive line consisted of rifle pits, or trenches, with the spoil of yellow-colored clay heaped in front, and forward of that the Rebels had laid obstructions of chevaux-de-frise* and abatis. Artillery batteries at the strongpoints were protected by bastions that gave many of the guns interlocking fire.

Grant set up headquarters in a farmhouse at the outer edge of his investment lines; he had no firm plans except to wait for the arrival of Foote's ironclads and the steady stream of reinforcements that Halleck was pushing down from Paducah. But the following morn-ing, Thursday, February 13, Grant had scarcely finished his cup of coffee when heavy firing broke out to the south where McCler-nand's division was posted. This did not bode well. Grant had given orders that under no circumstances was any commander to take action that might bring on a general engagement—and now this.

McClernand, a politician, not a military man, apparently had gotten into an argument with a pesky Rebel battery to his front and ordered one of his brigades to silence it. The brigade massed for the attack and marched forward, only to be brutally cut down in a crossfire of rifle and cannon fire. Instead of leaving it be, McClern-and obstinately ordered a second bloody assault, and then a third, which nearly decimated the outfit before it dawned upon him that the Rebel position was well nigh impregnable. Grant knew he would bear watching in the future.

---

* Chevaux-de-frise are sharpened wooden spikes designed to impale attacking troops.

There was shelling from the lone gunboat on the scene, *Caronde-let,* which fired 139 78- and 64-pound shot at the fort before taking a hit by a huge 128-pounder ball through her port iron casement. According to Captain Walke, this did a terrific amount of damage and bounded around inside "like a wild beast stalking its prey." But the rest of Foote's ironclads weren't due till the next day, and Grant used the time to strengthen his investment and usher the steady stream of reinforcements into the lines. Around sunset the wind shifted to the north and east and a cold rain began; by evening it had turned to sleet and ice, and later to snow, and the temperature dropped to 12 degrees. This made for the "severest deprivations and sufferings" among the men, who had no tents, had been ordered to build no fires, and had foolishly discarded their warm clothes on the march from Fort Henry the day before.

On Friday Foote's gunboats made their appearance, just as they had at Fort Henry, minus the luckless *Essex* and the flagship *Cincin-nati,* which were still in the yards for repairs. In their places were the *Louisville* and the *Pittsburgh.* Grant mounted his horse and found a high ridge overlooking the river where he could observe the proceedings. Foote's assault began at 3 p.m. when the ironclads, including *Carondelet,* formed a line of battle about two miles below the fort and began steaming toward it. The firing broke out at 3:30. The results were not encouraging.

Not only were the batteries at Fort Donelson situated well above high water, they contained heavier artillery and were manned by better gunners, or at least luckier gunners. As the distance closed within a mile the weight of the Rebel fire began to tell. "We heard the deafening crack of bursting shells, the crash of solid shot, and the whizzing fragments of shell and wood as they sped through the vessel," wrote Captain Walke aboard *Carondelet*. "A shot hit the pilot house, killing one of the pilots," Walke said. "They came harder and faster, taking flag staffs and smoke stacks and tearing off the side armor as lightning tears off the bark from a tree."

Without warning, the portside rifled gun exploded. One of the gunners described it: "It knocked us all down, killing none, but wounding over a dozen men and spreading dismay and confusion among us. Then the cry ran through the boat that we were on fire and my duty as pump-man called me to the pumps. While I was there, two shots entered our bow-ports and killed four men, and wounded several others. They were borne past me, three with their heads off."

Carondelet was within 400 yards of the fort, exchanging gunfire point blank, when Captain Walke noticed that they were alone. The other ironclads had taken enough punishment and "were rapidly falling back out of line." *St. Louis* and *Pittsburgh* had their wheel ropes shot away and were spinning uncontrollably downstream in the fierce current. *Louisville*, likewise, had become unmanageable. All of the ships had sustained grievous damage and loss of life. Commodore Foote had been standing in the wheelhouse of *St. Louis* when a shot entered and killed the pilot standing next to him and tore his own foot nearly off.

Walke stood in with *Carondelet* as long as he could, giving as good as he got and the Rebels banging away with everything they had. It was later revealed that the gunboat sustained 54 direct hits. But at last he, too, was forced to retire—to the humiliating sound of cheering from the Rebel emplacements—having shot up most of his ammunition. It was a bitter fact that Fort Donelson was not going to be carried by gunboat attack alone.

That night there was more arctic weather; again the wind howled, again the temperature dropped into the teens, and by morning there was three inches of snow on the ground. There were also 10,000 Rebels outside their rifle pits before dawn, massed for an all-or-nothing attack against Grant's right wing, which was in McClernand's bailiwick. From here on, one would have to search deeply in Civil War annals to find conduct as inept, irresolute, and, ultimately, as shameful as the Confederate command at Fort Donelson after it came under Grant's attack.

The previous day General Floyd had arrived at the fort accompanied by his brigade. As senior officer he was nominally in charge, but he deferred tactical operations to Pillow, who had been there a few days longer and presumably knew his way around. After a conference with the division and brigade commanders Floyd concluded that the fort was untenable "except with fifty thousand troops," and that it should be evacuated. It was decided that General Buckner would cover an evacuation at noon on the 14th, led by Pillow, south toward Nashville by the river road. Noon came, but Pillow for some reason countermanded the order and put the men back in their rifle pits. Then came the battle with the ironclads, and a wave of confidence swept over the Confederate garrison. That night another council was called, the issues debated, and the decision was made to attack the Union right at dawn to force open a route of retreat to Nashville. Fortuitously for the Confederates, the howling nighttime wind and bitter sleet and snow masked the Rebels' movement as they brought infantry, artillery, and cavalry unobserved, some of it right across the face of the Yankee line.

A thousand miles east in Washington, Abraham Lincoln's anxiety over Donelson was overshadowed only by concern for his 11-year-old son Willie, who lay deathly ill in a giant rosewood bed upstairs in the White House. Frustrated as he had been by the inaction of Halleck and Buell, the President was now convinced that the Confederates would go to any lengths to destroy Grant and save Fort Donelson. In fact, Lincoln saw the value of Donelson—and the calamity that its downfall would have on the rebellion—far clearer than any of the Rebels. Thus the President telegraphed Halleck he was not worried that Grant would be beaten by the Rebel army inside the fort, but that "Grant should be overwhelmed from the outside."

Lincoln had worked it all out in his mind. The assumption by Halleck and Grant that General Johnston would not bring his army to relieve Fort Donelson because it would allow Buell to walk into Nashville was false, the President insisted. The Rebels could burn the Nashville bridges over the Cumberland and by leaving only a small force there could keep Buell at bay for several weeks. Meantime, after crushing Grant, Johnston could then turn on Buell and do him in as well. Lincoln was convinced that the Confederates would spare nothing to save Fort Donelson and would bring reinforcements from Virginia. Therefore it was paramount to break all the rail connections possible.

So fearful was Lincoln that he concluded his telegram with this gloomy appraisal: "Our success or failure at Fort Donelson is vastly important, and I beg you to put your soul into the effort." For his part, Halleck was convinced that the Confederates down in Columbus were actually preparing to attack Cairo, and fretting about how to defend it. He hadn't the foggiest notion that they were evacuating Columbus and headed to Memphis and points south.

At daybreak the music of reveille in the Union camps surrounding Fort Donelson was suddenly eclipsed by a ferocious din of gunfire in McClernand's far right sector near the river. The Rebel attack had begun and was rolling up the Yankee line. The Union general Lewis "Lew" Wallace, a 35-year-old Indiana lawyer and politician who would go on to write the novel *Ben-Hur,* gave this colorful description of the action at midmorning: "The wood rang with a monstrous clangor of musketry, as if a million men were beating empty barrels with iron hammers. Buckner flung a portion of his division on McClernand's left, and supported the attack with his artillery. The roar never slackened. Men fell by the score, reddening the snow with their blood. Close to the ground the flame of musketry and cannon tinted everything a lurid red. Limbs dropped from the trees on heads below, as if shorn by an army of cradlers. The division was under peremptory orders to hold its position to the last extremity."

Whose orders these were Wallace does not say, but they would not have come from Grant at this juncture since he had, in fact, left the field. After the shellacking of his ironclads the day before, Commodore Foote, who had been seriously wounded and could not be moved from his flagship, had requested a conference with the commanding general to consider what to do next. Grant had gone down to the gunboats before dawn where Foote told him it would take ten days to have his ironclads repaired at Mound City, Illinois, and Grant agreed that he had best lay siege to Fort Donelson till then.

Whatever Grant made of the sudden rumbling and growling of artillery upriver in the direction of his lines is not reported, but as he rode away from the conference with Foote he was intercepted by a frantic messenger with news that the Confederates were attacking

McClernand in force and that his division was thrown back in disarray. This was the last thing Grant had expected, having assumed that Pillow and Floyd were bunglers who would have waited inside the fort and sooner or later run up a white flag. As he neared the battle area, Grant was shown haversacks from Confederate casualties containing extra rations, which he concluded was evidence that this attack was actually a retreat, and that the enemy was trying to cut their way out.

At length Grant came upon a traumatized McClernand in the company of Lew Wallace and, according to Wallace, "[Grant's] face flushed slightly, with a sudden grip he crushed the papers in his hands, and in his ordinary quiet voice said, 'Gentlemen the position on the right must be retaken.' " In reply McClernand muttered something—evidently aimed at Grant—that sounded like "This army wants a head." Grant, taken aback by such an impolitic remark, replied evenly, "It would seem so," and rode on.

Grant rode all over the battlefield, urging soldiers to replenish their cartridge boxes and go back into the line. Seeing their commander at the front, many of the men gave him a cheer and returned to the fight. "The one who attacks now will be victorious!" Grant declared to anyone who would listen, an axiom that he followed, rightly or wrongly, for the rest of the war. He soon told this to 55-year-old division commander C. F. Smith, who had been his commandant at West Point and was considered the epitome of martial manner and mien. Six feet three inches tall, with an upright bearing and a long, white mustache, Smith and his division anchored the Union far left. Grant ordered him to hit the Rebel line hard there, as a diversion from the fight in McClernand's sector. Smith replied in his soldierly way, "I will do it."

Grant then continued back down the line. Everywhere he rode the snow-covered ground resembled a slaughterhouse, bloodstained and littered with the crumpled bodies of the wounded, dead, and dying of both sides. Finally, revolted by these gory sights, Grant told his staff, "Let's get out of this dreadful place."

It is worth hearing Lew Wallace's account of General Smith's charge, which became something of a legend in the Army of the Tennessee (which it was not yet called): "The air about him twittered with minie-bullets. Erect as if on review, he rode on, timing the gait of his horse with the movement of his colors. He never for a moment doubted the courage of volunteers; they were not regulars—that was all. If properly led he believed they would storm the gates of His Satanic Majesty. A soldier said, 'I was nearly scared to death, but I saw the old man's white mustache over his shoulder, and went on.'

"On to the abatis the regiments moved, leaving a trail of dead and wounded behind. There the fire seemed to get trebly hot, and there some of the men halted, whereupon, seeing the hesitation, General Smith put his cap on the point of his sword, held it aloft, and called out, 'No flinching now, my lads!—Here—This is the way! Come on!' "

Now Dr. John H. Brinton, Grant's surgeon, picks up the story in a letter to a fellow physician. "You ought to have heard old C. F. Smith cursing as he led his storming regiments. 'Damn you gentlemen, I see skulkers! I'll have none of that here. Come on you volunteers! This is your chance. You volunteered to be killed for love of country, and now you can be! You are only damned volunteers! I'm only a soldier, and don't want to be killed, but you came here to be killed, and now you can be!' "

Wallace resumes: "He picked a path through the jagged limbs of trees, holding his cap all the time in sight; and the effect was magical. The men swarmed in after him—not all of them, alas! Up the ascent he rode, and up they followed. At the last moment the keepers of the rifle-pits clambered out and fled."

The effect of this action on the Rebel general Pillow was palpable. Upon hearing that an apparently successful attack was in progress in his rear, he told Buckner to cease the attack and get his men back in the trenches. When Floyd—who was in supreme command—heard this, he immediately countermanded the order, since he had just sent a telegram to Johnston stating, "The day is ours." Then, when he spoke to Pillow personally, Floyd proceeded to pluck defeat right out of the jaws of victory. He canceled his countermand and returned the army to the fort, much to the disgust of Nathan Bedford Forrest, who later wrote that not only had the Rebel attack that morning opened a road to Nashville, it had opened *three* roads before the soldiers melted back into their trenches and the Yankees again began closing the ring.

What went on in Pillow's mind seems beyond rational explanation, unless he felt it was necessary somehow to reorganize his men before beginning the retreat. Yet that alone does not make much sense, since the whole bloody enterprise was to get the troops *out* of Fort Donelson and on the road—any road—to Nashville, and urgently. The failure appears to have been a masterpiece of shilly-shallying by the commanding general, John Floyd, and his second in command, Gideon Pillow, for whom Grant now held an even more deserved contempt.

That night a final counsel of war was held within Fort Donelson, which may even have superseded the fantastic dithering of the day. With a mile-wide line of escape between the river and the pushed-back Union front still open to them, both Floyd and Pillow decided, over Bedford Forrest's continued objections, that the day was now lost and surrender was the only option.

Floyd, however, allowed that he did not wish to be captured personally, on account of the pending indictment against him in federal court in Washington and other accusations that might lead to the hangman's rope. Instead, he proposed to take the last remaining steamship out of Fort Donelson and make his way to Nashville where he might be of further use to the cause.

This suddenly put the onus on Pillow, who likewise took a pass. It seems that Pillow had made so boisterous a habit of publicly proclaiming "Give me liberty or give me death" that he feared becoming a laughingstock if he now gave up to the Yankees, and wanted to go away with Floyd. Thus the burden of surrendering the first Confederate army during the Civil War fell upon the good soldier Simon Bolivar Buckner, while his superiors cravenly made their escapes to safety across the river.

For his part, Bedford Forrest announced, "I did not come here for the purpose of surrendering my command," and he sought permission to take his cavalry out of harm's way. Buckner acquiesced, and by sunup, after wading through icy swamp water sometimes rump-high on their horses, Forrest and his cavalrymen made good their getaway, taking along with them a number of like-minded infantrymen.

At last the time arrived for Buckner to perform his repugnant duty. He wrote a letter to Grant alluding to his "present state of affairs" and asked for the appointment of commissioners to "agree upon the terms of capitulation," signing it, "Respectfully, your obedient servant, etc."

In the early hours of the morning a Confederate party came out of the fort and delivered Buckner's envelope to the nearest available Yankee command, which happened to be that of General Smith, whose evening rest had already been disturbed once that night when he accidentally gave himself a hotfoot by sleeping too close to his fire.

Smith delivered the letter to Grant himself, trudging through the snow after his famous day to the small farmhouse where Grant was sleeping on a mattress on the kitchen floor. He entered the room "half frozen," according to Dr. Brinton, and wanted a drink. Brinton produced a flask as General Smith warmed himself by the fire and had his drink and Grant read over Buckner's letter. "No terms to the damn rebels," said Smith to his former pupil, causing Grant to chuckle as he wrote out his reply: "No terms except an unconditional and immediate surrender can be accepted. I propose to move immediately upon your works." Smith, still standing by the fire, wiped his mustache and nodded in approval, and then, claimed Doc Brinton, the old soldier thrust out his foot revealing that the sole of his boot was nearly burned off and remarked sheepishly, "I slept too near the fire; I have scorched my boots!" Finally everyone could have a good laugh.

General Buckner's personal reaction to Grant's reply is nowhere recorded, but if he expected his old friend to let his men march out of Fort Donelson as the Confederates had when Fort Sumter surrendered the previous spring—under arms and with the Union flag flying—he was seriously misguided. He sent Grant a grumbling response that protested "the ungenerous and unchivalrous terms which you propose," then hauled down his flag and made himself a Union prisoner.

Grant immediately became a hero in the North. The press touted his line to Buckner about "unconditional surrender" and dubbed him U. S. "Unconditional Surrender" Grant. The papers reported that Grant had smoked a cigar during the heat of the battle and people began sending him cigars by the box, precipitating a habit that eventually would kill him.*

Fort Donelson did not come without cost: Combined casualties were more than 5,000; 507 Union soldiers were killed, 1,976 were wounded, and 208 were either captured or missing versus for the Confederates 327 killed, 1,197 wounded, and a small army, 12,392, were made prisoners.

The 25-year-old colonel William Camm, of the 14th Illinois, an Englishman by birth and a teacher by trade, went over the field where the Rebels had lost most of their men shortly after the surrender. The sight was frightful. "The dead are badly distorted," Camm wrote in his diary. "One poor fellow had fallen across a fire and was burned in two. Citizens, some of them women, were searching for relatives among the dead," he wrote. "I came across the body of what looked like a pretty girl quietly sleeping. The pale face was turned up, the rain had combed the auburn hair back from a high, smooth forehead, and washed all the blood from the hole where the bullet had gone through the temple."

As Camm gazed upon the dead soldier, who was in fact a young man, not a girl at all, he noticed an envelope in the breast pocket of his half-opened coat. The letter, Camm said, "was in a beautiful hand, from a mother to her son, urging him to be a good soldier,

---

* At that point Grant usually smoked a pipe; cigars were expensive.

to do his duty without fear, not to drink or swear, and if those he fought against fell into his hands, to be kind to them."

Camm replaced the letter and mulled its contents. He decided that the boy had come from a "quality" upbringing and concluded that it would have been better if the mother "had taught her handsome son to revere human freedom and justice . . . for the negroes," even at the expense of slavery.

Camm was among a small handful of military diarists or letter writers of the period who expressed abolitionist sentiments as opposed to salvation of the Union as the prime reason for their service. It is not to say that Camm himself was an active abolitionist. But when a young lieutenant off one of the gunboats remarked to him, "Colonel, you put your mark on these fellows, and put it on them good," Camm understood the irony and replied, "Yes, but we call ourselves Christians, and pretend to be civilized, yet we glory in such work as this." He added silently, and to himself, "Somewhere in human policy, there is a great wrong. I hope that we have found it, and that I am helping to blot it out—Slavery!"

―――――◆―――――

Now that the road to Nashville was open Grant wanted to take it, but Halleck inexplicably held him up. Nevertheless, Grant's accomplishment was impressive. Not only had he taken the fort with all its artillery and stores, he had captured an entire Rebel army of more than 12,000 and inflicted some 2,000 casualties, while taking nearly 3,000 casualties of his own. Here was the first great victory for the Union, and Grant was the hero of the hour.

From the Confederates' standpoint the loss of Fort Donelson was an unmitigated disaster. Why Sidney Johnston chose Floyd and

Pillow to defend it rather than more experienced generals such as Hardee or even Buckner remains a puzzle. Maybe it had to do with seniority, but that doesn't wash since a commanding general could certainly overrule it. Johnston might have gone forward with his whole army to face Grant, but then he would have left the path clear for Buell, who had been inching his way toward Bowling Green for weeks. In any case the failure was a severe blow. Kentucky was now lost, and from the Cumberland Gap to the Mississippi the whole Confederate line had collapsed. Nashville was now exposed, and Johnston ordered it evacuated by the military.

This caused a near panic as civilian mobs threatened to break into warehouses and military stores, but the timely arrival of Bedford Forrest and his cavalry troopers put an end to that, and order was quickly restored. Forrest organized the removal of hundreds of wagons containing food, ammunition, and uniforms, sending them south toward Atlanta and other Southern cities. He had his men dismantle arms factories and sent their precious machinery away on railcars. Forrest was a man with no military schooling—in fact little schooling of any sort—who had worked himself up from private to general by dint of courage, ingenuity, and raw military horse sense. There is much to be said for the suggestion that if he had held higher command sooner the war in the West may have had another outcome.

As the Yankees moved into town the Nashvillians shuttered themselves inside their homes and hoped for the best. Union commanders, however, had issued stern orders against looting or vandalism, and soon citizens began to reappear on the streets. Among the Union force was Capt. G. P. Thruston, adjutant of the First Ohio, who, while attending Miami University of Ohio, had become close friends with Joel Allen Battle, Jr., of Nashville, now Captain Battle of the 20th Tennessee, Confederate States Army. There had been a little clique of roommates and messmates at the college and Battle was among the most popular. "A handsome young Southern student, and refined," was the way Thruston described him, "with an intellectual face, graceful and cordial in manner. He seemed an ideal type of young American manhood and was greatly beloved by all his associates."

Most of his associates, however, were now officers in the Federal army, in particular Buell's army, which was soon to be on its way to Pittsburg Landing to join forces with Ulysses Grant. One day a local physician came into Thruston's camp south of the city seeking a pass through Union lines. When Thruston asked him, casually, if he knew Allen Battle, the doctor's face lit up and he replied that not only did he know him, they were closely related. Moreover the doctor, whose name was W. C. Blackman, insisted that Thruston come to his home for dinner and meet Battle's wife and sisters. This created a somewhat awkward situation for all concerned, since a southerner inviting a Yankee soldier into his home was at the least apt to raise suspicion, and likewise a Union officer venturing beyond his lines into what amounted to an enemy camp was taking his life in his hands.

Nevertheless, Thruston consented on grounds that Blackman was "a gentleman of high character and I felt safe in his promised protection," and Blackman presumably had enough standing in the community to ward off any misgivings. At the dinner party the Blackman family, and including Battle's wife and sisters, showered Thruston "with every kind, cordial, consideration," he said, and as he left he jokingly promised that "when we got down there and captured Captain Battle I would see that he received the kindest treatment," to which one of Battle's sisters assured him with a smile that her brother "would have no occasion to accept his kindness," adding that "it will probably be more than you can do to hang on to your own scalp."

On that happy note Thruston departed next day for Shiloh with the odd feeling that soon enough he might be in the business of killing his close friend—or vice versa.

Meantime, Sidney Johnston now had to draw himself a new anti-Yankee barrier—across the bottommost parts of Tennessee instead of the top—beginning at Chattanooga and stretching 300 miles to Memphis on the Mississippi. And he had to defend it with one-quarter fewer troops, thanks to the fiasco at Fort Donelson.

This new Confederate line also ran through an unkempt backwater in the far southwest corner of Tennessee, a place of no intrinsic military value. In fact, it had almost negative military value, with its dark, serrated flora and mazy terrain. There was a small wooden church there called Shiloh chapel, which meant nothing to anyone but the locals, that had taken its name from a Hebrew expression meaning "Place of Peace."

CHAPTER 6

THIS CRUEL WAR

ULYSSES GRANT HAD PRODUCED THE FIRST GREAT victory of the war, cleared two major arteries into the heart of the rebellion, and captured an entire Rebel army; in the process he managed to get most of his superiors angry at him. Halleck in particular was spiteful enough to go behind Grant's back to McClellan, accusing Grant of "neglect and inefficiency."

In a telegram on March 3, Halleck groused: "I have had no communication with General Grant for a week. He left his command without my authority and went to Nashville. His army seems as much demoralized by the victory at Fort Donelson as was that of the [Army] of the Potomac by the defeat at Bull Run. It is hard to censure a successful general immediately after a victory, but I think he richly deserves it. Satisfied with his victory, he sits down and enjoys it without any regard to the future. I am worn out and tired with this neglect and inefficiency. C. F. Smith is almost the only officer equal to the emergency."

As if this were not damaging enough, Halleck followed up a few days later with a postscript: "Word has just reached me that since the taking of Fort Donelson General Grant has resumed his former bad habits [the drinking]."

This unseemly outburst was prompted by Grant's failure to reply, on several occasions, to requests by Halleck for troop strengths and movements, and also a snide report from Buell that Grant had made an unauthorized trip to Nashville. In his memoirs Grant attributes the failure to communicate to a telegraph operator "who proved afterwards to be a Rebel; he deserted his post a short time later and went south taking [the] dispatches with him."

But McClellan—perhaps recalling the scene from Fort Vancouver, Oregon—deduced that Grant was probably up to his old tricks, and sent Halleck this reply: "Your dispatch of last evening received. The future success of our cause demands that proceedings such as Grant's should at once be checked. Generals must observe discipline as well as private soldiers. Do not hesitate to arrest him at once if the good of the service requires it, and place C. F. Smith in command. You are at liberty to regard this as a positive order if it will smooth your way."

Now both Halleck and McClellan were irate at Grant, but there is every indication that behind and beyond these charges was the green goddess jealousy. While "Unconditional Surrender" Grant was being celebrated on a national scale for marching on Fort Donelson, Halleck, the general in charge of the Department of the West, had been marching a desk in St. Louis, receiving no credit for the victory. Apparently Halleck was beginning to see a rival in Grant. Furthermore, Halleck had ordered Grant *not* to take Nashville after Grant had telegraphed that he could have it in Union hands—"in 8 days"—and Grant had found a way to disobey him in that matter also.

As it happened, a week after Donelson had capitulated a convoy containing the infantry division of William "Bull" Nelson came steaming up the Cumberland River and arrived at Clarksville, south of Fort Donelson, where Grant had gone the day before. Nelson, a portly and obstreperous giant with a full beard and side whiskers, had been given an army division after he set up a Union recruiting station in his native Kentucky. The division had been loaned to Grant as reinforcements from Buell on a temporary basis when it was thought a long siege would be necessary to capture Fort Donelson. Now Grant, being the good soldier that he was, and realizing that the occupation of Nashville would be an important prize in winning the war, had a bright idea. If he himself was not permitted by Halleck to take Nashville, *somebody* needed to, so Grant declared to his chief of staff, according to Dr. Brinton, who was present in Grant's office on the steamboat *Tigress:* "I have it, Rawlins! That must be Nelson and his command. I will order him to report to Buell in Nashville."

The fact that Buell was as yet many miles from Nashville, and "was headed thither at a snail's pace," did not faze Grant in the least. He saw a chance to capture and occupy a major enemy city and did not hesitate. Nelson and his people steamed up that night and occupied Nashville without a shot being fired. For his trouble Grant now had Buell—who complained to McClellan, "My troops are being filched from me"—furious with him too.

Under cover of McClellan's instructions, Halleck issued an order that relieved Grant of command and replaced him with C. F. Smith. "Remain yourself at Fort Henry," Halleck instructed Grant.

"Why do you not obey my orders to report troop strength and positions of your command?"

Grant was flabbergasted, and maintained that this was the first he had heard of Halleck's requests. His demotion could not have come at a worse time. Something important was brewing—a big expedition up the Tennessee River, and not just gunboats this time but a major infantry action. Ostensibly it was to be in the nature of a raid to break up the Memphis and Charleston Railroad to deny the Confederacy its ability to send reinforcements against McClellan's operations in Virginia. And, if successful, it would indeed have dealt the Rebels a severe blow. A worried LeRoy P. Walker, until recently the Confederate secretary of war, telegraphed to Richmond, "The Memphis and Charleston road is the vertebrae of the Confederacy, and there are no troops for its defense."

Grant's reaction to his demotion at first was disbelief, then indignation, and at one point it actually brought him to tears. "I was virtually under arrest," he said later, "and I had lost my command." He responded to Halleck in the tone of a hurt friend. "I am not aware," Grant wrote, "of ever having disobeyed any orders from headquarters—certainly never intended such a thing." In the throes of humiliation, he asked to be relieved from further duties in the department, but Halleck was silent on the request. Clearly, though, there was more to this than Grant simply not responding to Halleck's telegrams. Halleck could easily have sent his chief of staff down to Grant on a steamboat to find out what was going on.

While Grant remained in limbo at Fort Henry, with only his staff to keep him company, C. F. Smith organized and, with 60 steamboats, got the expedition under way into the darkest heart of Rebel territory. Grant had walked with his old commandant up and down the levee the night before the army departed, according to surgeon Brinton, who remained with Grant during this period. Unfortunately their conversation is lost to history. Brinton nevertheless put in his impressions: "The treatment received by General Grant at this time cut him bitterly. I formed the opinion at the time that General Buell's complaints had not a little to do in leading to the misunderstandings." Brinton characterized the action of Halleck and McClellan as "infamous," and concluded that "[Grant's] fault was in being too strong and active."

Now it was Halleck who found himself in an unenviable position, for word of Grant's travails had leaked out, as always it must in Washington, and among the recipients of the news was the President of the United States. Still in agony over the death of his son Willie, who at last had expired two weeks earlier, Lincoln at least was thankful to find a winning general—Grant—only to discover that he had asked to be relieved from duty. The lawyer in Lincoln quickly determined that almost all of the accusations against Grant were based on rumor and hearsay, and he told Halleck, in so many words, to "put up or shut up" (i.e., either court-martial him or return him to duty). Thus, on March 13, Grant received a letter from Halleck, saying, "You cannot be relieved from your command. There is no good reason for it. Instead of relieving you, I wish you as soon as your new army is in the field to assume the command and lead it on to new victories."

Grant was immensely grateful and reassured. The thing had blown over. He had not seen Halleck's treacherous correspondence, and would not until the war was over, and somehow believed it was all a simple misunderstanding. In fact, such was his naïveté that amid all this backstabbing he wrote to Julia, "There are not two men in the United States who I would prefer serving under than Halleck and McClellan." If Grant had one notable fault it was that he too often failed to discern the true character of his fellow men. This bedeviled his entire career, especially after he became President of the United States.

With Grant now out of the doghouse, another quirk of fate threw him together with the man who would become his closest confidant, almost his alter ego: William Tecumseh Sherman. Sherman had arrived at Cairo beneath an even darker cloud than Grant had just escaped from under, for it had been widely reported that Sherman was "crazy." Having rehabilitated himself from these accusations, Sherman was given command of a reinforced division of 9,000 raw recruits with which to spearhead operations against the Memphis and Charleston Railroad somewhere along the Tennessee-Mississippi border.

In time, the size and mission of the Tennessee River expedition was greatly expanded. Orders now were that when the railroad was destroyed, C. F. Smith was to select a base of operations deep in Rebel territory, where he would be joined by five more divisions totaling nearly 50,000 men. As well, Buell was to march 20,000 men of his army overland from Nashville and meet up with Grant at some point close to the river. Once established, this combined army was to "operate against the enemy" as the situation dictated. It was generally assumed that a large and decisive battle would be brought on, since the Confederates could not allow such a force to roam about their country unmolested. Grant was now headed south to take command. It would become Sherman's finest hour.

Sherman was born in Lancaster, Ohio, on February 8, 1820, into the comfortable family of a prominent lawyer and state supreme court justice. When he was nine, however, Sherman's father died, leaving behind his wife with nine children and an ocean of debt. From then on the family relied on relatives and friends for their survival, and young William was sent to live with the neighboring Ewing family. He developed into a tall, awkward redhead with a promising intellect and an edgy, anxious temperament. His foster father, Thomas Ewing, had become a United States senator and secured for him a place at West Point, which he entered in 1836 at the age of 16, proving to be a better than average student and graduating near the top of his class in 1840. In Sherman's final year, a plebe arrived at the Academy with the name of U. S. Grant, and Sherman often claimed that he was the one to nickname him "Sam," as in "Uncle Sam" Grant.

Sherman's military career took him to posts throughout the South where the wealth and prominence of Thomas Ewing opened doors for the young lieutenant. He mixed and mingled well with the upper crust of Southern society, for whom he acquired a lasting affection. In 1846 the army sent Sherman to California when war broke out with Mexico, and he got caught up in the Bear Flag Rebellion and the famous set-to between his boss Gen. Stephen Kearny and (then a colonel) John C. Frémont. With California occupied by the Americans, Sherman spent the duration consigned to supply duty and was present for the Gold Rush of '49 brought on by the discovery of nuggets at Sutter's Mill.

In 1850 Sherman returned to the East Coast and became engaged to his foster sister, Eleanor "Ellen" Ewing, a practice that was not uncustomary in the 19th century. By then Ewing had been named secretary of the interior, and Sherman's wedding was attended by nearly all the top political celebrities, including the President of the United States.

Unfortunately, the California gold rush had created such an overwhelming monetary inflation that it left Sherman, who had become a captain, almost destitute, and he resigned from the army and wound up running a bank in San Francisco. But the gold bubble soon burst and the bank failed, and eventually Sherman found himself in Cincinnati employed as, of all things, a bill collector.

At last his luck began to turn when he got wind through family channels from the new secretary of the army, John Floyd, that the state of Louisiana intended to establish a new military academy in Baton Rouge and was looking for a superintendent. Sherman applied for the job and was soon en route down the Mississippi to oversee the building construction and the education and military training of 56 cadets at the Louisiana Seminary of Learning and Military Academy, which would one day become Louisiana State University.

The institution officially opened its doors on New Year's Day 1860, and Sherman proved to be an excellent college president; he got on well not only with the students but with the Louisiana politicians from the governor on down. These were, however, ominous and uncertain times. The abolitionist John Brown had recently caused a great uproar with his famous raid, and his body had barely begun to molder in the ground when a schism over slavery split the Democratic Party and practically ensured the election of Lincoln. Residing in Louisiana, Sherman didn't need to read the tea leaves to see that this would lead to war.

His personal feelings were strongly antisecession. Sherman viewed the United States as an entity in which individual states could not be permitted simply to make off with themselves without the consent of the majority of states. Such a policy, Sherman said, would cause state after state to peel away until "we should reap the fate of Mexico, which is eternal war." On slavery, however, Sherman, like many if not most men, North and South, was a man of his time and loathed the notion of abolition almost as much as secession, because he worried that it would bring on civil war. "I would not," he wrote to Thomas Ewing, Jr., his foster brother, "abolish or modify slavery. Negroes in the great numbers that exist here must of necessity be slaves. All the congresses on earth cannot make the negro anything else but what he is." Sherman was more ambivalent about slavery spreading to the territories, a burning issue of the day, "but as to abolishing it in the south or turning loose 4 millions of slaves, I would have no hand in it."

Nevertheless, Sherman described himself as "an ultra" on the question of secession. "I believe in coercion [war] and cannot comprehend how any Government can exist unless it defend its integrity." But the two issues—national integrity and slavery—he wrote, "should be Kept distinct, for otherwise it will gradually become a war of Extermination without End." So said William Tecumseh Sherman.

As war clouds enveloped Louisiana Sherman one night after dinner delivered himself of a harsh and prophetic sermon to the academy's French instructor, whom he considered a friend: "You, you people of the South, believe there can be such a thing as peaceful secession. You don't know what you are doing . . . The country will be drenched in blood. You mistake the people of the north. They are a peaceable people, but an earnest people, and will fight too, and they are not going to let this country be destroyed without a mighty effort to save it . . . The North can make a steam-engine, a locomotive or railway car; hardly a yard of cloth or shoes can you make. You are rushing to war with one of the most powerful, ingeniously mechanical and determined people on earth—right at your doors. You are bound to fail!"

Having thus summed up the situation, Sherman had arranged by early February 1861 to extract himself from Louisiana, as the Southern states seceded one after the other. First, however, he wanted to set the affairs of the academy in good order and was in the process of doing so when without warning the governor seized the federal forts and arsenals. For Sherman, the straw that broke the camel's back came when wagonloads of rifles, "still in their old familiar boxes with U.S. scratched off," arrived at the school "for safe keeping." Thus, he wrote indignantly, "I was made the receiver of stolen goods."

Next day Sherman handed in his resignation and caught a steamboat north to St. Louis, where he accepted the presidency of a mule-drawn streetcar service. When war finally broke out after the firing on Fort Sumter in April 1861 Sherman's foster father Ewing and his brother John Sherman, now a U.S. senator, jerked a few political strings so that Sherman found himself colonel of the 13th U.S. Infantry, a regular army regiment. Three months later he commanded a brigade at the First Battle of Bull Run where he managed to put on an admirable performance despite the appalling Federal rout. Following this, he accepted assignment as second in command of the Department of the Cumberland, headquartered in Louisville, where the rumor started that he had gone insane.

The situation in Kentucky was confused, delicate, and extremely critical when Sherman arrived. The governor had been pressing for secession but the legislature was against it. Both Rebels and Yankees were raising troops there. Lincoln was trying everything he knew to keep Kentucky in the Union while Jefferson Davis was doing his best to keep it out. The man commanding the department was 56-year-old Gen. Robert Anderson, who had suffered the humiliation of surrendering Fort Sumter. Anderson had become feeble from the strain ever since Sumter, and the month after Sherman arrived, he stepped down and Sherman stepped up. It was not an agreeable job.

Scarcely had Sherman moved his things into Anderson's office than Simon Cameron, the U.S. secretary of war, arrived in Louisville on a fact-finding tour with an entourage of newspaper reporters, whom he insisted should remain in the room during the briefing. When Anderson asked Sherman's opinion of what it would take to quell the rebellion in his sector, Sherman replied that it would probably take around 200,000 men to subdue the entire Mississippi River Valley. Cameron was naturally taken aback, since there weren't 200,000 men in the entire army at that point, but nothing further was said.

When he returned to Washington, Cameron sent a note to the adjutant general asking him to prepare a memo of the conversation at the briefing, including Sherman's "insane" opinion that 200,000 soldiers would be required. Apparently the note and other information leaked to the press and soon newspapers were circulating reports that the commanding general of the Department of the Cumberland had "gone mad," "was crazy," "had gone insane." The more Sherman tried to straighten things out, the worse it became; news reports of his "insanity" snowballed, and in time the question of his mental stability seemed to become a self-fulfilling prophecy. Two of his close relatives, in fact, had been institutionalized, and Sherman himself found he was beginning to doubt his sanity.

This was also when Sherman's hatred of the press began to solidify. There had been a few unpleasant run-ins with newspapers while he was in California, but the harsh attacks on his sanity drove Sherman past the point of no return. According to the author Emmet Crozier in *Yankee Reporters, 1861–65,* when the *Cincinnati Appeal* correspondent Florus B. Plimpton met Sherman during one of his inspections south of Louisville, he handed the general a letter of introduction from his editor. Sherman looked the youthful reporter up and down, handed him back the letter, and replied, "The next train to Louisville goes at half-past one. Take that train. Make sure you take that train."

Startled, Plimpton protested, "But, General, the people are anxious, I'm only after the truth."

"The truth!" Sherman shouted. "That's what we don't want. No sir; we don't want the enemy any better informed than he is! Go on home; make no mistake about that train!"

In any case, things continued to wear on Sherman, and on November 5, 1861, less than a month after he had taken command, he asked to be relieved.

Whatever Sherman did during his leave of absence seemed to restore him, and he returned, bright eyed and eager, to find that Henry Halleck, whom he had known in California, had just been placed in command of the Department of the West. Halleck assigned Sherman to run the district of Cairo—Grant's old job—but with no army, since Grant had taken that with him to fight the battles of Forts Henry and Donelson. Cairo at this point was described by one observer as "a small place at the terminus of the Illinois Central railroad, a place of not much account, low and flat, and at some seasons entirely under water." Sherman's job was to keep Grant supplied and reinforced, and that was where they began a long-distance friendship that lasted through the war and afterward. He was extremely solicitous of Grant's needs and promised to send him anything "within reason," up to and including surgeons, nurses, officers' wives, laundresses—even himself. It was for his outstanding performance as Grant's supply officer that Sherman was rewarded with the 9,000-man division of green recruits and sent to spearhead the Southern invasion in early March 1862.

<hr />

On March 10 Sherman embarked his division on 18 steamboats up the Tennessee to Fort Henry. Two days later Gen. C. F. Smith arrived with three more divisions and told Sherman to "push on under escort of the two gunboats *Lexington* and *Tyler* and break up the Memphis & Charleston railroad between Corinth and Tuscumbia, Alabama." Smith said that he would be following with the rest of the army. At that point General Smith was "quite unwell," Sherman noted. Sometime earlier he had scraped his leg on a rusty piece of tin while getting into a small boat and it had begun to fester and swell. There were no such things as antibiotics, and Smith was in pain, and considerable danger as well. Even as they spoke it had begun to rain.

It was still raining and the river was high as Sherman's force passed by Pittsburg Landing. The captain told Sherman there had been a Rebel cavalry force there, and a battery, but the gunboats had disposed of them, killing half a dozen Confederates in the process. They steamed on below the Tennessee line and the river was in full flood. At a point where the river is the dividing line between Alabama and Mississippi they put in to the shore and disembarked.

The objective was the town of Burnsville, about halfway to Corinth, 30 miles distant. There the rail company maintained large repair and maintenance shops; the idea was to tear up as much track as possible, burn the shops and depots, and put the M&C out of business for as long as possible.

Well before dawn Sherman sent his cavalry forward, then followed them with the infantry and artillery. "It was raining very hard at the time," he said. "Daylight found us about six miles out, where we met the cavalry returning. They had made numerous attempts to cross the streams, which were so swollen that mere brooks covered the whole bottom." Several men had drowned. "It was raining in torrents," Sherman said. Word came from the rear that the river was rising very fast (in fact it rose 16 feet in 24 hours), and unless they returned immediately the way back would be impassable. Escape was "so difficult," Sherman reported, "that we had to un-harness the artillery horses, and drag the guns under water through the bayous."

They dropped back down the river and by that night, March 14, they had reached Pittsburg Landing, where they found Hurlbut's division waiting on boats. Sherman also left his men on the boats and steamed down to Savannah, where he found General Smith bedridden in the Cherry mansion, his leg having worsened during the past two days. Smith told him to take the army's chief engineer, James McPherson, and to land his division, and that of Hurlbut as well, at Pittsburg Landing, making camps "far back [from the river] to leave room for the entire army."

On March 17 Grant, now reinstated, arrived and took charge of the army. He made his headquarters at the Cherry mansion in Savannah along with Smith, but he usually went up to Pittsburg

Landing every day. Benjamin Prentiss's division soon arrived, as did McClernand's and Hurlbut's, and set up camps at Pittsburg. W.H.L. Wallace had assumed command of Smith's old division. Lew Wallace's division came up, but there wasn't room at Pittsburg, so it was debarked at Crump's Landing, about six miles north of Pittsburg. That gave Grant an army of 48,894 on the books. Buell, who was marching overland through Bowling Green and Nashville with 20,000 more, was expected April 6, a force that when combined would be irresistible.

———◆———

A month earlier, the Green River in southern Kentucky was also running high and Rebel troops, who were evacuating Bowling Green, had burned all the bridges across it when, on the morning of February 14, Buell, whose army had arrived on the east side of the river, ordered his artillery to shell the town. A blanket of snow covered the ground. Josie Underwood had spent the night in the city with a family friend, a Mrs. Hall, only to find that the war at last had come to Bowling Green.

"The place was alive with panic," she told her diary. "Soldiers were rushing wildly—cavalry and infantry—horses were being taken everywhere and everywhere found—citizens, men women and children, white and black, were fleeing over the hills to get out of reach of danger—whilst the steady Boom—swish, shriek, and bang of cannon shot and shell went on. One shell crashed through the corner of Mrs. Hall's kitchen and a piece of metal fell into the biscuit dough that Aunt Sallie [a cook] was kneading—she rushed into the house where we all were, all spattered with flour—saying—'Bless de Lord—a Union shell in my biscuit dough!' "

This was the day Josie and her family had waited for—the liberation of their state from Rebel influence. Fort Donelson would fall to Grant next day. But it was also a time of shock and sadness, for they had lost so much since those happy times at Mount Air and Memphis. They had lost in fact nearly everything since the war began ten months earlier.

It had been good to come home after her stay in Memphis, but not for long. "The feeling is growing more and more bitter between the Union people and secessionists, try as we will to maintain the same outward show of friendship," Josie said. All of the "substantial" people in town were Unionists, she said, and the Rebels were by and large a shabby lot. They had kept a close ear to the proceedings at Fort Sumter where Major Anderson was holding out against the Confederate force in Charleston. Anderson was "a personal friend and distant cousin" of her father's.

It wasn't long before Josie received "a warm and beautiful" letter from Tom Grafton, who had left the Shelby Grays to become a major of a regiment from his native Mississippi. Grafton said he "hopes the North will recognize the South's right to withdraw from a hated Union without bloodshed." William Western was visiting Mount Air when word came about Fort Sumter's fall. They were having dinner, and among the guests was Benjamin Grider, a Bowling Green lawyer who was married to Josie's sister, and whose own sister, Jane, had been Josie's traveling companion to Memphis. The two brothers-in-law were devoted to each other, according to Josie, but when news of Sumter arrived Western said, "I'll go to Memphis and fight with the South—for that's what she'll do now," to which Grider replied, "Well Bill, I don't reckon Kentucky can stay neutral now—and I'll raise a regiment to fight against you and whip you back into the Union." With that, they departed and Josie took a horseback ride around Mount Air.

"The air was so balmy and sweet. The country is so lovely with the redbud and dogwood in blossom . . . we came home just as the sun was setting, the most beautiful place in the whole country round. The peach trees all in blossom make it look like a huge bouquet of pinks and the perfume of the honeysuckle has wafted to us on the gentle breeze just as we rode up the Hill from the front gate—never was there a more peaceful happy home and never I believe a happier girl than I. It is too horrible to think of war devastating this beautiful land."

Yet that is exactly what happened. As spring turned to the summer of 1861, a few of Josie's former school friends from secessionist families "fell away," and there was an increasing coolness between Unionists and secessionists that often turned to outright hostility. William Western became a major in the cavalry of Nathan Bedford Forrest, and Ben Grider, as promised, raised his Union regiment, the Ninth Kentucky, of which he was colonel. Josie's uncle "Wint" (Winston Henry), a West Pointer, resigned his army commission, saying he "could not conscientiously fight any longer against the South." His sister, Josie's mother, said of him, " 'Oh! If he had only died or been killed defending the flag and the country for which his fathers fought!' She begged us never to mention his name to her again—to let him be as one dead—too bad! So sad!"

Josie "got another beautiful letter from Mr. Grafton. It seems cruel not to write him—even if I . . ." She did not finish the sentence. Josie's brother, Warner, only 15, ran off and joined the army against his family's wishes. Somehow he found he way into Ben Grider's regiment.

Then, at the end of the first summer of the war, General Johnston and the Confederate army came to Bowling Green and occupied the town. General Hardee brought an army of 27,000 to
anchor the line behind the Green River—west to Columbus on the
Mississippi and east to Virginia and the Cumberland Gap.

Josie had to give up her horseback rides. The soldiers overwhelmed the town and were camped in the orchards and fields
at Mount Air. "The fields all trodden down and the fences being
burned" (for firewood), she wrote. "Tonight as I looked out from
my window at the tents shining white in the moonlight, with here
and there a campfire, and hear the various bugle calls from far off
and near—there is something thrilling and beautiful in it all, in
spite of the underlying and ever-abiding sadness."

In early October, someone warned Warner Underwood that
he was under suspicion of spying for the Union and was being
"watched." A few days later a hundred soldiers "with gleaming axes"
marched to the house and began felling the large old oak and wal-
nut trees that had shaded the mansion for decades. The officer in
charge said that the hill upon which Mount Air rested commanded
a field of fire across the river and had to be cleared, and then they
were going to erect a fort with artillery batteries. They tore down
the cabin of an elderly slave, and when the man came to Josie's
father crying despair he could not be made to understand why
Underwood was powerless to stop the destruction.

Rebel families in town were bolder now and frequently insulting toward Unionists. On November 5 Josie turned 21, worried
about her father, who was being harassed, and her mother, who
had fallen into ill health. Rebel officers began to make themselves
at home at Mount Air. Josie's father received a letter from his

son-in-law Western, who was quite wealthy and had gotten wind of the situation at Mount Air. He offered to buy the property, slaves and all, for $50,000 in gold (more than $1 million today), reasoning that because he was a Confederate officer the place would be protected and the family could continue living there, just as they were. Underwood was tempted and grateful, but in the end the slaves changed his mind. When he tried to explain the situation to them, they could not understand it—only that they were being sold—and they implored against it wretchedly, Josie recorded: "I never would er believed Mars Warner you'd sell us!" "And dear Pa could not stand it—'and I never will!' he said. We will do the best we can together—come what may."

Over a bleak Christmas holiday Josie, her mother, and other Union women baked pies and cakes to take to Union prisoners who were being held by the Confederates in the Bowling Green stockade. When they returned to Mount Air the great blow came. Josie's father stood with three Confederate soldiers in the library by the fire and read a document he'd just been given. By order of the commanding general, A. S. Johnston, they were "to vacate the premises immediately." The Rebel orderly apologized, but the order stood. Underwood managed to get them a single day longer to pack and leave. They were banished.

All day they packed: Their books, the piano, some of the better furniture, and their clothing in trunks went into a wagon. They took up housekeeping in a small lent cabin in the woods about 15 miles from town. Even as the Underwoods left, Confederate officers were prowling the halls of Mount Air, staking out claims for living quarters. The cabin the family settled in had leaks through which icy rain dripped and Mrs. Underwood's health worsened.

They endured this dingy living through the worst of the winter.

One beastly night in late January the "biggest and most respectable secessionist in town"—and, as well, an old family friend—appeared at the cabin door, warning Josie's father that soldiers would arrest him the next day for treason, espionage, or both, and that he had best leave at once. With a heavy heart Underwood packed a few things, kissed his wife and daughter, and rode off "into the darkness and the cold night," hoping to sneak north through the Rebel lines. Next day the soldiers came. Informed that Underwood was not there, they searched the house. As they left, a lieutenant said to Josie, "I'm glad your father isn't here, Miss. I don't like this kind of job."

The dreary winter dragged on in agonizing uncertainty, and then good news. On February 7 word was received that Underwood had gotten safely through the lines and was at Columbia, Kentucky, with Grider and his regiment as well as his son, Warner. Soon it got out that a big battle was raging at Fort Donelson, about a hundred miles to the southwest. A few days after that, two soldiers appeared with a note from a Confederate colonel, saying, "Mr. Underwood—we are about to vacate your premises and advise that you take possession at once lest evil persons destroy the buildings."

Josie became ecstatic and told her diary, "We are going back to Mount Air. Oh! I am so glad!" Her mother suspected it might be a trick to trap her fugitive husband, but the family quickly mounted their carriage and rode toward Bowling Green. Josie wrote, "Goodbye poor little leaky cabin! And all the good, kind, ignorant people of these woods and this journal, till I can write again in my own old room at dear Mount Air!"

She would never do it. "Mount Air is in ashes!" her next entry cried. Their home was gone, burned to the ground by the time the carriage brought them there. Who did it, they never learned—some spiteful person or persons, civilian or military. Faced with the loss of Fort Henry, Johnston's army was evacuating Bowling Green, but the Rebel general Hardee had posted handbills warning that anyone caught torching buildings would be shot on sight.

As the Underwoods neared Mount Air it appeared that the house was still there, but that was a mirage; only the gable was standing, and it fell in with a crash just as they arrived and "helplessly watched the smoldering ruins of our once beautiful and happy home. Both orchards were cut down, as well as the avenue of big trees leading [down the drive] toward town—all were gone—not a fence left on the 1000 acres. Ruin, devastation and desolation everywhere!" Then it began to snow.

The Underwoods went to spend the night with Mrs. Hall in town, and next morning the shelling from Buell's artillery began that interrupted Aunt Sallie's biscuit bake. "Mike Hall [Mrs. Hall's bachelor son who lived with her] was so beset he didn't know what to do and at one point shouted, 'Great God! What will I do with all these women!' " Josie remembered her father telling her that if she was in a house in range of shot to go to the cellar, so that's what they did. Mike Hall passed a brandy bottle around while some of them prayed and Buell's shot and shell whistled and crashed into the town. Some of the people rushing by who saw the cellar door open jumped in, and soon they had "quite a heterogeneous crowd—among them the Catholic priest." As well, one of Josie's old suitors, Hugh Gwyn, arrived wearing his brand-new Confederate lieutenant's uniform, which he had just rescued from the tailor, who had not quite finished sewing up the collar. Josie noticed this, and "as the hours in the cellar wore on, the cannon keeping up the steady booms, everyone felt a little safer in the situation. I offered to sew [Gwyn's] collar—so he and I rushed out of the cellar into the house where I got Mrs. Hall's [sewing] basket and sewed it on, whilst he foraged in the pantry."

They took a picnic feast back to the cellar—half a ham, pickles, as well as the bowl of "cold beat biscuit" that the cook had been kneading when the cannonball entered the kitchen. Going back to the cellar Josie was nearly decapitated by a ball that "whizzed right in front of my face and buried itself in the ground not six feet from us."

Around dark the shelling slowed and then stopped. They later learned that a deputation of prominent men had gone across the river to convince Buell that the Confederates had all gone, including Hugh Gwyn, who said he was "off to my regiment, if I can find it." Soon Union troops entered the town. Josie's older sister Fanny was married to Ben Grider, and Josie and her mother took up residence in her home. The day after the shelling her father arrived, and next day so had her 15-year-old brother Warner, resplendent in his new blue lieutenant's uniform. They had lost much, but at least the family was together again. It would not be so for long.

CHAPTER 7

HE LOOKED LIKE
AN OLD VIKING KING

A FUROR CONVULSED THE SOUTH IMMEDIATELY after the loss of Forts Henry and Donelson and the evacuation of Columbus and Bowling Green. It was aimed mostly at Albert Sidney Johnston but also rubbed off on Jefferson Davis, since he was the one who had sent him west with such great expectations. On February 22, 1862, a second inaugural was held for Davis in Richmond, the new Confederate capital, during which he remarked, "Battles have been fought, sieges have been conducted and the tide for the moment is against us. We have had our trials and difficulties. That we are to escape them in the future is not to be hoped. It was to be expected when we entered this war that it would expose our people to sacrifices and cost them much, both of money and blood." He went on to predict that the South would overcome these difficulties and prevail, but the gloomy assessment by the president was unprecedented, and he was heavily condemned in the press.

Yet the press and the public seemed to reserve a special scorn for Sidney Johnston, whom they had been assured was to be the savior of the West. "Every hamlet resounded with denunciation, and every breast was filled with indignation at the author of such calamities," wrote Johnston's son Col. William Preston Johnston, who served on his father's staff. The general, the younger Johnston said, "became the special target of every accusation, including imbecility, cowardice, and treason." A deputation of politicians appeared at Davis's door to demand Johnston be relieved, to whom Davis sourly replied, "If Sidney Johnston is not a general, I have none." When Davis and others urged Johnston to defend himself, his answer underscores part of the reason Winfield Scott called him "the finest soldier I have ever commanded" and deserves close attention.

———◆◆◆———

Albert Sidney Johnston was near to a legend for men on both sides of the war who had served in the old army. Handsome and "powerfully made," he was over six feet tall with wavy gray hair and a piratical mustache, and he exuded the highest air of command. Phillip D. Stephenson, a private of the 13th Arkansas, hung around his headquarters one day in hopes of getting a glimpse. "If ever a man *looked* the 'great man' Albert Sidney Johnston did," Private Stephenson wrote later. "A martial figure, although dressed in civilian clothes. I saw him but once, a black felt 'slouch' had shaded his features as he walked head down as though buried in deep thought. He looked like an old Viking king!"

Johnston was born in Kentucky in 1803, the son of a physician, and studied at Lexington's Transylvania College, along with Jefferson Davis, who was two years behind him. Both men received appointments to the U.S. Military Academy, and Davis developed a strong admiration for Johnston during those years. In 1826 he graduated eighth in his class and served in the 1832 Black Hawk War as chief of staff for Gen. Henry Atkinson. In 1829 he had married Henrietta Preston, who soon contracted tuberculosis, and in 1834 Johnston left the army to care for her. After she died in 1836, he went to Texas and took up farming but enlisted in the Texas army during that republic's war for independence from Mexico. His exploits became renowned. People retold the story of how Johnston waded into a fight between a mountain lion and a pack of hunting dogs, clubbing the lion to death with the butt and barrel of his rifle. He rose quickly in the ranks and became adjutant general, and later commander, of the Republic of Texas Army.

This nearly cost him his life, as it seemed to be a common practice in the Texas of those days for a man seeking command of the army to issue a challenge to his opposition, just for the hell of it. Such a man was one Felix Huston, a Texan via Mississippi, who had come to the struggling republic with 500 men, staking his fame and fortune on the outcome of the new independent country. When Sidney Johnston was named head of the Texas army, Huston promptly challenged him to a duel on trumped-up grounds, which Johnston—who despised the practice—accepted and named the time as 7 a.m. the following day, February 7, 1837.

No proper dueling pistols could be found so it was decided to use Huston's giant horse pistols with foot-long barrels. The men met at the appointed time on a plain beside the Lavaca River where Johnston's second lodged a formal complaint that Johnston had never used such weapons before, but Johnston "waived the objection."

The duel was a very strange affair. If a man fired a pistol in a duel using hair-trigger weapons, often the sound of the report would cause his opponent's finger to twitch enough to set off his own pistol. Thus, relying on "his sense of moral superiority," as his son put it many years later in a biography of his father, Johnston quickly fired first into the air, causing Huston—who was said to be an excellent duelist—to reflexively shoot wild.

At any exchange Huston could have declared that he was "satisfied," but he chose not to do so, and the bizarre dance of death continued five times, with Johnston discharging his pistol quickly into the air and five times Huston's shots going wild. On the sixth time, however, Huston finally caught on and shot Johnston in the pelvis, a wound from which doctors on hand declared he could not recover. Huston then approached the stricken Johnston and, of all things, apologized, before slinking back to his quarters for breakfast. It took Johnston many months to heal, but in defiance of the surgeons' forecast he was once more able to resume his role as commander of the Texas army.

In 1843 he married Eliza Griffin and began a new family, settling on his plantation called China Grove. When the Mexican War broke out in 1846, Johnston commanded the First Texas Rifle Volunteers under Gen. Zachary Taylor and fought at the battles of Monterrey and Buena Vista. After the war he returned to his cotton plantation until, in 1849, Taylor, by then President of the United States, appointed him as paymaster to the U.S. Army with the rank of major. In 1855 Johnston was appointed colonel of the soon-to-be-famed Second U.S. Cavalry, which fought in numerous Indian campaigns in Texas and the Great Plains. The regiment became remarkable for the number of its officers who would become prominent in the Civil War, including Robert E. Lee, who was Johnston's second in command; future Confederate generals William J.

Hardee, Earl Van Dorn, Edmund Kirby Smith, Fitzhugh Lee, and John Bell Hood; and the future Union generals George H. Thomas and George Stoneman.

In 1857 Johnston commanded a force to chastise the Mormons in Utah Territory, who were reported to have set up a religious government and were practicing polygamy in defiance of U.S. law. Beginning in 1847 some 30,000 Mormons had migrated to areas around the Great Salt Lake after being abused and run out of various towns in Illinois and Missouri. The newly organized Republican Party ranked polygamy along with slavery as an immoral and illegal sin and pressured the government to step in. Johnston managed to subdue the Mormons without serious bloodshed, for which he received a promotion to brigadier general and was appointed command of the Department of the Pacific, based at Alcatraz Island in San Francisco Bay.

Abraham Lincoln had been elected President when Johnston and his family sailed for California in December 1860. Talk of secession was already in the air, but he had hardly unpacked when news arrived that Texas had seceded. Johnston deplored the notion of disunion, but, as in the great majority of cases where Southern loyalties were torn, he remained steadfast with his adopted state, which in those times usually commanded a higher allegiance than did the national government in Washington, D.C.* On May 3, 1861, his resignation from the U.S. Army was officially accepted.

Ordinarily Johnston and his family would have sailed for New York, but that was complicated by the war. His older son, William Preston, sent a letter warning that if he arrived in New York

---

* In those days it was known as Washington City, presumably to distinguish it from Washington Territory.

he would probably be arrested. Indeed, Albert Sidney Johnston was an influential and coveted officer, a fact everyone understood, from the President on down. The adjutant general had suggested to Winfield Scott that Johnston be promoted to major general as an inducement to remain with the Union, which was immediately approved by Lincoln, and a letter containing the promotion was mailed, but not in time for Johnston's resignation.

Then, in Los Angeles, where Johnston had gone with his family after resigning, word was spread falsely that he was involved in a treasonous plot to seize arms from the U.S. arsenal and take over California for the Confederacy. This was clearly ridiculous, but the word soon came that federal authorities intended to arrest Johnston in California. This prompted him to put his wife and children aboard a ship, and then, on June 16, join up with a dozen other U.S. officers for a tortuous and harrowing journey by horseback across the southwestern deserts to Texas. Along the way they dodged various U.S. troops who had been ordered to capture them; were revolted by the rotting bodies of stagecoach passengers recently massacred by Apaches; nearly died of thirst; and were awed by the Great Comet of 1861 that suddenly appeared one evening after sunset and sparkled nightly in the skies above their wasteland trek. Johnston saw it as "a good omen."

Johnston and his party reached civilization at San Antonio, two months and 1,500 miles later, and Johnston continued on by steamship and train to Richmond, which he reached in early September. There he was immediately taken to Jefferson Davis, who remarked afterward, "I hoped and expected that I had others who would prove to be generals, but I knew I had *one,* and that was Sidney Johnston." Accordingly, Johnston was made one of the two full generals in the Confederate States Army and named commander of Department 2, the Department of the West. He was 58 years old. The clock had begun to tick.

Now, after only a few months into his command, Sidney Johnston had become the object not only of scorn but of ridicule, yet he remained obdurate. "I observed silence because it seemed to me the best way to serve the cause and the country," Johnston wrote Jefferson Davis from Decatur, Alabama, on March 18. "The facts [regarding Fort Donelson] were not fully known, discontent prevailed, and criticism or condemnation were more likely to augment than to cure the evil.* I refrained, well knowing that heavy censures would fall upon me, but [was] convinced it was better to endure them for the present . . . What the people want is a battle and a victory. That is the best explanation I can make. I require no vindication. I leave that to the future."

Heavy censures aside, Johnston had more than enough cause to be alarmed. Two large Federal armies were converging on him, each larger than his own. After evacuating Bowling Green and then Nashville, Johnston seemed to flounder, beset, in the words of the historian T. Harry Williams, by "a fog of mental paralysis induced by the crisis he was facing."

He seemed unable to understand the loss of his army at Donelson because he had ordered Floyd by telegram beforehand that, if it appeared he could not hold the fort, he must "get [his] troops back

---

* Here he alludes to the disgraceful behavior of Generals Floyd and Pillow. By the time of Johnston's letter to Davis both Floyd and Pillow had been suspended pending an investigation.

to Nashville." It did not seem to occur to Johnston that he had sent Floyd and his men into a trap, which Floyd himself had sprung.

Nevertheless, Johnston was with his army in Decatur, having marched it through the middle of Tennessee to the nearest rail-head on the Memphis and Charleston, and was boarding it now on the cars for Corinth, Mississippi, 150 miles to the west. Johnston was afterward criticized by many—and continues to be by modern historians—for not putting himself in the Big Picture, that is, for electing to stay with a part of the army at Bowling Green instead of making his headquarters at some more convenient location the better to command it. In other words, these critics charge that Johnston was behaving more like a division or corps commander rather than the commander in chief of a department.

There is something to be said for these criticisms, since during the four months between the time he first arrived in the department and the fall of Forts Henry and Donelson, Johnston had neither distinguished himself nor provided the sort of leadership that inspires men to battle. Possibly this was owing to his advancing age or to the arduous overland journey across the Southwest, but most likely it had to do with the immensity of the task before him. It couldn't have helped that the supply of military arms and equipment was wanting, as was the supply of men. When Johnston asked Richmond for a number of trained military engineers, he was told there were only four of these people who were unassigned, and one was on court-martial duty! These day-to-day nightmares seemed without end, crowding out the time to plan strategy. What Johnston needed was a superior second in command to handle the mundane issues, but what Richmond sent him instead was General Beauregard, with his Napoleonic complex and outsize imagination for grand strategies.

Beauregard's most shining characteristic was certainly not attention to detail; in fact, he was a famous delegator. He was most interested—often to the point of obsession—in fleshing out elaborate war-ending battle plans. Indeed, he had a flair for strategy, diagnosing upon his arrival at Bowling Green on February 6 that the army was posted in a salient that stuck out invitingly to any enemy who wished to attack its flanks. After a while Johnston sent him away to deal with the force at Columbus—i.e., its evacuation—but even from that distance Beauregard continued to bombard the department commander with plans and strategies for the conquest, or reconquest, of everything up to and including the Ohio River and St. Louis.

———— ◆ ————

Pierre Gustave Toutant-Beauregard was among the most flamboyant and intriguing of the Rebel generals, beginning with his colorful name and rich Gallic heritage. In the early part of the war he was idolized throughout the South, known in the press as "the Great Creole," hero of Fort Sumter, despite the fact that there was little heroism in turning the entire artillery defenses of Charleston, South Carolina, on a nearly helpless detail of Yankees hiding in the fort, which sat like a large duck at the entrance to the Charleston harbor.*

Beauregard was born May 28, 1818, into a family that traced its Gallic lineage back 500 years. He grew up on a thousand-acre sugar plantation 20 miles south of New Orleans in St. Bernard Parish,

---

* It is noteworthy that after the white flag had been run up Beauregard remained in his room and sent a subordinate to accept the Union surrender, rather than humiliate Maj. Robert Anderson, his former artillery instructor at West Point and a good friend from the old army.

where French remained the common language and most of the Creole gentry actually *still* considered themselves French despite the fact that Louisiana had been purchased by the U.S. government in 1803. They tended to regard Americans as boorish parvenus and awaited the day when some new Napoleon would arise and return them to French rule. Meantime, they clung to their Gallic heritage and customs like bats to a cliff, commanding their slaves in French and educating their young men in Paris.

Young Pierre was somehow different from his peers, we are told. His best friend growing up was a slave boy his age named Tombie, whose father, Placide, practiced voodoo and was the plantation's designated hunter, spending all his days in the woods to put deer, game birds, and waterfowl on the master's dinner table. Pierre became absorbed by the notion that he would one day be a great hunter, and spent his days with Tombie hunting and fishing in the fertile forests and bayous, using an old "Brown Bess" muzzleloader left behind by the British after their defeat at New Orleans in the War of 1812.

At the age of eight Pierre was sent to a private tutor outside New Orleans where the lessons were taught in French. When he turned 12 his father broke with tradition and, instead of sending him to school in France, enrolled him in what was known as the French School in New York, run by two brothers who had fought as officers under Napoleon. Here Pierre was for the first time confronted with the need to learn English, which he learned quickly but never completely mastered, as his later letters, orders, and other military correspondence clearly demonstrate. The emphasis in class was on mathematics and commerce, but the brothers' tales of great European battles so enthralled Pierre that he began reading whatever he could find on the Napoleonic Wars and soon left his family aghast by announcing that he wished to make the U.S. Army his career. This would necessitate an appointment to the Military Academy at West Point, which his father reluctantly obtained by way of the Louisiana governor, with whom he was friendly.

Even while the family fretted that Pierre was becoming too Americanized, he removed "Toutant" from his surname by dropping the hyphen, presumably to make himself seem less foreign. When he entered West Point at the age of 16, Beauregard was short but muscular, swarthy, and exceedingly handsome, with wavy black hair and a barbershop mustache. He had a quick mind, a quick temper, and a long memory. No doubt Beauregard took his share of ribbing because of his accent, but he made friends easily with such classmates as George Meade, John Sedgwick, Joe Hooker, and Irvin McDowell, who went on to become Union generals, and Braxton Bragg, Jubal Early, and William Hardee, who joined the Confederacy. At the Academy he was known as an excellent equestrian and dedicated scholar of military history with a firm grasp of Jomini and other military authorities. Most especially, he is said to have idolized Napoleon, probably because of his French heritage, which would call into question his generalship during the Battle of Shiloh. He graduated in 1838 number 2 in his class of 45 and joined the engineers, the army's most exclusive branch. His biographer T. Harry Williams tells a story with significant elements of plausibility about a tragic love affair that Beauregard is said to have had with the daughter of Winfield Scott, soon to be general in chief of the army.

As the story goes, the year he graduated Beauregard fell in love and became engaged to 17-year-old Virginia Scott, but the Scotts disapproved because they believed her too young to marry. Mrs. Scott proceeded to take her daughter on a five-year grand tour, but each had promised to write the other. However, as time passed no letters were received by either party, and Beauregard, "offended and embittered," in 1841 married someone else. While in France, the heartbroken Virginia converted to Catholicism, and upon returning to America she entered a convent in Virginia where, in 1845, at the age of 24, she found herself on her deathbed. From there she summoned Beauregard to tell him that she, too, had become embittered after he apparently dropped her, only to learn recently that her mother had intercepted all the letters and destroyed them.

However long Beauregard remained "offended and embittered," he did marry the beautiful sister of his friend Charles Villerè, a member of one of the most prominent Creole families in New Orleans, upon whose plantation downriver at Chalmette the Battle of New Orleans was fought. Marie Laure Villerè Beauregard bore him two sons before dying in 1850 during childbirth.

Beauregard's army engineering career was mainly in Louisiana overseeing forts and other military structures. He once challenged a fellow officer to a duel over what he considered insulting language in a letter regarding a most trivial matter, thereby demonstrating what, according to some, was a lingering vestige of Mediterranean hotheadedness. As with the duel of Thomas Grafton, Beauregard's affair was broken up by police before it could come to pass, which was a lucky thing, since the man he challenged, Lt. John C. Henshaw, had chosen shotguns and buckshot at 30 yards—and if a second shot became necessary the range would decrease to 25 yards, and so on.

Beauregard served with distinction under Winfield Scott in the Mexican War, was wounded several times, and showed intense personal valor, fortitude, and military acumen, becoming one of the first U.S. soldiers to enter Mexico City. After the war he resumed engineering duties, but, like many officers of the period, he began to tire of the army because of the low pay and slow promotions. He toyed with the idea of joining the filibustering* expedition of William Walker, the freebooting soldier of fortune from Nashville who had recently taken over the government of Nicaragua. When Walker offered Beauregard a job as his second in command, one of his army superiors talked him out of it. This, too, proved a fortuitous intervention, for when Walker and his cronies attempted to filibuster Honduras they found themselves on the wrong side of a firing squad.

On the eve of civil war Beauregard married one of the Deslonde sisters of St. James Parish, who was also the sister-in-law of John Slidell, the distinguished U.S. senator from Louisiana. By then, Beauregard had enrolled his two boys at the Louisiana Military Academy at Baton Rouge, where William T. Sherman was the superintendent. With the presidential election of 1860 approaching, and the South threatening to secede if Lincoln was elected, Beauregard wrote to Sherman giving his opinion that this crisis, like those that had preceded it, would somehow blow over.

It did not, of course, blow over, and within weeks of Lincoln's election, as the Southern states began voting to leave the Union, Sherman resigned his position as superintendent of the Louisiana Military Academy, and Beauregard, by then an avowed secessionist, became, of all things, superintendent of the United States Military Academy at West Point. Considering the precarious political situation, this astonishing event can be explained only by the likelihood that Beauregard believed the superintendency of West Point would be a feather in his cap when it came time for being assigned rank in the Confederate army.

---

* In that day to "filibuster" was to take over a nation by force.

In any event, his superiors quickly realized the mistake they had made, and, even though his appointment had come courtesy of his powerful brother-in-law Senator Slidell, Beauregard's stay at West Point was a remarkably short one. The very day after he took over, in fact, word arrived from Washington that his orders were rescinded, and he returned to New Orleans, only to discover upon arrival that Louisianans had voted to secede. He immediately resigned his commission in the U.S. Army, expecting to be made head of the Louisiana state military, but that honor fell to Braxton Bragg, a former army officer who had become a planter in the state. Beauregard considered this such an affront that he enlisted himself as a private in a battalion called the Orleans Guards that was composed of Creole high society.

Soon Beauregard was writing letters to Jefferson Davis and other key Confederate officials offering his military services. Davis responded by ordering Beauregard to take charge of the Rebel forces at Charleston, where the Confederacy was demanding the evacuation of Federal troops from Fort Sumter. A "peace commission" had been sent to Washington to work out an orderly transfer of military installations and other government property located in the seceded states, but the Lincoln Administration refused to meet with them. At last it was determined that negotiations were impossible, and when Lincoln attempted to resupply the fort Beauregard, upon the instructions of Davis and his cabinet, opened fire.

After Sumter fell, Lincoln called for the states to provide volunteer troops to invade the South and put down the rebellion, prompting Virginia, North Carolina, Arkansas, and Tennessee also to secede. Beauregard was put in command of the forces in northern Virginia defending the so-called Alexandria Line that covered the junction of the Orange and Alexandria and Manassas Gap railroads, located near a stream called Bull Run.

The Federal army, under Irvin McDowell—who had been Beauregard's West Point classmate, ranked number 23, to Beauregard's number 2—had crossed the Potomac, taken Alexandria, and occupied Arlington, the immense estate that Robert E. Lee's wife had inherited from her father. Beauregard deduced that the next move would be for the Federals to attack him and occupy the Manassas railhead, which was vital to transportation to and from Richmond as well as to the rich Shenandoah Valley. He immediately began to fortify as reinforcements poured in from the Southern states.

On July 10 a pretty 16-year-old girl named Bettie Duval appeared in Beauregard's camp and produced an encoded message hidden in her hair.* This was courtesy of Mrs. Rose Greenhow, a fixture on the Washington social circuit since the Presidency of Andrew Jackson. The note warned that the Federals would begin their forward movement in less than a week. Mrs. Greenhow obtained intelligence of Union movements by a variety of reliable sources and found ways to communicate them to the Confederates until 1862, when she was arrested and imprisoned by operatives of Allan Pinkerton's detective service, and soon afterward she was deported to Richmond, Virginia.†

---

* The code had been devised by Col. Thomas Jordan, Beauregard's chief of staff, who will figure prominently in the Battle of Shiloh.

† Rose Greenhow, 1814–64, a Marylander from a slaveholding family, became a secessionist through her friendship with South Carolina's John C. Calhoun. In 1864 she drowned off the entrance to North Carolina's Cape Fear River as the small boat she was in was being pursued by a Federal blockade vessel.

Beauregard had about 22,000 in his army to face 35,000 in McDowell's, but by sound military supervision he managed to commandeer an additional 8,000 troops under Joseph E. Johnston, who had been holding back more than twice that number of Yankees in the Shenandoah Valley. These men arrived at the eleventh hour on the Manassas Gap railway, just as the Battle of Bull Run was reaching its most pitiless intensity, and soon turned the tide of battle into a disgraceful rout of the Federal army.*

Throughout the South Beauregard's status as the hero of Fort Sumter became even more exalted as word got around that he had ridden along the lines in heat of battle, raised sword in hand, exhorting the men to hold firm, doffing his hat to them. At one point his horse was shot from under him, but he remounted and continued on, displaying wonderful bravery and leadership, now urging the men to attack. Ladies showered him with gifts and mash notes; newborn babies were named in his honor, as were streets, hotels, and Rebel gunboats. The press named him the Colossus of Manassas. President Davis promoted him a full "general of the army," right up there with Sidney Johnston, the highest rank possible. Beauregard was on top of the world until he ruined it by making himself obnoxious, mainly by writing inflammatory letters to newspapers.

It was likely a feature of his Mediterranean heritage that Beauregard was excitable, flamboyant, opinionated, and bursting with

---

* Notable in this victory was the arrival of the brigade under Thomas J. Jackson, who earned the sobriquet "Stonewall" that day by standing firm against a Union charge.

ideas. To the reserved, self-possessed FFVs* in Richmond he must have seemed a strange creature—and President Davis was more like them than like him. In any case, Beauregard's new rank seemed to go to his head, and he began to buttonhole politicians and cabinet members with suggestions, plans, strategies, and proposals for campaigns and bombard them with letters of advice and complaint. It was one of these latter that landed him in trouble with the one man he didn't need trouble with—Jefferson Davis. T. Harry Williams points out that because both men's personalities were so volatile "it was inevitable that they would clash." Perhaps not, if Beauregard had been able to muster a modicum of professional self-restraint. Alas, he could not, and he became embroiled in an unseemly quarrel with Davis that went public and spoiled relations with his commander in chief, one of the few men in the Confederacy who could outhate even Beauregard.

The great victory at Manassas was less than a week old when Beauregard wrote a letter to two former aides who had become Confederate congressmen, complaining bitterly that the army could have marched on after the battle and taken Maryland—perhaps even Washington itself—were it not for a want of food from the army's commissary in Richmond. The letter was read in secret session but produced a ferocious reaction against the Davis administration. Davis made the matter worse by trying to defend himself, and naturally it leaked to the newspapers, whereupon the furor erupted again in an irate cloud of "could have beens" and "should have beens."

---

* In the South—or at least in Virginia—being an FFV (First Family of Virginia, i.e., those whose ancestors colonized Jamestown and similar sites) is the equivalent of having arrived on the *Mayflower*.

The trouble quickly simmered down, but the damage was done. Beauregard shared command of the army with Joseph E. Johnston, another full general, who was senior in rank, an awkward arrangement since the two were absolute opposites in terms of strategy—Johnston (as he would remain throughout the war) was cautious and defensive minded, whereas Beauregard was itching to launch an offensive and lure the Union army to its doom. (Mrs. Greenhow in Washington kept sending messages— "Come on. Why don't you come on?" meaning an attack on the U.S. capital.) Beauregard argued that a quick march by the army would easily clear Federal troops out of Maryland south of Baltimore and isolate the capital city, but to no avail. Jefferson Davis remained aloof in Richmond, clinging to his 1,600-mile "barrier" from Virginia to New Mexico and resting on the proclamation he made at the outset of war: "The South wants only to be left alone." Davis's idea was to conduct defensive warfare only and avoid any invasion of Northern territory, which might make the conflict appear abroad as a civil war rather than a war of separation, which he believed it was. In fact, recognition by Britain, France, or other European powers remained the linchpin of Davis's strategy at this stage of the war. Later, of course, he would have to change his mind.

When Davis failed to develop an offensive, Beauregard requested a transfer to New Orleans, which he believed was in danger of being attacked. His request was refused. Beauregard then became involved in a series of acrimonious squabbles with cabinet members, principally Judah Benjamin, the secretary of war. Beauregard dragged Jefferson Davis into this tasteless imbroglio by asking him to overrule his closest subordinates. Instead, Davis tried to console Beauregard, who seemed to be working himself into a perfect swivet as he continued to produce adversarial letters against the administration. It seemed to some that the Creole was deliberately trying to provoke the president of the Confederacy, but more likely, in the vernacular of the day, his Gallic blood simply was up. He was in a pugnacious frame of mind, and if he could not fight a war of weapons against the Yankees, he would fight a war of words against anyone in the administration who opposed his ideas.

On November 3 Beauregard published a letter in the Richmond *Whig,* which began, "Centerville, Va. Within the hearing of the Enemy's Guns."

The dateline itself was enough to start people snickering. The gist of the letter was that he had no intention of running for president against Davis, but it rambled on against the Davis administration in a pretentious, egotistical manner. Clearly, things could not long continue this way.

When the army went into winter quarters, Beauregard's eclectic mind and unbridled enthusiasm tackled another kind of military quandary—namely, the problem of distinguishing Rebel troops from Yankees in the smoke and fury of battle. At Manassas there had been instances on both sides of troops firing on themselves, and Beauregard concluded that the armies' flags looked too much alike. Thus he designed a new "battle flag" for the Confederacy: two crossed blue bars with white stars on a bloodred field.*

---

* This became the well-known Confederate battle flag that today symbolizes the conflict, as distinguished from the official flag of the Confederacy, which was two red bars on a field of white with a wreath of stars on a blue square.

The last straw broke in Beauregard's war of words when he submitted his report on the Battle of Manassas to the Confederate Congress. Again it excoriated the Davis administration, and Davis was understandably irate. By then Beauregard had fallen in with a handful of powerful men who disliked Davis and were seeking ways either to thwart him or get him out of office. Among them were Vice President Alexander Stephens; generals Joseph E. Johnston, James Longstreet, Gustavus W. Smith; and several prominent editors in Richmond and Charleston. Another of these was Robert Toombs of Georgia, an upstanding lawyer and Davis's secretary of state during the first few months of the war. Toombs was one of the fire-eaters, and like Beauregard had believed from the beginning that the South should have waged an aggressive war against the Union and brought it quickly to its knees, rather than sit pompously behind a defensive line giving the North time to organize its vast resources against the Confederacy.

One day in February 1862 a Colonel Pryor arrived at Beauregard's headquarters with an important question for the Creole. It was not an auspicious time, since Beauregard had recently undergone a serious operation on his throat in Richmond and was still in some pain. History does not tell us what the throat surgery was, but even as a boy there are indications that he had trouble with his throat, and it had become so bad that the doctors had risked this operation, leaving him "swathed in bandages."* Colonel Pryor, a member of the Military Committee of the Confederate Congress,

---

* Any operation was hazardous in those times, but anything to do with internal surgery carried special risks because antibiotics had yet to be invented.

was close to Davis. He had come to get Beauregard's consent to "a plan under consideration in Richmond."

The plan was Beauregard's transfer to the Department of the West. Pryor explained that all the higher authorities, Davis included, were deeply concerned with the situation in Sidney Johnston's command—the defeat of Zollicoffer in Kentucky and the loss of Forts Henry and Donelson in Tennessee had shaken everyone. Johnston needed help to reverse the tide of defeat and reinvigorate the army. The consensus was that Beauregard was the man to help him do it.

Beauregard asked for time. Toombs had gotten word of the plan and advised him against it. "Once you are ordered away," he told the Creole, "you will not be ordered back." Beauregard considered the matter further and accepted his transfer. He might disagree with Jefferson Davis, he might even dislike him, but he refused to believe that Davis was the kind of man who would intentionally hurt the Confederate cause by sending him—or any officer—away from the place he could do the most good. Beauregard prepared immediately to depart.

After ordering the evacuation of Columbus, Kentucky, Beauregard established his headquarters first at Jackson, Tennessee, and then at Corinth, Mississippi, from where he began organizing an army to fight the great battle for the fate of the West. Johnston and his army were on their way via the Memphis and Charleston road. Beauregard immediately wrote the governors of a number of nearby Deep South states, appealing to them for new troops. Davis and the authorities in Richmond recognized that the manpower shortage was critical and ordered 10,000 men under Braxton Bragg in Pensacola to board cars for Corinth. Likewise 5,000 under Daniel Ruggles in New Orleans were pressed to Beauregard's command. By the time Johnston reached Corinth on March 22, the Confederate force under Beauregard totaled more than 25,000, and more were arriving every day. Combined with Johnston's 20,000, they would make a formidable force, but a hitch quickly developed. Corinth, it seemed, was groaning unhealthily under the strain of so many men. Although it was an important rail junction, it had no large sources of fresh water as had Bowling Green or, for that matter, Pittsburg Landing, and sanitary conditions rapidly deteriorated. The sick list expanded until doctors began to fear epidemics of fever, cholera, or worse.

There was, however, a brighter element in the mix. On March 8 Gen. Earl Van Dorn had lost the Battle of Pea Ridge in far northwest Arkansas but was retreating south with at least 10,000 men. Although this force might be dejected after its loss, Van Dorn had telegraphed that he was headed with all possible speed to join the Rebel army at Corinth. It was mainly a matter of getting the troops across the Mississippi where they could be transported to Corinth on the M&C cars. Johnston and Beauregard were delighted. Van Dorn's arrival would alter the equation in their favor.

Beauregard, meanwhile, continued to erupt with innovative notions, one of which earned him a measure of ridicule from some of his fellow officers. This was the famous bells-into-cannon appeal that he made to the planters of the Mississippi River Valley. Somewhere in his military history reading Beauregard had been informed that in times of war Europeans often melted down large bronze bells to make cannons, and in times of peace the reverse was true.*

Beauregard suggested melting down church bells and court-house bells, and in fact an artillery battery was formed after that fashion in 1861 called the Edenton Bells, out of Edenton, North Carolina. He composed an exhortation to the planters of the Mississippi valley that appeared prominently in newspapers from Memphis to New Orleans. It was pure Beauregard: "We want cannon as greatly as any people . . . I, your general, entrusted with the command of your army embodied of your sons, your kinsman and your neighbors, do now call upon you to send your plantation bells to the nearest railroad depot, to be melted into cannon for the defense of your plantations . . . Who will not cheerfully send me his bells under such circumstances?"

Surprised and delighted at this startling request, the poets went to work.

Melt the bells Melt the bells
. . . That the invader will be slain
By the bells.
. . . And when foes no longer attack
And the lightning cloud of war
Shall roll thunderless and far
We will melt the cannon back,
Into bells.

---

* In 1528, for example, the tsar of Russia melted down the world's largest bell to make the world's largest cannon to protect the gates of the Kremlin.

Braxton Bragg was disdainful, saying they already had more metal in New Orleans than they could use, which was not really so, since the Confederates were reduced to using cotton bales instead of iron plate to protect their gunboats ("cottonclads"). Stories circulated that some 500 bells were found in the former U.S. customs house when New Orleans fell to Union forces, and that they were sent to Boston by the Yankee commander Gen. Benjamin "Beast" Butler to be auctioned off. Documents uncovered later, however, suggest that far fewer bells were collected.

When Sidney Johnston arrived in Corinth and was briefed on the military situation, he immediately agreed with Beauregard that they must strike Grant at Pittsburg Landing before Buell came up with his army of 25,000. Reports from scouts and spies had Buell about two weeks' march from Grant. Then Johnston did a strange thing. Noting the dark cloud of opprobrium that surrounded him after the loss of Kentucky and Tennessee, he offered Beauregard command of the army.

Beauregard naturally was surprised at this turn of events, and he declined the offer. He later said in his memoir of the battle that Johnston made the gesture "to restore the confidence of the people and the army, so greatly impaired by reason of the recent disasters."

In a letter to Johnston's son Preston after the war Beauregard recounted his conversation with Johnston on the subject of command.

"I came to help you," Beauregard said, "not to supersede you. You owe it to your country, and to your own reputation, to remain at the head of this army. We are now concentrated and can strike a decisive blow. The enemy is not prepared for it. This is not the time to resign. One great victory and everything will be changed for you."

Beauregard then said that Johnson agreed. "Well, be it so, Together we will do our best to insure success."

Preston Johnston in his biography disputes this version and says Beauregard "misinterpreted the spirit and intention" of his father's offer. Preston Johnston says his father offered Beauregard the army because he was already presiding over most of it at Corinth and knew more of the ground firsthand and of the enemy lying at Pittsburg Landing. "The truth was that, coming into this district which he had assigned to Beauregard, Johnston felt disinclined to deprive him of any reputation he might acquire from a victory," the younger Johnston wrote.

Whatever the reasons, the matter was settled. Beauregard would act as second in command and also be responsible for drawing up the attack order against Grant. To this latter task Beauregard detailed his chief of staff, Colonel Jordan, who had organized and operated the Rose Greenhow spy ring in Washington, D.C., and had been Cump Sherman's West Point roommate. Like Beauregard, Jordan was a student of Napoleon Bonaparte, and thus the battle plan he drew was essentially Napoleonic in its character and design. It was said that he kept on his desk a copy of Napoleon's marching orders at the Battle of Waterloo—not, perhaps, a good sign.

First, the army was to be reorganized into four division-size corps. The I Corps was composed of 9,136 men under the bishop general Leonidas Polk; the II Corps, 13,589 under Braxton Bragg, who would also serve as Johnston's chief of staff during the planning; III Corps, 6,789 under the tactician William Hardee; IV Corps, 6,439 under John Breckinridge of Kentucky, formerly the Vice President of the United States. All were West Pointers except Breckinridge, a Princeton man who was also a lawyer.*

The plan itself was straightforward. The corps would make their way north toward Pittsburg Landing by various country roads and, once there, assemble in successive lines of battle across the front of the mouth of the cornucopia, inside which Grant's army was blissfully encamped. Hardee's III Corps would strike first along the three-mile front, followed closely by Bragg's large II Corps and, behind that, Polk's 9,000-man I Corps. Breckinridge's IV Corps would be held in reserve to take advantage of enemy weaknesses or to shore up, if necessary—these latter movements to be directed by Beauregard.

The main thrust of the attack was to fall on the Union left, the object being to drive a wedge between Grant's army and the river, rolling up the Yankee army northwestward until it was floundering in irretrievable disorder in the miry wastes of Owl Creek, cut off from the landing and any hope of escape. That, anyway, was the plan on paper.

---

* There are many various troop strength figures afloat. Illness, details, and other distractions make any exact count meaningless. These numbers come from the Official Records (OR).

CHAPTER 8

I WOULD FIGHT THEM
IF THEY WERE A MILLION

⊸◆⊷

E VEN AS MORE REBEL TROOPS ARRIVED IN COR-
inth, Beauregard's throat had not yet healed and continued
to cause him trouble and pain, and he was often unable to provide
anything but advice and consultation. Still, he insisted on being
informed of any important intelligence. In the late hours of April 2,
a Wednesday, the commander of a detachment at Bethel Station
on the Mobile and Ohio line, about 25 miles north of Corinth,
telegraphed headquarters that a mass of Union soldiers had been
maneuvering for what appeared to be an attack toward Memphis.
Since Bethel Springs was north and east of Pittsburg Landing, the
Union troops undoubtedly belonged to the division of Lew Wallace, who was camped at Crump's Landing about five miles north
of Grant's main body.

From his sickbed Beauregard scribbled a note on the bottom of
the telegram saying, "Now is the moment to advance, and strike

the enemy at Pittsburg Landing." He had Colonel Jordan personally deliver it to General Johnston. Johnston consulted Bragg, who,
when aroused from sleep in his quarters across the street, studied
the message and Beauregard's recommendation and gave it his
approval as well.

Still, Johnston wasn't so sure. The soldiers needed more instruc-
tion, he said, and he wanted to wait for Van Dorn, who would
add 10,000 battle-tested men to his army. None of Johnston's soldiers had been in battle, as at least some of Grant's had at the river
forts. Many did not yet understand the drill commands, so critical
in combat, or for that matter a sense of discipline and duty and,
worse, total commitment to honor and to the cause. They were
green, all right; some had been recruited barely a week earlier.

Bragg pointed out that every day they waited, they ran the risk
that Buell's army would arrive, or that Grant would himself recognize the danger he was in and begin to fortify. Johnston relented
and told Jordan to see that each of the troops was issued a hundred
rounds of ammunition and three days' cooked rations. Green or
not, they would prepare to march on Pittsburg Landing by 6 a.m.*

This was far easier ordered than done, for heavy rains had muddied
the two narrow dirt roads between Corinth and the landing so as to
make them almost impassable for troops, let alone artillery, ammunition trains and supply wagons, and the thousands of other vehicles and
animals that would have to pass over them during the 20-mile march.

---

* Neither army ate well in the field, but the Confederates seemed particularly ill fed, surviving on a diet consisting primarily of flour and grease—
with molasses, if available. To prepare for a march, they fried bacon and
used the grease and flour to make biscuits ("tougher than a mule's ear"),
which they wrapped in cloth and kept in their haversacks.

By 10 a.m. next morning, Thursday, April 3, Jordan was still working on the marching order. Johnston, however, decided to start the troops anyway, without waiting for the written order. Utter disarray quickly descended upon the endeavor, owing to the obstinacy of General Polk.

Polk had resigned his officer's commission almost immediately after graduating from West Point, some 35 years previous, to go into the ministry, and apparently he had not absorbed a sufficient appreciation of real-world military problems beyond his student days—or, as one of his fellow officers put it, "He had been in the cloth too long." Polk's corps, it seems, was encamped in the narrow streets of Corinth, through which led the only roads to Pittsburg Landing, with its artillery, baggage, supplies, and thousands of troops clogging the way. By late afternoon it was discovered that Polk had idiotically refused to move without a written order, resulting in gridlock that reminded one officer of "the temple scene in *Orlando furioso.*"* Thus Polk prevented the departure of Hardee's corps, scheduled to attack first, and Bragg's, which was next. When it was finally sorted out the shadows were long lengthened and Hardee's people, marching in the dark, would not reach their appointed destinations that night, further disordering the plans.

The expression "confusion reigned supreme" is rarely, if ever, more apt. Brigades, divisions—indeed, whole corps—detoured down wrong roads and paths or encamped in places where other brigades, divisions, and whole corps needed to pass. The plan had

---

* A Vivaldi opera in which the frenzied knight Orlando battles gorgon-like statues in a temple. It was not uncommon in those times for officers to show off their knowledge of the classics.

been for the army to be on the march at 3 a.m. on April 4, so as to attack at sunrise on the fifth, but along with the marching order foul-up, a torrential all-night downpour drowned these hopes. Streams swelled their banks and covered bridges; roads washed out; men became "anxious to keep their powder dry."

Units consistently became lost—even guides became lost. Entire trains of overloaded baggage wagons and artillery had to be manhandled to the sides of roads to let troops pass. Sergeants argued with teamsters mired in axle-deep mud, staff officers yelled at unit commanders, and the air became blue with frustrated profanity. Hardee somehow reached his line of departure on time and deployed in line of battle, but Bragg's corps became entangled with Pope's and Breckinridge's, and the end result was a delay of 24 hours, which was probably fatal.

By midmorning, April 4, as Johnston prepared to leave his Corinth headquarters in Mrs. William Inge's "Rose Cottage," the hostess approached him, saying, "General, will you let me give you some cake and a couple of sandwiches?"—to which he replied with a bow, "No thank you, Mrs. Inge, we soldiers travel light." Sixty years later she remembered, "I curtsied, but I did not say anything. Nobody ever contradicted General Johnston. But I quietly went out into the kitchen and wrapped up two sandwiches and put them in his coat pocket."

Cavalry scouts were still reporting that the Yankees had not fortified, and there were no signs that Buell had arrived. After spending the night on the road, Johnston and Beauregard arrived on the field in front of Grant about seven next morning, April 5, expecting to launch the attack. But Bragg was short an entire division, which he could not find. After waiting most of the morning Johnston looked at his watch and cried in disgust, "This is perfectly puerile! This is not war!" He rode to the rear, where he found Bragg's lost division once more obstructed by Polk's troops. By the time that was sorted out it was past two, and past four by the time Polk got in line, and Breckinridge was still bringing up the rear.

Both Johnston and Beauregard agreed that it was too late to launch the attack that day, and that evening Beauregard got cold feet about the whole plan. About 4 p.m., as Polk was placing his men into a line of battle behind Bragg, he was told that Beauregard wanted to see him immediately. When he reached Beauregard's headquarters Polk found the second in command talking excitedly with Bragg, and soon Breckinridge rode up. "I am very much disappointed at the delay," Beauregard "said with much feeling," according to Polk, who replied, "So am I sir," and began to explain what he saw as the reasons for his tardiness (namely Bragg). But that was not what Beauregard meant.

"He said he regretted the delay exceedingly," Polk remembered, "as it would make it necessary to forgo the attack altogether; that our success depended on our surprising the enemy; that this was now impossible, and we must fall back to Corinth." Polk was in shock. Here they were within a mile and a half of the enemy camps and Beauregard wanted to call it off?

There were reasons other than surprise that also caused the excitable little Creole to lose his nerve. Reports had come in that because of the delay many of the soldiers had consumed all their rations, and there was now every likelihood that Buell would soon be arriving. But most seriously was the matter of the firing they had heard sporadically that afternoon from Hardee's positions at the front. "Now," exclaimed Beauregard, "they will be entrenched to the eyes!"

At this point Johnston appeared and "asked what was the matter."

When Beauregard repeated his gloomy assessment, the army commander replied, "This would never do." He asked Polk what he thought, and the bishop general gave his opinion that his troops "were in as good condition as they ever had been; that they were eager for the battle; that to retire now would operate injuriously upon them, and I thought we ought to attack."

At this a "warm" discussion broke out among the corps commanders, but Johnston's "blood was up," and he interrupted with a conclusion that ended the argument: "Gentlemen, we shall attack at daylight to-morrow." He disagreed that the Yankees were on high alert, but in any case remarked to one of his staff officers as they walked away, "I would fight them if they were a million. They can present no greater front between those two creeks than we can, and the more men they crowd in there, the worse we can make it for them."

That night the men slept on their arms and built no fires, even though the air was chilly. From time to time after midnight there was desultory firing from the front line. Practically none of these men had seen battle before, but they had at last arrived at the place where the elephant lived. Promptly at 4 a.m. the troops were quietly awakened all along the line, given some time for morning ablutions, such as they were, and a hasty breakfast of cold bacon and biscuits. Then the hundreds of companies were formed into hollow squares where the captain read a short address from the commanding general: "I have put you in motion to offer battle to the invaders of your country . . . you can but march to victory over the mercenaries sent to subjugate you and despoil you of your liberties, your property and your honor . . . The eyes and hopes of eight

millions of people rest upon you; you are expected to show yourselves worthy of your lineage, worthy of the women of the South
. . . and with the trust that God is with us, your generals will lead
you confidently to the combat—assured of success."

After that, the army was arrayed in two successive lines of battle, each about two miles long, one corps after the other, 800 yards
apart, facing north—Hardee first, then Bragg—then Polk when he
came up, with Breckinridge in the rear in reserve.

Johnston had originally envisioned an order of battle in which
the three corps would attack abreast—Bragg on the right, Hardee
in the center, and Polk on the left. This is what he telegraphed to
Jefferson Davis on April 3. But as it turned out the three corps were
strung out laterally for two miles or more, going into battle one
behind the other. Just how this happened remains one of the many
mysteries of Shiloh.

Johnston's original idea seems like the more sensible formation,
since it allowed each corps commander the flexibility to fight his
own corps on a front of a mile or less, instead of being spread out
in a long line that was certain to become entangled as the other
corps moved into the fight. But either Johnston did not communicate this correctly or emphatically enough to Beauregard or Beauregard ignored it. After the war some, including Jefferson Davis,
and Bragg in particular, accused Beauregard of deliberately changing Johnston's plan without consulting the commanding general.
It may be so, because apparently the first Johnston heard of the
order for the three corps to attack *en echelon* was on April 4, the
day the army went on the march. It has been suggested that Johnston simply gave in to Beauregard's plan because it was too late to
change it. Perhaps he felt that way at the time; we will never know.

In any case, Johnston was the commander, and in the end the decision to go into battle with such an awkward formation was his responsibility. In Bragg's estimation, years later, Johnston's original battle plan was "admirable," but "the elaboration (Beauregard's), simply execrable."

The sky changed from gray to pink while some of the generals, including Beauregard, huddled around the campfire at Johnston's headquarters. According to Bragg, Beauregard's argument of the previous evening was suddenly renewed, "with Beauregard again expressing his dissent."

At almost the same time from the distant forest toward Pittsburg Landing came a rising crackle of rifle fire and then the boom of a cannon.* At this, General Johnston closed the discussion. "Note the hour, please," he said. "The battle has opened, gentlemen." Mounting his big thoroughbred charger Fire-Eater, Johnston declared to the little assembly, "Tonight we will water our horses in the Tennessee River."

He and Beauregard rode down Bragg's front line offering encouragement to the division and brigade commanders. At some point word got back that the men wanted to see Beauregard, resplendent in his full Confederate gray and gold uniform, topped by the snappy red-trimmed French kepi he always wore. The Creole was reluctant at first, but he assented with the condition that there must be no cheering to alert the enemy.

---

* This was likely precipitated by the predawn Union reconnaissance patrol of the unfortunate Major Powell, including the German immigrant Private Ruff, which so defiantly held up the advance of Hardee's left that General Prentiss had time to get his division in line to absorb the Rebel blow.

Johnston approached Gen. Randall Gibson, of Bragg's corps, commanding a Louisiana brigade. "I hope you may get through safely to-day," he said, "but we *must win a victory.*" He placed his hand on Col. John Marmaduke's shoulder and said, "My son, we must this day either conquer or perish." To Thomas Hindman, commanding Hardee's First Brigade and wearing a long brown duster, Johnston said, "You have *earned* your spurs as a major-general. Let this day's work *win* them."

Deep in the ranks of Hindman's brigade, in a regiment called the Dixie Grays, at the very center of the front line attack, stood a 21-year-old Welsh bastard named Henry Morton Stanley who three years earlier had escaped a British workhouse and jumped a ship bound for New Orleans—and who, ten years later, would become the world-famous journalist and African explorer who "found" the missing missionary David Livingstone in the Belgian Congo by famously greeting him, "Doctor Livingstone, I presume?"

Next to Stanley was a boy of 17 named Henry Parker. "I remember it," Stanley wrote in his memoirs, "because, while we stood-at-ease, he drew my attention to some violets at his feet, and said, it would be a good idea to put a few into my cap," because "perhaps the Yanks won't shoot me if they see me wearing such a sign of peace." They plucked the violets and arranged them in their caps, "while the men in the ranks laughed at our proceedings."

Evidently these were moments of great clarity for the Rebel soldiers, who, unlike their counterparts across the way—mostly innocent and ignorant at their breakfasts—knew full well they were marching into a terrible battle against what they understood was a Yankee army of 50,000 men. "Newton Story, big, broad, and straight," Stanley remembered, "bore our company banner of gay silk, at which the ladies of our neighbourhood had laboured.

"As we tramped solemnly and silently through the thin forest, and over its grass, still in its withered and wintry hue, I noticed that the sun was not far from appearing, that our regiment was keeping its formation, that the woods would have been a grand place for a picnic, and I thought it strange that a Sunday should have been chosen to disturb the holy calm of those woods."

Preston Johnston dramatized it this way: "The two armies lay face to face: The Federal host, like a wild boar in his lair, stirred, but not aroused by the unseen danger; its foe, like a panther hidden in the jungle, tense in wait to spring . . . Long before dawn the forest was alive with silent preparations for the contest, and day broke upon a scene so fair that it left its memory on thousands of hearts. The sky was clear overhead, the air fresh, and when the sun rose in full splendor, the advancing host passed the word from lip to lip that it was the 'Sun of Austerlitz.' "*

───────◆◆───────

The initial strike of the Rebel army was less a clash than a collision between Hardee's corps and the Federals of Prentiss's division, whose camps were pushed out slightly farther south than Sherman's, so as to bear the brunt of the initial assault. A Mississippi cavalryman in Ben Cheatham's Tennessee division sat on his horse watching the attack begin. "We could see the lines of our army for long distances,

---

* At the Battle of Austerlitz (1805) the French army advanced in early morning fog until at the last moment the legendary "sun of Austerlitz" ripped apart the mist and revealed so many of Napoleon's soldiers that the Russian defenders fled in fright.

right and left," he said, "as they advanced with marvelous precision, with regimental colors flying, and all the bands playing 'Dixie.' " When the Confederates got within earshot of the Federal camps they began the spine-chilling Rebel yell that so many have told of yet found so hard to define. It has been described variously as high-pitched, frantic, even manic, somehow distantly reminiscent of the native Indians or perhaps a colossal pack of beagles. Whatever it was exactly, it could be terrifying. Now it came from thousands of throats, drawing nearer, drowning out the music of the bands, drowning out everything, even the gunfire, with profound malice. Thus was Hardee's attack, more than 9,000 strong, launched on Sunday morning, April 6, 1862.

Hardee's regiments consisted mostly of soldiers from Arkansas and Tennessee, with men from Alabama and Mississippi mixed in. They were typically backwoodsman, or small farmers, who found themselves in the ranks of the Confederate army because their country—or what they considered their country—had been invaded. They had been taught from earliest youth that northern-ers were their enemies. Now their enemies had come, as General Johnston had warned them, to subjugate—to despoil their liberty, their honor, their homes, and their women—and they intended to dispose of them just as they would the Goths.

The late Civil War historian Shelby Foote liked to tell of the time a Union colonel was interrogating a captured Rebel private after one of the early battles in Virginia, and at one point the officer demanded to know why he was fighting against the Federal soldiers. "Because you are here," the indignant Confederate replied. These men—most of them—were willing to lay down their lives for a political idea that had set in motion these great armies with banners.

The Federal soldiers in the foremost camps of Prentiss's division—men from the upper Midwest and from Missouri—had far less time to contemplate their motives and could only look in awe and wonder at the approaching storm.

In just a few minutes Hardee's line emerged from the wood and crossed into open fields named for the families that farmed them—Seay Field, Fraley Field, Rea Field, Spain Field. The Mississippi cavalryman who had been watching from a high piece of ground as the line emerged to the tune of "Dixie" observed that "the engagement soon became general and the enemy were evidently yielding to the hammer strokes." From his vantage point he took in "the roar and rattle of musketry, the belching of cannon, the screaming of shells, the whistling bullets, all united to beget emotions which words cannot describe. The deafening sounds, the stunning explosions, and the fiery flames of battle seemed to pass along the line in great billows from right to left."

Down in the din the racket and the violence was, of course, far more shocking and horrifying. In the nearest Union camp Colonel Peabody, who when we last left him was riding toward the sound of the guns after being chastised by General Prentiss for starting the battle in the first place, had led about 1,200 of his 12th Michigan and 25th Missouri regiments to the northern lip of a wooded and brambled ravine that he expected the Confederate troops would have to cross to get to the Federal camps. No sooner had he formed them in a quarter-mile-long fighting line than Major Powell arrived from his harrowing reconnaissance excursion. When Powell informed Peabody that the Rebels were breathing down his neck and crossing Seay Field just beyond the woods, the 31-year-old engineer told him to have his men fall in and prepare for a fight.

About 7:30 a.m., without forewarning, a large body of Confederates appeared atop the opposite crest and began a double-quick descent into the ravine. This was the brigade of Col. Robert G. "Fighting Bob" Shaver, an Arkansas lawyer who believed in hitting the enemy hard and quick. The Dixie Grays, including Henry Morton Stanley, were among the troops who had gone into the ravine armed with out-of-date smoothbore muskets that were loaded with "buck and ball"—three buckshot and one large .50-caliber lead ball, a deadly enough combination for the kind of close-up work they would be doing today.

Stanley described the terrifying exhilaration as they surged into the ravine: "We trampled recklessly over the grass and young sprouts. Beams of sunlight stole athwart our course. The sun was up above the horizon . . . A dreadful roar of musketry broke out from a regiment adjoining ours. It was followed by another further off, and the sound had scarcely died away when regiment after regiment blazed away and made a continuous roll of sound."

People found various ways to describe the racket of massed rifle fire. Some likened it to the crackle of wildfire sweeping through a thicket of dry cane; others said it sounded like heavy hail falling on a tin roof. Up close it simply drowned out everything else. As they reached the bottom of the ravine Stanley's friend Henry Parker remarked, "We are in for it now." But so far they had "seen nothing." Beyond a thicket the regiment overtook its skirmishers when suddenly there was a cry, "There they are!" and a shout from the captain, "Aim low men!"

Stanley saw nothing to shoot at but was still advancing. "I at last saw a row of little globes of pearly smoke streaked with crimson, breaking out, with spurtive quickness, from a long line of bluey figures in front; and, simultaneously, there broke upon our ears an appalling crash of sound, the series of fusillades following one another with startling suddenness, which suggested a mountain upheaved, with huge rocks tumbling and thundering down a slope. Again and again these loud, quick explosions were repeated with increased violence until they rose to the highest pitch of fury. All the world seemed involved in one tremendous ruin!"

Peabody's audacious stand blunted Shaver's attack, but soon Shaver was joined on the right by the brigade of the 51–year-old general Adley H. Gladden, a South Carolinian turned New Orleans merchant who had fought with valor in the fabled Palmetto Regiment in the Mexican War and reached the top of New Orleans society by becoming president of that city's exclusive Boston Club. When at the last moment it became apparent that Hardee's corps was not large enough to cover the entire front, General Johnston had personally ordered Gladden—who belonged to Bragg—to extend Hardee's line toward the Tennessee River.

Consisting of four Alabama regiments plus Gladden's old First Louisiana, this brigade had come up from Bragg's second line, which had been following 500 yards behind Hardee's corps before Shaver's men were halted by Peabody's fire. And on Shaver's left the large seven-regiment brigade of 38-year-old Alabama lawyer and editor Sterling A. M. Wood added its weight to the fray.

Down in the ravine in the midst of all the banging and whizzing and roaring Stanley lay flat, shaken and terrified, but continued to load and fire "as if it depended on each of us how soon this fiendish uproar would be hushed." The man behind Stanley was lying so close that the muzzle of his gun stuck out in front of Stanley's face, "mak[ing] my eyes smart with powder. I felt like cuffing him."

He looked forward and "saw the banner raised over Newton Story's head, and all hands were behaving as though they knew how long all this would last."—which remains the eternal question on the mind of every infantryman in battle since time immemorial.

On Shaver's left a disaster was in the making. From some particularly thick woods two regiments—one Mississippi, the other Tennessee—had just emerged onto more open ground when hundreds of Peabody's ranks suddenly rose up from cover and let off a horrific blast of fire almost in their faces. These were new men, raw recruits, who immediately panicked and ran away screaming "Retreat!" As they passed through another Rebel regiment coming up from behind, their wild behavior became infectious and nearly started a general stampede before it was checked by quick action from the higher ranking officers and their staffs bringing up the rear. Brigade commander Wood, division commander Hindman, and General Johnston himself—accompanied by the now exiled Tennessee governor Isham Harris, who had attached himself to the commanding officer as an aide during the battle—galloped forward to halt the fugitives, re-formed them into ranks, and ushered them back into the advance with encouraging words and ferocious threats.

━━━◆━━━

In the Union lines on the left of Peabody's brigade stood 2,000 men of Prentiss's other brigade, composed of regiments from Wisconsin, Missouri, and Illinois and commanded by 51-year-old Madison Miller, another former Mexican War hero who had been wounded at Buena Vista, was president of a Missouri railroad and a Missouri state legislator, and was formerly the mayor of Carondelet, Missouri. For some reason unknown to military science, Prentiss had posted Miller's people at the edge of woods astride the eastern Corinth Road at the *southern* end of Spain Field, instead of behind good natural cover at the northern end, where they would have had all day to shoot at any Confederates crossing into the open to get at their camps. Posted a good 500 yards to Miller's rear were the two six-gun artillery batteries of Emil Munch and Andrew Hickenlooper. Only the day before, Munch's Minnesotans had been transferred from Sherman's division to Prentiss's, and Hickenlooper's Ohioans had literally just gotten off the boat at Pittsburg Landing.

Off to their right Miller's infantrymen and the artillerists could see and hear the smoke and din of Peabody's fight, but where they now stood nothing stirred, not the faintest breeze, and no birds sang. But each man knew or at least must have suspected what was coming and wondered what it would be like when it did.

An 18-year-old corporal named Leander Stillwell of the 61st Illinois was among those waiting. Until recently he had been a farm boy raised in a log cabin in the fertile southern tip of Illinois known as "Egypt" for the way the Mississippi flooded over each spring like the Nile. Nearly all of that section of the state had been settled by southerners or their descendants and leaned toward the Confederacy—even sent soldiers to the Rebel army, as we soon shall see.

Young Leander's father was a strong Union man, but Leander did not respond to Lincoln's first call for troops, nor to the second; then, after the North's humiliation at the Battle of Bull Run, like so many others he joined up, unwilling to see the Union split asunder or, more directly, "to be pointed at as a stay-at-home coward."

Stillwell and his comrades had been enjoying the relaxation of a Sunday morning when their peace was disturbed by the deep *pum* of artillery somewhere off to the right. "Every man sprung to his feet as if struck with an electric shock," he said later, "and looked inquiringly into one another's faces." Soon enough there came "a low, sullen, continuous roar. There was no mistaking that sound," he said. The drums beat the long roll, and in due time the 61st Illinois was posted in woods at the southern edge of Spain Field, from where they could see "the blue rings of smoke curling upward among the trees off to the right" (where Peabody was having his fight at Seay's Field), "and the pungent smell of gunpowder filled the air."

As they stood waiting for the enemy to appear, Stillwell's thoughts drifted back to his old log cabin and his father and mother, "who would be getting my little brothers ready for Sunday school; the old dog lying asleep; the hens cackling about the barn." He did not have long to dwell on these things, however, for within minutes "Suddenly to the right there was a long, wavy flash of bright light, then another, and another! It was the sunlight shining on bayonets—and—they were here at last! A long brown line with muskets at a right shoulder shift, in excellent order, right through the woods they came." As many in the Federal ranks remarked that morning, when the Rebel lines came crashing through the woods they were preceded by a diaspora of frightened wildlife: bounding rabbits, leaping deer, whirring coveys of quail, even flights of wild turkeys sailing high overhead; it wasn't as though the Confederates were actually sneaking up on anyone.

The order to open fire was given at once and "from one end of the regiment to the next leaped a red sheet of flame." At this the Confederates stopped and fired a volley of their own, and the air was suddenly filled with zinging hot lead and a layer of dense white smoke. Stillwell was trying to peer beneath the smoke in hopes of sighting an enemy soldier when he heard someone "in a highly excited tone calling to me from the rear, 'Shoot! Shoot! Why don't you shoot!'" He looked around to find one of the second lieutenants "fairly wild with excitement, jumping up and down like a hen on a hot griddle." "Why lieutenant," Stillwell replied, "I can't see anything to shoot at," to which the lieutenant replied, "Shoot! Shoot anyhow!" and shoot he did, thinking, however, "that it was ridiculous to shoot into a cloud of smoke."

Behind this smoke was the brigade of the Rebel general Gladden, whom General Johnston had directed to the right to close on Lick Creek, the eastern boundary of the cornucopia's opening, which was supposed to be the far right of the Confederate army. But first it became necessary for Gladden to deal with these Federal troops who were in the way, which happened to be Miller's brigade of Prentiss's division, including Leander Stillwell shooting at smoke. Apparently, Gladden's "blood was up," along with everybody else's that morning. After he was informed that Bragg and Johnston wanted Gen. James Chalmers's brigade to swing out behind him even farther toward Lick Creek, Gladden was overheard saying to the messenger orderly, "Tell General Bragg that I have as keen a scent for Yankees as General Chalmers has."

This roar of gunfire had no sooner informed Prentiss that his second brigade was now engaged in battle than orders came, "for some reason—I never knew what," Stillwell said, to fall back across the field to their original positions on the northern side in front of their tent camps. There ensued some of the fiercest fighting of the battle.

Stillwell remembered jumping down behind a tree and thinking he had disturbed a hive or swarm of bees "because of the incessant humming above our heads," until it dawned on him those were bullets "singing through the air." This was also where he saw his first man killed that day. The man was hiding behind a tree to load his weapon, then whipped out around the tree, fired, ducked, and reloaded. But the next time Stillwell turned his head the man was "lying there on his back, at the foot of his tree, with his leg doubled under him, motionless—and stone dead. I stared at his body, perfectly horrified," Stillwell said; he had been hit "square in the head. Only a few seconds ago that man was alive and well." It came near to "completely upsetting me," Stillwell said, adding ominously, "I got used to such incidents during the course of the day." Such was his baptism of fire.

Over in Peabody's part of the line the fighting had become so severe that from his point of view the issue was in doubt. Confederate Henry Stanley and his regiment had continued to load and fire at Peabody's men from cover while the officers organized a charge, the only way to break the stalemate. It was near 9 a.m. when the order came, Stanley said, to "Fix Bayonets! On the double-quick! Forward! We continued advancing, loading and firing as we went. The Federals appeared inclined to await us," he said, " but at this juncture we raised a yell."

Stanley and thousands of his comrades rushed at Peabody's line, yelling wildly, stopping occasionally to fire, but pressing forward through the smoke and din. The yelling was good for them, Stanley said, somehow heartening, encouraging, and relieving of the tensions of the battlefield.

As the Rebels attacked and the shooting became heavier and more men began to fall, some of Peabody's troops began to melt away to the rear. It was difficult to detect them at first because of the woods and underbrush, but the attrition soon became substantial, and roads to the rear were soon clogged with fugitives and stragglers as well as steadily increasing numbers of wounded. Then Peabody himself was killed and the brigade fell apart.

Peabody had sent his aide to ask the colonel of his left regiment if he could hold; meantime Peabody went to find Prentiss to ask for artillery support and troops. Failing to locate the general, he galloped back to his position, where he found that the situation had deteriorated. Men had continued to desert, and those who hadn't were falling back into their own camp, firing but retreating in the face of heavy Confederate pressure. When Peabody's aide returned with an affirmative answer as to whether the left regiment could hold, he found his commanding officer sprawled over a log, shot through the head. He had been trying to rally his disheartened troops when suddenly he threw up his hands and reeled backward off his horse, dead.

About a year earlier, not long after he had joined the army, Peabody had had a premonition that he would be killed, and he wrote to a friend about having "a sort of presentiment that I shall go under," adding that, "If I do, it shall be in a manner that the old family will be proud of it—Good-by old fellow." Even as he was mustering the brigade to the long roll earlier that very morning he told a fellow officer that he would not live to see the result of it. It was too true. The gallant Peabody had already been shot four times that morning—wounded in the hand, thigh, neck, and body— before meeting the bullet to the brain that killed him. Joseph Ruff, the German private who had accompanied Major Powell on his reconnaissance patrol the night before, came across Peabody's corpse just to the west of the regimental camps: "He had evidently been shot from his horse for he lay with his legs over a log and his head and shoulders on the ground," Ruff remembered. At age 32 Peabody was already an exceptional man; there is no telling how far he might have gone.

——————◆————

General Shaver's charge against the remnants of Peabody's regiment came roaring and yelling up from the ravine scattering everything in its way. " 'They Fly!' was echoed from lip to lip," exulted Henry Morton Stanley, who was screaming his lungs out with the rest. "Then I knew what the Berserker passion was . . . at such a moment, nothing could have stopped us."* Of the bluecoats he said, "When we arrived upon the place where they had stood, they had vanished. Then we caught sight of their beautiful array of tents!"

As for Private Ruff, after he returned from the hazardous patrol he did not seem to grasp the severity of the situation. It was his turn that week to serve as cook for his squad, so when he got back to Peabody's camp that morning he grabbed a pail and started for a spring about half a mile away to get water to cook with. All along his walk there came the rising noise of battle, and on his return trip he saw Sherman's troops in great disorder, some running away from the battle sounds, others toward it, and bullets filled the air. When Ruff arrived back at Peabody's camp the bullets were riddling his own tent, causing him to conclude that "it did not look as though

———————————

* Berserkers (from which the word *berserk* descends) were old Norse war-
   riors who dressed in wolfskin or bearskin shirts and worked themselves
   up to a trancelike frenzy when going into battle.

there would be any breakfast" that morning. Ruff set down his pail and picked up his gun just as Prentiss's line began to break for the rear. As he emerged into the company street he could see "brown and gray-clad soldiers among the big white tents."

As Ruff and his comrades fled northward, Shaver's Confederates stopped to enjoy the fruits that the Union encampment yielded: uniforms, shoes, swords and other weapons, knapsacks, trunks, and utensils—all was plunder—as, in some regiments, was breakfast, still warm upon the table or hot upon the stove or fire, a feast for the famished Confederate soldiers. "I had a momentary impression," Stanley said, "that with the capture of the first camp the battle was well-nigh over; but it was only a brief prologue of the long and exhaustive series of struggles that day."

———◆———

Way out on Peabody's left, blackened by gunpowder and shaken by the terrific shooting of the six guns of his battery—one shot fired by each gun every 30 seconds or so—Captain Hickenlooper felt close to exhaustion though the fighting had gone on less than an hour. Each of the three times the Confederates charged Miller's brigade, his gunners had loaded double-shotted canister,* "which tore great gaps in their ranks and drove them back to cover," Hickenlooper said. In the meantime, his men were dropping like flies. "Each man and officer takes his assigned position," then "the

---

* A diabolical projectile consisting of a can containing 27 iron spheres about the size of Ping-Pong balls, which turned the cannon into an enormous shotgun. Double-shotted meant they used two cans.

minies buzz and sing about their ears."* When a gunner "drops from his place, another fills the gap; and thus the work goes on with a system and regularity marvelous in its perfection."

Attesting to how well this "system" worked was its effect on General Gladden's Confederate attack, which was thrown back several times as the Rebel soldiers attempted to cross Spain Field. Powder smoke hung so heavily in the air that at one point Gladden rode forward through the jumbled, mangled bodies of his dead and wounded to get a better look at the Union position. He had not gone far when a terrific cannon blast blew him off his horse; members of his staff were horrified to find that his left arm had been shredded and nearly torn from its socket by a ball or exploding shell fragment. He was carried away "pale, faint, but still smiling" to a field hospital in the rear where the arm was amputated, but he died a few days later, the first, though not the last, general officer to be mortally wounded in the battle.

This development left Col. Daniel Adams, a Louisiana lawyer, in charge of what was fast becoming a Rebel calamity. Hickenlooper's cannon fire had dispirited the Confederates, and they started streaming to the rear, until Adams seized the colors and rode slowly through the retreating troops, crying, "Will you come with me?" Which they did, he reported later, "with great alacrity, and leading them close to the enemy lines I ordered a charge which was promptly and effectively executed."

---

* Short for minié ball, the standard bullet on both sides of the Civil War, a .52-caliber conical lead slug named after the French officer who developed it.

As the battle seemed to reach its most pitiless intensity, an order from Prentiss reached Hickenlooper's battery directing, of all things, a "change of front to the right"—meaning that the guns should be turned 90 degrees, "a difficult movement to execute under fire," Hickenlooper complained, "in woods filled with dense under-growth, horses rearing and plunging and dropping in their tracks." It was a mistake, said the battery captain, "which the enemy imme-diately took advantage of by a direct charge on our now exposed and defenseless left flank."

Gladden's—now Adams's— men came on in three lines of bat-tle, at last unmolested by Hickenlooper's cannon fire. Infantrymen who were guarding the battery rose up and fired a volley, which at first caused the Confederates to waver and hesitate. But they soon recovered and came on again "with a Rebel Yell that caused an involuntary thrill of terror to pass like an electric shock through even the bravest hearts," Hickenlooper said. Another volley from the infantry soldiers produced a similar result. Many Confederates fell, but the companies closed ranks and came on once more, "their colors moving steadily forward."

Hickenlooper realized that it was time for him to get out, and had just given the order to limber up "when there comes a crash-ing volley that sweeps our front as with a scythe, a roar that is deafening, and the earth trembles with the shock." Confederate artillery had been turned upon them. Every horse in that section of the battery went down—as well as most of the men—including Hickenlooper's own horse, Gray Eagle, upon whom he had been mounted. The infantry guard arose and fled, "in wild dismay, leav-ing the wounded, the dying and the dead." Using such horses as remained,* Hickenlooper managed to get away with four of his guns, abandoning the 6-pounders to the Rebels.

His flight was spectacular, with teams of horses hauling guns and caissons, "bounding through underbrush, over ditches, logs, each driver lashing his team." Back they raced through their own camps, past the deserters and the stragglers and the wounded, until they found a line about a mile north where Prentiss had planted his colors and intended to make a stand near a peach orchard along an old wagon track that was later called the "Sunken Road," Hickenlooper recalled, "for its having been cut for some distance through a low hill."

⇥◆⇤

On the heels of Hickenlooper's mad dash Miller's brigade also collapsed after officers warned that "the troops on our right [Peabody's regiment] had given way, and we were flanked," reported Leander Stillwell. He rose from behind his log and had started for the rear when, like Private Ruff, he saw "men in gray and brown clothes running through the camp on our right." But also, he remembered, "I saw something else, too, that sent a chill all though me. It was a kind of flag I had never seen before; a gaudy sort of thing with red bars. The smoke around it was low and dense and kept me from seeing the man who was carrying it but I plainly saw the banner. It was going fast, with a jerky motion, which told me that the bearer was at the double-quick." As he ran down his company street Stillwell considered retrieving his knapsack from the mess tent, but

---

* A Confederate officer later counted 59 of Hickenlooper's horses "lying dead in their harnesses all piled up in their own struggles."

"one quick backward glance made me change my mind. I never saw my knapsack or any of its contents afterward."

Sixteen-year-old private George W. McBride of the 15th Michigan had an even more harrowing tale to tell. His regiment had arrived at Pittsburg Landing only the previous afternoon, and that morning as the fight heated up was led onto the battlefield on the extreme left of Prentiss's division with no ammunition whatsoever. At one point they found themselves standing at ease and order arms when they observed several long lines of men in brown and gray coming down a slope opposite them. "The first line moves down the hillside, crosses the little creek, enters the clearing, halts, and fires into us," McBride recalled. "Not a man in our company has a cartridge to use. A few men fall. We are ordered to shoulder arms, about face, and move back, which we do."

After finally being issued ammunition, McBride's regiment was put back into the fight. "There was the crash of musketry, the roar of artillery, the yells, the smoke, the jar, the terrible energy. At intervals we can see the faces of the foe, blackened with powder, and glaring with demonic fury, lost to all human impulses, and full of the fiendish desire to kill. Somebody calls out, 'Everybody for himself.' "

As he ran back through the brigade camps, McBride reported that the Confederates "were sweeping the ground with canister; the musket fire was awful. The striking of the shot on the ground threw up little clouds of dust, and the falling of men all around impressed me with the desire to get out of there. The hair commenced to rise on the back of my neck. I felt sure that a cannon ball was close behind me, giving me chase. I never ran fast before, and I never will again. It was a marvel that any of us came out alive."

Thus, the collapse of Prentiss's line was complete.

The battle everywhere had now become so intense that it was unsafe in practically the entire battle area, not just where the troops were fighting. Many of the rifles could be deadly, though not accurate, at up to a mile. A rifleman in battle was supposed to be able to load and fire three aimed shots a minute. Theoretically, then, if every rifleman in a brigade fired three times a minute, that would put 12,000 bullets in the air in that single minute, and from that one brigade only. At Shiloh there were more than 30 brigades in the fight, so one can only imagine the amount of deadly metal flying through the air in any given minute.

Our Mississippi cavalryman, for example, who had been observing from his high vantage point on the Confederate left, explained the effects of artillery fire on men standing a mile or more from the main battle line. "We could hear heavy missiles whizzing around and above us; some of them too were distinctly visible. One great solid shot I shall never forget. As it came through the air it was clearly seen. Capt. Foote saw it as it ricocheted, and spurred his horse out of the way. Lieutenant T.J. Deupree was not so fortunate. This same shot grazed his thigh, cut off his sabre hanging at his side, and passed through the flank of his noble stallion which sank lifeless in his tracks. It also killed a second horse in the rear of Lieutenant Deupree and finally, striking a third horse in the shoulder, felled him to the ground without disabling him, and not even breaking the skin. The ball was now spent. My own horse, 'Bremer,' in the excitement and joy of battle raised his tail high, and a cannon ball cut away about half of it, bone and all; and ever afterwards he was known as 'Bob-tailed Bremer.' Many solid shot we saw strike the ground, bounding like rubber balls, passing over our heads, making hideous music in their course. Colonel Lindsay at this time countermarched the regiment and took shelter in a neighboring ravine."*

———◆———

For Sidney Johnston and Beauregard the gunfire was music to their ears; by barely 10 a.m. the center of Grant's position had been pushed back halfway to Pittsburg Landing. The slaughter had been appalling, but this was war. To destroy this Union army would produce repercussions far beyond the mere elimination of troops from the Federal forces. England and France would certainly be watching; a lifting of the Yankee blockade and freedom of international commerce were in the offing. But all that was wishful thinking. The battle raged and Sherman was now taking his turn at the meat grinder.

---

* There are Civil War stories, some, perhaps all, apocryphal, of the soldier who, seeing one of these apparently slow-moving iron cannon balls bound over the ground, sticks out his foot to stop it only to have the missile carry away the foot.

CHAPTER 9

ALL THE FURIES OF
HELL BROKE LOOSE

———◆◆◆———

B ECAUSE HE HAD CONSISTENTLY SNEERED AT REPORTS of an enemy attack, Sherman was now forced to eat his words. But wisdom dictates the adage "If you have to eat crow, eat it while it's hot."

"It was a beautiful and dreadful sight," Sherman admitted, almost in awe, "to see them approach with banners fluttering, bayonets glistening, and lines dressed on the centre." Having watched his own orderly shot dead before his eyes ("the fatal bullet," he said later, "which was meant for me"), Grant's senior division commander ordered Colonel Appler of the 53rd Ohio to stand his ground, then galloped back to his headquarters at the Shiloh church, sounding the alarm to nearby commanders and sending warnings to Generals McClernand, W.H.L. Wallace, and Hurlbut, whose divisions were encamped in the rear, a mile or so north. Prentiss already knew.

As a Confederate battery began shelling his camps, Sherman later said—in what must be one of the most profound understatements of the war—"I became satisfied for the first time that the enemy designed a determined attack on our whole camp." As the historian of one of his regiments later wrote, Sherman's "great genius finally condescended to notice the practical fact that a great battle had commenced."

The fidgety Appler had already changed his regiment's battle line at the Rea family farm three times that morning. First it faced south. When one of his officers, half dressed and just out of bed, came running up hollering, "Colonel, the rebels are crossing the field," Appler ordered the regiment reoriented toward the east. Just as that had been accomplished, "bright gun barrels of the advancing line shone beneath green leaves" to the south, and Appler's adjutant told him, "Colonel, look to the right," whereupon, "with an expression of astonishment," Appler cried, "This is no place for us!" He ordered the 53rd to about-face and marched it northward, back through its camps, shouting, "Sick men to the rear!" placing the regiment in yet another position in some brush on an elevation behind the officers' tents, according to the adjutant, 22-year-old Lt. Ephraim Cutler Dawes, who less than a year earlier had graduated from Marietta College in Marietta, Ohio, and was the second youngest officer in the regiment.

After the war, Dawes wrote a comprehensive and intelligent paper entitled "My First Day Under Fire at Shiloh," which he presented to the Cincinnati chapter of the Military Order of the Loyal Legion of the United States. In detailing his own experiences and those of his regiment on that fateful Sunday morning, Dawes's paper expresses in vivid microcosm the thrust of events affecting his and the other 11 regiments in Sherman's 10,557-man division while the Rebel attack unfolded.

The 53rd Ohio was the vanguard of Sherman's line, with its camp projecting out only slightly less to the south than Peabody's camp over in Prentiss's division. It was approximately 7 a.m., Dawes wrote, "and the view from the high ground where I stood at this time was never to be forgotten. In front [Rea Field] were the steadily advancing [Rebel] lines marching in perfect order and extending until lost to sight in the timber on either flank. In an open space on the Corinth Road a [Rebel] battery was unlimbering. Directly in front of the spot where General Sherman's orderly lay dead there was a group of mounted officers and a peculiar flag—dark blue with a white center."

Lieutenant (later promoted to major) Dawes was describing the regimental flag of the Rebel general Patrick Ronayne Cleburne, which would be his standard as a brigadier, and later a major general, commanding a division when Cleburne had become known in Southern circles as the "Stonewall of the West." It was said that as the war wore on, Union soldiers dreaded the sight of Cleburne's colors, which were almost Arabic-looking, silk and velvet midnight blue with a gleaming moon in the center. The 34-year-old Cleburne, a native of County Cork, Ireland, was six feet tall, slender, and ramrod straight, with striking blue eyes and a rust-colored mustache that tapered into a handsome Vandyke. Orphaned at 18, he had served with the British army in the 41st Foot Infantry regiment, but in 1849 he immigrated to the United States, where he wound up in Helena, Arkansas, becoming in time a lawyer and newspaper owner.

Cleburne could claim some military knowledge from his days as a British soldier, but, like many of Johnston's officers, this was his first fight. His most valuable asset was his soon-to-be-legendary personal bravery and almost fanatical determination to win battles. As Cleburne led his brigade forward that morning he soon encountered an "impassable morass" near the confluence of Shiloh Creek and its eastern branch. It was a swampy quagmire of jungly marsh, trees, and brambles so thick a snake could barely wriggle through it, let alone a brigade of infantry, and as Cleburne himself tested it his horse became bogged down and he was thrown headlong into a sea of mud that caked his entire body. Emerging from this indignity, Cleburne extricated himself "with great difficulty," instructing his commanders to avoid the bog, but in so doing it split his brigade in half so that only two regiments—the 24th Tennessee and the 6th Mississippi—came up in Rea Field. There they found themselves in front of Appler's 53rd Ohio, lying in wait about 600 strong, posted behind hay bales, stumps, logs, and other cover. Behind this Yankee line were the six rifled cannon of Capt. A. C. Waterhouse's battery, loaded with canister.

"The camps of Buckland's and Hildebrand's brigades were in sight," Dawes wrote, "and all the regiments were in line." Sherman had arrayed three of his brigades across the southwestern mouth of the cornucopia as follows: McDowell's was posted on the far right near Owl Creek; Col. Jesse Hildebrand's—to which Dawes's 53rd Ohio belonged—was to the east with its left flank resting on the Shiloh church; Col. Ralph Buckland's was farther east across the Corinth Road with its right flank resting on the church. (By an odd fluke, Sherman's remaining brigade, David Stuart's, was detached from the rest, far away to the east on the left of Prentiss near the Tennessee River, and would have to fight its long fight alone.)

"From the rear of all the camps," Dawes said, "hundreds of men were hastening to the rear. These were the sick, the hospital attendants, the teamsters, the cooks, the officers' servants, and some who should have been in the line. There was a sharp rattle of musketry far to the left on General Prentiss' front [this was the beginning of Shaver's and Wood's attack on Peabody]. The long roll was beating in McClernand's camp. The Confederate battery fired, its first shot cutting off a tree top above our Company A.*

As Cleburne's men came through the line of the Union officers' tents, Colonel Appler gave the command to fire, and there was an enormous crash of musketry along the whole front of Hildebrand's and Buckland's brigades. "The battle was fairly on," said Dawes.

Up close, it felt considerably more personal. When Appler's gunfire and artillery opened up at short range, Cleburne said, "It swept the open spaces between his tents with an iron storm that threatened certain destruction to every living thing that would dare to cross them." It was about that time that Cleburne lost his artillery support because the men were unable to see the Yankee lines or artillery positions. The consequence was a "terrible fire, and a quick and bloody repulse" of the two regiments.

The 23rd Tennessee retreated about a hundred yards before staff officers—including their old commander, a Col. Matt Martin (later badly wounded)—managed to round up perhaps 20 percent of

---

* During the Civil War soldiers learned to be particularly leery of cannon fire in the woods, because the solid shot were fully capable of bringing down huge tree limbs with a terrific crash, and though there are no recorded figures it is safe to say many men were killed or injured being crushed or struck by these objects.

them. On the other hand, the Sixth Mississippi rallied on its own, re-formed with about 100 men fewer, and made another charge with even more disastrous results. As the regiment emerged past the tents of the 53rd Ohio, the blue-clad line rose up in a tremendous blast of rifle fire that left the entire Confederate attack line writhing with bloody Mississippians. Out of a force of 425 who had gone into the fight a few minutes earlier, some 300 officers and men were left dead or wounded on the battlefield, including its colonel and its second in command, and the Sixth Mississippi, for all practical purposes, ceased to exist.

But here something bizarre happened—Colonel Appler lost his nerve. Dawes reported: "The first fire of our men was quite effective. The Confederate line fell back, rallied, came forward, received another volley, and again fell back, when our colonel cried out, 'Retreat, and save yourselves!' "

Several companies immediately skedaddled to the rear, but several others did not hear Appler's order and stayed fighting until they realized they were alone, whereupon they retreated to a ravine farther north. At this point General McClernand appeared and ordered Appler's fugitive companies to make a line with men from his division in front of Sherman's headquarters by the Shiloh chapel. Here the fight became hot and heavy. "Waterhouse's battery was firing down a ravine between our camp and the 57th Ohio Camp. A good many men in our left were shot here by a fire which they could not return because of McClernand's regiment in our front," Dawes wrote.

"As I turned to go back to the right," continued Dawes, "I saw the 57th Ohio falling back, despite the efforts of the gallant lieutenant colonel, A. V. Rice, the only field officer with it." It seemed to Dawes that even what was left of his regiment might save the line by

An artist's rendering of the Shiloh church or meetinghouse right before the battle. Afterward, Union soldiers picked it to pieces for souvenirs.

Ulysses S. Grant. Shiloh was by no means Grant's finest hour, but he stood to the test and was the victor.

Henry Halleck, in charge of the Union's western theater, connived against Grant behind his back.

President Lincoln despaired of getting his western armies into action before Grant; then he despaired of the result.

Gen. Don Carlos Buell arrived on the battlefield in the nick of time but later insinuated that he won the battle.

William Tecumseh Sherman had been considered "crazy" until he redeemed himself at Shiloh.

Charles F. Smith was considered the ideal soldier, but a minor scrape proved fatal.

John A. McClernand was a "political general" who stirred up trouble.

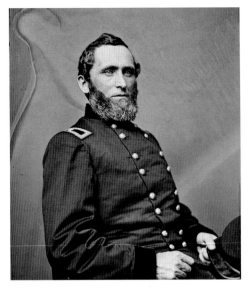

Benjamin M. Prentiss held firm in battle but lost his division in the process.

Lew Wallace went famously "missing" at Shiloh. Later he would write the most beloved novel of the 19th century.

Stephen A. Hurlbut, a hard-drinking former South Carolinian, performed well at Shiloh but later was suspected of embezzlement.

W.H.L. Wallace took over Smith's division and shared his fate.

*Before the war, Albert Sidney
Johnston had been considered
the "finest soldier" in the army.
At Shiloh he would give his life
trying to prove it.*

*Jefferson Davis, president of the
Confederacy, had lost faith in
Beauregard after the Battle of
Bull Run, or Manassas. After
he sent Beauregard west, Davis's
worst nightmare came true.*

*P.G.T. Beauregard, the Great
Creole, idolized Napoleon and
adopted Napoleonic tactics
that had failed at Waterloo.*

William J. Hardee wrote the manual on infantry tactics in the old army.

Leonidas Polk, West Point comrade of Jefferson Davis, was the Episcopal bishop of Louisiana when the war began.

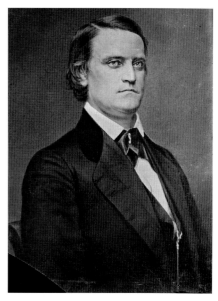

Though his men were among the most disciplined and combat ready in the Confederate army, Braxton Bragg was disliked.

The only Rebel commander without a West Point education, John Breckenridge was formerly Vice President of the United States.

Pittsburg Landing a few days after the battle. The steamboat second from right is said to be the Tigress, *Grant's command vessel.*

U.S. senator Charles Sumner, whose harsh antislavery rhetoric on the Senate floor led to a national incident that further hardened North and South against each other.

U.S. senator Ben Wade, a rough midwestern backwoodsman and abolitionist, set his Southern colleagues on edge with dark threats of dueling challenges.

The U.S.S. Carondelet, *one of the city-class ironclads that proved so effective for the Union effort in the West.*

The U.S.S. Lexington *and U.S.S.* Tyler, *which did yeoman's service at the Battle of Shiloh. These so-called timberclads were early efforts to introduce a war vessel with effective protective armament— the armament in their case being made of stout wood.*

Shiloh, second day of battle. The recapture of artillery by the First Ohio and other regiments in a contemporary drawing published in Frank Leslie's Weekly *magazine.*

A gun crew from Louisiana's renowned Washington Artillery at Shiloh.

Henry Morton Stanley in his Great White Hunter uniform was a private in the Rebel army at Shiloh. Later he became world famous for "finding" Dr. David Livingstone in Africa.

An artist's rendition of Hurlbut's division at the Peach Orchard as it appeared in Frank Leslie's The Soldier in Our Civil War.

Col. Oscar Malmborg, a Swedish immigrant who bamboozled Confederate troops during the battle by employing a European-style "hollow square" drill formation.

Col. David Stuart, with his brigade on the far left of the Union line, held out till late afternoon, possibly saving Grant's army. Stuart had hoped the war would erase a dreadful stain on his character but it proved indelible.

Ambrose Bierce was a youthful Union officer in Buell's army. Afterward he became one of America's best known writers.

Col. Thomas Jordan was Beauregard's chief of staff who drew up the faulty battle orders for the Confederate attack at Shiloh.

Ann Wallace had traveled to Shiloh to surprise her husband, Union general W.H.L. Wallace, and was actually at the battlefield when the fighting broke out.

Panicked Union soldiers flee to Pittsburg Landing as the Rebel army advances. It was said that at one point up to 10,000 Federals were cowering beneath the bluff.

Artist's rendition of the fighting at the Hornet's Nest on the first day at Shiloh.

Rebel general Randall Gibson, Yale graduate and prosperous Louisiana lawyer, whose brigade casualties were among the highest at Shiloh, was wrongly lambasted by Braxton Bragg as "an arrant coward."

Old Daniel Ruggles, "with a head bald as an egg and the beard of an Old Testament prophet," finally broke the Union Hornet's Nest with the greatest artillery barrage yet heard in the Western Hemisphere.

A photo of the Hornet's Nest, and possibly the sunken road, taken several decades after the battle.

Bombastic, hard-drinking Union general William "Bull" Nelson suffered the strangest fate of any high-ranking officer on either side.

Nathan Bedford Forrest tried to warn Beauregard of the danger of Buell's arrival at Shiloh but lost his way in a rainstorm.

The Bloody Pond at Shiloh became a place of refuge for soldiers of both sides, who declined to kill one another while partaking of its waters.

These big siege cannons had been transported to Shiloh on steamships to help destroy the Confederate fortifications at Corinth. But they proved invaluable at repelling the final Rebel attack at twilight on Grant's last possible line. Note their enormous size in comparison with regular infantry field guns.

First there was the Battle of Shiloh; next came the "battle of the books"; then came the "war of the monuments."

At top, staring down at the former Confederate position, is the Illinois State Monument dedicated in 1904 and featuring the bronze figure of a woman ready to draw a sword and renew the battle if necessary.

Just down the street the Confederate monument (above) features defiant and angry figures "fraught with insubordination and veiled with more awful meaning than a Greek tragedy."

The arguments over the Battle of Shiloh will apparently go on indefinitely.

moving to the right, and he ran "to where the colonel [Appler] was lying on the ground behind a tree, and stooping over, said, 'Colonel, let us go and help the fifty-seventh. They are falling back.' He looked up; his face was like ashes; the fear of death was upon it; he pointed over his shoulder in an indefinite direction and squeaked out in a trembling voice: 'No, form the men back here.' "

The young lieutenant was already shaken and now appalled. "Our miserable position flashed upon me. We were in the front of a great battle. Our regiment never had a battalion drill. Some men in it had never fired a gun. Our Lieutenant Colonel had been lost in the confusion of the first retreat. Our major was in the hospital, and our colonel was a coward. I said to him, with an adjective not necessary to repeat here, 'Colonel, I will not do it.' He jumped to his feet and literally ran away," Dawes testified.

Wells S. Jones was the senior captain commanding a company in the line when Dawes informed him, "Captain, you are in command; Appler has run away; I have ordered the regiment to close up to the right; let us help the fifty-seventh." Jones agreed and Dawes went down the line telling the company commanders what had happened. The first one he came to, "brave old captain Percy of Company F, swung his sword in the air and said: 'Tell Captain Jones I am with him! Let us charge!' "

Dawes considered it would be better to get everyone together before doing anything like that, but right then the regiment from McClernand's division ahead of them broke to the rear, and the retreat continued with the Rebels in hot pursuit. Soon Dawes and what was left of the 53rd Ohio encountered the remnants of the 77th Ohio, which had been likewise mauled "by a series of sledgehammer blows, kept up almost incessantly," according to

18-year-old Pvt. Robert H. Fleming, a brigade clerk who found himself on the firing line with his regiment when the battle began. Fleming was one of those disturbed by the effect of artillery fire in trees, noting, "My particular fear at that time was being killed by a falling limb."

As the battle heated up, "the artillery fire trebled in volume," Fleming remembered, "and all the furies of hell broke loose at once could not have made more din." When Appler's 53rd Ohio gave way it left the 77th with its left flank "in the air," or unprotected, and, according to Fleming, "the men in the left companies were firing at the enemy in the *rear* of the position once occupied by the fifty-seventh Ohio," which meant the 77th had been completely outflanked.

At that point Fleming himself was shot, "And as I fell, I felt that deathly shiver, and felt the blood spurting out and I thought I was done for." But Fleming was not done for, and he made his way to a field hospital just as the chief surgeon ordered it evacuated in the face of the Rebel assault.

Other Confederate brigades had come up from Braxton Bragg's second Rebel line to press Sherman's shattered ranks. Cleburne's men had been sacrificed in the first wave and many of his regiments, in the hyperbolic words of one historian, "were reduced to a burial squad." Most of the survivors were sent to the rear "to reorganize," some weeping, some cursing, all gasping, horrified at what they had just been through. But the damage they had done to Sherman's men was palpable; the Yankees had been very roughly handled and knew they were not up against pushovers. In the words of one Yankee soldier who had watched the Confederate lines storm forward into almost certain death: "If they were willing to do that to themselves, what would they have done to *us*?"

Dawes, with what was left of the 53rd Ohio (by then eight companies—most of the regiment—had fled to the landing), found
himself in a dangerous position. Prentiss's retreating soldiers were
passing behind him on the run, and he was taking fire from both
east and west. From the ranks of the retreating 17th Illinois Dawes
plucked a man he knew to be a veteran of earlier battles and hoped
he might help shore up Dawes's wavering greenhorns. "He was a
brave, cool man," Dawes said. "First he found some Enfield rifle
cartridges for company A, and filled their nearly empty boxes. Next
he went along the line, telling the men he had seen the elephant
before, and had learned that the way to meet him was to keep cool,
shoot slow, aim low. He said, 'Why it's just like shooting squirrels—only these squirrels have guns, that's all!' Pretty soon he called
out, 'Good-bye,' and as he hurried to his company I saw his regiment moving by the left flank."

But Sherman's line continued to collapse. By then the Rebels
had captured three of Captain Waterhouse's guns and seriously
wounded Waterhouse himself. "They were swarming around them
like bees," Dawes remembered. "They jumped upon the guns and
upon the hay bales and yelled like crazy men." Forty soldiers were
all that remained of the 53rd Ohio, and Captain Jones was trying
desperately to join them with the remnants of the 57th Ohio, which
was still making some kind of fight around the Shiloh church.

"No orders had been issued in our brigade in regard to the care
of the wounded," Dawes complained. "No stretcher bearers had
been detailed. When a man was wounded, his comrades took him
to the rear, and thus many good soldiers were lost to the firing
line." Disorder ruled, remembered Dawes, observing that many of
the men were nearly out of ammunition and that "there were three

different kinds of guns in our brigade and six within the division, all requiring ammunition of a different caliber."

Hildebrand, the 61-year-old brigade commander, "had disappeared," according to Dawes, who conceded that "during the fight he had displayed the most reckless gallantry, but when the 57th and the 53rd were driven from their camps he assumed that their usefulness was at an end, and rode away and tendered his services to General McClernand for staff duty."

This had been a mistake; there were still about 400 men left (of the brigade's original 2,467 who had been present for duty at the start of the battle), and they wanted a leader. By then, Dawes said, "bullets came from many points of the compass," which was aptly illustrated by a man who was shot in the shin of his leg. "Go to the rear," said Captain Jones, and the man staggered off into the brush. Presently he staggered back, saying, "Cap'n. Give me a gun. This blamed fight ain't *got* any rear!"

Dawes and the other Federal units continued a fighting retreat with the Rebels pressing upon them like a fiery hot breath. "The Confederates charged; there was a brisk fire for a few moments. Our line gave way at all points," Dawes said. When the lieutenant was finally able to survey the situation he found that the 53rd Ohio had been reduced to himself and seven men. As they struggled northward they came upon a brass cannon that had somehow got stuck between two trees, and upon one of the horses that was hauling it sat a man, crying. Dawes detailed his men to free the piece and moved on.

"I had no idea where we were, and I think no one else had," Dawes continued. "All around was the roar of musketry, but immediately about us was literally the silence of death. The ground was strewn with the slain of both armies." Then up ahead Dawes saw the sergeant major of the 77th and called out to ask him if he knew where his regiment was.

"I don't know," the sergeant major replied. "I was captured this morning and just escaped."

"Come with us," shouted Dawes.

"No," he said, "I am going with this regiment," pointing to "a regiment in full ranks, marching through a field on lower ground, uniformed in blue, marching smartly by flank to a drum beat." Dawes was suddenly perplexed. "It did not seem possible," he said, "that a Union regiment in such condition could be coming from the battle line." He moved nearer and took a closer look, then tugged at the sergeant major, and hissed, "They are Rebels."

"They are not," insisted the sergeant major, but just then "the wind lifted the silken folds of their banner. It was the Louisiana State flag!" This was, in fact, the illustrious Orleans Guards battalion Gardes d'Orle'ans, the Louisiana French-Creole regiment mentioned earlier who went into battle in their prewar blue Federal militia uniforms and at one point were attacked by soldiers from their own side.

Dawes and his little band of fugitives continued to wander north, seeking some sign of their regiment or brigade—even their division. Someone pointed out a man on a horse wearing a long brown duster, about 200 yards distant, and said, "There is major Sauger" (one of Sherman's staff officers). "I ran towards him (wherever I went the seven men of our regiment followed)," Dawes said, "waving my hat to attract his attention. I came up with him and [saluting] said, 'Major, where is our brigade?' "

"I don't know where anybody is," came the reply, and as the officer turned Dawes was startled to see revealed a uniform of Confederate gray under his long, brown duster.

"At just that moment," said Dawes, "a stand of grape [shot] came whirring through the air and struck just under his horse, the horse ran away and I never heard the rest of the story." It was only afterward Dawes learned that he had just reported to the Rebel general Thomas Hindman.

At that point a Confederate battery set up uncomfortably close and began throwing shot and shell Dawes's way. "It did not seem best to try to drive it away with seven men," he said, but concluded that its line of fire was most likely pointed to where the Union troops were, so Dawes decided that, "if we could follow [the Rebel shells] and not get shot, we could surely find somebody."

By this point it must have seemed like they were marching toward the end of the world, but about half a mile down an old farm road they came upon Colonel Hildebrand, their erstwhile brigade commander, "sitting on his horse by an old log barn, intently watching the swaying lines and waving banners of troops fighting in a long open field to the south."

"Now we are all right," Dawes told his men, and he went up to the old colonel, asking, "Where is the brigade?"

"I don't know," was the reply. "Go along down that road and I guess you may find some of them."

Dawes suddenly became indignant, and then insubordinate. "Why don't you come with us, get the men together and do something?" he demanded.

"Go along down that road," Hildebrand snapped. "I want to watch this fight."

"Cannon shot were whizzing through the air, bullets were spatting against the old barn," Dawes said. "It was not an ideal place to tarry." He marched his seven men down the road that the colonel had suggested, presently coming upon a fellow officer, Lieutenant Henrickle, "a typical battle picture. His arm and shoulder were covered with blood where a wounded man had fallen against him. His coat was torn by a bullet; his face was stained with powder; his lips were blackened by biting cartridges; he carried a gun. His eyes shone like fire. He was the man we had long sought. I said to him, 'Jack, where is the brigade?' He pointed across a ravine and said, 'Part of your regiment and part of mine are right down this way a little.'

"I felt like falling on his neck and weeping for joy," Dawes said.

Captain Dawes's odyssey that morning, or something like it, was being played out all through the rest of Sherman's brigades and regiments, who were being driven relentlessly back by the Rebel onslaught. Men lost, men confused, men frightened; men surrounded by death and hating themselves for becoming inured to it, or for being scared by it; men who were trying to do their duty and men who had abandoned it. They were not ready for this contest—but the Confederates were just as green. Death was in the air, and there was nothing left but to fight it out and let the devil take the hindmost.

Very soon after rejoining the 53rd Ohio, now reduced to 250, Dawes and his seven faithful men were placed in a long, jagged line containing the remnants of Sherman's and Prentiss's divisions, as well as men from the divisions of W.H.L. Wallace, McClernand, and Stephen Hurlbut, who were girding themselves for a last stand along a stretch of the battlefield more than a mile back from their original line. What would happen during these next few hours would stand prominent in history alongside Gettysburg's Cemetery Hill, Pickett's Charge, and the Bloody Lane at Antietam. But those things were all in the future, including the next two hours at

Shiloh, and the American people at that point had no idea, no context, for grasping the scope of the devastation and the overwhelming suffering caused by this civil war. They would learn it, though, as it hit them periodically, like terrible shock waves, one after the other, when the battle news came in.

During all of that violent and gory morning Sherman had been riding around his collapsing lines trying to shore people up and redirecting traffic as best he could. He had been shot twice, including the painful wound in his hand he'd got in his original encounter. He had wrapped it in a handkerchief and stuck it inside his tunic and kept going. Three horses, including his favorite mare, had been shot from under him.

An aide from headquarters who appeared at midmorning to check on how things were going found Sherman resting briefly beneath a tree. "Tell Grant if he has any men to spare I can use them. If not, I will do the best I can. We are holding them pretty well just now, but it's hot as hell."

CHAPTER 10

WHAT FOLLOWED, NO MAN COULD WELL DESCRIBE

—▸◆◂—

ULYSSES S. GRANT, FROM HIS HEADQUARTERS at Savannah, Tennessee, had boarded the steamboat *Tigress* for Pittsburg Landing. By most reckonings that would have been between 7 and 7:30 a.m., and it would probably have taken *Tigress* about two hours to make the nine-mile trip upstream against the swift current of the flooded river.*

Before leaving, Grant fired off a message to Buell, who had arrived during the night on the outskirts of town with an advance party, saying there was a battle in the works and he had best prepare

---

* A question arises about why Grant took so much time to get to the battlefield. But traveling by horseback would have been problematic; Grant would have had to steam up to Crump's Landing, where there was still six miles of tricky terrain to cross—and not knowing where the Rebels were. And if he had chosen to travel on the Savannah side of the river, there would be nine miles of swamp to navigate. The steamer was safer and surer.

to march his men toward a spot opposite Pittsburg Landing where they could be ferried across by the available steamboats. Meantime, Maj. Gen. "Bull" Nelson—the gigantic Kentuckian and Annapolis graduate whom Grant had sent to take Nashville after the fall of Fort Donelson—was stewing in his own juice. Nelson's division, the vanguard of Buell's army, had arrived just outside Savannah the afternoon before, where Nelson somehow developed a premonition of a Confederate attack on Grant's army.

On Sunday morning, just as his troops were preparing for inspection, the noise of battle began to drift from Pittsburg Landing toward Savannah and stirred Nelson into action. "He had not yet arisen," recalled an aide, when "he sprang from his couch. He called for Lieutenant Southgate . . . and ordered him to have the brigade commanders to have their men in readiness to move at any moment." Then he sent another aide to see if any transports had arrived during the night. As the firing continued, the aide said, Nelson, "still awaiting Grant's orders, chafed like a lion caged. He ate no breakfast, paced up and down before his tent, could not be pacified, and would not be pleased with anything or anybody."

Finally, "unwilling to endure his torturing suspense, he mounted his horse and galloped to Grant's headquarters," only to find that the commanding general had left. But soon after that—the aide gives the hour at a little past 8 a.m.—Nelson received Grant's orders to march his division "to a point opposite Pittsburg," saying, "You can easily find a guide in the city." It was a good thing, too, that Grant had thought to set these people in motion; he was going to need all the infantry divisions he could get.

A little less than halfway up the Tennessee from Savannah to Pittsburg was Crump's Landing, where the division of Lew Wallace had been parked because it was felt there was not enough room for it to camp at Pittsburg. As they neared Crump's Grant told the steamer skipper to run in close. There, in anticipation, Lew Wallace was waiting on the shore and shouted out, "My division is in line, waiting for orders."

Grant hollered back that as soon as he reached Pittsburg Landing and found out where and what the attack was he would send him orders. This Grant did, but for reasons never quite fully explained Lew Wallace's division never arrived on the battlefield that day.

Grant continued on toward the sounds of the firing, which became alarmingly heavy the farther south they steamed. It was going to be a difficult day all around for Grant: Two nights earlier when his horse slipped in the darkness of a rainstorm he'd fallen on his ankle, badly spraining it, and he was reduced to using crutches.

When he reached Pittsburg Landing, Grant was mortified by what he saw. Streams of stretcher bearers were carrying wounded to hospital boats. Officers were shouting madly to get men moving off of other boats, and even to keep boats from fleeing. Horse and mule wagons hauling cases of cartridges and artillery ammunition were driven in clouds of astonishing profanity to the top of the bluff where they could be distributed along the fighting front.

Most galling, the entire slope from brow to basin was thronged with thousands of panic-stricken shirkers and stragglers who were cowering beneath the cover of the bluff—and more coming in all the time—many of them crying out to anyone who would listen, "We are whipped! We have been cut to pieces!" Grant seemed to exhibit a rare sort of sympathy toward them, unlike some of the officers in his and Buell's armies who threatened to have them hanged or shot or (Buell's own preference) have the navy gunboats turn loose their cannons on them.

"It was a case of Southern dash against Northern pluck and endurance," Grant wrote later in his memoirs. "Three of the five divisions engaged on Sunday were entirely raw, and many of the men had only received their arms on their way from their states to the field. Many of them had arrived but a day or two before and were hardly able to load their muskets according to the manual."

In any case, Grant realized that most of these men "would rather be shot where they lay" than return to the fight, and he wasted no time on them. Hoisted upon his horse with the crutches strapped to his saddle, he rode off the steamer plank where he was met by his adjutant John A. Rawlins, who told him the attack was general, all along the Union lines. Thus informed, Grant and his staff rode up the hill toward the shooting.

Lt. William R. Rowley, one of Grant's aides, trotted up after watching the influx of stragglers and other fugitives from the fighting.

"General, this thing looks pretty squally, don't' it?" he asked.

"Well, not so very bad," Grant replied. "We've got to fight against time now. [Lew] Wallace must be here very soon."

"Firing grew sharp upon the left where the troops were breaking very badly," according to A. D. Richardson, one of Grant's early biographers. "Grant and his staff galloped to a little open field in front of a deserted cabin. Across the field was a rebel battery, which instantly opened upon them. The first shell struck just in front of the General.

" 'We must ride fast here,' said Grant.

"They rode behind the cabin a moment, but shells crashed through the roof, covering them with shingles.

"Grant: 'The old building don't seem to be a very good shelter; suppose we move on.'

"As they did, a bullet struck the General's scabbard and threw it up into the air. The sword dropped out and was never recovered," Richardson wrote.

<hr />

Lying on one of the hospital ships at the landing was Pvt. Robert Fleming, the clerk in Colonel Hildebrand's headquarters who had found himself wounded in the fighting and thought he was "done for." After the surgeon of the field hospital where he'd gone for help had ordered the place evacuated, Fleming made his way to one of the hospital boats at the landing. Men with stretchers were kept busy, Fleming said, carrying the wounded onto the boats, and also "carrying men off the boats as quickly as they succumbed to their wounds, and laying them in a row on a level ledge about halfway up the bank."

Somehow Fleming found out that his brother, a sergeant two years his senior, was also on the boat, desperately wounded. Fleming went to him but "saw at a glance that death was written on his face." A doctor had already told Fleming's brother that his wound was mortal, and there was little Fleming could do but make him a pillow of his own shirt, filled with hay, and wait for him to die.

Fleming also noticed that one of these men being carried to the dead line "attempted to raise his head. Two Sisters of Charity who were on the boat quickly went to his aid, and brought him back aboard."

The Sisters were among some 600 Catholic nuns from a dozen different orders generically referred to as the Sisters of Charity, who truly were angels of mercy on the battlefields during the Civil War.

They were looked at askance in some quarters because they nursed both Union and Confederate wounded—and some were even accused of spying—but the torn and dying men and boys seemed profoundly grateful to have a woman's touch in their distress, which often reminded them of home.

The work the Sisters did was not a "proper" type thing that women engaged in during the mid-19th century. One Sister described the deck of a hospital ship she was serving on as "looking like a slaughterhouse, with doctors tossing overboard arms and legs to a watery grave." When one of the doctors' wives suggested to a nun that this was not a fit place for women, the Sister paraphrased Jesus from the Bible, "Whatever ye do not doest to the least of these, ye do not doest to me."

There were women other than the Sisters of Charity at Shiloh that day. Officers' wives often visited their husbands in the field and even though it would not have been approved of at Pittsburg Landing because of the impending operations, 29-year-old Ann Wallace, wife of one of Grant's division commanders, General W.H.L. Wallace, had come down by steamer. The trip would become the ordeal of her life.

She had come aboard the steamer *Minnehaha,* which brought a cargo of fresh Iowa troops to Pittsburg Landing before dark. During a brief stop at Savannah, Mrs. Wallace had learned that her husband was now in the field commanding the division of Gen. C. F. Smith, who was lying ill in the Cherry mansion.

Wallace was a 41-year-old Illinois lawyer, Mexican War veteran, and friend of Abraham Lincoln, who had received his military training in the state militia. He was tall, spare, and balding, with a beaklike nose on a narrow face, a recessed chin, and tufts of hair that stuck out on the top and sides of his head so that he resembled a contemporary image of Washington Irving's timid schoolteacher Ichabod Crane. But in fact Wallace was a solid, highly competent, and courageous officer who, according to the well-known journalist Charles C. Coffin, "could bring order out of confusion and by a word, a look, or an act, inspire his men." Unbeknownst to Ann Wallace, as the steamer pulled into Pittsburg Landing, with all of its chaos, her husband, out on the battlefield, was undergoing a trial of the severest nature.

Respectfully, a captain in an Illinois regiment offered to walk Mrs. Wallace out to her husband's headquarters. "We heard a great deal of firing," she said, "but it was accounted for by the return of the night pickets and the discharge of their guns.* I had put on my hat and gloves, when Captain Coats suggested that perhaps it would be better for him to first find out how far it was, and perhaps I had better ride. So I remained on the boat.

"Before half an hour Captain Coats came back wounded in two places, one painful wound in the hand, but neither of them dangerous. I learned that a big battle was in progress and that my husband had moved with his command to the front. The only thing then to do was to wait where I was. That long day on that steamboat, its scenes and sensations, are beyond description," Mrs. Wallace said. "The wounded were brought by hundreds onto the boat. I did not hear a groan or murmur except those unconscious under influence

---

* Once loaded, most Civil War–era rifles and muskets could not easily be unloaded, and the quickest method of disarming them was to fire them off.

of chloroform or sleep. I passed from place to place holding water and handing bandages for the surgeons until it became so crowded I felt I was in the way."

Another woman caring for the Union wounded that day was 44-year-old Mary A. Newcomb, whose husband had been in General Wallace's division before he died of wounds received in the Battle of Fort Henry. She'd had the devil of a time even getting him buried in Effingham County, Illinois; because of the strong Rebel sentiment no Presbyterian minister would preside over the funeral, and she'd had to settle for a Methodist preacher. Mary had become a sort of unofficial nurse and surrogate mother to her dead husband's regiment, the 11th Illinois Volunteers. Even Grant had joked that he'd commit himself to the hospital if Mary was doing the cooking.

━━━━◆━◆━◆━━━━

Grant and his staff had charged up to the top of the bluff at Pittsburg Landing and started inland. They rode perhaps half a mile when they met W.H.L. Wallace, who was trying to support Prentiss in his crisis. From Wallace, Grant received further confirmation that the attack seemed to be the full force of the Confederate army. Grant dispatched Rawlins to hurry back to the landing and direct the quartermaster Capt. A. S. Baxter to hurry *Tigress* down to Crump's Landing and tell the other Wallace—Lew Wallace—to bring his division to Pittsburg on the double.

Grant's orders had been verbal, but when Rawlins reached the landing Baxter wanted them written out to eliminate any chance of mistake. The substance of the order was that Wallace would come up by the River Road—the shortest route, about five miles—and "form a line of battle at a right angle with the river and be governed by circumstances." This should have been simple to accomplish, but it was not, and so has spawned acrimonious controversy down the years until the present day, as we shall see. In any event Lew Wallace that morning took the wrong road, and with it the critical weight of his 7,200-man infantry division was removed from the battle.

Meantime, Grant continued to visit his divisions, lending encouragement, hastening up ammunition and supplies, and "sending his aides flying over all parts of the field" with orders to commanders or to collect information. The fact that a lot of lead and iron was flying through the air did not seem to deter Grant in the least. Among his aides that morning was Capt. Douglas A. Putnam, a paymaster, who had come up on *Tigress* that morning and volunteered to assist Grant when he got to Pittsburg Landing. Riding after the general with Rawlins, Putnam began to notice the first signs of battle and, "in [his] inexperience," asked Rawlins if the little pitter-patter he was hearing in the leaves was rain—"to which Rawlins tersely said, 'No, those are bullets, Douglas.' "

According to Putnam Grant had, against his habit, donned his full major general's uniform that day, "complete with buff sash, making him "very conspicuous," causing Rawlins and McPherson—who was serving that day as chief of staff—"to remonstrate with him for so unnecessarily exposing himself," but Grant brushed them off.

He visited Sherman in the bullet-pocked clearing of his old drill field near the peach orchard, and found him grimy, bloodstained, and just as feisty as ever, with his collar pulled around sideways, "so that the part that should have been in front rested under one of his ears," Putnam said. It was a grim meeting of few words, with Grant asking questions and Sherman vowing to fight on.

The problem was that Sherman's command simply wasn't standing up to the Rebel assault. Pat Cleburne's men were flooding into the ravines leading toward Shiloh church, and Sherman's brigades were in danger of being cut off—especially McDowell's men, who were guarding the far right end of the Federal line way out by the Owl Creek bridge. About 10 a.m. Sherman sent orders for the entire division to withdraw to a line farther north. When word of this got to McDowell, he rode out and ordered the brigade to fall back to the new line. As this order was passed down, the lieutenant colonel commanding McDowell's old regiment, the Sixth Iowa, "about-faced the left wing and marched it back to the field fence, leaving the other four companies standing in line in the woods," according to the regimental historian. Puzzled by this unusual maneuver, McDowell rode over to the regiment to find out what it meant. "It means, sir, that the colonel is drunk," was the answer he got, whereupon McDowell had the colonel arrested and relieved of his sword.

Alcohol use on the battlefield was not limited to the Union army alone. Around the time of the Sixth Iowa incident, and just to their left, was a Rebel company in Bushrod Johnson's brigade consisting of about 60 men from southern Illinois who had sided with the Confederacy. They were protecting Capt. Marshall T. Polk's Rebel battery of six guns, which was shooting it out with a Yankee battery across the way.

The Illinois men were among a small but defiant group of Illinoisans from the "Egypt" area who identified with the grievances of the South. Known as the Southern Illinois Company, they served in the 15th Tennessee, in Johnson's brigade, a part of General Polk's corps.

During the battle that morning the firing became heavy and hot, and it appeared that Sherman's people, led by Col. Joseph

Cockerill's 70th Ohio, were going to storm Polk's battery and possibly capture it. After all other senior officers of the 15th Tennessee were shot down, Johnson told the captain of the Southern Illinois Company to take command and defend the guns, which he did, according to the regimental historian, despite the fact that "Brevet Lieutenant Harvey Hays, who was drunk, did little more than yell a litany of curses at the blue-clads." The Rebel guns were successfully repositioned in a fierce fight that earned the Illinois Confederates their full "twelve minutes of fame," or so it was maintained by witnesses at the Battle of Shiloh.

After Sherman, Grant next visited Prentiss, who was in the fight of his life in the center of the line, having been pushed back nearly a mile. Grant told him to hold his position "at all hazards," and that he would send him reinforcements—meaning from Lew Wallace's division—soon as it arrived. For better or worse, Prentiss took him to heart. Grant said the same thing to his other division commanders. Lew Wallace was now the army's reserve, the only large-size unit not then already engaged. Grant insisted to everyone that Wallace was near at hand. His presence on the battlefield was critical, as Grant well knew; it could mean the difference between self-preservation and defeat.

By then it was midday and the Rebel attacks were at their most furious intensity. Nothing better illustrates the level of violence and desperation of the attacks—and the Union defense— than the trial of Colonel Camm of the 14th Illinois, whom we first met as he studied the face and the diary of the beautiful dead Rebel soldier at Fort Donelson.

By midmorning the first waves of the Confederate attack— Hardee's corps and, soon after, Bragg's—had crested and broken over the regiments of Prentiss and Sherman, whose divisions had been posted in the southernmost lines of the Union position. In so doing these Confederates had practically sacrificed themselves: The Sixth Tennessee, for instance, endured 70 percent casualties, but they had also taken a fearful toll on the Union defenders, who were falling back in almost as wretched a condition.

However, they were falling back on their second lines, which consisted of the camps of Major General McClernand and Brig. Gen. W.H.L. Wallace's divisions, and also the division of Brigadier General Hurlbut, who was nearest the landing itself. Now they were being additionally swamped by the Confederate army's second waves, consisting of Polk's corps and Breckinridge's reserve.

In his diary, Camm had written, "April 6th. Began with a bright beautiful morning. The trees were budding, the birds were singing, but none of us dreamed what a dark and bloody ending the day would have. It was a morning for lambs to gambol on. As we saw it last that evening, a great red globe of blood."

The 14th Illinois was assigned to Hurlbut's division but soon after the attack started Sherman asked for help from Hurlbut and McClernand, and Camm's was one of the regiments sent south to plug a gap between Sherman and the hard-pressed Prentiss. Right away Camm "noticed something that I did not like." Some of the junior officers, he said, were swapping their coats with shoulder straps and insignia for the coats of privates, and when one of them tried to involve Camm in the scheme he replied, "I am proud of my straps," adding that he would need them in the confusion of battle and "I would die with them on if I have to die." Thus said, Camm rode off toward the sound of the guns, "which had settled into a steady roar."

For the remainder of the day we see in Camm's regiment the difference between how men in desperate battle fight under resolute commanders, as opposed to what we have already seen of the 53rd Ohio, deserted by its colonel.

When Camm rode ahead to clear the road to the battle line so the regiment could pass, he met a wagon carrying, among other baggage, a wounded soldier whose leg had been blown off below the knee. "He stuck the stump, with the shattered bone almost sticking out into my face," Camm said, and in a strong voice he cried above the din, "Give 'em hell for that, Colonel!"

"The earth was shaking now," Camm said, "and above the cannon and rifle fire we could hear the treble of the rebel yell as the storm came towards us." When they came to the Review Field, where they used to drill, "the bullets began to whiz by." Camm was riding with the regimental chaplain and "admonished him to go to the rear and prepare to succor the wounded; at the same time, " he said, "I handed him my pocket book, which contained several hundred dollars, asking him to send it to my father should I be killed."

The regiment went into the line south of the Purdy road, facing southwest with a battery of five rifled guns and an old brass howitzer. They were supporting an Ohio regiment and so were told to lie down and wait. Camm noticed that one of his color bearers, a boy named Fletcher Ebey, was kneeling, trying to get a look around, and before Camm could order him down a bullet through the heart "laid him down dead, and bleeding on his flag." Moments later, Camm said, a lieutenant named Opitz was sitting on a stump, messing with the tobacco in his pipe, when a bullet "struck him in the end of the nose and cut the top of an ear off as it came out. I could see the Jonnies running from tree to tree and popping away at us as they came. They had driven everything before them so far, and seemed to think they could drive us, too.

"The battery was belching like a volcano, but only seemed to attract the fire of the enemy's guns and the rush of heavy shot and head-splitting crack of bursting shell all about us were adding to the increasing roar." Camm heard a bugle and saw the Confederates ahead massing for a charge, and also a tall Union artillery sergeant double-shot the brass cannon. The regiment was ordered forward but did not fire until the Confederates were in close range.

"What followed," Camm said, "no man could well describe, until the Rebels were repulsed. I saw our handsome orderly of company 'G' fall with blood spurting from both temples. Regimental Color Sergeant John E. Kirkman rolled the body of his dead comrade off the national colors and rose with both flags in his hands, and as he did so a shot passed through the folds of the Stars and Stripes, cutting a gap in the staff and then passing through Kirkman's cap and grazing his head.

"The enemy were checked but were very stubborn, and we murdered each other down at close range," Camm wrote. "Our brigade commander rode down the line and I asked him to turn us loose with the bayonet. 'No, no,' he said, 'you would lose every man.'

"My horse was struck behind the saddle and lunged among the men, so I let him go; I tried to get the men to charge but between us [and the Rebels] was a struggling mass of wild and wounded battery horses, many of them harnessed to the dead, and I could not get them started. But I got far enough forward to see a Confederate soldier trying to lead his men into our line. I covered him with my pistol but he was behaving so bravely that I hesitated firing.

"He pointed me out to a black-bearded soldier on his left," Camm continued, "and as his piece covered me, a quiet and not unpleasant feeling came over me, and I let the point of my saber drop to the ground. I seemed to hear the bullet hiss." Just then somebody shot the Rebel officer and, moments later, the soldier with the black beard. Camm, who had dismounted, was hit in the thigh by a shot that glanced off his saber. Walking back across the Union line he encountered two officers, a captain and a lieutenant, who had been shot. "Blood was running through Sibley's fingers," Camm said, "and Simpson's hand was mangled.

"New troops seemed to have come against us. The 15th [Illinois] on our right with Ellis and Goddard both killed, gave way. Our right wing followed. [Colonel] Hall rushed up with orders—'back, back.'" The regiment backed up about a hundred paces and re-formed on the Purdy road. Among the last men to get in line was a sergeant, "well-dressed, almost a dandy. Tears were running over his cheeks and he was exhorting his comrades to die upon the line, rather than to break again."

At that point there was a lull in the battle, "but before our muskets could cool," Camm wrote, "the enemy came on again, and the fight became fiercer than ever." A young man named Noble Stout, "whom the men used to make sport of because of his innocent simplicity," staggered up to Camm, crying, "Oh, Colonel, I'm shot." He had been hit in the stomach. Camm led him behind a fallen tree but afterward noticed "the pale face, the closed eyes, the livid parted lips, and supposed him dead. But," he added, "a burial party tells me they could not find the body."

A man came up with a rifle whose stock had been shot away, saying, "That is the fourth gun smashed in my hand. What shall

I do?" Camm pointed to a gun on the ground and the man threw down his broken weapon and "was soon blazing away. Nearby stood Hankins, blood spouting from his breast at every inspiration," said Camm. "He loaded and fired till a shot struck him in the chin and went through the neck killing him.

"Up the road through a rift in the smoke I saw a confederate officer mounted in front of their colors waving a bright sword, leading his men on, but before the smoke hid them again, officer, horse, and colors all went down," blown apart by a battery of heavy guns in Camm's rear. Outflanked again, Camm's regiment again gave ground, with such officers as remained doing all they could to rally the men. Camm grabbed a color bearer and led him on the run to a ravine in the rear where he began to shout for the fleeing men to "rally on the colors."

This many of them did, and in a short time "the remnant of our regiment was ready for our foes," said Colonel Camm. They had gone into the battle at 10:30 a.m., and now, at straight-up noon, there was only the glaring sun overhead to remind them that they were not already dead and rotting.

CHAPTER 11

LIKE SHOOTING INTO A FLOCK OF SHEEP

As the Confederates drove Grant's army northward, what remained of the civilian population of Pittsburg Landing made do as best they could while the drama unfolded. Shortly before the battle nine-year-old Elsie Duncan had been "sitting outside beneath a blooming hollyhock bush watching the bees on flowers." The night before the battle, as she tells it, "Mother said that we would have to trust in the Lord to take care of us. Margie [a servant] brought a cat into the room. Mother prayed and she and Margie sang some songs. Then we all went to bed and left everything to the Lord.

"Next morning," Elsie continued, "when I waked and saw my mother sitting there by the fire with the baby in her lap, it seemed that she was sitting there by the bed when we went to sleep and still sitting there when we got up. I always felt safe when I was with my beautiful mother—with her hazel eyes and black hair, rosy cheeks and lady-like ways. She had the most beautiful white hands I ever saw.

"And then I jumped out of bed and said 'Oh Mother, what is that noise!' With a beating heart I rushed to her side. 'Is that the fighting?' I was frightened and I said, 'Oh mother, do you think that [her brothers and half brothers] Jim and Joe and [illegible] are there?' She said 'I'm afraid they are.' Father, being a chaplain," Elsie wrote, "we knew he would not be in the battle. But when I heard the cannon roar and the guns popping and the horses screaming it seemed as if everything was lost."

Elsie left the house for a short while—apparently to seek a safer shelter—for when she returned, she said, "I saw that my father [a local preacher and Confederate army chaplain] had come home. He was bending over the bed and mother was tearing a cloth into strips. I went into the room and saw a rebel soldier boy with his hip all shot up. I gave one look and saw that it was one of our neighbor's boys. I could not bear to look at him. When they were through with him his folks came and took him home."

Just where on the battlefield Elsie was located is hard to determine, since the family apparently had several dwellings in the vicinity. Maps show that "Duncan Field" was located just north of the Hamburg-Purdy road near the intersection of the Main Corinth Road, which would have put it close to where Colonel Camm and his 14th Illinois were having the fight of their lives with the men of Hardee's corps, including Pat Cleburne's survivors and the brigade of A. P. Stewart. Reports say that "Cleburne joined Stewart at 12 noon in an attack upon positions at Duncan House, where some of Cleburne's men were taken prisoners by the Seventh Illinois." Later, the house was in the midst of the Hornet's Nest fighting.

One shudders to think that a family of civilians was actually in the middle of the kind of fighting that characterized that part of the field, but according to Elsie, wherever it was she called "home" that day saw something of the battle.

"The fighting began at our gate, just past the house," she wrote. "As the battle raged it got further away leaving dead men and horses behind. My father and other old men were behind the lines helping all they could. I went into one house where they had taken wounded and dead men. The floor was covered with blood. As I went back I saw a woman screaming and wringing her hands and mother was trying to quiet her. She could not do anything with her. She said that she had two sons in that battle—one on each side fighting against each other."*

Harriett Duncan told the woman she had her own children in the battle and that she must "bear up," but the woman continued on "toward the firing line. We heard that one [of her sons] was killed in his own backyard," Elsie said. (At least two soldiers' accounts report a lone woman walking across the battlefield in the midst of heavy fighting.) "Nobody had left their homes," Elsie said, "they did not expect the battle to be fought there."

During the day, various people came and went in Elsie's house. An old man arrived looking for his sons; a slave asked for a drink of water before going off to find his 17-year-old "master" who had gone into battle. Elsie tells of a grandmother who shooed her daughter and two grandchildren to the landing where they cringed under the bluff with the slackers from the Federal ranks. "They stayed

---

* Not unlikely since both Confederate and Union forces recruited heavily from the local area in the days before the battle.

under there three days and two nights without food or water, and only came out Tuesday."

In the far southeast of the Pittsburg Landing camp a Yankee picket named William Lowe had stationed himself 50 yards from a house and was lost in lonely meditations as the firing neared, when suddenly "a man emerg[ed] from the brush on the right of the road and went to the house. His hat was pulled down over his eyes and he did not see me, but I was pointed out to him by a woman at the door.

"He came over to where I was," Lowe said. "The tears were coursing down his cheeks. He had been over in the rear of the Confederate army and said they were killing men by thousands. He had been to get their general to move his family back out of the reach of the battle."

Lowe told the resident that he would be better off moving his family behind the Federal line, but the man demurred, saying he had no preference for either side, he just wanted out. "He insisted on bringing me a chunk of pone and some milk," Lowe said, "which I declined." Lowe questioned the man about the size of the Rebel army, "but I could get nothing out of him except that they were 'a powerful sight.'"

———— ✦ ————

As the Battle of Shiloh rolled northward, Beauregard moved his headquarters along behind and by noon was nearing the Shiloh church where Sherman's headquarters once had been. He continued feeding troops into the cauldron of battle, but by now most units were already committed. Following the practice of his hero Napoleon, Beauregard sent troops marching toward the sound of the loudest fighting, for which he was later criticized, since much of the present fighting was in the Union center and it had been Sidney Johnston's clear intention to roll up the Yankee left flank, which was anchored on the river. Johnston's purpose was to separate the Federals from any escape or reinforcements via Pittsburg Landing and the river transports and drive them to surrender in the swamps of Owl and Snake Creeks. That this was not done owed in part to a lack of concentration of Confederate troops on the far right, and in part to the heroic and sanguinary stand by the shattered scraps of General Prentiss's and W.H.L Wallace's divisions, and of Sherman's isolated brigade on the far left of the Union line. Let us begin with the latter.

By about 10 a.m. it had become apparent that the Confederate line of battle was short by perhaps a mile from reaching the bottoms of Lick Creek and the Tennessee River in order to form a perfect and totally closed front against the Union forces. Not only that, but a Confederate engineer sent to scout the area reported seeing a large Federal force apparently maneuvering for a flank attack on the Rebel army. (This "large Federal force" was actually the isolated brigade of Sherman's division, which was trying to figure out how to meet the Rebel attack.)

At that point General Johnston himself pulled the second and third brigades of Jones Withers's division—commanded respectively by Brigadier General Chalmers and Brig. Gen. John K. Jackson—out of the fight where, along with Gladden's brigade, they had just collapsed Prentiss's line. Johnston encountered Chalmers's men in the process of looting the tents of the recently departed 18th Wisconsin, and the commanding general was particularly incensed to see one of his officers, a lieutenant, emerge from a tent with an armload of Yankee booty. He sharply reprimanded the young man, saying, "None of that, Sir, we are not here for plunder!"

In those days and times, for a young officer to be personally censured by someone of Sidney Johnston's stature would be a fate almost worse than death, and the lieutenant's humiliation was palpable. Seeing this, Johnston softened and tried to relieve the lieutenant's discomfort by taking from him a small tin cup, saying, "Then let this be my share of the spoils today," he smiled. Afterward, Johnston used the cup for attention, at times lifting it like a sword, and sometimes striking it for emphasis on the bayonets of the soldiers. Johnston personally led Chalmers and Jackson due east to the bottoms of Lick Creek, with orders to sweep north along the Tennessee riverbank to Pittsburg Landing. Like many things, it proved far easier said than done. In fact, nothing was easy that day. Nothing.

Blocking the way was Sherman's lone Second Brigade that he had posted there weeks earlier to guard approaches near the river before any of the other divisions arrived. For some reason Sherman had left it out there even after McClernand, Prentiss, W.H.L. Wallace, and Hurlbut came up, and with nearly a mile-wide gap between it and Prentiss's leftmost regiment.

Commanded by Col. David Stuart, a 46-year-old Amherst graduate, Michigan lawyer, and former U.S. congressman, the brigade's three regiments, 2,335-strong, were well posted on hills and elevations around the intersection of the Hamburg-Purdy and Hamburg-Savannah roads. One of these regiments was the 55th Illinois, camped in the Peach Orchard, which was just coming into its fragrant pink blossoms when war found it.

In the ensuing years there was a great deal of righteous indignation and acrimonious finger-pointing on both sides of the battle, but perhaps none so furious as that of the 55th Illinois and 54th Ohio, which composed the bulk of Stuart's brigade that morning. Stuart's shorthandedness was due to the disgraceful bugout of the brigade's third regiment, the 71st Ohio, which, led by its commanding officer, "that globule of adipose pomposity, Col. Rodney Mason,"* ran off in its entirety—never to return—at the first shots from some Rebel skirmishers.

The bulk of the regimental finger-pointing, however, was directed at none other than the division commander himself, General Sherman, who, according to survivors of the battle, "left [the brigade] off two miles, detached from his division—left it during the battle, without artillery, without his orders, and apparently without a thought, and left it in his report, with a mere allusion never after corrected or elaborated."

There appears to be some justification for this bitterness—especially the part about getting short shrift in Sherman's after action report, since Stuart's brigade suffered the second highest casualty rate (340 killed, wounded, and missing) of any of Sherman's four brigades, and held its position—and the army's critical left flank—until late in the day.†

The morning had started strangely for the Second Brigade. A day earlier, in an artillery realignment, Grant had stripped Stuart of his battery, which was reassigned to W.H.L. Wallace's division. From an early hour Stuart's men had listened apprehensively to

---

*   This description courtesy of the regimental historian of the 55th Illinois, who also identified Mason as a onetime Ohio attorney general and offspring of a highly prominent Ohio family. Grant himself referred to Mason as a "constitutional coward," and he was cashiered from the army later that year.

†   To Sherman's credit he admits in his report that he had not yet received the report of Colonel Stuart, who had been wounded, and was thus unable to account for the activities of the Second Brigade.

the sounds of battle on their right as the Confederate line crashed into Sherman and Prentiss, but as the minutes, and then the hours ticked by, nothing appeared on their front. As the sun rose in the sky some men began to think the brigade had been bypassed in the attack, but Stuart knew it was just a matter of time—especially after he "discovered the Pelican flag advancing in the rear of General Prentiss's headquarters."* Stuart immediately dispatched a warning to Hurlbut that Prentiss's front had been turned, and Hurlbut in response sent one of his batteries and two regiments, but they wandered down the wrong road and became lost.

One problem Stuart faced was that the particular spot of ground he had to defend was among the most cut-up terrain of all Pittsburg Landing, broken with steep ravines, creeks, bluffs, and heavy timber, and it was difficult to estimate just where an enemy attack would appear and how to receive it. Thus Stuart spent much of the morning having the brigade change fronts based on the noise of battle on their right.

At one point, after a report that Rebel cavalry had been sighted, a controversial order for a hollow square was issued by the assistant brigade commander, a Swede, whose description in the official regimental history of the 55th Illinois is worth listening to: "As the regiment was filling its ranks [earlier that year] there appeared upon the scene one Oscar Malmborg, around whose name hung a vague mystery of noble lineage and military glory—the former never to be verified and the latter scarcely confirmed. From that time on, the country round

---

* This was likely the Louisiana state flag carried by the First Louisiana. The 18th Louisiana had its own pelican flag but was in another part of the field.

about resounded with such orders as: 'Column py fyle,' 'Charge pea-nuts,' with an occasional exasperated inquiry like: 'What for you face mit your pack?'—all uttered in ferocious tones and foreign accent."

Malmborg, who had worked in the emigrant department of the Illinois Central Railway, and been schooled in European infan-try tactics, ordered the regiments formed up in hollow squares, a favorite European defense by infantry against cavalry attack. But this, according to the sentiments of the men, was "totally ludicrous" under the circumstances—especially since, just as the 71st Ohio was floundering around that morning trying to organize itself into some similarly unwieldy formation, as soon as the first Rebel skir-mishers appeared and fired off a few random shots it so spooked that 667-man regiment that the 71st ran off toward the landing, Colonel Mason and all.

The panic likewise infected the other two regiments, the 55th Illinois and the 54th Ohio, which, caught by skirmish fire in the middle of a turning movement, began a dash to the rear only to be outrun by Stuart himself, on horseback, who galloped ahead, then wheeled and drew himself up to face them. "Halt, men!" he cried; his stentorian voice cut the air like a saw. "Halt!" He swung his sword "like a medieval knight" and swore oaths at them and called them cowards. "Halt!" Whereupon they stopped running and "froze in their tracks, and shamefacedly returned to the fight."

Stuart had saved the day; in fact, he held powerful sway over the men of the regiment. He was a stern taskmaster but fair and a man of good humor, but behind this lay the stain of a great pubic shame for which he was trying to atone, and the brigade too would find itself drawn in to the atonement. The fact was, Colonel Stuart was a man with a past.

In 1855, Stuart had moved his law practice from Detroit to Chicago, and in a short time he became one of the city's wealthiest and most socially prominent citizens. Then, in 1860, he became entangled in an infamous scandal. He was named as correspondent in one of the most notorious divorce cases of the century, which ruined him socially and politically, and when war broke out the following year he saw it as the only way to redemption.*

Stuart pledged to personally raise and equip a regiment but was thwarted by the Illinois governor, who was pressured by the Chicago Bar Association, the press, and public outrage against Stuart. He then went to the War Department and offered to raise an entire brigade. He was granted authority to do this but was able to organize only one regiment—the 55th Illinois—before the war in the West required putting troops in the field. In time he was given command of Sherman's Second Brigade, of which his 55th Illinois was part.

His men came to adore him. He could talk their turkey. On the steamer trip up to Pittsburg Landing, according to the regimental history, Stuart, "magnificently dressed, walking the decks like a king," gathered the men together on the hurricane deck to deliver a lecture against drunkenness, promising that at the end of the war he would take them to New Orleans "where we would all get drunk together." In an incident described in the annals of the regiment's history, Stuart set an example of the evils of intemperance by posting one Private Welsh, of B Company, upon the hull of an

---

* Isaac H. Burch, a Chicago banker, accused Stuart in a divorce proceeding of having had an affair with his wife, a daughter of the influential Corning family from New York. Divorce was quite rare in those times, and the case was prominently celebrated in the newspapers with all the sniggling innuendos of Victorian times.

upturned ship's boat to stand in the sun in penitence for his insobriety and for the amusement of the men who packed the decks.

Suddenly wheeling upon the culprit, Stuart puffed himself up
in the manner of an actor and vehemently proclaimed: " 'There is
Welsh; he got drunk last night, fell into the river, and lost his gun.
He is his own horrid example of intemperance.' Addressing Welsh
directly, Stuart demanded accusingly, 'Welsh, you were drunk last
night, weren't you?' Welsh replied, 'Yeas, about half-drunk,' whereat
the colonel roared, 'Half-drunk—damn you! Well, why didn't you
get whole drunk like a man?' "

The men ate it up. They respected him, even though they all
knew about his disgrace because so many of them were from Chicago where it had been front-page news for months. It was this
kind of closeness that allowed Stuart to give his noncommissioned
officers what surely must rank as one of the strangest speeches in
military history. Shortly after they had encamped at Pittsburg Landing Stuart minced no words: "I am a man of somewhat damaged
reputation, as you all well know. And I came into the army solely to
retrieve that reputation, and I depend upon this regiment to do it."

Doubtless this news had spread down to the ranks, for as they
streamed past him that Sunday morning of battle they took him
in, seated upon his horse in the middle of the tall oak forest, "his
voice bellowing like a trumpet" for them to halt. Even the dimmest
among them must have felt a sense of loyalty to the man, some kin-
dle of his authority and his magnetic personality that caused them
to rally upon him; otherwise, they simply would have kept on running. "If Stuart had died then," the regimental biographer wrote,
"he would have been canonized in the hearts of his men." They were
young and full of life and had it all before them, and inexperienced

as they were as soldiers they knew that this was not just a fracas, or push-shove, or even a fistfight; here their very lives and limbs were at stake. Otherwise, they would have kept on running.

━━━━◆◆◆◆━━━━

James Chalmers, a 31-year-old University of South Carolina–educated lawyer and former district attorney for Holly Springs, Mississippi, was short, slight, belligerent, and later in the war one of Bedford Forrest's finest cavalry commanders. Today his 2,039-man infantry brigade had been entrusted with the key to Sidney Johnston's battle plan for the undoing of the Union army. Unfortunately Beauregard, charged with feeding reinforcements into the fight, was all the way over on the Confederate left, several miles from where Chalmers's effort was being undertaken. And Beauregard was still operating under that Napoleonic fixation of his—that reinforcements must be ordered to the sounds of the heaviest fighting, which, in his case, was the battle right in front him involving the dispute with the divisions of Sherman and Prentiss.

Chalmers was the first of the two brigades sent to affect the turning movement on the far Confederate right. He commanded four regiments of Mississippians plus the 52nd Tennessee, which, like its opposite the 71st Ohio, at the first sign of trouble that morning had "broke and fled in the most shameful confusion," according to Chalmers, who sourly added that, "After repeated efforts to rally it, this regiment was ordered out of the lines, where it remained during the balance of the engagement."*

---

*   With the exception of two companies "who fought gallantly in the ranks of the Fifth Mississippi Regiment," according to the Official Records.

With his right flank on Lick Creek and facing north, Chalmers ordered his brigade forward until they came to an orchard about 400 yards wide behind which was "a steep and perfectly abrupt hill" with deep underbrush and lined by a fence, "behind which the enemy was concealed."

Chalmers called up his six-gun battery of Alabama artillery commanded by Capt. Charles P. Gage. He then gave the order for the brigade to advance against the enemy. "My line moved on across the orchard in most perfect order and splendid style," Chalmers said later, "and to my great surprise not a shot was fired until we came within 40 yards of the fence." The result was an instant bloodbath from buck and ball in which Chalmers's men "suffered heavily in killed and wounded" but "after a hard fight drove the enemy from his concealment."

At that point, Chalmers said in his official report, his men needed to replenish their ammunition, and half an hour was given over to this task. Resupply was one of the greatest impediments to the Confederate attack at Shiloh. Unlike the Yankees who, as they gave ground, actually backed closer to their ammo dumps, the Rebel brigades struggled to replenish their ammunition from wagons that often had the utmost difficulty keeping up as the assault rolled through the dense forests, ravines, creek beds, and swamps that characterized the terrain.

Stuart, still holding the far left of the Federal line, and still waiting for something to happen, said that between the loss of the 71st Ohio and fugitives who had fled from his 55th Illinois and 54th Ohio, he could count only 800 rifles in his ranks to defend against

Chalmers's 1,200 remaining men and Jackson's 2,600, coming up on his left. From about 10 a.m. on, the two sides skirmished, taking pot shots at each other, with the Confederates lobbing in some artillery shells. One of these Rebel pot shots hit Stuart in the shoulder, and although he stayed with the brigade he turned over immediate command of the 55th Illinois to Colonel Malmborg, with his quaint Scandinavian military ways. Then, at 11:30, Chalmers attacked, and the sight of hundreds of Confederate soldiers in battle line with flags flying caused members of the 55th Illinois to quaver once more.

Malmborg again ordered the regiment to form into a hollow square, a maneuver that brought the Rebel charge up short. The Confederates "had never seen a hollow square, or even heard of it," and they were intensely suspicious, some crying out, "It's a Yankee trick!" They were wary that the Yankees had masked batteries hidden somewhere, "or perhaps something more mysterious and dreadful."

When the hollow square made no further moves, the Confederate line went forward again, but Malmborg ordered the square to withdraw a few hundred yards. The Confederates halted again and began discussing it with one another. They could not believe the weird formation they were seeing, as it scuttled backward bristling like an angry blue porcupine with its fixed bayonets sticking out on all sides—it seemed somehow deceitful, as if it must be trying to lure them into a trap. The Rebel officers prodded, cajoled, and cursed and the Confederate line advanced once more. And once more the hollow square withdrew.

At length, Malmborg discovered he had gone as far as he could go, finding himself at the brink of an enormous ravine at least a hundred feet deep. There he ordered the hollow square to disburse, cross the ravine, and form in line of battle on an elevation in the rear, which proved to be a perfect defensive position, at least for the next two hours, but it was as bloody a two hours as any on a field where nearly all the fighting was horrific and pitiless.

Pvt. Robert Oliver, of the 55th Illinois, was lying behind a log firing when 2nd Lt. Theodore W. Hodges came up beside him "and knelt on one knee with the point of his sword on the ground, saying, 'Oliver, as soon as you get your gun loaded take Ainsbury to the rear. Then he was hit with a canister shot in the head. He hung to the hilt of his sword until his hand came to the ground, bending the sword double, and when he let go it bounded six feet into the air. That was the last command he ever gave."

A Rebel soldier remembered that his regiment "fought like Indians," from behind trees, brush, rocks, and logs. It was here that the Rev. M. L. Weller, chaplain of the Ninth Mississippi, was slain giving succor to the wounded.

After the death of Lieutenant Hodges, Private Oliver located the wounded Ainsbury and turned him over to another soldier headed to the rear. Then he heard the voice of a friend, "who called out, 'Robert, for God's sake don't leave me.' I looked back and saw James D. Godwin of my regiment," Oliver said. "He had everything off except his pants, and was as red as if he had been dipped into a barrel of blood. I said, 'Never—put your arm around me and I will do the best I can for you.' " As he lugged Godwin back he felt more bullets slam into his friend, and when he finally found a surgeon, "upon cutting the shirt off, to my horror there were seven bullet holes in that boy, not yet seventeen years old," Oliver said.

Capt. L. B. Crooker, also of the 55th Illinois, had been hit in the legs and collapsed beneath a large elm tree where he encountered orderly sergeant Parker B. Bagley, who inquired, "Crooker, are you hurt, too?" Crooker asked for water and then, because their position seemed to attract many Rebel bullets, they began to crawl away. But Crooker collapsed again. Bagley took him by the arm and slung him over his shoulder when, Crooker said, "a burning sensation passed along my back, and we both fell together." The bullet had hit him "crosswise, under the shoulder and passed on, killing poor Bagley. Lying beneath him I could feel his hot blood run down my side, and hear . . . his dying groan."

With its superior numbers, Chalmers's left flank began to wrap around the Federal right, and Stuart ordered a withdrawal across yet another ravine just behind them, to what he thought was a more defensible position. This was accomplished, but not without horrible bloodshed for, as Captain Crooker explained, "Almost instantly the ground [we had] left was occupied by swarms of exultant and yelling rebels, who now, without danger to themselves, poured a shower of bullets down upon and among the fugitives." A Major Whitfield of the Ninth Mississippi said (after the war), "We were right on top of you. It was like shooting into a flock of sheep."

Not only that, but a battery from Jackson's brigade added to the carnage, firing canister and grapeshot point blank at the helpless Yankees, who were trying to scramble up the steep sides of the ravine. One Confederate compared it with shooting "fish in a barrel." About 200 of Stuart's men were killed or wounded while fleeing across the ravine, but the remaining 400—who had set up on a rise at the opposite lip of the ravine—gave an excellent account of themselves for yet another hour, bringing the Confederate assault on the far left to a standstill, but not without a price.

"Only the excitement of battle could sustain a man in the midst of such carnage," wrote Lt. Elijah Lawrence. "As man after man was shot down or mutilated, a feeling of perfect horror came over me at times, and I berated the powers that placed us in such a position and left us alone to our fate. Can it be wondered at when forty-three out of sixty-four of my own company were killed or wounded in that short time?"

The bloodshed continued unabated until near 3 p.m. when Stuart's men were down to their last bullets and the Confederates had worked their way to within 20 feet of Stuart's line. Right about that time the Federal gunboat *Tyler* came alive and began diabolically lobbing its huge nine-inch shells into Chalmers's positions. Nobody was hurt, but the shock of the explosions gave time for the remnants of Stuart's brigade to escape through the woods toward Pittsburg Landing, which was the only place they had to go. They had held the line against a combined Confederate force five times their number and, by many accounts, saved the Union's left flank.

For his part, when the shells from the gunboats began to land amid his positions, Chalmers "pressed rapidly" out of the area, and toward the Union center, "where the battle seemed to be raging fiercely." That may have sounded good in his after action report, but why didn't he pursue Stuart's people right to Pittsburg Landing? Chalmers doesn't tell us, nor does anyone else. It may have had to do with exposure to the gunboat firing, or because tactical policy in Johnston's army always dictated marching "to the sound of the guns." But one thing for sure was that even as late as 3 p.m. the way to Grant's supply base and main line of communication had been wide and clear.

Even less clear is what General Jackson and his brigade had contributed to the enterprise. For much of the time Jackson seemed inert. At the beginning Jackson put himself "in support" of Chalmers, but when the fighting was the heaviest, and the weight of his 2,200 men could have changed the balance, he was not in it. Initially, Jackson was ordered by Johnston, who had ridden over for a look-see, to charge the camps of the 55th Illinois in the orchard.* But the camps proved to be very nearly deserted. After that, Jackson faced a force commanded by the Yankee general John McArthur, whose brigade wore Scottish tams and marched to bagpipe music. But most of the time when Chalmers was having his fight against Stuart, Jackson's brigade did not seem to do more than exchange fire. Late in the battle, when Chalmers was hard pressed, he rode back to Jackson's position and got two regiments as reinforcements, and though they helped turn the tide it was becoming very late in the day.

In short, what was later estimated to be no more than 600 Yankees and no artillery held off two Rebel brigades of 3,600 men and two artillery batteries of six guns each. It was one of the oddest, and most unequal, fights of the day, and if the men of Stuart's brigade had not made their stand the landing might have fallen into Confederate hands. In other words, a checkmate.

After Stuart's retreat Jackson, like Chalmers, marched his brigade left toward the Union center, to the rising *pop-pop-pop* and *boom* of the guns, where both ran straight into the 19th century's version of a buzz saw. Later it would become known as the Hornet's Nest.

---

* Johnston had mistakenly called it the 59th Illinois.

CHAPTER 12

IT WAS ALL A GLITTERING LIE

B Y LATE MORNING THE REBEL ARMY HAD PRESSED the Federals northward all across the wide mouth of the cornucopia for nearly a mile toward its narrowing base. From Sherman's positions near Owl Creek in the west to Stuart's ravine along the Tennessee River the Federals were giving way.

By noon the line of battle had assumed the shape of a boomerang, in which the remnants of Prentiss's division—now barely a regiment—bulged out in the center, with Hurlbut's brigades slanting away slightly to the Union left and W.H.L. Wallace's slanting away slightly right. It finally began to look as if the conflict was sorting itself out from the earlier chaos and confusion. But this was not so.

The difficulty was that the topography rendered Pittsburg Landing as inefficient a place imaginable to launch an offensive attack and nearly impossible for a commander to keep under control. What had been intended by Beauregard and Johnston as an orderly battle had devolved into a series of individual fights, mostly between brigades, of which there were 33 total for both sides at the height of the Shiloh fight on Sunday. It would seem then that Grant's ground had been chosen well, but this was not so either, even if it was better suited for defense than attack. In short, generalship on both sides was problematic; it had become mostly a fight between colonels commanding regiments.

Ever since he arrived on the battlefield, Grant had been seeing to his various division commanders. He'd told Prentiss in the late morning that he must hold his ground in the Union center "at all extremities." Prentiss then formed an obstinate defense about half a mile in length, with the remnants of his division, along with Hurlbut and W.H.L Wallace—about 5,700 men at the peak, all that remained of their once powerful divisions—in a wooded thicket along an old wagon rut, which came to be known as the Sunken Road. It was a strong, protected position, defended by six batteries containing 25 guns. Here was the so-called Hornet's Nest, a place of dark horrors where the most awful slaughter of the Battle of Shiloh took place.

Private Henry Morton Stanley, who had been in the vanguard of Shaver's Confederate brigade when it overran the camps of Prentiss' division about 9 a.m., had been briefly under the impression that the Battle of Shiloh "was well nigh over." But he had barely found time to start ransacking Yankee loot from the big white tents of Peabody's routed regiment when he discovered that the fight he'd just been in "was only the brief prologue of the long and exhaustive struggles which took place that day."

Line officers began forming up the men for a further advance, and soon Stanley reported, "We came in view of the tops of another mass of white tents and, at almost the same time, we were met with a furious storm of bullets, poured on us from a long line of blue coats, whose attitude of assurance proved that we should have tough work here. After a few seconds we heard the order 'Lie down men and continue your firing.' "

Stanley found a large fallen tree to hide behind, where "the shells plunged and bounded and flew with screeching hisses over us," he wrote many years later in his autobiography. Spellbound by the tumult around him, Stanley fancied that the cannonading was like "the roaring of a great herd of lions," the rifle fire like "the yapping of terriers," the whisk of shells like "the swoop of eagles," and the zipping of bullets like "the buzz of angry wasps."

He wrote, "I marveled, as I heard the unremitting patter, snip, thud, and hum of bullets, how anyone could live under this raining death. I could hear the bullets beating a merciless tattoo on the outer surface of the log, pinging viciously as they flew off at a tangent to it, and thudding into something or other at the rate of a hundred a second. One here, one there found its way under the log and buried itself in a comrade's body.

"One man," Stanley said, "raised his chest as if to yawn and jostled me. I turned to him and saw that a bullet had gored his whole face and penetrated into his chest. Another ball struck a man a deadly rap on the head, and he turned on his back and showed his ghastly white face to the sky." Another cursed the enemy and "raised his head a little too high, when a bullet skimmed over the top of the log and hit him fairly in the center of his forehead and he fell on his face."

Stanley and the rest of Shaver's brigade were undergoing one of the most vexing of infantry predicaments—a large body of men exposed and pinned down by enemy fire, with casualties mounting. To remain there was suicide, to retreat unthinkable. There was but one choice and the difficulty of executing it was testimony to the valor necessary among the officers and noncommissioned officers of that day and time. Slowly, agonizingly, with jaws clenched and muscles tensed, the officers rose up from their hiding places and stood to the front. "Forward, forward!" they cried. "Charge!"

"Just as we bent our bodies for the onset," Stanley said, "a boy's voice cried out, 'Oh stop, please, I've been hurt.'" It was Stanley's squad mate and friend, the 17-year-old Henry Parker, who had picked the violets for their caps, "standing on one leg, and dolefully regarding his smashed foot on the other." Stanley looked at him and turned away. "In another second we were striding impetuously toward the enemy," Stanley said, loading and firing as they went.

A Rebel battery galloped up, halted in a cloud of dust, and opened fire on the blue line with canister and shell, resulting in a slackening of Yankee fire. Big Newton Story, the flag bearer marching forward with the colors, had advanced so fast he found himself 60 yards ahead of the Dixie Grays. He stopped and looked back with a smile, shouting, "Why don't you come on, boys?" Their response was the Rebel yell, "taken up by the thousands," according to Stanley, "and the advance then moved forward at quick-time."

The line of bluecoats seemed "scornfully unconcerned," at first, Stanley said, but as they took in the "leaping tide coming at a tremendous pace, their front dissolved and they fled in double-quick retreat." As the Rebel attack rushed through the second camp of white tents, Stanley became physically exhausted; they'd been fighting for five hours, and as he paused a bullet struck him in the stomach and he tumbled to the ground.

These white tent camps represented the far left of General McClernand's line—four Illinois regiments under Col. Julius Raith, who found that command of the brigade had devolved upon him by default after two senior colonels were either absent or ill. A prosperous Illinois flour mill owner and Mexican War veteran, Raith was a popular officer among his fellow Illinoisans, but he found that his sudden authority did not command the requisite respect necessary to conduct matters in the present emergency. First of all, when he sent orders for his regiments to fall in for battle that morning, he was scoffed at, much as Sherman scoffed to the worrywarts in his lines and insisted that the shooting in front was only picket firing. When the command was at last organized it was positioned too late and too far back to prevent the flanking and shameful rout of Hildebrand's brigade over in Sherman's division, which had resulted in the dismal odyssey of Lieutenant Dawes and his little band of fugitives from the 53rd Ohio after their colonel had deserted them.

Things did not go perfectly for the Confederates either as the morning progressed. In the Federal center and right the forest was more tangled with thick scrub underbrush. As the melee raged on, no breeze blew, and the gun smoke pancaked upon the battlefield like a London fog, making control of troops more a matter of instinct than anything else. Rebel units marching at various angles to get to "the sound of the heaviest fighting" wound up firing into each other with devastating effect, causing regiments and entire brigades to halt, and even withdraw, until the situation clarified itself.

For example, in the brigade of the Rebel general Sterling A. M. (SAM) Wood, which was advancing just west of Shaver, two regiments, one Alabama, the other Tennessee, were in the process of charging and routing a Federal battery and capturing its six guns when a line of Confederates—possibly from A. P. Stewart's brigade—appeared in their rear, "and as they reached the crest of a hill the men (as their officers said) without orders, fired into us, killing at first fire 5 in Major Kelly's battalion, a lieutenant in the Eighth Arkansas, and wounding many others," according to the official report of General Wood.

When the alarmed and outraged Wood galloped toward them shouting cease fire, "another volley from this entire line was hurled on us." Wood's horse was shot, panicked, and threw him, but Wood's foot caught in the stirrup and he was dragged at length through the Federal encampment of General McClernand with serious injuries that kept him out of the fight for much of the afternoon. This was but one of the foul-ups of the Confederate attack as it advanced relentlessly northward, in bloody fits and starts.

Ben Cheatham's division encountered the Hornet's Nest as it was beginning to form about 10 a.m. He had been ordered by Beauregard to "ascertain the point where the firing was heaviest and there engage the enemy at once." Marching east, from the far left of the Rebel line, Cheatham came to an open cotton field on the other side of which he "discovered the enemy in strong force behind a fence and an abandoned road." For an hour Cheatham's artillery tried without success to silence a Yankee artillery battery that covered their approach; then Colonel Jordan (of Beauregard's staff and the author of the attack plan) appeared on behalf of Beauregard and ordered Cheatham to charge the battery.

Cheatham put his Second Brigade in motion across the field, 300 yards wide, whereupon "the enemy open upon us from his entire front a terrible fire of artillery and musketry." The brigade continued through this maelstrom until the men reached the center of the field and "another part of the enemy's force, concealed and protected by the fence and thicket to our left, opened a murderous cross-fire on our lines, which caused my command to halt, and return their fire. After a short time, I fell back to our original position," Cheatham said. He had lost many of his best officers in the charge, including, apparently, a young boy, John Campbell, whom Cheatham described as being part of "my military family." While acting as aide-de-camp that day, "he fell dead, his entire head having been carried away by a cannonball." Cheatham stated later in his official report of the battle that "He was a noble boy, and showed the qualities of a brilliant and useful soldier." So ended the first Rebel encounter with the Yankee's Hornet's Nest.

Braxton Bragg, who was serving as Johnston's chief of staff, and a corps commander as well, was in his usual black mood that day, disapproving of the undisciplined troops, the unschooled officers, the organization—or disorganization—of the army in general and of the broken and cut-up ground of the battlefield and of his own corps in particular. He was therefore pleasantly surprised when right after first light, "Within less than a mile the enemy was encountered at the encampments of his advanced positions, but our first line brushed him away, leaving the rear nothing to do but press on in pursuit."

These early good tidings did not last, however, for soon General Hindman's division of Bragg's corps also encountered, as Bragg said, "the most obstinate resistance of the day, the enemy being strongly posted, with infantry and artillery, on an eminence immediately behind a dense thicket. Hindman's command was gallantly led to the attack, but recoiled under a murderous fire," Bragg wrote. "The valiant leader fell, severely wounded, and was borne from the field he had illustrated with a heroism rarely equaled." This was, of course, from Bragg's official report made some weeks after the battle, but it concisely sums up that quandary of homicidal dismay they named the Hornet's Nest.

With General Hindman out of the battle, by Bragg's orders it fell on Shaver's brigade of his division to attack and dislodge the Federals "posted in considerable force in the dense undergrowth and heavy woods," where, like Cheatham, General Shaver said the enemy had placed a battery "the presence of which was so completely concealed I was not aware of it until it opened."* Shaver marched as Bragg told him, "until my left was in about 50 and my right about 60 yards from their lines when a terrific and murderous fire was poured in on me from their lines and battery. It was impossible to charge through the dense undergrowth," Shaver said, "and I soon discovered my fire was having no effect upon the enemy, so I had nothing left me but to retire or have my men all shot down."

Providentially, Pvt. Henry Morton Stanley, of Shaver's command, had not been dispatched by the bullet to his stomach earlier. Instead, it was mostly spent and had struck his belt buckle, denting it, merely knocking the wind from him. But by the time he

---

* In battle, one of the greatest dreads on both sides was to march into range of hidden, or "masked," batteries. At close range the damage they could do firing canister rounds was horrendous.

recovered, his brigade had marched on out of sight, and it was left for Stanley to overtake it, which led him on his own chilling odyssey down the butcher's path. When he recovered from the shock of being struck by the spent bullet, Stanley had remained on the ground for a period of time, exhausted; then he crawled to a tree and ate ravenously from his haversack for the first time since dawn. Now, with the sun high in the sky, he "struck north in the direction which my regiment had taken, over ground strewn with the bodies and the debris of war.

"The ghastly relics," Stanley said, "appalled every sense." Somehow he felt curious to see who among his comrades had fallen and quickly came upon the body of "a stout English sergeant of a neighboring company . . . conspicuous for his good humor, and nicknamed John Bull." Next to him was a young lieutenant who "judging by the gloss on his uniform must have been some father's darling. A clean bullet hole in the center of his forehead had ended his career."

Soon Stanley came upon about 20 bodies, "lying in various postures, each by its own pool of viscous blood, which emitted a peculiar scent, which was new to me then. Beyond these, a still larger group lay, body overlying body. The company opposed to them must have shot straight." He lumbered on, shuddering at the sight of "those wide open dead eyes," ruminating much later that this "was the first Field of Glory I had ever seen . . . and the first time Glory sickened me with its repulsive aspect, and made me suspect it was all a glittering lie."

Trudging on through the woods toward the racket of gunfire where his brigade was fighting, Stanley "moved, horror-stricken, through the fearful shambles where the dead lay as thick as sleepers in a London Park on a bank holiday." He noticed from the piles of dead bodies that "every half mile or so [the Yankees] stood and contested the Confederate advance. I overtook my regiment about one o'clock," he said, "and found that it was engaged in one of these occasional spurts of fury."

Stanley's arrival coincided with Shaver's repulse at the Hornet's Nest. Shaver reported to Bragg his "inability to dislodge the enemy, and that his command was very much cut up," including the death of the colonel of the Seventh Arkansas. He was told to stay put and await orders. "We lay down and availed ourselves of trees, logs, and hollows, and annoyed [the Federals'] upstanding ranks," Stanley said, "battery pounded battery, and meanwhile, we hugged our resting places closely." The Hornet's Nest remained dark, dangerous, and thus far insurmountable.

———————————

Cheatham's and Shaver's Rebel brigades had run up against Col. James Tuttle's First Brigade of Gen. W.H.L. Wallace's division, consisting of the 2nd, 7th, 12th, and 14th Iowa regiments, holding tenuously to the Federal right flank of the Hornet's Nest. They were ensconced along the abandoned wagon track known as the Sunken Road, described thusly by a man who was there: "The old road ran along a slight elevation and was so water washed in places as to afford good shelter to men lying down to fire on an advancing enemy—a sort of natural rifle-pit, though rather thin in places. There was an open [cotton] field extending to the front about 500 yards to the timber occupied by the Confederates."

Next Bragg ordered Colonel Gibson and his Louisiana brigade to try the Yankee bottleneck. Gibson was a tall, sober-looking, 29-year-old New Orleans lawyer and aristocrat—scion of a prosperous sugar planter—with intense blue eyes and a handlebar mustache, who had graduated from Yale where he was a member of Scroll and Key, one of the secret societies on campus second only in prestige to the fabled Skull and Bones.

No sooner had Gibson appeared with his brigade in Barnes Field than he found himself in Bragg's doghouse for seeming to be insufficiently aggressive. In his defense (he later called for a court of inquiry in the matter) Gibson testified that he had been ordered by one of Bragg's own staff officers "to move more slowly and keep at a greater distance from the front line." For his part, Bragg claimed Gibson had been holding back. "I had not been able to force [Gibson] into battle up to twelve o'clock."

Gibson formed his brigade in a line of battle two ranks deep and prepared to send his soldiers across the cotton field, but before this could happen, in the misty haze of the battlefield, a section of Cheatham's men fired into the rear of Gibson's far left regiment, the Fourth Louisiana, composed mostly of new troops and commanded by Col. Henry W. Allen, killing and wounding at least 27 men. "This was a terrible blow to the regiment," Allen said, "far more terrible than any inflicted by the enemy. It almost demoralized the regiment, who from that moment seemed to dread their friends much more than their enemies." The enraged Louisianans—most of whom were French Creoles who spoke little or no English—were on the verge of firing back at their tormentors when, of all things, a woman wearing a long dress and sunbonnet appeared before them, deliberately crossing the field between the battle lines as if on a vital mission, and the firing died down on both sides for a few moments. Quite possibly this was the distraught woman, alluded to by Elsie Duncan, who was fearful of her sons' safety on the battlefield.

Like Cheatham and Shaver before him, when Gibson marched his brigade across the field and got within 40 or 50 yards of the thicket where the Yankees lay, he was suddenly greeted with the same lethal sheet of flame and smoke from a dense line of hidden riflemen, and "a murderous fire of grape and canister from the masked batteries and rifle pits." Two of his regiments actually managed to enter the thicket only to be caught up in a nearly impenetrable tangle of blackjack oak. They undertook to push the thick leafy trees and branches aside with their gun butts and barrels, and even their hands, but sight was lost except for a few feet and control quickly became impossible.

At one point a frantic message was sent from the colonel of Gibson's First Arkansas to Allen's Fourth Louisiana, saying, "For God's sake cease firing," that "we were killing his men and he was killing ours."

Col. B. L. Hodge commanding the 19th Louisiana stated afterward that, even while his men were being shot down all around him, he could see none of the enemy in the thick brush, and "from the manner of the men looking through the bushes, as if hunting an object for their aim, it was apparent that they were unable to descry the concealed foe, and were only firing at the flash of the enemy's pieces." It was maddening.

The dense canopy of trees kept the wind from blowing the smoke away, and the noxious powder burned the men's eyes and noses, causing their eyes to water uncontrollably. They kept firing and reloading, firing and reloading, into the thick smoke until their gun barrels became too hot to handle. At one point "a horse galloped through the woods nearby, its belly ripped open and intestines trailing; it became entangled in its own guts and fell to the ground."

Hodge's predicament quickly became desperate for, as he said later, "my men were rapidly being shot down, and I [had] no reason to believe we were inflicting equal injury on the enemy." Therefore, Hodge "gave the order to cease firing and charge bayonets." This proved even more futile since after his men had plunged 20 or 30 steps into the scrub oak jungle they could still see no enemy other than the flashes of rifle fire that were fast depleting the regiment. At some point a brush fire had started in the dead leaves on the ground and suddenly began sweeping through the woods where many of the wounded and dead lay, burning men alive. Hodge ordered his men to commence shooting again, but also to withdraw across the field to their original positions.

As Colonel Gibson re-formed his brigade he sent an urgent message to Bragg requesting an artillery battery to silence the Union guns that were causing them so much grief. The messenger returned to say not only that the request was denied but that Bragg had ordered them to charge the Hornet's Nest *again,* immediately. In fact, Bragg even sent one of his staff along to see that it was done correctly.

When this staff officer encountered Colonel Hodge, he was told "to say to the General that I thought it impossible to force the enemy from this strong position by a charge to the front," adding, helpfully, that an artillery battery "playing on [the enemy] flank, simultaneous with a charge [on the flank], would easily carry the position."

No dice. They charged again as ordered, headlong, and again were driven back with great loss of life and limb. Colonel Allen, of the Fourth Louisiana, who was shot through both cheeks, would later say, "The brigade was sacrificed by three separate charges, and without the aid of any artillery whatever, although we had it at hand ready to open on the enemy." The major commanding the 13th Louisiana had been killed, and the captain succeeding him wounded, and the air filled with Gallic cries and curses as an artillery projectile went clear through each member of a six-man squad, spraying blood and bits of brains and other organs on nearby troops. Hodge's charge was repulsed.

But Bragg wasn't through. Apparently he intended to teach Gibson and his brigade some sort of lesson in martial fortitude. Furious at the sight of Colonel Allen's Fourth Louisiana streaming back in retreat across the Davis Wheat Field, Bragg ordered his engineer officer Captain Lockett (who earlier had mistakenly identified Stuart's lone brigade as an entire Yankee division) to ride out to the Fourth Louisiana and "take its colors and carry them forward."

"The flag must not go back again," Bragg said.

Lockett "dashed through the line of battle, seized the colors from the color bearer, and told him, 'General Bragg says these colors must not go to the rear.'" As he spoke these words, the color bearer was shot down in front of him, leaving Lockett alone on his horse in the middle of the battlefield, holding the regimental colors of the Fourth Louisiana.

A few moments later, Lockett said, "An officer came up to me," with a bullet hole in each cheek, blood streaming from his mouth, and asked, "What are you doing with my colors, Sir?"

"I am obeying General Bragg's orders to hold them where they are," Lockett replied.

"Let me have them," demanded the officer, "if any man but my color-bearer carries these colors, I am the man. Tell General Bragg I will see that these colors are in the right place. But he must attack this position in flank; we can never carry it alone from the front."

The officer "was Colonel H. W. Allen, later governor of Louisiana," Lockett later wrote, then dashed off to deliver another message, while brave, shot-up Henry Allen stood out in front of his lines with bullets whistling around him, holding the colors of the regiment he commanded and defiantly facing the enemy.

Then, in an act of total misunderstanding or breathtaking condescension, Braxton Bragg himself came up to Allen right before he launched the final charge and said, "There will be no faltering now, Colonel Allen." Rightfully incensed at this utterly thoughtless remark, Allen, a 42-year-old widower, native Virginian, and Harvard Law graduate—transplanted to Louisiana and owner of one of that state's largest sugar plantations—simply sneered at the corps commander and, with blood still streaming from his cheeks, lifted his sword, shouting, "Forward! Here boys, is as good a place as any to die!"

As they reached the place where the last charge had failed, a Louisiana private named Richardson remembered, "I looked to my left and saw Colonel H. W. Allen with elevated sword, urging his men to stand firm. His chin was bleeding from a wound. There too was my schoolmate, Captain Hilliard, commanding his men to rally when he fell dead."

The regiment stood to the fight for nearly half an hour, firing into the smoke, the men continuing to fall with horrifying regularity. Gibson had his second horse of the day shot from under him. Ultimately this charge also failed.

Col. James F. Fagan of the First Arkansas summed up the experience this way: "Three different times did we go into that valley of death, and as often were forced back by overwhelming numbers entrenched in a strong position." No matter how well Braxton

Bragg trained his men he was an awful battlefield commander. The Yankees simply could not be dislodged the way Bragg was doing it, sending his forces in piecemeal, one regiment at a time.

What is telling here, however, is that although the fighting at Shiloh was confused it was not always chaotic. Officers would lead their units into battle, most of them conspicuously on horse-back, making themselves easy targets. The men would advance until encountering such heavy fire that prudence dictated it was no longer wise to go forward; instead, they halted and returned fire. If the return fire silenced or sharply subdued the enemy, they continued the advance. If not, they would usually stand and fight, shooting at the enemy until it became apparent that nothing was being accomplished, and then they would usually retire, often on the order of their officers.

There were of course times when the men would simply retire on their own. Anyone who has been under fire understands that unless the feelings of helplessness and hopelessness can be over-come, and a fair chance to conquer the enemy is apparent, discre-tion becomes the better part of valor or, put in the vernacular of the day, "endurance was no longer a virtue." The role of the officers is paramount here; the men look to them for courage and a sense of security in the belief that their officers are trying their utmost to get them through safely. If the men do not sense this they will not give their best effort

There were units, however, frequently untried or poorly trained, which would not stand up to fire, usually owing to the presence of soldiers or officers who were constitutionally unfit for battle. Experienced combat soldiers know that fortitude is tied directly to their comrades in arms, and that what compels them to persist in an otherwise perfectly insane act is a combined feeling of allegiance to, and fear of humiliation by, their fellow soldiers.

Of the approximately 2,300 men in Gibson's brigade who went into action at Shiloh, 682 were killed, wounded, or missing—among the highest Confederate casualty ratios in the battle. But that did not satisfy Bragg, who in his disgust, humiliated the brigade by ordering it to retire behind the line, out of the fight, and in his official report he publicly charged that the failure of Gibson's brigade to take the Hornet's Nest was due to "want of proper handling"; privately, he condemned Gibson as "an arrant coward." Such was the thanks to Randall Lee Gibson and his First Brigade, Ruggles's division, Bragg's corps, for their part in the ordeal of April 6, 1862, the first day of the Battle of Shiloh.

CHAPTER 13

I WILL LEAD YOU

M EANWHILE, NO FEWER THAN TEN CONFEDERATE brigades were then closing on the Hornet's Nest; not only had the bishop general Polk come into the fight with his corps, but most of Breckinridge's reserve corps had also been committed to the battle by Beauregard and Johnston. Bragg—as irate as ever because of the inevitable tangling up of the different corps lines—worked it out with Polk that he would take the right side of the battle line if Polk would take the center, leaving the left to Hardee. Considering earlier casualties, straggling, and other losses, they were together probably 15,000 to 18,000 strong.

One of these brigades belonged to Col. Winfield S. Statham from Breckinridge's reserve corps, who was about to attack the Federal center-left in a sector just to the east of the outermost point of the Hornet's Nest salient. It was defended by the Yankee colonel Isaac Pugh commanding—after the wounding of the previous commander—Hurlbut's First Brigade, which consisted of three Illinois regiments and one regiment of Iowans. As Statham's people moved up, they marched over areas where the battle had swept through a short while earlier, and a private in the 15th Mississippi took in the appalling scenery. "Here and there we saw the bodies of dead men—friends and foes lying together—some torn to mincemeat by cannonballs. Some still writhing in the agonies of death," recorded private Augustus Harvey Mecklin. "The cannon seem to be carrying on this contest wholly among themselves. Though at some distance from us. Some of the balls reached us and while we were halted one struck a tree nearly a foot through & splitting it asunder tore a poor fellow who was behind it into a thousand pieces."

Statham's brigade marched to Spain Field where they were told to rest. "It was very warm," Mecklin wrote. "The sky was clear but for the horrible monster death . . . on all sides lay the dead and dying. Before us were the rifle pits dug by the Yankees, behind them lay the camp. While resting here, Gen. Beauregard, as I suppose, came charging by [actually it was General Johnston and his staff, banners flying]. Our men greeted him with a deafening cheer. We were not allowed to rest long," Mecklin said.

Like so many Mississippians of the era, Augustus Mecklin's parents had migrated from the Atlantic states during the 1840s—in his case, South Carolina—in hopes of cashing in on the cotton boom. Mecklin instead felt a calling to the Lord, and after college in Tennessee he entered the Theological Seminary at Columbia, South Carolina, studying for the Presbyterian ministry. But when war broke out he immediately returned home to Choctaw County and enlisted in the 15th Mississippi—at the age of 28, older than most of his messmates, and better educated as well.

Colonel Statham formed up his brigade to charge the Yankee position, much of which lay in the Peach Orchard of the widow Bell where the bullets clipped the blossoms, which floated down like pink snowflakes. And here is where something went very wrong that led to tragedy, if it can be called that, on a day when tragedy reigned supreme.

They had no sooner marched over the brow of a hill when "We were saluted by a violent volley from the enemy," Mecklin wrote. "For the first time in my life I head the whistle of bullets." Unbeknownst to Mecklin, apparently because he was farther back in the ranks, this "violent volley"—delivered by a thousand-plus muskets of Colonel Pugh's 41st and 32nd Illinois—blew the head off of Statham's column and sent it reeling back in confusion.

Mecklin's company had taken cover in the former camp of the 71st Ohio, from which that regiment had made its disgraceful bugout from Stuart's brigade when the first shots were fired, and from there Mecklin's people engaged in a shooting contest with the Illinoisans and Iowans of Hurlbut's division.

"We took shelter behind the tents and some wagons & a pile of corn & returned the fire of the enemy with spirit," Mecklin said. "Soon men were falling on all sides. Two in Co. E just in front of me fell dead shot through the brain. I fired until my gun got so foul that I could not get my ball down," Mecklin told his diary. He got a man nearby to throw him a gun from a wounded soldier and fired until it, too, became hopelessly fouled with powder.

Others however, found this kind of fighting unpalatable and began drifting off individually or in units down the slope and out of close range. Among these was the 45th Tennessee, which had sulkily retreated behind a fence along the Hamburg-Purdy road near the bottom of the hill. "Squads of men would leave the ranks, run up to the fence, fire, and fall back into place; but the regiment would not advance," said an aide to General Breckinridge. Statham was mortified and did his utmost, talked himself blue in the face, in fact, but the 45th Tennesseans declined to fall in and steadfastly refused to go back up the slope.

This was not an uncommon thing in 19th-century armies. All soldiers are understandably apprehensive when told to form a line and march into certain gunfire, knowing there would be a considerable number of dead and wounded. It was when many, if not most, of the soldiers refused to make the charge that trouble came. Most of the time they responded to pleas and speeches by their officers or higher-up officers. Rarely would a regiment flat out refuse to make a charge, for they would then be sent to the rear in disgrace and become the butt of jokes, antipathy, and condescension by the other regiments in the division.

In any case, "General Breckinridge, foiled and irritated, rode to General Johnston and complained he had a Tennessee regiment that would not fight," wrote former Union brigadier Manning Force in his history of the battle. Tennesseans who would not fight—it was almost unimaginable.

Watching from a knoll in the distance, Sidney Johnston had seen Statham's column waver, then bend, and of the Union soldiers he remarked to the Tennessee governor Isham Harris—in exile since Buell took Nashville and serving as an aide to Johnston— "Those fellows are making a stubborn stand here; I'll have to put the bayonet to them."

John Breckinridge had fully taken charge of this far right of the Rebel line. He was described by one officer as "the finest-looking man on the field that day, in his shiny jacket of new Kentucky jeans." Indeed the 41-year-old Princeton graduate and former U.S. Vice President was a daunting figure—tall in the saddle, with a prominent aquiline nose set between piercing blue eyes and a drooping handlebar mustache. Alone among the senior commanders in having no formal military training, Breckinridge was anxious to prove himself and chafed much of the morning as the battle raged in his front and no call came for his brigades.

Now his hour had arrived. He had seen Statham's line waver and fall back. He had set Gen. John Bowen's brigade in motion. But here was the rub, as it had rubbed all day. To get at the enemy, Statham's men would have to cross an exposed ridge, descend one slope, and ascend another into the Peach Orchard—probably 100 yards—all the while "raked by this deadly ambuscade." Although, as Private Mecklin has testified, the brigade was "delivering and receiving fire" that Governor Harris called "the heaviest as any I saw in the war," they could not, Preston Johnston wrote, "drive the enemy from his stronghold by fire, nor without a charge that meant death for many." Breckinridge's adjutant, Colonel Hodge summed it up: "The crisis of the contest had come; there were no more reserves, and General Breckinridge determined to charge."

It was near 2 p.m. and General Johnston was confident at last that he had organized a combined force that would drive the Yankees from the Hornet's Nest. They had been fighting there for four hours straight, during which time the Federal right had been broken and Sherman's and McClernand's men pushed nearly into the swamps, while on the Federal left Stuart was making his last stand and was about to be routed.

"Only the center had not been moved," declared Preston Johnston.

At last a concerted effort was being made. Four Confederate brigades—those of Stephens, Statham, Bowen, and Jackson—were in line of battle, preparing to push the enemy into the swamps or the river to complete the victory. Instead of Bragg's piecemeal stabs at the Hornet's Nest, there would now be one grand assault: Johnston had placed the brigades in line himself—on the Rebel right, where there was good fighting ground, away from the left and the dreadful Sunken Road.

A while earlier, talking with his aide Maj. Edward Munford, Johnston expressed confidence that he was closing the ring. "We sat on our horses, side by side, watching [Chalmers's] brigade as it swept over a ridge," Munford said, "and, as the colors dipped out of sight, the general said to me, 'That checkmates them . . .' He laughed and said, 'yes, sir, that mates them.'"

And then came Breckinridge to report he had Tennesseans who would not fight. As Sidney Johnston sat astride his horse watching the progress of the battle in the distance, he was anything but pleased by news that his army contained a regiment of cowards. Cowardice was contagious and could not be tolerated. Before Johnston responded, however, Governor Harris became animated and spoke up, "General Breckinridge, show *me* that regiment." Breckinridge nodded apologetically toward the commanding general, but it was Johnston's call; he said, "Let the governor go to them."

Harris rode off toward the front and "with some difficulty put the regiment in line of battle on the hill," wrote Preston Johnston, but "after some delay the wavering of the line [was] still increasing."

Johnston had no sooner ordered all brigades to prepare for the charge when General Breckinridge reappeared, "in a highly emotional state," saying he "feared he could not get his brigade to make the charge." A regiment was bad enough, but now an entire brigade.

"Then I will help you," Johnston said, and the two of them rode to the front, soon joined again by Harris. Johnston rode down the line, speaking reassurances in his commanding voice. As he had feared, the cowardice of the 45th Tennessee had infected Statham's other regiments; he sent Breckinridge to speak to one section, accompanied by Breckinridge's 17-year-old son, whose "beautiful composure and serene fidelity" was remarked on by many eyewitnesses. Down the other way—where the 45th Tennessee was posted—Johnston sent Governor Harris, who "galloped to the right, and after a sharp harangue, dismounted and led them on foot, pistol in hand, up to their alignment, and [was] in the charge when it was made."

Johnston, meantime, rode along past the reluctant ranks, extending his little looted tin cup that he held in his hand and clinking it on the upright bayonets of the men in line, saying to them, "These must do the work! Men, they are stubborn; we must use the bayonet!" When he reached the center, he turned and faced them on his big thoroughbred bay and cried, "I will lead you!"

His son and biographer Preston Johnston spoke to, or corresponded with, many eyewitnesses to the scene and reported that Johnston's "voice was persuasive, encouraging and compelling (it was also inviting men to death—but they obeyed it). But most of all it was the light in his gray eye, and his splendid presence that wrought them."

Statham's men responded with a mighty Rebel yell, and then marched out toward the Hornet's Nest. Certainly there was no more star-studded brigade charge in the history of the Civil War—leading in the center Albert Sidney Johnston, the highest ranking field officer in the Confederate army; leading on the left the former Vice President of the United States John Cabell Breckinridge, and on the right the Confederate governor of Tennessee, Isham Harris, pistol in hand. As Preston Johnston told it: "A sheet of flame burst from the Federal stronghold, and blazed along the crest of the ridge. The line moved forward at a charge with rapid and restless step. There was a roar of cannon and musketry; a storm of lead and iron hail. The Confederate line withered, and the dead and dying strewed the dark valley. But there was not an instant's pause. Right up the steep they went. The crest was gained."

The Peach Orchard lay before them, now almost stripped of blossoms, and they went in at the double-quick, driving the Federal forces with the bayonet. Augustus Mecklin and his 15th Mississippi were among them. "Many of our boys fell in this fatal charge," he said. "Never was there such firing."

Among those who fell in the charge was Joel Allen Battle, Jr., a recent graduate of Miami College of Ohio and now adjutant of the 20th Tennessee, which was commanded by his father, a wealthy Nashville planter. All day the younger Battle had galloped the field carrying messages and orders, collecting stragglers, and urging men forward. His arm was in a sling from a wound received in the earlier Battle of Mill Springs, or Fishing Creek, in which General Zollicoffer was killed. It was a sad day for the Battle family. Not only was Joel Allen killed but his younger brother was also, and the elder Colonel Battle was captured. The 20th Tennessee, however, was one of the regiments in Statham's brigade that stood its ground and did not have to be led to the fight by General Johnston. That fact was recorded many years later by then Gen. G. P. Thruston, whose First Ohio had been opposite his old college friend's regiment during the fray.

———◆———

One of those lucky enough to elude the Confederate dragnet was 16-year-old Yankee John A. Cockerill, who shouldn't have been there at all. Cockerill had enlisted a few months earlier as a musician fourth class in the 24th Ohio Volunteer Regiment of Buell's army—and he was carefully placed in a company where his brother was a lieutenant and could look after him. But on the morning of April 6, 1862, John Cockerill found himself temporarily assigned to the 70th Ohio of Sherman's division, in a regiment that was commanded by his own father, Joseph Cockerill. The transfer had been due to young Cockerill's illness, but on that Sunday morning he had recuperated and was feeling fine and sitting down at the mess table for breakfast "when I heard ominous shots along our picket lines." Everybody at the table scattered, Cockerill remembered, and "at the first alarm I dropped my knife and fork and ran to my father's tent, to find him buckling on his sword."

There, he retrieved his "beautiful Enfield rifle with its beautiful curly maple stock," which his father had gotten for him, and loaded his cartridge box with ammo. By the time he had finished, "my father was mounted outside and the bullets were whistling through the camp and shell were bursting overhead."

Uncertain of what to do, Cockerill "ran to the old log Shiloh Church," from where he beheld "regiment after regiment, and brigade after brigade of Confederate troops" marching toward him. "The sun was just rising in their front and the glittering of their arms made a gorgeous spectacle for me." It was here that he saw

Sherman and his staff pushing on toward the battle—"the splendid soldier, erect in his saddle, his eye bent forward, he looked like a veritable war eagle." No sooner had Sherman passed than a Union artillery battery began to fire until a Confederate shell blew up in its midst, Cockerill said, killing the captain and a number of horses, and the second in command fled with what remained "and was not seen at any other time, I believe, during the two days' engagement."

It fast became obvious to Cockerill that remaining at the church would probably be injurious to his health, and so he hightailed it back to his regiment's camp, where he found the tents shot to rags and a mass of wounded men being carried to the rear. Since, as a musician, Cockerill was technically a noncombatant, and responsible during battle for care of the wounded, he joined a carrying party that was moving a badly wounded officer to the rear. With that duty fulfilled, Cockerill became uncertain of what to do, and, finding himself comparatively alone, he started for Pittsburg Landing on the river.

He had gone perhaps a mile when he encountered the Highland brigade of General McArthur, wearing their Scottish tams, with their regimental bands playing and their flags flying. Young Cockerill found them "the handsomest body of troops I ever saw."

"As I sauntered by, a chipper young lieutenant, sword in hand, stopped me and said: 'Where do you belong?'"

He replied, "I belong to Ohio," to which the lieutenant answered, "Well, Ohio is making a bad show of itself here to-day. Do you want to come and fight with us?"

Not knowing what else to do, Cockerill nodded his assent. The lieutenant took out a notebook and wrote down his name and regiment, "in case anything should happen to me," which is how a

16-year-old Ohio boy found himself fighting with a brigade of Illinois Scotsmen on the far, far left flank of the Hornet's Nest.

Cockerill stood there for a while bewildered at what he had done. He knew no one, and no one spoke to him. Then one of the bands struck up "Hail Columbia" and the brigade fell in, turned, and marched toward the boom and rattle of the fighting. The first task assigned to Cockerill's regiment was support of an artillery battery, one of the most disagreeable jobs for infantry troops in battle. This was because the opposing artillery naturally opened "counterbattery" fire at the earliest opportunity, and owing to the imprecision of the artillery of the day a great many of the shells fell among the infantry troops supporting (guarding) the battery. Then, if things went as planned, the enemy would deliberately concentrate its attack so as to fall upon the artillery battery and silence it, which meant hot work for the infantry supports. Suffice it to say there were many groans of profanity whenever it was learned that supporting the artillery would be the fate of the troops that day.

For what seemed like hours Cockerill and his companions hugged ground around the roaring artillery battery on the far Federal left and said whatever passed for prayers. "Everything looked weird and unnatural," he remembered years later, "the very leaves on the trees seemed greener than I have ever seen leaves, and larger. The wounded and butchered men who came up out of the blue smoke in front of us, and were dragged or sent hobbling to the rear, seemed like bleeding messengers come to tell of the fate awaiting us."

General McArthur went by, his hand, like Sherman's, wrapped in a handkerchief from a wound. Suddenly the Rebel charge broke upon them and the enemy line stopped to fire. "The bullets shrieked over our heads and in our ranks," Cockerill said, "soon the dry leaves were on fire, and the smoke added to the general obscurity. At this moment the young lieutenant [the one who took Cockerill's name and regiment] who was gallantly waving his sword at the front, was struck by a bullet and fell instantly dead, almost at my feet. I shuddered at the thought—*dead and unknown.*"

By that time the fire "became so terrible that we were driven back into the ravine. I was crouched down loading my piece when a man who had been struck above me, fell on top of me and died by my side." Cockerill kept firing until he ran out of cartridges, and then he saw the Rebel charge: "I saw the gray dirty uniforms of the enemy. I heard their fierce yells. I saw their flags flapping in the grimy atmosphere. That was a sight I have never forgotten. I can see the tiger ferocity in those faces yet; I can see them in my dreams."

This proved too much and the blue line wavered, then broke. Everyone turned and ran for the rear. A private fleeing next to Cockerill suddenly "gave a scream of agony" and began dragging one of his legs. Cockerill stopped and the soldier leaned on his shoulder and begged for help. "I half carried and half dragged him for some distance, still holding to my Enfield rifle, with its beautiful curly stock," Cockerill said, but something between duty and compassion forced upon him a hard choice.

Regretfully, he said, "Seeing that I must give up the role of Good Samaritan or drop my rifle, I threw it down." All the while, "the bullets were whistling more fiercely than at any time during the engagement. My companion was growing weaker all the time." Finally Cockerill sat him down beside a tree and watched him bleed to death. "I knew nothing of surgery or how to staunch the flow of blood," he said. Another soldier passed by, took a look, and remarked, "He's a dead man."

When the wounded soldier died Cockerill resumed his flight, walking down a road, when he encountered some cavalry engaged in stopping stragglers. One of them he recognized as a man from his father's regiment. When the boy inquired about the regiment the trooper told him that "it had been entirely cut to pieces, and that he, personally, had witnessed the death of my father—he had seen him shot from his horse."

Sixteen-year-old John Cockerill, musician fourth class, bearing this awful news, trudged toward Pittsburg Landing, not because he felt he would find anything better there but simply because he couldn't think of any other place to go.

✦

The charge of Statham's brigade, led by the commanding general Sidney Johnston, marked the beginning of the collapse of the Hornet's Nest. On the Federal left, Colonel Pugh and his Illinoisans, and the brigade of General McArthur—with all their artillery, including young John Cockerill—fell back nearly half a mile to a new line astride the Hamburg-Savannah road at the southern edge of Wicker Field. But the Rebels, led by Chalmers's brigade, which had finally disposed of Stuart, were sidling around farther north and fast closing in on the Union left flank.

After getting Statham's charge under way, General Johnston and Governor Harris had reunited in the rear as the Rebel line continued to press forward. Johnston was sitting alone on his horse when Harris found him. "I had never, in my life, seen him looking more bright, joyous and happy," Harris recalled afterward. Occasional bullets still whistled around them, fired by small bands of Yankee survivors who, by Preston Johnston's account, "delivered volley after volley as they sullenly retired."

In those brief minutes while Johnston, in the front, had led the brigade forward, his horse Fire-Eater had been shot a number of times and Johnston himself had been clipped by bullets in three places, but seemingly he had come through the experience unhurt.

He said, "Governor, they came very near to putting me *hors de combat** in that charge," and the general pointed to his foot, where a shot had ripped the sole off of his boot from heel to toe and left it flapping. "Are you wounded?" Harris asked; the answer was "No."

Harris asked if there were any messages he wished delivered; just then Federal artillery opened up, enfilading the new Rebel line that continued to press forward. Johnston told Harris to ride to Statham and tell him to "silence that Yankee battery." Harris galloped to Statham, no more than 200 yards away, and returned within a few minutes.

As he rode up to Johnston with the news that Statham had set his artillery in motion, the governor saw the general reel in the saddle as if he were about to fall from his horse. Harris grabbed him by the neck and pulled him upright, exclaiming, "General, are you wounded?" to which Johnston replied, "in a very deliberate tone, 'Yes, and I fear seriously.' " These were his last words.

Harris immediately dispatched one of Johnston's captains for a surgeon. By the sheerest of ironies, earlier that morning Johnston had sent his own surgeon, Dr. D. W. Yandell, to treat wounded Federal prisoners of the 18th Wisconsin. When Yandell protested

---

* From the French, meaning "out of the battle" or disabled.

that his duty was to serve the commanding general, Johnston told him, "No, those men were our enemies but are our prisoners now, and deserve our protection." It would prove to be a fatal decision.

Johnston suddenly went slack and dropped his reins. Harris, still supporting him in the saddle, seized the bridle and guided both horses to a ravine about 150 yards behind the lines. He dismounted near a large oak, where he eased Johnston out of the saddle and to the ground, asking, frantically, where he was wounded. But the general gave no reply.

Harris undid Johnston's cravat and tore his shirt open but found no wound. A "profuse amount of blood" had run out onto the ground from the general's knee-high right boot, but Harris felt that Johnston's wound must be something more serious than that. By then several of the general's aides had arrived. Harris raised Johnston's head and tried to pour some brandy down his throat, but most of it only dribbled from his lips.

Johnston's former brother-in-law and best friend, Col. William Preston, leaped from his horse and rushed to the general's side crying, "Johnston, do you know me?" but the general was unresponsive. Preston also tried pouring brandy into Johnston's mouth, but it only gurgled in his throat. "He had neither escort nor surgeon near him," Preston said. "His horse was wounded and bleeding. He breathed for a few minutes after my arrival, but did not recognize me." Albert Sidney Johnston expired at 2:30 p.m. or thereabouts.

It need not have been so. The "profuse amount" of blood that had run from his boot and pooled up on the leaves beneath the tree told the story. A bullet had clipped his right popliteal artery, which lies behind the knee, and he had bled to death in perhaps 15 minutes. Had Johnston himself or anyone else with the slightest medical experience known it in time, the field tourniquet that the general carried in his own pocket could have been used to seal off the blood flow above the knee long enough to get him to a surgeon. The circumstances surrounding the death of General Johnston stand out among the many mysteries and contradictions of Shiloh. Eyewitnesses have placed the time between his wounding and his death at anywhere from 15 to 45 minutes. Just who among his aides did what, and when, remains in dispute.*

Terrible shock among the living set in; tears were shed. Johnston was more than a general, he was an icon. His loss, especially at the high tide of battle when Confederate brigades were sweeping the field, was devastating.

Colonel Preston, as chief aide-de-camp, scribbled a note for Harris to carry to Beauregard: "General Johnston has just fallen, mortally wounded, after a victorious attack on the left of the enemy. It is up to you to complete the victory." Thus command of the army, and the battle, now fell to General P.G.T. Beauregard, the Great Creole.

Governor Harris's horse had run off in the confusion, and when he mounted Fire-Eater, who had remained beside his master's body, Harris found him so badly crippled that he dismounted only to discover that the horse had been shot in three legs. Harris was able to obtain a fresh horse from Johnston's orderly and galloped off to where he had last known Beauregard to be, but by then Beauregard had moved his headquarters forward to Shiloh church.

---

* For years it was assumed the fatal shot was fired by a Yankee soldier, but some modern historians now contend that Johnston was accidentally shot by his own men. Considering the amount of firing that was going on, and absent any concrete proof, any such speculation would seem to be just that.

Stunned at the news of Johnston's death when Harris finally reached him, the Creole read Preston's note, then said—much as a question—"Everything else seems to be going on well on the right," to which Governor Harris "assented." Then, said Beauregard, according to Preston Johnston's account, "the battle may as well go on." It seemed an odd thing to say.

By then it was about 3 p.m. and practically everyone on both sides agreed that a lull had occurred in the fighting. This break lasted for about an hour, a very critical hour, for the sun was now beginning to sink. The pause was attributed to various reasons, the most controversial of which was that Beauregard had somehow "let down"—that he did not press the fight hard enough just as the Yankees were beginning to crack. There is something to be argued along this line of reasoning, mainly because Beauregard remained seriously ill with his throat ailment. His pulse, taken earlier in the day, was said to have been 100, and he was weak and could hardly speak. The surgeons wanted him confined to his ambulance. Clearly the Great Creole was in no condition to take to the field as Johnston had, to rally the troops and lead men in battle charges.

In any case that was not his job, as Beauregard himself was quick to point out in his memoirs. In fact he condemned Johnston's going to the front as "behav[ing] like a division or corps commander, instead of the commanding general of an army." After his conversation with Governor Harris, Beauregard sent word to all of his corps commanders telling them of Johnston's death and that the battle must be vigorously prosecuted. He also told them to keep the death a secret, so as not to alarm or dishearten the troops.

Back at the death scene, beneath the tree in the ravine, Johnston's aides concealed the general's body in a blanket and carried it to his headquarters in the rear. An examination was performed, which concluded that Johnston had been hit four times that day: Marks from two spent bullets were found on his legs, plus the one that had cut his boot sole, and then the fatal one behind the knee, which he himself apparently did not feel.

Next day the body was escorted to Corinth by his entire staff, Colonel Preston leading the way, back to his headquarters before the battle, which was the home of Mrs. William Inge, the admiring lady who had secreted the little lunch parcel in the general's coat. In 1925, on her deathbed, 91-year-old Augusta Evans Inge recalled the scene for the notable Shiloh historian Otto Eisenschiml.

"They brought his body back to my house, wrapped in a muddy blanket," she said. "Together with an old friend of mine, Ellen Polk,* I cleaned his face and uniform, and in his pocket I found half of one sandwich and a small piece of cake. He had eaten most of it."

They laid the body out in the front parlor of the cottage, and his orderlies stood guard over it while they waited for the train to New Orleans. Sixty-three years later, Mrs. Inge reached out to Eisenschiml, trembling. "Look at these hands," she said. More than half a century after his death Albert Sidney Johnston remained a great Southern hero. "These are the hands that wrapped the Confederate flag around the body of General Johnston, before they took him South."

———————◆◆◆———————

The lull in the battle continued until half past three in the afternoon. Not a complete lull, of course; tens of thousands of men

---

* A cousin to both President James K. Polk and the Rebel bishop and general Leonidas Polk.

continued to shoot at one another, but a relative break, nonetheless. Past the Peach Orchard there was a swale out of immediate firing range where Statham's exhausted Confederates fell down, wretched with thirst after their successful charge. Near it was a large pond around which "the dead of the enemy lay thickly, & down in the bottom of the pool of clear blue water there was a dead man in one edge of it," Augustus Mecklin wrote in his diary. "Our boys rushed to the water and with their cups drank deeply. If the water had been mixed with blood it [was] all the same." This became known as the Bloody Pond, and during the day men of both sides used its waters to drink, or soak, or wash off wounds, with an unspoken agreement not to kill each other there.

Referring to the lull, Basil W. Duke, the famed Kentucky cavalryman and later brigadier general who was shot in the shoulder at Shiloh while attempting to saber a Union soldier, made this colorful analogy: "It went on all day like the regular stroke of some tremendous machine. There would be a rapid charge and fierce fight—the wild yell that would announce a Confederate success—then would ensue a comparative lull, broken again in a few minutes, and the charge, struggle, and horrible din would recommence."

After Sidney Johnston fell, though, Preston Johnston wrote, "There was no general direction nor concerted movements. The spring and alertness of the onset flagged. The determinate purpose was lost sight of."

Here Preston Johnston seems to be blaming Beauregard, but he might as easily have blamed the corps commanders, especially Breckinridge, who commanded the right. One explanation for the lull, however, was that the Yankees on the right had withdrawn nearly half a mile after Statham's charge, and it took time to catch up with them and renew the fight; besides, the Rebel soldiers were exhausted and out of ammunition.

Still, they were without Johnston's imposing presence at the front and a vacuum had arisen with his loss and no one, neither Breckinridge, nor Bragg, nor Polk, nor Hardee, nor Beauregard, could fill the empty space. Time was now working against them; the sun was three-quarters down in the western sky. And what they did not know was that, in those very same moments, Buell's army of some 20,000 was close to crossing the Tennessee and swarming onto the field, and that Don Carlos Buell himself was at Pittsburg Landing.

———◆———

Buell had reached the landing "midway in the afternoon," furious, as he steamed up from Savannah, at the "stream of fugitives that poured in a constantly swelling current along the west bank of the river." The mouth of Snake Creek, he said, "was full of them swimming across. The face of the bluff was crowded with stragglers from the battle. The number there has been estimated at from five thousand in the morning to fifteen thousand in the evening," the outraged Buell complained.

At the landing he found Grant and several of his staff "on his boat, in the ladies' cabin," Buell wrote curtly in the 1880s, after Grant was dead. According to Buell, "There was none of that masterly confidence [by Grant] which has since been assumed with reference to the occasion." Grant, Buell continued, "appeared to realize that he was beset by a pressing danger," and seemed "much relieved" by Buell's arrival. "He held out his sword," Buell snipped, "to call my attention to an indentation which he said the scabbard had received from a shot." However, according to John Rawlins, then Grant's adjutant general, when Buell inquired of Grant, "What preparations have you made for retreating," Grant responded, "I have not yet despaired of whipping them, General" and told Buell that he expected the arrival of Lew Wallace's 7,200 fresh troops at any moment, which would allow him to regain the momentum.

Buell wrote that he "proposed [to Grant] that we should go ashore, but as we reached the gangway I noticed that the horses of himself and his staff were being taken ashore. He mounted and rode away, while I walked up the hill; so that I saw him no more until the attack occurred at the Landing late in the evening." So stated Major General Buell 20 years after the war.

Grant had in fact become increasingly anxious about the whereabouts of Lew Wallace since midmorning. His aide Captain Rowley remembered that about 11 a.m., two hours or more after he had sent Captain Baxter with orders for Wallace to move to Pittsburg Landing *immediately*, Grant had "expressed considerable solicitude [i.e., anxious concern] at the non-appearance of General Wallace, and sent an orderly dashing off to the extreme right to see if he could see anything of him, remarking that it could not *possibly* be many minutes before he would arrive." In this Grant was quite wrong.

Shortly after noon, Rowley continued, "a cavalry officer rode up and reported to General Grant, stating that General Wallace had positively refused to come up unless he received *written* orders." Grant all but exploded and ordered Rowley to ride to Lew Wallace and "tell him to come up *at once*," and that "if he should require a written order of you, you will give him one." Grant added for Rowley to make sure he had writing materials in his haversack and "see that you don't spare horse flesh."

Rowley and the aforementioned cavalry captain hightailed it up toward Crump's Landing on the River Road but found no sign of Wallace and his division. When they reached his camp, six miles north, he was not there either, except for a lone baggage wagon that was just then moving off. When they inquired of the teamster as to Wallace's whereabouts, they were told that the division had marched off down the Purdy road, leading toward the southwest, which would have put Wallace on the battlefield near Sherman's camp at a bridge over Owl Creek—except that Sherman was no longer in his camp, which was now occupied by General Beauregard and about one-third of the Rebel army.

A mile or so down the Purdy road Rowley came across signs that the division had veered off down a road known as the Shunpike. After riding what he estimated as five or six miles, Rowley came upon the rear of Wallace's division, which was stretched out for nearly two miles.

"They were at rest, sitting on each side of the road," Rowley later wrote in his official report, "some with their arms stacked in the middle of the road. When I reached the head of the column I found General Wallace sitting upon his horse, surrounded by his staff, some of whom were dismounted and holding their horses by their bridles."

When Rowley told Wallace it had been reported to Grant that he refused to march without written orders, Wallace "seemed quite indignant, saying it was a 'damned lie!' in proof of which he said, 'Here you find me on the road.' "

To which Rowley replied that "I had certainly found him on *a* road, but I hardly thought it was the road to Pittsburg Landing." In fact, Rowley said later, judging by the sound of the firing, Wallace was now considerably farther away from the battlefield than he had been at his original camp. Wallace responded that this was the road his cavalry had led him down, "and the *only* road he knew anything about," and that it led around Snake and Owl Creeks to Sherman's camps.

"Great God!" Rowley said. "Don't you know Sherman has been driven back? Why, the whole army is within half a mile of the river, and it's a question if we are not all going to be driven into it."

Just then Wallace's cavalry rode up and delivered the same embarrassing news, that if he kept marching down this road the Confederate army in fact would be between Wallace and the Union army. Digesting this disagreeable turn of affairs, Wallace ordered his division to countermarch. He also ordered Rowley to remain with him as guide, rather than ride back and explain the situation to Grant.

Wallace's order to countermarch further delayed things, for instead of simply ordering the entire division to about-face so that the last regiment in line became the first, the order to "countermarch" required the head of the column to peel off and march back toward the rear—with the rest of the 7,200 troops waiting, then following, front to rear—so that the original head of the column would remain in the lead. Wallace later explained that he wanted to have "certain regiments whose fighting qualities commanded my confidence" at the front of his columns. Just so, but precious minutes were slipping away, as the fighting at Pittsburg Landing grew more desperate with every tick of the clock.

Wallace's division countermarched for nearly three hours before reaching a side road that would carry it into River Road, down which Grant had expected them to march in the first place. By then it was 3:30 p.m. and they were still about four and a half miles from the battlefield. At the intersection of this side road, Wallace was intercepted by Colonel McPherson and Adjutant General Rawlins, who had subsequently been sent by Grant after Wallace still had not shown up.

"I understood him [Wallace] to say that his guide had led him wrong," McPherson said in his official report. In any event, Wallace had marched a good ten miles out of the way—five miles down the wrong road and five miles back. McPherson told him to "For God's sake move forward rapidly," but it seems Wallace was cursed with the slows that day. For one thing, he was marching with his artillery—by far the least hasty of his components—in between his First and Second Brigades, so that the entire column was compelled to move at the pace of the artillery.

When McPherson pointed this out, Wallace had the artillery move off the road so the brigades could pass on, but this, according to Rawlins, occasioned a delay of "a full half an hour, during which time he [Wallace] was dismounted and sitting down." No sooner had the column gotten under way again than a report came that the bridge over Snake Creek was in the possession of the Rebels. The column was again halted while this information was investigated and proved false.

In the meantime, according to Rawlins, "the artillery firing at Pittsburg Landing became terrific, and we who had been there knew it was our heavy guns," by which he meant the big siege guns that were posted right above the landing itself, suggesting that the army was at its last extremities and in danger of being driven into the river. Such was the state of affairs vis-à-vis General Lew Wallace and his missing infantry division as the sun began to sink over Pittsburg Landing and the Battle of Shiloh approached its dramatic climax.

Even while the battle had seemed to slow down in midafternoon, at the same time emotions and impelling motions were building up like an enormous head of steam in a boiler, and then, "about half-past-three o'clock, the struggle at the centre, which had been going on for five hours with fitful violence, was renewed with the utmost fury," wrote William Preston Johnston. "Polk's and Bragg's corps, intermingled, were engaged in a death grapple with the sturdy commands of Wallace and Prentiss." The lull, it seemed, was over.

This latest eruption at the Hornet's Nest almost had to be endured to be believed, so ferocious was the fighting. It had been precipitated by the Rebel general Daniel Ruggles, the irascible 52-year-old Massachusetts-born, West Point–educated Mexican War veteran, with a head as bald as an egg and a long, white beard like an Old Testament prophet.

As the stalemate at the Hornet's Nest continued to confound, Ruggles had impetuously commanded his aides to, "Bring forward every gun you can find," on the theory that if the Confederates were unable to shoot the Yankees out of the nest with their rifles, or to prod them out with their bayonets, then by damn they would literally blow them out of it with the most spectacular concentration of artillery yet seen on the American continent.

By half past four Ruggles's people had assembled some 62 cannons of various weights and calibers, which he lined up and pointed at the Hornet's Nest in general and the Sunken Road in particular. When Ruggles gave the order to fire they said the whole ground shook as in an earthquake, and "the sky lit up in a blaze of unearthly fire." What is more, this stupendous demonstration of firepower coincided with the simultaneous ("though unconcerted") advance of the whole Confederate line.*

The artillery barrage utterly stupefied the defenders of the Hornet's Nest, prompting 26-year-old Corp. Leonard B. Houston of the Second Iowa, W.H.L. Wallace's division, to write his friends, "I don't know how our Regiment escaped . . . it seemed like a mighty hurricane sweeping everything before it when men and horses were dying; at this moment of horror . . . the *little birds* were singing in the green trees over our heads! They were as happy as if all were perfect calmness beneath them."

If the birds seemed happy, the Confederates were decidedly not, emerging as they were from the tree line across a broad expanse of field, thousands upon thousands of bayonets at the ends of their gun barrels gleaming menacingly in the afternoon sun. It takes a great deal of single-minded determination—let alone raw courage—to behold such a sight and not feel a strong urge to flee, which is what the Yankees in the Hornet's Nest finally did after fighting valiantly for six long and ghastly hours. The very primitiveness of so many men headed straight for them, bearing long gleaming knives come to kill them close-on, was apparently more than they could bear.

---

* In recent years there has been some disagreement among historians over the precise number of guns in Ruggles's gigantic battery. For more than a hundred years the figure stood at 62. Some now argue 50-something, others 60-something; I say after all this time it probably doesn't matter.

Worse, not only was the entire Rebel front line moving on them but both flanks had collapsed, as no fewer than seven Rebel brigades closed in on the nest's tenants from both sides and the rear.

The first to give way was Hurlbut's division on the Union left, which was being confronted by three brigades under Breckinridge and Bragg—Chalmers's, Jackson's, and Bowen's. Clearly the Federal commanders had gone well past the point when "further endurance was no longer a virtue." The lines to the left and to the right of them had fallen back, and Hurlbut's position became a salient that stuck out like a sore thumb.

In taking to heart Grant's charge to hold out "at all hazards," Prentiss, and to a lesser extent Hurlbut and Wallace, had essentially outfortituded themselves and now faced total annihilation or surrender. They chose the latter, some deliberately, even with the formality of white flags and officers surrendering their swords, but in many cases the men simply slipped away from the lines after seeing Rebels at their flanks and rear. When the tally count was made, more than 2,200 Yankee soldiers had been made prisoners, including a division commander, Benjamin M. Prentiss himself.

In their official reports, Hornet's Nest commanders from the top down unanimously registered sentiments to the effect that "It was therefore useless to think of prolonging a resistance which could only have wasted their lives to no purpose." Or, "To have held out longer would be to suffer complete annihilation." Still, about half of the Hornet's Nest defenders, maybe more, made it out of the trap, especially those closer to the landing.

General W.H.L. Wallace nearly got out himself but didn't. When he was notified of the impending collapse of the brigade on his left flank and Wallace went to see about it, an aide, who was also

311

his brother-in-law, Lt. Cyrus Dickey, directed the general's attention to a mass of Confederate infantry about to pitch into his last remaining regiment in that part of the field. As Wallace rose off his saddle to get a better look, a bullet struck him in the back of the head and exited through his left eye, blowing it out. The general fell headlong to the ground, evidently killed.

The horrified Dickey instructed Wallace's orderlies to conduct the general's corpse to the rear, but soon the Rebel advance nearly overtook them and they quickly moved the body out of the road, placing it by some ammunition crates to protect it from being trampled. Then all fled the scene. It was then past 5 p.m.—by some accounts, closer to 6—when the Confederate line swept through the Hornet's Nest.

A regiment was detailed to escort the huge catch of Yankee prisoners back to Corinth, while Prentiss was taken to the Shiloh church to meet General Beauregard. The Rebel line continued on until at last it came upon what remained of Grant's army, drawn up defiantly for one last stand at Pittsburg Landing.

CHAPTER 14

MY GOD, MY GOD, IT IS TOO LATE!

———◄◆►———

A T LONG LAST, MUSICIAN FOURTH CLASS JOHN Cockerill reached Pittsburg Landing, "almost too scared to be put on any sort of duty." From the crest of the bluff he looked down upon a hive of breathtaking commotion, which he compared to a disturbed bed of ants. "Below lay thirty transports, at least," he remembered, "all being loaded with the wounded, and all around me were baggage wagons, mule teams, disabled artillery teams and thousands of panic-stricken men. Some of the stragglers were being forced to carry sandbags up to fortify batteries of heavy siege guns."

The cabin on the bluff that had once been used as Grant's head-quarters was "turned into a temporary field hospital," Cockerill said, grisly as a charnel house, "where hundreds of wounded men, brought down in wagons and ambulances, were being unloaded, and where their arms and legs were cut off and thrown out to form gory, ghastly heaps."

It seemed to Cockerill that everyone was yelling at once, and the air continued to fume with curses and threats by officers who were variously ordering or pleading with the thousands of fugitives to return for the one final stand against the Rebel onslaught. Even Grant joined in this effort, Cockerill said, yelling at the men that "Buell's army would soon be on the field, and he did not want to see his men disgraced."

Cockerill said that Grant told them if they did not return to the fight, "he would send his cavalry down to the river to drive them out," and indeed did just that, for "a squadron of cavalry soon appeared, divided at either end of the landing, and riding toward each other with sabers drawn. The majority of the skulkers climbed up the bank," Cockerill said, "hanging by the roots of the trees, and after the cavalry had passed they were back in their old places again."

About that same time, said Cockerill, a most welcome sight appeared on the opposite side of the river, "where I saw a body of horsemen emerging from the low canebrakes back of the river. In a moment I saw a man waving a white flag with a red square in the center. I knew that he was signaling, and a few minutes later, I saw the head of a column of blue emerge from the woods beyond." It was Buell, and they were saved, or so Cockerill believed.

———◆◆———

Twenty-nine-year-old Ann Wallace had remained aboard the *Minnehaha* all through that Dantesque day, while teamsters loaded wounded men aboard the steamboats that were, in fact, about the only structures at Shiloh remaining in Union hands.* Buell's men on the far side of the river had to make a road down to the water, but soon all the steamers at the landing, including the *Minnehaha,* were going "over and back, over and back," Ann Wallace recorded, ferrying fresh troops to the battlefield. Overtaxed surgeons on the upper, or hurricane, decks were tending to the wounded, while Buell's soldiers were loaded below.

Half of Ann Wallace's family was on that fatal battlefield, or so it seemed, and she was nearly beside herself because of it. In addition to her husband, the general, her father, a colonel, and both of her brothers as officers, two of her husband's brothers, as well as a number of more distant relatives, were in the fight. The noise of the battle had been drawing ominously nearer throughout the day and was now practically on top of her.

"As I sat there I saw these shells strike the sides of other steamers and cut off limbs of trees near where the road was made, and pass buzzing across our deck," she wrote in a letter shortly after the battle. Adding to the beastliness of the scene were the shrieks and moans of wounded who faced the surgeon's saw, or the frightened, searching eyes of silent sufferers. "I felt dazed and horrified, yet enthused by some means," said Ann Wallace, "so I was not afraid . . . I knew the danger, but felt lifted above fear of it.

"The panic-stricken raw troops seemed perfectly insane," she remembered. "The steamer would have to keep a slight distance from the shore, or it would have been swamped by the rush of officers and

---

* The Federals also had the camp and tents of W.H.L. Wallace's division, but everything else was in Confederate hands.

men." At one point a Union officer, half crazed with fear, somehow got aboard and came into the pilothouse where Ann Wallace was sitting. He produced a revolver and threatened to kill the pilot if he did not take his men aboard. The pilot stalled, pretending to obey, "giving the frenzied man time to come to his senses" and put his pistol down. "I felt it would be safer below," she said, "but the feeling that exhibition of fear on my part would make it a little harder for that pilot to stand at his post kept me from going down."

As the battle seemed to be nearing a wild, frantic peak, Ann Wallace turned to see the Rev. Charles Button, whom she knew from Springfield and as chaplain and elder of her husband's former regiment, "with a worn and depressed look," coming up the gangway, partially disabled by a spent bullet while he had been tending to the wounded.

"This is an awful battle," he said to her. She replied, "Yes, but these fresh troops will yet win the day." He hesitated. "You have a great many relations on this field, you cannot hope to see them all come in safe." Ann somehow deflected the statement, but he had come up behind her, where she was sitting, and once more said, "It is an awful battle."

It was his tone of voice. "The dread truth fell on my heart like a thunderbolt, like the cold hand of steel," she cried. "Words needed not to tell it. I was stunned, chilled, almost paralyzed! Suffering came hours afterwards." Soon Lieutenant Dickey, her brother, arrived and was "spared the task of telling me my life had darkened," she said. Dickey provided some details of Wallace's last moments and the attempt to return the body, but to Ann Wallace it was nearly beside the point. "My husband was dead, and the enemy had possession of the ground where he lay. 'Twas all they could tell me, and it was enough."

Ann Wallace spent the miserable remainder of that night, she wrote later, "bathing the fevered brows and limbs of the sufferers around me. Action was a relief, and it was a slight help to aid men who were suffering in the cause for which Will had given his life." These were the words of a general's wife.

———◆———

Buell's army arrived on the opposite shore with understandable trepidation. Since late morning they had marched the ten miles from Savannah through the most obnoxious jungles and swamps alongside the Tennessee River, down an old wagon road, in places barely a rut, "dank and unwholesome," led by a native guide, and impeded by fallen trees, shallow, scummy ponds, and "slippery mire shoe-top deep." It seemed with each passing minute the noise of the battle was sharpened, said a private from Ohio, naturally reinforcing everyone's realization that "it was no child's game going on ahead of us."

It was about 4:30 p.m. when Buell's leading regiments emerged from the swamp into a large cornfield and meadow opposite Pittsburg Landing, from which the view across the Tennessee River was appalling.

Ambrose Bierce, destined to become one of America's best-known literary figures, was a first lieutenant with the Ninth Indiana in Col. William B. Hazen's brigade of Nelson's division. As they slogged through the greasy swamps, in his mind the battle became a "dull, distant sound like the heavy breathing of some great animal below the horizon"; then, as they surfaced into the cornfield, "the air was full of thunder and the earth was trembling beneath [our] feet. Below us ran the river, vexed with plunging shells and obscured in spots by blue sheets of low-lying smoke."

Across the river, the smoke mostly blanked out the landing itself but, on the bluff above, Bierce saw "the battle burning brightly enough; a thousand lights kindled and expired every second. Through the smoke, the branches of the trees showed black; sudden flames burst out, here and there, singly and in dozens, fleeting streaks of fire [that] crossed over to us, followed by the musical humming of the fragments as they struck the ground on every side, making us wince, but doing little harm."

"The air was full of noises," Bierce continued, "distant musketry rattled smartly and petulantly, or sighed and growled when closer. There were deep shaking explosions and smart shocks. The death-line was an arc of which the river was the chord, filled with the whisper of stray bullets and the hurtle of conical shells; the rush of round shot. There were faint, desultory cheers. Occasionally, against the glare behind the trees, could be seen moving black figures, distinct, but no larger than a thumb; they seemed to be like the figures of demons in old allegorical prints of hell."

Such was Bierce's first impression of the unearthly spectacle unfolding before Buell's army as it reached its place opposite the landing—a vivid, articulate account of what it must have been like to see the very gates of hell across the river Styx. One of Buell's signalmen set up a wigwag* station, which is what 16-year-old John Cockerill saw from his perch atop the opposing bluff where the battle raged in earnest. Soon a transport, and then another, emerged from the blanket of sulfurous, flame-stabbed smoke around Pittsburg Landing and steamed toward them.

---

* Wigwag, or semaphore, is communicating by signal flags, in which messages waved out by a signalman could be conveyed over relatively long distances (with the added use of telescopes).

As more Federal regiments began to arrive at the cornfield they found themselves sharing space with a sizable gathering of local "country folks," who exhibited "an intense anxiety to see every movement visible on the farther side of the river.

"One of these worthies," wrote a private in the Sixth Ohio, "was hailed by our company," whose members apparently held the locals in fairly low esteem. "Say, old feller!" he was asked. "How's the fight going on over there?"

The man, the soldier said, was "an old and somewhat diminutive specimen, grizzle-haired, stoop shouldered, and withered from the effects of the sun and tobacco." After hesitating for a moment he turned and, "with a side-long glance of his eyes, answered slowly: 'Well, it are'nt hardly decided yet, I reckon; but they're driving your folks—some.'"

This perfectly diplomatic and truthful answer was greeted with howls of derision from the Sixth Ohio men, who called him a "damned old sesesh"* and sent him on his way with kicks and jeers and other, harsher expressions inappropriate for this story.

Pandemonium reigned on the riverbank as Buell's men and horses were herded onto the boats. Owing to the poor road through the swamp, all of the division's artillery had to be left behind at Savannah and brought up later in transport ships, but that didn't matter. What was needed now was men, or rather cannon-fodder, but—with any luck—fodder that would fight.

At the head of his division was 300-pound Bull Nelson, in fine spirits astride Ned, his magnificent black stallion, "the very picture of satisfaction and good humor," calling out to the men,

---

* A Northern derogatory term for a Southern secessionist or Rebel.

"Now, gentlemen, keep the columns well closed up!" This statement so stunned the private Ebenezer Hannaford of the Sixth Ohio (unaccustomed, as he was, to being referred to as a "gentleman," and certainly not by a major general) that he concluded it must have to do with the way the prospect of impending battle worked on the psyche of his rotund division commander. Hannaford decided that Nelson was a war lover and psychologized afterward that "Some natures seem to find in antagonism and conflict their native element—almost as much a necessity to them as the air they breathe."

For his part, Lieutenant Bierce acknowledged "there was no elephant on the boat that took us across that evening," adding that, instead "we had a woman. She was a fine creature, this woman; somebody's wife. Her mission, as she understood it, was to inspire the failing heart with courage, She stood on the upper deck, with the red blaze of battle bathing her beautiful face, the twinkle of a thousand rifles mirrored in her eyes; and displaying an ivory-handled pistol, she told me in a sentence punctuated by the thunder of great guns that if it came to the worst she would do her duty like a man!" Whether Bierce and his company were aboard the *Minnehaha* with Ann Wallace as it transferred troops from bank to bank is unknown. Mrs. Wallace is silent on this, and so is history, but it's certainly an interesting possibility to contemplate.

Bierce's writing here turns as purple as the darkening skies when the sun dipped below the horizon of the battlefield. But outside there was still light and time for one more charge by the ragged and exhausted Rebel army. It would be the one out of many they would talk about, and write about, and argue about, for decades to come, the charge that became known as "the Lost Opportunity."

———◆———

After the breakdown of the Hornet's Nest, a crisis was at hand for the Union army. Captain Putnam, one of Grant's aides that day, spoke of "a great disaster that seemed imminent." Streams of soldiers straggled to the landing in the face of the Rebel onslaught, and the steamer carrying Private Hannaford and the Sixth Ohio was just landing. "How shall I attempt to set that picture forth," Hannaford wondered. "All about us, thousands of panic-stricken wretches swarmed from the river's edge far up toward the top of the bluff; a mob in uniform; a surging herd of humanity smitten with a very frenzy of fright and despair; every sense of manly pride, honor, or duty, paralyzed and dead to every feeling except terror."

"Whenever a steamboat would land," observed Ambrose Bierce, "this abominable mob had to be kept off her by bayonets; when she pulled away they sprang upon her, and were pushed by scores into the water, where they were suffered to drown one another in their own way. The men disembarking insulted them, struck them. In return they expressed their unholy delight in the certainty of our destruction by the enemy."

Bull Nelson, who had decorated his hat with a large ostrich feather, dyed black, mounted Ned, at 17 hands high nearly as enormous as his owner, and led the men off the boat, roaring, "Gentlemen, draw your sabers, and trample these sons-of-bitches into the mud! Charge!" According to one of his aides, Lt. Horace C. Fisher, they "cut through the mob of runaways, who tumbled over each other in abject terror," with Nelson continuing to abuse them, bellowing, "Get out of the way, you damned cowards! If you won't fight yourselves, let these men off that will!"

With the collapse of the Hornet's Nest the Yankees were compressed into a half-mile-long line with its left resting on Pittsburg Landing and the gunboats and running almost due west to the Hamburg-Savannah road, their backs against the miry bottoms of Snake Creek. But of the roughly 49,000 men originally under his command, Grant could put up a fighting front of no more than 15,000 to 18,000, and probably not even that many. Since morning, more than 7,000 had been killed or wounded and 3,000 captured. Another 7,000—namely Lew Wallace's division—had still not arrived on the field. The balance—some 15,000 or more—were either cowering under the bluff at Pittsburg Landing or otherwise absent from their units.

As luck would have it, when it became clear that the collapse of the Hornet's Nest was imminent, Grant's chief of staff 51-year-old Joseph D. Webster, a Dartmouth man from New Hampshire and a retired veteran of the army's Corps of Topographical Engineers, began riding desperately along what he thought would have to become the new Union line, dragooning all the loose artillery batteries he could find and organizing them into some semblance of military order.

When he was finished Webster had actually fashioned a strong position consisting of six depleted brigades consisting of 20 or so regiments that had retained some vestiges of order, all of it protected by—depending on whose version is taken—25, 41, or 60 guns, including a battery of five tremendous 24-pounder siege cannons, each weighing in excess of 3,000 pounds, which had been intended for reduction of the Confederate fortifications at Corinth.

Still, as the Rebel batteries on the hills opposite the Dill Branch ravine poured fire into the Union ranks, men continued to desert their posts. The steamboat *Rocket,* loaded with ammunition and powder, took off at full speed from the landing to get out of range as the Rebel balls and shells burst around.

"As we sat on our horses we saw the flotsam and jetsam of Gen. Grant's army drift by in flight toward The Landing," said Lieutenant Fisher, "we saw double-decked ambulances galloping wildly with well men on the front seats prodding the horses with bayonets and swords, the ghastly load of wounded men inside shrieking in agony as the ambulances collided with each other or with trees in their flight. Shells were shrieking through the air and trees were breaking and casting their branches upon the ground. Nor were the bullets less vicious as they ripped around us. In a word, it was pandemonium broken loose."

Bull Nelson began deploying his troops on the left of the Union line, near the top of the bluff, telling them, "Don't stop to form, colonel, don't stop to form…we shall all be massacred if you do! There isn't a man out yonder on the left between us and the Rebels! For God's sake, hurry your men forward!"

Captain Putnam remembered that the artillery, including the fire of the gunboats, "made a noise not exceeded by anything I ever heard afterward." Grant and his staff were riding along near the bluff when a Captain Carson, one of his cavalry scouts, arrived to make a report. He then dismounted and was holding his horse by the bridle "when a six pound shot carried away all of Carson's head, bespattering Grant's clothing with blood." Lieutenant Fisher, who was present at the grisly incident, later wrote, "I heard a thud and some dark object whizzed over my shoulder. It was Captain Carson's head."

As Private Hannaford reached the top of the bluff where the battle was raging he passed a drummer boy furiously beating on his drum for no apparent reason. Lieutenant Crooker of the 55th Illinois remembered that "the belligerent little drummers nearly all preferred to fight, and were found along the line, gun in hand, as fierce as fighting cocks, with no notion of shirking."

To Lieutenant Fisher, the Union situation seemed desperate as the battle drew to its violent climax with the sinking of the sun. As the Rebel army, banners flying, began menacing for a final charge, he could hear them yelling and cheering across the ravine.

Grant had asked Nelson for the loan of one of his aides, and Fisher had been selected. As he and Grant rode down the line, "I could see no organized force to resist any serious attack," Fisher said. As the Confederate brigades appeared on the opposite ridge and he and Grant stopped to watch the attack, Fisher "decided that within a short time all of us would have been captured." Then, he wrote years later, "I heard [Grant] say something. I rode forward, saluted, and waited for his order. He paid no attention. His eyes were fixed to the front. Again I heard him mutter something without turning, and I saw that he was talking to himself: 'Not beaten yet by a damned sight,' " Grant was muttering.

At last, in the vesperal twilight, Beauregard had cornered the beast. In 13 relentless hours of savage combat the Confederate army had driven Grant back on himself, to the very edge of the Tennessee River and the Snake Creek swamps, where he'd first come ashore and where his army may have been hanging on by a fingernail—though it was a sharp fingernail, as we shall see. Grant's situation at this point was most precarious, and yet the only person in the Federal army who didn't think so seemed to be Grant.

In the gathering dusk McPherson, his engineering officer, returned from an assignment to assess the condition of the army and reported that fully one-third was hors de combat, and the rest "much dispirited." Grant merely nodded. "Well, General Grant," McPherson asked, "under this condition of affairs, what do you propose to do, Sir? Shall I make preparations for a retreat?" Grant's reply was short and quick. He had fought in the Mexican War and at Belmont, been the victor at Forts Henry and Donelson; he was no greenhorn, no amateur. "*Retreat?*" he blurted out, "*No!* I propose to attack at daylight, and whip them."

Experienced hunters say the most dangerous time to stalk a wounded animal is when he goes into his lair; there he somehow gathers unnatural strength, ferocity, and a singular resolve. Grant seemed to feel or sense this strength, the saving of his best blow for last, and he so remarked to others. But there are different analogies for his situation, and one that might have been more appealing to Beauregard and the Confederates comes from bullfighting lore.

Soon after the bull enters the ring he will select a spot for himself known to matadors as the *querencia,* to which the bull will return when he feels threatened. As the fight progresses, and the bull is worn down or wounded by the picadors' lances, after each encounter he will always go back to his querencia. Often it is located near the entrance to the ring, where he came in, as though the bull somehow feels the gate will be opened and he can escape. But he can never escape, and each time he returns to his querencia he becomes more predictable, more vulnerable, so that in the end the matador is able to kill him because he always goes back to the place where he feels most secure.

There is no evidence of course that Beauregard ever heard of this analogy, let alone employed it as a military tactic. Still, it was an

325

inescapable fact that all day his army had been driving the Federals toward Pittsburg Landing, and now, in their last extremity, the Yankees had drawn up for one last stand. From the Rebel side of things the position looked formidable enough, but neither unassailable nor impenetrable, because they had been assailing and penetrating Grant's defenses all day, up to and including the impenetrable Hornet's Nest. Too much blood had been shed—the countryside all around was fairly saturated with it—and now was the time for conclusions, to close it out.

That theme was on Braxton Bragg's mind. The querulous general had been vexed all day by the tendency of his victorious soldiers to stop and plunder enemy camps or forage for food (never mind that most hadn't eaten anything since breakfast), and Bragg had expended a good deal of energy pushing commanders to keep hammering, move forward, drive the enemy. But now the men were at the very edge of their endurance. The physical exertion associated with rushing forward, crawling, dodging bullets, and even hand-to-hand fighting is nothing compared with the toll exerted by the mental exhaustion of battle. The terror, exhilaration, horror, and revulsion of just a few minutes in combat—to say nothing of a full day's worth of it—overtaxes the body's adrenaline and drastically drains the soldier of energy.

At the fall of the Hornet's Nest, as surrenders had to be taken and prisoners dealt with, rumors circulated that the whole Yankee army had surrendered. Out of this disorder Bragg now anxiously tried to reassemble a fighting front to push through to the landing and complete the victory. "One more charge, my men, and we shall capture them all!" he cried.

Closest at hand Bragg had Withers's division, consisting of Chalmers's and Jackson's brigades plus the survivors of Gladden's brigade, now down to a mere 220 men commanded by Col. Zach C. Deas, after Gladden's successor Dan Adams was shot in the head during the melee at the Hornet's Nest. Also there was Patton Anderson's brigade from Ruggles's division as well as the lone remnants of Wood's brigade from Hardee's corps and about 30 guns—20 of them commanded by Maj. Francis A. Shoup, which had been part of Ruggles's grand battery at the Hornet's Nest. For some reason, none of the other corps commanders nearby—neither Polk nor Breckinridge—was able or willing to produce forces to join Bragg in the final assault. Bowen's and Robert Trabue's brigades were several hundred yards to the rear and far right of Bragg's line, while on the left Preston Pond's brigade was too far away and too isolated to participate in the assault. The other brigades simply had not come up.

Bragg drew up this Confederate line of battle—eight or ten emaciated regiments, certainly fewer than 5,000 men—at Dill Branch, a stream at the bottom of a steep ravine that emptied into the Tennessee less than a quarter mile south of Pittsburg Landing. Unfortunately for the Rebels, the recent flooding of the river—the same flood that had drowned out Fort Henry—also worked against them here.

In slack times the river ran 16 feet lower, which would have drained the Dill Branch ravine nearly empty. Now the river flooded the mouth of the ravine, not only making it impassable but raising the level of the river, which lifted the Yankee gunboats *Lexington* and *Tyler* to point-blank range straight down the gap in the bluff where Bragg's men would have to cross to get at Grant's army.

These powerful "timberclads" were the first of the river gunboats acquired by the U.S. Army and crewed by the navy and were old friends of Grant, having participated in his seizure of Paducah and the attack on the Confederates at Belmont and Fort Henry. Their monster 32-pounder guns were many times more powerful than the standard army field cannons, but they were not very accurate at long range.* Nevertheless, the mere sounds of their shells passing over and the superviolent explosions that followed took a severe psychological toll on the Confederate troops—and now, as Bragg's men prepared to charge down into the hollow of Dill Branch, the Union gunboats in fact had the close range they required.

It fell to Chalmers's brigade, which had been fighting since 8 or 9 a.m. and now anchored the Confederate right along the river, to cross Dill Branch nearest the gunboats. Colonel Camm, who had just escaped capture in the Hornet's Nest and was positioned opposite Chalmers's men in the Union line, peered out into the impending gloom as the Rebel line massed for its charge: "Again the battle was opened afresh, but for a time nothing was used but cannon; the sun looked like a ball of fire as it went out of sight, and the clouds of powder smoke hastened the gloaming. The scene was grand but fearful and the thunder terrific. We could see the red flashes of our own and the enemy's guns, and shells burst all about us. A mounted man had his buttocks cut off and the horse's back broken. I saw one cannon shot that seemed to jump out of the ground. It cut the top out of a bush my hungry horse was biting at, brushed my body and mangled a soldier sitting on a log a hundred feet or so behind me. One could not help wondering how any living thing could escape wounds or death.

---

* A contemporary report claimed that these 8-inch guns hurled a shell "as big as a full-grown hog."

"The Confederates attacked from the southwest," Camm said, "the worst point they could have chosen, for it forced them to cross a hollow that opened into the river, and exposed them to the fire of the gun boats *Tyler* and *Connestoga*." (In fact it was the *Lexington*.) The large-bore guns aboard the boats had been double-shotted with canister and "the execution was dreadful," said one Rebel who watched the charge. The cannon fire from the vessels, he said, was "continuous."

Farther to the Confederate left, things were not much better. Captain Gage's Mobile, Alabama, battery unlimbered on a prominent ridge and began to pour shot and shell into the Federal line. It was struck so many times by counterbattery fire, however, that it was forced to retire. Jackson's and Anderson's brigades had to descend the 60-foot-deep ravine in front of the center of Grant's line, which was protected by the battery of siege guns that had also been double-shotted with canister. Many of the men were out of ammunition but, as daylight was fast fading, they were instructed to charge with bayonets alone. As soon as the Rebel line appeared over the crest of the ravine they were slaughtered by close-quarter artillery fire in their faces.

The commanders managed to get the men to charge two more times, but after each their ranks were so decimated by gunfire that the charge stalled, then failed. The ravine began to fill with dead and wounded, and some of the wounded drowned in the bloody water that had backed up from the river. At last the exhausted men retired below the lip of the ravine and refused to continue unless there was "support" by strong reinforcements. General Withers was in the process of ordering these reinforcements when, he said in his official report, "to my astonishment, a large portion of the command to my left was observed to move rapidly from under the fire of the enemy."

Withers immediately ordered his adjutant to "go and arrest the commanding officers, and place the troops in position for charging the batteries." Word soon returned, however, that General Beauregard himself had ordered the army to retire for the night, a decision that became as controversial as Lee's so-called Lost Order at Antietam, or Longstreet's tardiness on the second day at Gettysburg. Among the famous what-ifs of the war, Beauregard's directive soon entered Confederate lore as the "Lost Opportunity."

Shiloh church, where Beauregard had kept his headquarters since Sherman's retreat in midmorning, was a good two miles from where Bragg was having it out with Grant's die-in-the-last-ditch defense. Beauregard had been in command of the army for nearly three hours, and he was deeply concerned that it was falling apart. Aides had reported that, among other things, all the roads were clogged with Confederate stragglers, regiments had been separated from their brigades, and companies from their regiments, and that at least a third of the army was engaged in plundering Yankee tents. Now he could hear with his own ears the tumultuous cannonading by the big Yankee gunboats and became fearful they were slaughtering his troops near the river.

Visitors to Beauregard's tent during this time were surprised, if not startled, to find the general tending to a large bird sitting on his lap. It was some sort of pheasant, the gift of a soldier who had picked it up on the battlefield that afternoon and offered it to Beauregard as . . . well, as dinner. Instead, the Creole took pity on the creature, which was dazed and confused by the shelling and suffering from a broken wing. He had taken to stroking it and apparently decided to nurse it back to health, for he had ordered a box to be altered as a cage so he could carry it along with his baggage after the Shiloh fight was finished. At least that was one story; another was that the general intended to save the pheasant and eat him later. In any case, anxiety over the disorganization of the army as well as its safety had become Beauregard's paramount concerns as darkness fell.

As is usual when matters of great import such as Shiloh are resolved by questionable decisions, memories often become "improved" with time or, put more directly, a great deal of lying goes on. The liar in chief in this case seems to be Beauregard, who, afterward, in justifying his order to stop the fighting, raised all sorts of reasons that he could not possibly have known at the time, sitting in his headquarters at Shiloh church, such as the arrival of Buell's army and the artillery strength of Grant's defensive line.

What we do know, however, is that Beauregard had just come into possession of a piece of intelligence that must have made him shiver with delight. A courier had ridden up from Corinth bringing a telegram from the Rebel general Ben Helm* in north Alabama, which revealed that Buell's army had been seen marching south toward Decatur, instead of west toward Pittsburg Landing.

---

* Benjamin Hardin Helm was, of all things, Abraham Lincoln's favorite brother-in-law, having married Mary Todd Lincoln's younger sister Emilie. Helm graduated from West Point in 1851, the same year his father was elected governor of Kentucky. He was killed at the Battle of Chickamauga in 1863, sending the President of the United States into deep, but very private, mourning.

Actually, it was only one division of Buell's army that had been spotted by cavalry scouts in Alabama, but it gave Beauregard the false impression that he would have all of tomorrow to finish off Grant before Buell could arrive.

Then there was the matter of Prentiss, who was delivered to Beauregard shortly after he was seized by Rebel troops. Prentiss later boasted that he deceived Beauregard by telling him that Buell was nowhere near Pittsburg Landing, and thus took credit for tricking the Creole into believing that he faced nothing more than Grant's badly mauled army next morning. But Colonel Jordan tells a different tale. When he rode into Beauregard's headquarters that evening he was introduced, he said, to a Federal general, who turned out to be Prentiss, and was charged with keeping him prisoner that night.

There was a great deal of jocularity among Jordan, Prentiss, and Col. Jacob Thompson, who had known Prentiss before the war. According to Jordan, as they were bedding down for the night Prentiss, "With a laugh . . . said, 'You gentlemen have had your way to-day, but it will be very different tomorrow. You'll see! Buell will effect a junction with Grant tonight, and we'll turn the tables on you in the morning.' " Jordan, "in the same pleasant spirit," or so he said, produced a copy of the dispatch from Corinth, but General Prentiss was having none of it. "He insisted it was a mistake, and we would see," Jordan later wrote in a magazine article, and when the morning broke with heavy firing from the landing, Prentiss exclaimed, "Ah, didn't I tell you so? There is Buell!" The discrepancy here is too wide for mere misinterpretation. Somebody is lying.

In the half-light while the battle still raged near the landing, Beauregard dictated a telegram to Richmond in which he informed Jefferson Davis and the Confederate government of the death of

General Johnston, as well as the "Complete Victory" of Confederate arms that day. The enemy, he said, had been thoroughly beaten and "the remnant of his army driven in utter disorder to the immediate vicinity of Pittsburgh and we remained undisputed masters of his . . . [camps]." The announcement was premature, of course, and later the Creole lamented, "I thought I had Grant just where I wanted him, and could finish him up next day."

So Beauregard sent a messenger, his old friend Maj. Numa Augustin from New Orleans society days, with an order telling all commanders to call off the battle and withdraw to the shelter of the Yankee camps. It had been Augustin's arrival at the Dill Branch fight that caused the withdrawal that precipitated General Withers's "astonishment"—to say nothing of Bragg's dumbfounded reaction when Augustin finally got around to him. Bragg was convinced, as he stated later in his official report, that he was in the midst of "a movement commenced with every prospect of success."

"Have you given that order to anyone else?" Bragg demanded. He had been acting, during the attack, as Beauregard's chief of staff.

"Yes sir, to General Polk, on your left, and if you look, you will see it is being obeyed," Augustin told him. Bragg was aghast as he watched the gray-clad Confederates fade back from the battle line.

"My God, my God," Bragg cried. "It is too late!"

CHAPTER 15

I INTEND TO
WITHDRAW

━━━◆◆◆━━━

G ENERAL BRAGG'S LAMENT WAS TOO TRUE. EVERY
fifteen minutes or so, steamers brought another several hundred of Buell's men across to the landing, and before morning he would have more than 17,000 fresh troops on the field. Not only that, but well after dark the much sought division of Lew Wallace at last concluded its bizarre odyssey from Crump's Landing and emerged from the Owl Creek swamps near Sherman's position at the far right end of the Union line. This now gave Grant nearly 25,000 completely new troops—more men than Beauregard could muster in the entire Confederate army at that point, considering the casualties and stragglers.

It seems almost a criminal error of military intelligence that nobody—not Sidney Johnston, Beauregard, or anybody else—thought to put a close watch on the routes Buell might have used to march to Grant's relief. But in those days and times the term "military intelligence," if not exactly an oxymoron, was at best an expression of a vague and more or less unrefined concept that smacked of being "undignified." Spying on the enemy—though it is absolutely necessary—was considered somehow "sneaky," even "ungentlemanly," and usually was relegated to the cavalry.*

In fact there *was* somebody watching out for Buell, and for whatever else lurked in the Confederates' far right quarter, and that somebody was Nathan Bedford Forrest along with his cavalry regiment. All day Colonel Forrest had been itching to do something useful with his horsemen, but in a fight like Shiloh, often the best thing cavalry can do is stay out of the way and guard roads and bridges. Forrest tested that notion once and found that it was held for a good reason. Late in the morning as the battle raged around the Peach Orchard, Forrest chafed at his orders to guard against any Federal attempt to cross Lick Creek, nearby where Stuart and Chalmers would soon be having their fight. As the roar of battle swelled in the west, Forrest reportedly told his men, "Boys, you hear that shooting? And here we are guarding a damn *creek!* Let's go and help them!"

Upon reaching the battlefield Forrest rode to the sound of the loudest firing, which, unfortunately, happened to be the Sunken Road in the Hornet's Nest at its worst, and immediately he sent for permission to charge the enemy. But division commander Ben Cheatham demurred, saying that his infantry brigades had already charged several times without success and needed some rest and

---

* The stigma on spying and collecting military intelligence continued way into the 20th century when Secretary of State Henry L. Stimson, later Franklin Roosevelt's secretary of war, famously shut down the so-called Black Chamber, in 1929, by declaring, "Gentlemen do not read each other's mail."

reorganization, to which Forrest was reported to have declared, "Then I'll charge under my own orders."

He formed his command into a column of fours in support of a regiment of Alabama infantry that was trying to drive a body of Federals from a fencerow and charged toward the Sunken Road. Blasted by massed artillery and infantry fire—both of which are anathema to cavalry—Forrest's bold riders lurched into the knotty thickets of the Hornet's Nest and immediately found themselves and their mounts hopelessly entangled in the branches of the thick scrub oak. They—most of them, anyway—somehow managed to extricate themselves from the jungled thicket, but it was obvious now, if it wasn't before, that mounted cavalry has little business in the middle of a serious infantry fight.

After that, Forrest led his regiment to the far Confederate right and hovered behind a series of Indian mounds along the Tennessee River, watching for trouble, of which Buell's army was the paramount example. In the distance Forrest's scouts could see some kind of activity on the far shore of the river, and the moving of steamboats, but when they attempted to get closer one of the Federal gunboats opened up and drove them back into the woods.

Night found Forrest suspended between curiosity and suspicion, and he ordered a squadron to strip a dozen dead Federals of their uniforms and sent a reconnaissance team under a Lieutenant Sheridan, dressed in Yankee blue, to get a better look at Pittsburg Landing. Soon they returned during a tremendous rain and electrical storm with news that was at once ominous and promising. Buell's army had indeed arrived and was crossing the river, Sheridan said, but in his opinion there was such disorder at the landing that a surprise night attack might end the affair on the spot.

Forrest immediately set out in search of a superior officer, the closest being Brigadier General Chalmers, who was asleep. After being awakened he replied that Forrest needed to find a corps commander, if not Beauregard himself, for such a portentous operation. Continuing on, Forrest came upon corps commander Hardee and told him that if the Rebel army did not immediately launch a night attack, "[We] will be whipped like hell before ten o'clock tomorrow." Hardee replied that Beauregard was the man to see, but somehow, in the rainstorm and the dark, Forrest was unable to locate Beauregard's headquarters at the Shiloh church. About 2 a.m. he returned to Hardee but was told only to "maintain his pickets." If there was in fact a "lost opportunity" for the Confederacy at Shiloh that was probably it.

For most of the men, that night must have been at the least an absorbing experience. The storm drenched everyone to the bone— even the Confederates who were now occupying the Yankees' Sibley tents were soaked, for the canvas had been riddled with holes during the day's fighting. All had been up since daybreak and were completely exhausted, and now even sleep was denied them. From the woods and the fields there came a kind of low, constant, monosyllabic sighing from the wounded, interspersed with the screams of those in acute agony. All day hundreds of wagons had been carting the wounded off toward Corinth, but it had not been enough. In places where the fighting had been heaviest, the wounded and the dead lay thick like a carpet, their countenances made more ghastly by the lightning flashes. As the storms broke up, a pale moon shone between the racing clouds, basking the horrid tableaux in an unearthly shade of yellowish blue.

Even more nauseating was the appearance of feral hogs, which began eating the dead and the wounded alike. Augustus Mecklin, who had survived the charge of Statham's brigade at the Peach Orchard, heard them, "unmistakable, quarreling over their carnival feast." Bierce, too, later told of recoiling in horror at the droves of man-eating hogs on the battlefield.

All of this was punctuated throughout the night by terrific explosions from the big 8-inch cannons of the gunboats, which had been firing at 10- or 15-minute intervals since sundown to harass the Rebel army. Confederates hid in hastily scraped-out pits or beneath houses and corncribs; one even told of crawling into a hollow tree trunk. Since it was unaimed fire, most of the shells fell harmlessly in the woods, but some did not. Four Rebel soldiers were found next day, stone dead but completely intact and without apparent wounds, seated around an oilcloth they had spread on the ground in a Sibley tent to play cards. A burned-out candle sat atop a bayonet stuck in the ground. "Each had three cards in his hand," said one of the soldiers who found them, "and four cards lay in the middle of the blanket." The mere proximity to such huge explosions was enough to fatally stop the human heart.

* * *

Don Carlos Buell was a stern old martinet with a superiority complex who from the beginning did not like Grant or anything else about the Battle of Shiloh. He was most especially disturbed by the horde of stragglers at Pittsburg Landing and hinted—or so Sherman claimed—that he was considering not bringing his army across at all rather than have it mingle with such cowardly riffraff. To Sherman it suggested that the ever cautious Buell didn't want to risk the possibility of his army getting whipped by the Confederates, just like Grant's had been. But Buell rebutted this years later by pointing out that he began bringing his army across to the landing as soon as it arrived on the opposite bank of the river. Brig. Gen. Thomas Crittenden, however, one of Buell's division commanders, worried that the cowardice in Grant's army would be contagious and found himself "so disgusted" by the mob at the landing that "I asked General Buell to let me land a regiment and drive them away. I did not wish my troops to come in contact with them."

Grant seemed unperturbed by any of this. When the rainstorm began he sought shelter in the cabin atop the bluff, which had once been his headquarters, but found that it had been turned into a surgery that was still operating at full capacity. Repelled by the gory work, he returned to the tempest and took refuge beneath a large oak tree, which is where Sherman found him in the pouring rain stretched out in his overcoat, his slouch hat pulled down, and smoking his eternal cigar.

"Well Grant, we've had the devil's own day, haven't we?" Sherman remarked.

"Yes," replied Grant. "Lick 'em tomorrow, though."

There were many in the army, if not most, who would have declared that Grant was living in a fool's paradise—but not all. Colonel Camm at least was confident that they were safe from the Rebel onslaught.

"For the first time we had a continuous line," he wrote in his diary. "There was no chance to flank us, and of the men who bore the brunt that day there was none left in the ranks that would not have died on the line."

———◆———

For the Yankee army, April 7, 1862, began before sunrise, which was slightly after 5 a.m. What Grant had in store for the Confederates

340

was almost the exact opposite of what they had planned to do to him the day before. Starting from Pittsburg Landing, the Union line would attack in a giant wheeling motion, pivoting on Sherman and Lew Wallace, who held down the far western end of the line, sweeping across the battlefield until they drove the Rebel army against the boggy wilds of Owl Creek, where it would have to surrender. As with everything else at Shiloh, this was easier said than done. Unlike yesterday's fighting, though, at least it was a plan.

Buell's divisions, which were nearest the landing, moved out first, crossing Dill Branch, now deserted except for the dead. Musician fourth class John Cockerill, who had been told that his father, the colonel of his regiment, was shot and killed on Sunday, had a miserable night at the landing. He had been near enough to witness the grisly beheading of Captain Carson by the cannonball and had curled up in the rain beside a hay bale but was unable to sleep because of the constant firing of the gunboats.

"There was never a night so long, so hideous, or so utterly uncomfortable," he wrote later. At dawn, however, young Cockerill was awakened by, of all things, strains of the overture from *Il Trovatore*,* "magnificent[ly]" rendered by the 15th Infantry Regiment band, serenading from the top deck of the steamboat *War Eagle*.

"How inspiring that music was!" wrote Cockerill. "Even the poor wounded men lying on the shore seemed to be lifted up, and every soldier received an impetus"—including Cockerill himself, who grabbed a rifle and, after a jolt from a swig of "Cincinnati whisky," joined up with the 15th Infantry Regiment and marched

---

* The tragic opera by Giuseppe Verdi, in which most of the interesting characters are killed off.

on the enemy. As they crossed Dill Branch, it didn't look like the same ground anymore—and it wasn't.

Cockerill noted that "the underbrush had been literally mowed off by the bullets, and great trees had been shattered by artillery fire." Moving on, he found "In places the bodies of the slain lay upon the ground so thick that I could step from one to the other . . . I remember a poor Confederate lying on his back, while by his side was a heap of ginger cakes and bologna sausage. [He] had evidently filled his pockets the day before with edibles from a sutler's tent, and had been killed before he had the opportunity to enjoy [them]."

Farther on, Cockerill "passed the corpse of a beautiful boy in gray, who lay with his blond curls scattered about his face, and his hands folded peacefully about his chest. He was clad in a bright, neat uniform, well garnished with gold, which seemed to tell the story of a loving mother and sisters who had sent their household pet to the field of war. He was about my age," Cockerill said wistfully, and later, when reminded of it, he broke into tears.

All across the line of march it was the same. "The blue and the gray were mingled together, side by side. Beneath a great oak tree I counted the corpses of fifteen men, lying as though during the night, suffering from wounds, they had crawled together for mutual assistance, and there all had died."

As they neared the Peach Orchard, Cockerill remembered, they came upon "an entire battery of Federal artillery which had been dismantled in Sunday's fight, every horse of which had been killed in his harness, every gun of which had been dismantled, and in this awful heap of death lay the bodies of dozens of cannoneers."

Among the most piteous sights, everywhere on the field "were the poor wounded horses, their heads drooping, their eyes glassy and gummy, waiting for the slow coming of death. No painter ever did justice to a battlefield such as this, I am sure," said the musician John Cockerill.

Soon enough they encountered the Confederate army. Lieutenant Bierce had found himself experiencing an odd sort of disappointment that morning when Hazen's brigade moved out "straight as a string" but through woods that seemed strangely unmarked by yesterday's battle. But shortly, "we passed out of this oasis that had singularly escaped the desolation of battle, and the evidence of the struggle was soon in great profusion." Bierce marveled that every single tree that remained standing was covered in bullet holes "from the root to a height of ten to twenty feet," [and] "one could not have laid a hand [anywhere on the trunk] without covering several punctures." Soon they began to come upon the dead, and a few of the living wounded, including a Federal sergeant whose brains were oozing out through a hole in his skull. So brutalized had things become that one of Bierce's men asked if he should put the victim out of his misery with his bayonet, but Bierce said no. "It was [an] unusual [request], and too many others were looking," he said.

The brigade kept moving through open fields and past the Bloody Pond and the Peach Orchard. Ahead they caught glimpses of Rebel cavalry, but no infantry, and Bierce had convinced himself that the Confederates, "disheartened" by the arrival of fresh Union troops, had retreated to Corinth. Onward they marched unmolested, until they came to "a gentle acclivity, covered with an undergrowth of young oaks." He could not have known it then, but Bierce was looking at the rear of the Sunken Road.

The brigade pushed into the open field and halted; then there were orders to press forward. When they reached the edge of the oaks, Bierce said, "I can't describe it—the forest seemed all at once to flame up and disappear with a crash like that of a great wave upon the beach." There was "the sickening 'spat' of lead against flesh, and a dozen of my brave fellows tumbled over like ten pins. Some struggled to their feet, only to go down again. Those who stood fired into the smoking brush and retired. We had expected, at most, a line of skirmishers"; instead, he recalled bitterly, "what we found was a line of battle, holding its fire till it could count our teeth."

If there could be any humor in such a sanguinary encounter Bierce was the one who found it, relating the "ludicrous incident of a young officer who had taken part in this affair walking up to his colonel—who had watched the whole thing—and gravely reporting, 'The enemy is in force just beyond that field, sir.' "

From the tangled protection of the Sunken Road the Confederates were giving the Yankees a dose of their own medicine. Advance was impossible for the Federal troops, and the two armies "flamed away at one another with amazing zeal," Bierce said, "while the riddled bodies of my poor skirmishers were the only ones left on this 'neutral ground.' "

Cannons were brought up. Nelson's division artillery had been left behind at Savannah because it could not be moved on the mud march through the swamp, but Buell sent him two batteries from elsewhere, including one commanded by Capt. William Terrill, a West Point–educated Virginian, the rest of whose family was in the Rebel army.* This was a heavy battery consisting of 12-pounder

---

* Terrill rose to the rank of general and was killed six months later at the Battle of Perryville; his brother James, also a brigade commander, was a general in Lee's Army of Northern Virginia and was killed in a battle near Richmond in 1864. A third, younger, brother joined the Confederate cavalry and was killed near Winchester, Virginia.

cannons that "did much execution," and it fell to Bierce's platoon to protect, or "support," them. "The shock of our own pieces nearly deafened us," Bierce groused while his men lay in the woods with the battle "roaring and stammering" all around them. "Oh, those cursed guns," he said with trademark sarcasm. "Had it not been for them, we might have died like men."

———◆———

What had happened was this. At dawn the noise of heavy firing from the direction of Owl Creek had startled Beauregard, who with almost a sense of leisure savored the notion of finishing off Grant and destroying the main Federal army in the West; in fact, the Great Creole halfway expected to find the Yankees had evacuated downriver during the night.

Grant, of course, had done no such thing, and Beauregard, now alerted that strong reinforcements must be on the field, hastily began assembling a defensive line with which he at least hoped to halt the Federal offensive and turn it into a stalemate. He sent Hardee to the far right, Bragg to the far left, and Polk and Breckinridge to the center to put regiments in place and make a stand.

If Beauregard had sent people to keep close tabs of Buell's whereabouts, at least he could have ordered the men to construct defensive fortifications during the night, which likely would have made all the difference in the world. Instead, he found himself in the same position that the Yankees had been in yesterday—having to defend against massed assaults with whatever protection was at hand. The fact that the Hornet's Nest provided good natural cover was some consolation; it would have to be, since Beauregard could scarcely muster 20,000 men of arms in the entire Confederate army.

The main Union thrust would be in the center, around the Hornet's Nest, just as the Confederates' efforts had been the day before. There the Rebels had gathered an odd assortment of depleted regiments and the ragtag of a few brigades totaling probably no more than 4,000 men to contend with the roughly 9,000 fresh troops of Nelson's and Thomas Crittenden's divisions.

The fighting, some of it hand to hand, seesawed all morning and into the afternoon, with Confederates pushing the Yankees back across farm fields and into woods, only to find themselves ambushed by fresh Federal troops and driven back to their original line. As the day wore on, Beauregard was hard pressed to shuffle regiments from one part of the field to another as more commanders cried for help. It was as maddening as using one's fingers to plug ever multiplying holes in a bursting dike.

During one of these attacks and counterattacks by the Second Texas Infantry, Sam Houston, Jr., son of the great Texan, found himself face to face with the remnants of Hurlbut's chewed-up command. He remembered the silence of his brigade marching across a wide, open field "with not a command given, nor a word spoken" as "I kept asking myself, 'Where is the enemy?' " Then a fence line before him "transformed into a wall of flame, and . . . our line seemed actually to wilter and curl up."

After the smoke drifted away, Houston said, "In front of us, and on both flanks, the very earth swarmed with Federals. So nearly had we approached the enemy that the ornaments on their caps were readily distinguished, and I remember noting even in that terrible moment, that our adversaries were the 3rd Iowa Infantry." And on the left, in Bragg's quarter near the Shiloh church, Private

Johnnie Green of Kentucky's "Orphan Brigade"* experienced what amounted to a miracle. He was raising his gun to fire when a bullet hit him in the chest, knocking him down. At first he thought he was killed, but on further inspection he found "one piece of the bullet laying against my skin inside my clothes just over my heart. The ball had passed through the stock of my gun, split on the iron ramrod, and the other piece had passed through my jacket and buried itself in a little testament in my jacket pocket."

The future explorer Henry Morton Stanley, presently of the Dixie Grays, found himself in the unfortunate position of having outrun his company during one of these sorties and was made a Yankee prisoner. "Even to my unexperienced eyes the troops were in ill-condition for repeating the efforts of Sunday," he said, but in short order they were "moved forward resolutely." When the shooting began Stanley was "in an open, grassy space, with no convenient tree or stump," but he quickly spied a shallow hollow in the ground ahead and made a dash for it.

From there he commenced firing and "became so absorbed with some blue figures in front of me" when "to my speechless amazement I found my companions had retreated!" As he rose from his hollow, the next words Stanley heard were, "Down with that gun, Secesh, or I'll drill a hole through you!" Then, he said, "Two men sprang at my collar, and marched me into the ranks of the terrible Yankees. I was a prisoner."

It went on like this all morning, small, fierce, desperate attacks—until the weight of numbers began to tell and the Rebels

---

* There were "orphan" brigades from Kentucky and Missouri, so called because their states were under Union control.

began to give ground. Back across the bloodstained Peach Orchard they went, across Sunken Road, giving up ground but making the Yankees pay for every yard. Pat Cleburne's brigade, the mere sight of whose once proud white-moon-on-a-black-field flag had shaken the Yankee soldiers, could now put only 800 men in the line out of his original 2,700.

When Ambrose Bierce's company of Federals was finally relieved of its support duty at Terrill's battery, he found himself wandering in a part of the now emptied Hornet's Nest that had caught fire yesterday, which proved to be a loathsome experience. "Death had put his sickle into this thicket," Bierce said," and fire had gleaned the field." Here lay the bodies, "half buried in ashes; their clothing was half burnt away—their hair and beard entirely," he said. "Some were swollen to double-girth, others shriveled to manikins."

As the hours wore on, more were wounded and carried off or killed. Most men in the Confederate ranks began to sense they were fighting a futile battle; by now most everyone knew that Buell and Lew Wallace were on the field, and the implications thereof were clear. Still they persisted, sullen, bitter, and deadly, though without the savage fury of yesterday because they had been simply fought to a frazzle.

The tension mounted as Beauregard watched the Yankee host prepare to drive his troops from the Shiloh church. It was about 2 p.m. and men were streaming back from the roaring, flaming, stinking cauldron of the fight on Bragg's front. The Creole found himself surrounded by reluctant regiments that balked at returning to the fray. No one wants to be the last man killed in a losing battle, and words could not move these shaken men; their commanders tried, Beauregard tried, Governor Harris of Tennessee tried—to no avail.

So Beauregard "seized the banners of two different regiments and led them forward to the assault in the face of the fire of the enemy," recorded Colonel Thompson, one of his aides, adding in a pensive note, "I became convinced that our troops were too much exhausted to make a vigorous resistance." No one could say that Beauregard was not a brave leader. Thompson rode to him with a plea that "you should expose yourself no further, . . . but to retire from Shiloh Church in good order."

This seemed the crux of the battle. The Shiloh church soon was recaptured; the Yankees were closing in; nearly all the gains of the previous day had been lost. Still Beauregard fought on, more out of a sense of honor and fury than anything else. Finally Colonel Jordan, the original planner of the battle, rode up and, employing a Napoleonic-sounding military figure of speech, compared the present condition of the Rebel army to "a lump of sugar, thoroughly soaked with water, yet preserving its original shape, though ready to dissolve—would it not be judicious to get away with what we have?" he asked.

With this dainty metaphor jangling harshly in his ears, Beauregard surveyed the mounting chaos in front of him, as more and more men straggled out of the fight, and solemnly replied, "I intend to withdraw in a few moments."

Breckinridge was sent for and told to serve as rear guard. With that, the Confederate army began its painful withdrawal from the Battle of Shiloh. The wounded continued to be carted off in heaps, but much of the captured artillery and other valuable loot from the Yankee camps was lost due to lack of transportation. Beauregard did, however, get away with 34 national, state, and regimental stands of colors to prove the Confederates had not come to the fight as pikers. Night soon closed in over another smoke-stained, fiery sunset and, as if to add insult to injury, as the Rebel army slouched south toward Corinth a dismal drizzle of rain began to fall.

The march back was excruciating—far more so than when they had marched out of the city four days earlier. Here is Braxton Bragg's personal assessment in a note to Beauregard written the next morning at 7:30 a.m. "My Dear General: Our condition is horrible. Troops utterly disorganized and demoralized. Road almost impassable. No provisions and no forage; consequently everything is feeble. Straggling parties may get in tonight. Those in rear will suffer much. The rear guard, Breckinridge commanding, is left at Mickey's in charge of wounded & etc. The enemy, up to daylight, had not pursued. Have ordered Breckinridge to hold on till pressed by the enemy, but he will suffer for want of food. Can any fresh troops, with five days' rations, be sent to his relief?"

He added, almost as an afterthought, "It is most lamentable to see the state of affairs, but I am powerless and almost exhausted.

"Our artillery is being left along the road by its officers; indeed I find but few officers with their men. Relief of some kind is necessary, but how it is to reach us I can hardly suggest, as no human power or animal power could carry [even] empty wagons over this road with such teams as we have."

For a man with Bragg's military decorum and combative disposition to have sent such a plaintive note to his commanding officer more than speaks for itself. A determined effort by Grant to pursue the retreating Confederate army likely would have ended the Civil War in the West in a fell swoop. But when it became apparent that the enemy was withdrawing, Grant—like McClellan later at Antietam and Meade after him at Gettysburg—simply found his army too exhausted to pursue. As if the two sides were warring jungle beasts, Grant was content to pant and bleed and lick his wounds, still master of his territory, and let the loser slink off, bloodied but unbowed, to fight again another day.

Sherman wasn't buying it, however, and while he also wasn't about to try to pursue the Rebel army immediately, by next morning he'd put together a heavy force of two brigades plus a cavalry regiment—strong enough, he felt, to press Beauregard and see what he could see—and maybe even sweep up a Rebel brigade or two and get revenge for his humiliation of the previous day. Instead, Sherman received a lesson from a man who knew how to teach them well.

As he marched his force south down the Corinth road, Sherman found no Confederates to kill but many Rebel hospital tents containing hundreds of dead and dying of both sides and those too injured to be moved. These unfortunates were being tended by overworked surgeons, whom Sherman arrested and then released on a promise that they would continue treating the wounded but, afterward, turn themselves in to General Grant as prisoners.

About five miles out, Sherman encountered a sizable Rebel camp near a clearing consisting of a large number of fallen trees.* Seeing gray-clad cavalry inside the camp, Sherman ordered an attack; an infantry regiment was sent out as skirmishers, backed up by an infantry brigade in line, plus his own cavalry regiment hovering on the flanks. If Sherman had known who was inside the enemy camp, he might have thought twice about attacking it, or at least proceeded more cautiously, because the man in charge of the Rebel

---

* This was either an old logging site or, just as likely, a natural clearing made by one of the fierce tornadoes that are so common in that part of the country.

cavalry was Nathan Bedford Forrest, whose mantra soon engulfed him: "War means fightin', and fightin' means killin'."

Instead of doing the prudent thing and galloping off, Forrest took one look at the Yankee host marching toward him and gathered his own people plus some 220 mounted Texas Rangers, along with several other scattered cavalry companies, and immediately charged pell-mell into Sherman's advance, shooting, shouting, and slashing with sabers.

The shock of this audacious performance caused the Federal skirmishers to drop their weapons and run away, followed by the Yankee cavalry, as Forrest's horsemen tore into them too. Sherman suddenly found himself in the unenviable position of a man who has stalked and cornered a beast in the woods, only to find it is meaner than he is. Aghast at the sight of his fleeing men, he ordered the brigade to move quickly into a defensive position.

Known for his almost superhuman courage and daring, Forrest meanwhile had galloped so hard that he had outraced his own men and abruptly discovered he was alone amid the disorganized but still dangerous enemy, who closed in shouting, "Kill him, kill him!" With saber in one hand and blazing pistol in the other, his horse rearing and plunging, Forrest fiendishly slashed out until one blue-coat pushed the barrel of his rifle against Forrest's side and pulled the trigger, sending a bullet tearing into his back. Enraged, Forrest reached down and snatched one of his tormentors by the collar and jerked him up behind him on the horse. Then, using this startled passenger as a shield, Forrest galloped through the furor of gun-fire and bayonets back to his own lines, where he unceremoniously dumped the amazed Yankee soldier on the ground.*

---

* Forrest's wound turned out to be painful but not serious.

After that, Sherman decided he had had enough, and what was soon known as the Battle of Fallen Timbers became the last engagement of the Shiloh Campaign.

No one could have been more shocked, or more delighted, at Sherman's return to the old camp at the Shiloh church than musician fourth class John Cockerill, when who should come trotting up at the head of one of Sherman's regiments but his *own father,* not dead at all but fresh from having served in the Fallen Timbers fiasco. Father and son had not seen each other for three days, and the reunion was dramatic, according to the younger Cockerill, who said his father "Dismounted and gave me the most affectionate embrace my life had ever known."

As the Confederates retreated the previous afternoon, young Cockerill had left his position in the lines and, with nowhere else to go, found the road leading back to the old camps of the 17th Ohio, his father's regiment, which had just been recaptured from the Confederates. The camp was deserted, the regiment gone, vanished, and "no one could tell me when it would return," he said. The tents were riddled with bullet and shrapnel holes and completely pillaged, including Cockerill's own personal possessions, but there was likely no happier boy on the battlefield, or, for that matter, on earth, now that his father had returned from the dead.

It did not always turn out that way. Ann Wallace, following her dreadful night on the *Minnehaha,* received stupendously uplifting news at ten o'clock next morning when her brother Cyrus Dickey arrived with word that her precious "Will had been brought in (after the rebels had been put to flight) and, Oh joy! He was

353

breathing. I flew to the adjoining boat where he was," she said, and found him on a narrow mattress on the floor. "His face was flushed, but he was breathing naturally, so like himself, save for that fearful wound in his temple." He seemed to recognize Ann's voice and squeezed her hand. "He knows me! He knows me!" she exclaimed. "I could appreciate all the feelings of Mary and Martha at the tomb of Lazarus."

The boat took the Wallace party to Savannah, to Grant's headquarters at the Cherry mansion, in the same room where lay the injured general Charles F. Smith, now gravely ill. Ann Wallace sat by her husband's side for three more days, holding his hand and trying to speak with him. Others of his staff and his brothers held his hand as well, but he responded only to Ann, she thought, because his touch recognized her wedding bands. Predictably, infection set in and hope faded. Wallace became delirious, and on Thursday "he pressed my hand long and fondly to his heart," she said, "then he waved me away and said, 'We meet in heaven.'" He died shortly afterward.

"Those last days had been so cherished, so unexpected," Ann wrote later. "I raised my heart in grateful thanks for this, and also that [his] dearest friends were with him at his death. God had led me there so that I should not meet the great sorrow alone."

The sorrow of course was not confined to the Wallace family. Captain Thruston recalled the sad discovery of the body of his friend Captain Battle the evening of the second day of Shiloh. Two of his college roommates had found him and notified a third, Maj. John R. Chamberlain of the 81st Ohio. "The last time I saw Allen Battle alive was in June, 1858, at Miami University, the year I graduated," Chamberlain wrote. "When I saw him next it was April 8,

1862, dead in the camp of Hurlbut's division on the battlefield of Shiloh." Two of his classmates were watching over him, Chamberlain said. "There was a smile on his face, his right hand was raised, the forefinger extended as if pointing to some object, when the fatal bullet struck him down."

His friends fashioned a rude coffin made of cracker (hardtack) boxes, and a deep grave was dug on sloping ground in the rear of the 31st Indiana Regiment. Chamberlain used an ax to cut a big chip out of a large black oak tree facing the grave, "so as to guide us to the spot should we ever be required to do so." As the coffin was lowered into the ground, wrote Captain Thruston, "none of us had any thought other than that we were laying to his last rest a gallant soldier, a sincere man, who thought that the cause for which he fought was the right thing to die for." At that point the carefree days of college, for these old chums, must have seemed a million miles away.

———— ◆ ————

At last the final results of the Battle of Shiloh reached Richmond. Beauregard had tried to smooth it over by noting all of the enemy regimental colors and Yankee officers the army had captured, and restating at length the "glorious, heroic," and nearly victorious sweep of the field Sunday, before he retired the army out of "discretion" in the face of a superior enemy force. Now it finally sank in to Jefferson Davis that Albert Sidney Johnston, his friend since boyhood, had indeed been killed, and he wept bitterly in private, moaning, "The cause could have spared a whole state, rather than that great soldier." Later he wrote, "When he fell, I realized that our strongest pillar had been broken."

Davis, an accomplished West Point–trained soldier, illustrious colonel in the Mexican conflict, and former U.S. secretary of war, immediately read through all of Beauregard's latest posturing about "victory," but he did not retract the promising statement he had read before the Confederate Congress a day earlier, which had been based on Beauregard's original telegram. Like the Creole, Davis decided to leave the best face on it, for the South needed all the bucking up it could get. George McClellan had recently landed a Yankee army at Hampton Roads, below Richmond, and was slowly working his way up the peninsula toward the Confederate capital with an estimated 120,000 men.

Yet Davis never forgave Beauregard for calling the army back on Sunday evening. In his memoirs he wrote, "At the ensuing nightfall our victorious army retired from the front and abandoned its vantage-ground on the bluffs, which had been won at such a cost of blood. The enemy thereby had room and opportunity to come out from their corner, reoccupy the strong positions from which they had been driven, and dispose their troops on more favorable ground."

CHAPTER 16

AH! TOM GRAFTON—
HOW MISTAKEN
YOU WERE!

———◆◆◆———

UNLIKE BEAUREGARD, GRANT DID NOT SEND GLOWING reports about the battle either to St. Louis or to his nation's capital; in fact, according to Halleck's testimony in the Official Records, Grant's report of the event did not "give any satisfactory information."

Furious that a battle had been brought on against his orders, Halleck telegraphed to Grant on April 8, after it was over, "Your army is not now in condition to resist attack. It must be made so without delay." Halleck also apparently made the recommendation that Grant retreat his army across the river, a suggestion that Grant declined on grounds that it would "demoralize" his soldiers. Then, on April 9, the supreme commander of the Union army in the West boarded a steamboat in St. Louis and proceeded toward Pittsburg Landing to relieve Ulysses Grant and take charge of the army himself.

357

The report on the battle that Grant submitted begins, "It becomes my duty to report another battle fought between two great armies, one contending for the maintenance of the best government ever devised, the other for its destruction," but it was painfully short on details, leaving Lincoln and the government to learn the particulars through the newspapers, which of course sensationalized the event. Horace Greeley's *New York Tribune* complained, "Gen. Grant's lame dispatch is as foggy as are most others," and the *Cincinnati Commercial* condemned Grant's report as "loose, rambling [and] slovenly."

Word quickly spread that there had been a terrible battle and a Northern victory at Pittsburg Landing, but the first comprehensive story was written several days after the fighting ended by Whitelaw Reid of the *Cincinnati Gazette*. The story was widely reprinted in the eastern press. In more than 19,000 words Reid's gloomy narrative was not about "a great victory for the Union, but a near disaster," in which he chronicled all the blunders that had nearly shattered Grant's army. Grant himself came in for his share of the blame, as the North (and the South as well) tried to absorb the mind-numbing slaughter.

When everything was said and done, the combined casualties at Shiloh amounted to 23,741, which is more, as historian Shelby Foote has pointed out, in a single battle than in all America's previous wars—American Revolution, War of 1812, and Mexican War—*combined*. The butcher's bill included 1,754 Union dead, 8,408 wounded, and 2,885 missing or captured for a total of 13,047. Confederate losses were 1,723 killed, 8,012 wounded, and 959 missing or captured for a total of 10,694. The casualties at Shiloh were fully *twice* those in all the earlier battles of the Civil War.

Nothing like it had ever happened before in the Western Hemisphere, and the Northern people's initial elation at a great Union victory soon turned to shock, and then to outrage, as the casualty lists came in.

For Grant, it was the end of a grand illusion. Based on the mediocre performance of the Confederates at Bowling Green, Nashville, and Forts Henry and Donelson, Grant, like so many others, had convinced himself that a Union victory in a single great battle would cause the Confederacy to dissolve. However, after Shiloh, he reversed himself entirely with the stark conclusion that the Union could be restored only by the total conquest and subjugation of the South.

The Shiloh story that Whitelaw Reid told was even grimmer than the harsh casualty figures suggested; his was a tale of blundering, stupidity, cowardice, and sloth. All of the mistakes glared out prominently: the failure to fortify, failure to reconnoiter, failure to read the signs of impending attack, failure even to have a battle plan in case of attack—all of this in addition to the sordid spectacle of the cringing masses below the bluff who had deserted the Union lines.

Soon other stories circulated, accusations such as that Grant's army had been so surprised that hundreds of Union soldiers were bayoneted to death in their tents or while eating their breakfast; that Grant had been dallying at a mansion ten miles from the battlefield instead of staying with his troops; that he had so little control of his army that most of it ran away at the first shot; that he had been saved only by the miraculous, last-moment arrival of Buell; and that he had been negligent in not pursuing Beauregard's beaten army and destroying it. For his part, Grant did not enhance his reputation when he denied being surprised, telling a newspaper that even if the Rebels had told him where and when they planned to make their move, "we could not have been better prepared," nor when he continued to insist that he had been attacked by 70,000 Confederates.

Next were the usual charges of drunkenness and incompetence; references were made to Grant's indifferent military bearing and his inattention to his troops. Presently the lieutenant governor of Ohio arrived at Pittsburg Landing to report back to the Cincinnati *Commercial Appeal* that there was an "intense feeling [in the army] against Generals Grant and Prentiss that . . . they ought to be court-martialed and shot." (This abrupt public animus against Prentiss appears to have been caused by the fact that in his official report Grant failed to credit Prentiss with stemming the Confederate onslaught by holding out in the Hornet's Nest until nearly dark; thus, all that most people knew was that Prentiss had surrendered to the enemy with nearly his entire command.)

So, instead of being hailed as the victor of Shiloh, Grant was suddenly denounced from the halls of Congress to the White House as a hapless blunderer and alcoholic, and a chorus arose for his removal. Soon the clamor was such that Lincoln was forced to deal with it. Popular lore has it that he told the critics, "Find out what kind of whiskey Grant drinks and send a barrel of it to my other generals." There is no firm evidence that he said this, but there *is* evidence that Lincoln said of Grant, "I can't spare that man, he fights."

For the most part, Grant sloughed off his detractors, but the furor nearly unhinged Sherman, who wrote a volcanic letter to the offending Ohio lieutenant governor that stopped just short of challenging him to duel. He accused the politician of "preferring camp stories to authentic data then within your reach," and "circulating libels and falsehoods."

The fiery Ohioan reserved his most caustic scorn, however, for editors and reporters, who, he claimed in a letter to his wife, "are the chief cause of this unhappy war—they fan the flames of local hatred and keep alive those prejudices which have forced friends into hostile ranks. In the North the people have been made to believe that those of the South are horrid barbarians, unworthy of Christian burials, whilst at the South, the people have been made to believe that we wanted to steal their negros, rob them of their property, pollute their families [an allusion to miscegenation], and to reduce the whites to below the level of their own negros."

Warming to his subject, Sherman continued, "If the newspapers are to be our government, I would prefer Bragg, Beauregard . . . or any other high Confederate officers instead." "The American press," he wrote his brother Senator John Sherman, "is a shame and a reproach to a civilized people. When a man is too lazy to work, & too cowardly to steal, he becomes an editor & manufactures public opinion."

Halleck arrived in the middle of this uproar to personally take charge of the army—or, more precisely, three armies: Grant's, Buell's, and a third army belonging to newly promoted Maj. Gen. John Pope, who, on the same day as the ordeal at Shiloh, had defeated and captured the Rebel forces at Island Number 10 in the Mississippi and was on his way to Pittsburg Landing.

Grant was rewarded with nothing for his troubles at the Shiloh fight, except what amounted to a demotion. He was named second in command under Halleck, but for all practical purposes the general was shunted aside, since Halleck barely spoke to him and consulted with him not at all. When Grant protested, Halleck slapped him down with this rejoinder, "For the last three months I have done everything in my power to ward off the attacks made upon you." This was mostly a gratuitous falsehood, since Halleck himself was behind many of them; for instance, he had just mailed a letter to a fellow general in Washington describing Grant as "little more than a common gambler and drunkard." Still, when Lincoln had demanded to know the reason for the shocking casualty rate at Shiloh, Halleck at least had the decency not to hold Grant responsible; instead he put the blame on "the Confederate generals and their soldiers."

Now with an enormous army of some 120,000 men, and 200 guns, Halleck announced to his superiors in Washington that he would "leave here tomorrow morning and our army will be before Corinth by tomorrow night," a statement that proved to be ridiculous. Whatever compelled Halleck to say such a thing is beyond puzzling, given that it took him a full month to move the army a mere 20 miles to attack the Rebel bastion.

From the first day, Halleck marched his army as if he were conducting a kind of long-distance siege. For him the wilderness of northern Mississippi was filled with ghosts and shadows and a Rebel behind every tree. At first Halleck estimated Beauregard's force at 75,000, but with each day the estimates grew until it became 200,000. In fact, even when the Rebel general Van Dorn finally arrived from Arkansas with his 15,000, Beauregard could muster no more than 52,000 men actually fit for duty, owing to the Shiloh casualties and to a terrifying outbreak of diseases due to lack of sanitary facilities in the cramped town.*

---

* Situated in dense terrain with little access to running water, antebellum Corinth could at best muster about 2,000 residents. The concentration of the Rebel army suddenly swelled this population to more than 70,000 with the arrival at last of Van Dorn's men from Arkansas. With warm weather coming it became one of the most unhealthy places on Earth.

To ward off any chance of being surprised, as Grant had been at Shiloh, Halleck each morning would creep his army less than a mile forward toward Corinth, then spend the rest of the day having it dig in and construct elaborate fortifications along an eight-mile front, as if a Rebel attack were imminent. This nonsense continued day after day under the scorching Mississippi sun, and the men began complaining about the relentless excavations; there was even talk of mutiny. But "Old Brains," whom one of his colleagues described as "short, stout, and rather stupid-looking," was taking no chances.

———•◆•———

For his part, Beauregard realized he was in a grave situation. With his army wracked by disease and devastated by the fighting at Shiloh, it was certainly in no shape to withstand the ordeal of a siege by the huge Union host now closing in. Likewise, the Creole understood that his army was still the South's last best hope for staving off the Yankees in the western theater. Desperate times called for desperate measures, and Beauregard, if nothing else, was inventive.

As Halleck's armies began to converge on Corinth, their cavalry scouts were unsettled by the noise of train whistles and the sounds of cheering within the city, signs that the Rebels were being reinforced. They saw intimidating siege guns protruding from embrasures in the enemy fortifications. When deserters wandered into Federal camps and were placed under interrogation, they told of many new regiments arriving from other Confederate commands. Gen. John Pope reported to Halleck, "The enemy is reinforcing heavily, by trains, in my front and on my left. The cars are running constantly and the cheering is immense every time they unload in front of me. I have no doubt, from all appearances, that I shall be attacked in heavy force at daylight."

As Halleck absorbed all of this, his notion of a total envelopment of the city evaporated from his bookish mind. He decided to stay outside the Confederate defenses and await developments, which were not long in coming.

The music of military bands wafted across the parapets of Corinth's fortifications into the Federal camps close to the front; during pauses in such patriotic or sentimental tunes as "Dixie" or "Sweet Lorena," the Yankees caught the martial blare of bugles calling men to action. At night they could see Rebel sentries, backlit by campfires, who seemed oddly impervious to sharpshooters' bullets.

Beauregard, of course, was pulling off the greatest con of the war. Withdrawal in the face of an enemy is among the most difficult and dangerous of military maneuvers, and the Creole did it with such daring and finesse that when Halleck's men finally entered Corinth they found practically nothing to indicate that the Rebels had even been there.

Most of the sick and wounded had been moved out south on what were supposed to be "reinforcement trains." Military stores, arms, and artillery had been evacuated as well, and there was nary a man to shoot at. The arriving "troop trains" were the work of a lone Confederate locomotive that ran day and night up and down the various tracks that converged on Corinth. Every so often it would stop and blow its whistle, a signal for everyone in hearing range to start cheering. The bulletproof "sentries" were cornfield scarecrows in worn-out Rebel uniforms, and the fearsome-looking siege guns were only "Quaker" artillery—tree trunks stripped of bark and painted with thick tar pitch, mounted on busted and useless artillery caissons. The informative Rebel "deserters" were plants sent by Beauregard himself to falsely report heavy reinforcements to the Confederate army. It is ironic that—aside from his performance at First Manassas—the Corinth hoax became, arguably, Beauregard's finest achievement during the war.

***

It was during this slow advance to Corinth that the Union army nearly lost Ulysses Grant. As he sat in his headquarters tent day after day, puffing incessantly on his cigar, Grant finally reached his limit of tolerance for Halleck's shabby treatment and decided to resign from the service. He made arrangements for a 30-day leave, but when Sherman went to see him he found that Grant's staff had packed up all his camp desks and trunks and records and stacked them for shipping next morning. "Sherman, you know I am in the way here," Grant said resignedly. "I have stood it as long as I can." When Sherman asked where he was going, Grant said St. Louis, and when Sherman inquired if he had any business there, Grant replied, "Not a bit."

To Sherman, this was the worst possible thing that could happen to the army. He had not only become close to Grant, he had begun to see in him the makings of a great military marshal. The two of them seemed to have a kind of subliminal understanding of each other, and Sherman was determined not to let Grant abandon his career. He insisted that Grant would be miserable sitting on the sidelines while other generals fought the war. He argued that their real problems were nothing more than the made-up lies of his own personal nemesis, the press, which, he reiterated, was "dirty, irresponsible, corrupt, malicious, etc."

Sherman saved his sharpest invective for the rumors and tales that Grant was a drunkard and forecast that the press would soon "drop back into the abyss of infamy that they deserve." In fact, he used himself as living proof, noting that only a few months ago he had been pilloried as "crazy," but now, after the Battle of Shiloh, he was lauded in the newspapers as a great hero and a wise military leader. If Grant remained in the army, Sherman said in conclusion, "some happy accident might restore him to favor and his true place."

Sherman's passionate disquisition had the desired effect. Grant canceled his plans to resign and in less than a week the "happy accident" that Sherman had predicted came about after George McClellan suffered a humiliating defeat by Robert E. Lee at the gates of Richmond, and "Old Brains" Halleck was called back to Washington to replace him as general in chief of the army. This, in turn, restored Grant as commander of the Army of the Tennessee, as it had now been formally styled, and ultimately wrote him onto one of the larger pages of history.

While Lee inflicted woeful damages to a series of Union commanders in the East, fortune seemed to smile on the Federal forces in the West. After Island Number 10 fell, Memphis was taken by the gunboat fleet of Commodore Foote, Grant's old colleague from the Forts Henry and Donelson days. But Foote wasn't there to celebrate. The wound that he suffered at Fort Donelson never healed well, and he was forced to retire from the active list and later died from complications of the injury. About the same time as Memphis capitulated, Adm. David Farragut steamed his big "salt water" navy up from the Gulf of Mexico and captured New Orleans, the largest city in the Confederacy. That left Vicksburg, then a town of considerable size and strength, as the only bottleneck that prevented the Union from free access to the Mississippi. Grant took it upon himself to rectify that omission.

After nearly half a year of false starts—some of them costly—Grant brought the Vicksburg defenders to bay in a three-month siege that finally ended with surrender on the Fourth of July, 1863—the same day that Lee brought his defeated army south from Gettysburg. Grant was finally hailed as a great hero, and when Lincoln called him East to face Lee he became the fifth commanding general of the Army of the Potomac. It took nearly two more bloodstained years, but Grant finally laid siege to and subdued the Rebel army near Richmond. After the surrender at Appomattox he became not only the man of the hour but the man of the age.

In 1868, after serving as general in chief of the U.S. Army, Ulysses Grant was elected President of the United States on the Republican ticket. His term was generally unremarkable, except that toward the end his administration was wracked by unprecedented scandals and corruption that damaged his personal reputation. For some reason he had allowed cronies to control him, and Reconstruction measures in the South went beyond the punitive into pure dishonesty.

Afterward he and Julia took a world tour during which he was celebrated by kings and emperors as the greatest soldier of his time. When he returned in 1880 he was persuaded to form a brokerage firm, which failed despite his fame and reputation. He was thrown into bankruptcy and forced to give up his trophies, swords, and souvenirs for unpaid loans. He obtained an army pension but remained deeply in debt until Mark Twain encouraged him to write his autobiography. He went to work on what would become *The Personal Memoirs of U. S. Grant,* which was published in 1885 and became one of the most phenomenal successes in the history of publishing, earning some $450,000 (nearly $10 million in today's money).

But Grant did not live to enjoy it. His longtime smoking habit (upwards of 12 cigars a day) had brought a diagnosis of throat cancer, which, toward the end, rendered him speechless, and he was forced to write notes to communicate with his editors on the memoirs project. He died on July 23, 1885, and his remains, along with Julia's, lie in a mausoleum that is still a prominent landmark high above the Hudson River in New York City.

Sherman continued under Grant as a division and later a corps commander, and at one point he was made military commandant of Memphis. There, apparently, he first indulged the pyromaniacal urges that brought him to infamy in Atlanta and other Southern cities, by ordering that if any Union vessel on the Mississippi received gunfire from the shore the nearest town would be burned to the ground.

It had not taken Sherman long to become a "hard war" man, whose military philosophy was quite opposite the modern notion of "winning the hearts and minds of the people." In fact, today's experts on counterinsurgency would no doubt be dismayed, if not shocked, by Sherman's attitude toward Southern civilians who, he said in late 1862, must be made to understand that "we will remove & destroy every obstacle, if need be take every life, every acre of land, every particle of property, every thing that to us seems proper, and we will not cease till the end is attained, that all who do not aid [us] are enemies, and we will not account to them for our acts. If the people of the South oppose [us] they do so at their peril, and if they stand by, mere lookers on the domestic tragedy, they have no right to immunity, protection, or share in the final result . . . I would not coax [the South] or even meet them half way," he said, "but make them so sick & tired of war that generations would pass before they would again appeal to it."

At Vicksburg Sherman was Grant's right-hand man, and after Grant was sent east Sherman was given Grant's job of commanding the Federal armies in the West. His victory at the Battle of Atlanta ensured Lincoln's reelection in 1864 and, in the North, propelled Sherman into hero status almost equal to that of Grant.

After the Confederate surrender Sherman became magnanimous toward his former enemy, declaring, "The South is broken and ruined, and appeals to our pity. To ride the people down with persecutions and military exactions would be like slashing away at the crew of a sinking ship. I will fight as long as the enemy will fight, but when he gives up and asks quarter, I will go no further." This earned Sherman the wrath of the radical Republicans in the administration and in Congress. Halleck was so incensed that he leaked to the newspapers that Sherman "must have some screw loose again."

A despiser of politics, Sherman was granted permission to go west and supervise fighting the wild Indians, whose suppression had been neglected during the war. But when Grant became President, Sherman took over as general in chief of the army, a post he held until 1884. From that position he began to see Grant falling under the influence of unscrupulous politicians, but when Sherman tried to warn him it was to no avail, and in time he distanced himself from his old friend. Still, Sherman retained an abiding affection for his wartime companion, and once he quipped, "Grant stood by me when I was crazy, and I stood by him when he was drunk."

Like Grant, Sherman published his memoirs, entitled *General William T. Sherman, by Himself,* which to no one's surprise was controversial but highly entertaining and sold 25,000 copies, earning him $25,000. He lived in New York City after his retirement and maintained a lively social life, especially as guest of honor at countless reunions of the Grand Old Army of the Republic, as the Union veterans called their organization. His wife, Ellen, died in 1888, and he followed her three years later. Of all his pithy sayings, Sherman is perhaps best known for his response to a group of politicians who were pushing him to run for President. "If nominated, I will not run," he declared, "if elected, I will not serve."

Of the other notable Union commanders at Shiloh, the much idolized general C. F. Smith died at Savannah just over two weeks after the battle of the leg infection he'd suffered when he scraped his knee getting into a boat. Simple antibiotics that are available today would easily have cured him.

Prentiss spent several months in a Confederate prison before being exchanged. He continued in the army but resigned in 1864, still angry that Grant had slighted his role at Shiloh. Grant, however, rectified the omission in his memoirs, referring to the "valiant" performance of Prentiss's division.

Stephen Hurlbut replaced Sherman in command of Memphis, but his administration there was tainted by scandal and corruption and he was accused of embezzlement. After the war Hurlbut was named U.S. minister to Colombia and, later, to Peru.

John McClernand went on with the army to Vicksburg but continued to be a thorn in Grant's side, trying to upstage and sabotage him at the same time. At last Grant had enough and fired him, and McClernand returned to Illinois and to politics, but he became nearly destitute and strings had to be pulled to secure a pension for him before he died in 1900.

Lew Wallace had a most interesting career. Following his tardy performance at Shiloh he was relieved and put in charge of the defenses of Cincinnati, a sinecure. But he managed to get back in good graces and served well throughout the war. He later became governor of the New Mexico Territory, where he had dealings with the notorious Billy the Kid, and served as U.S. minister to the Ottoman Empire. He also became an accomplished poet, playwright, and novelist, and his 1880 novel *Ben-Hur: A Tale of the Christ* became the best-selling American novel of the 19th century. It is said to have been partially based on his experiences at the Battle of Shiloh. He spent the rest of his life trying to prove that he had not been dilatory at Shiloh, but the argument continues even today. In his memoirs, however, Grant largely absolves Wallace of blame, observing that if Sherman had not been pushed back more than a mile by the Rebel army the original road Wallace had taken to get to the battlefield would have been the correct one.

The elephantine general William "Bull" Nelson had a stellar but all-too-brief career after Shiloh. His division was the first to march into Corinth after Beauregard's evacuation, and he later served prominently in Tennessee and Kentucky, where on September 29, 1862, not quite six months after the battle, he was murdered in Louisville's Galt House hotel by, of all people, a fellow Union general with the ironic name of Jefferson C. Davis. The two men had quarreled earlier, and after Nelson had publicly shamed Davis in the hotel lobby, Davis borrowed a pistol from another officer and shot Nelson through the heart. There was talk of court-martialing Davis but, oddly (and outrageously), nothing came of it, and he served through the rest of the war.

James B. McPherson, Grant's chief engineer at Shiloh, rose rapidly, as predicted, in the officer corps, succeeding Sherman to command the Army of the Tennessee. But Sherman's earlier foreboding that McPherson would rise to the top of the army only "if he lives" proved eerily true. During a reconnaissance at the Battle of Atlanta McPherson blundered into the Rebel lines and was shot to death trying to escape. Sherman broke into tears when the body of his friend was brought into his headquarters. He had it laid out on an unhinged door placed between two benches and grieved over it the rest of the day. McPherson, as commander of an army, has the dubious distinction of being the highest ranking Union officer killed in the war.

Henry Halleck received public condemnation for letting the Confederate army escape at Corinth, but he served in Washington after being named general in chief until Grant superseded him. After the war, and presumably at Grant's pleasure, he was put in charge of a military division headquartered in Louisville, Kentucky, where he died in 1872. Grant was President by then, and apparently he had learned from military correspondence of Halleck's earlier double-dealings. Halleck was never a leader of men but more of a manager, and he did not command their respect even in headquarters positions. Lincoln, in fact, regarded him as "nothing more than a first rate clerk."

Of the prominent Confederate commanders at Shiloh who lived through the war, Pierre Gustave Toutant Beauregard probably suffered the most. Jefferson Davis, who disliked the Creole anyway, was furious when he learned that Beauregard had called off the

Shiloh assault just as the Confederates seemed poised to force a surrender, and doubly so when he heard the Creole had abandoned the critical rail junction at Corinth. Under the best circumstances, communications between Richmond and the West were never good, and Davis's opinion was doubtless clouded by letters and other exchanges from officers who were unsatisfied with Beauregard's performance.

Not long after Corinth was evacuated, Beauregard took a leave of absence (without consulting authorities in Richmond) in hopes of curing his still ailing throat. When Davis learned of this, he immediately appointed Braxton Bragg to command the army. Efforts by Beauregard's political friends to have him restored proved futile, and he was sent to command the coastal defenses of South Carolina and Georgia, a second tier position. Even while he fumed in private, Beauregard did a creditable job, all the while dreaming up fantastic schemes for the South to win the war with submarines, unique warships from England, and initiating secret treaties with supposedly disaffected midwestern states such as Indiana. Nothing came of them, of course, as Beauregard remained on Jefferson Davis's blacklist. In 1864, however, Davis brought him to Virginia to assist in the final stand that Lee presided over at Petersburg, and he and Joe Johnston, who had begun the war together at First Bull Run, were among the last of the senior officers of the Confederacy to surrender.

After the war Beauregard worked as an executive for Louisiana railroads, but these enterprises ultimately failed. During this time he submitted his entry in what became known as the War of the Books by surreptitiously co-authoring, in 1884, *The Military Operations of General Beauregard During the War Between the States,* and from the 1880s until his death he carried on a bitter and unseemly public fight with Jefferson Davis and others over who lost the war.

Because of his status and credibility as a former Rebel general, Beauregard was offered a post as the drawer of winning tickets in the Louisiana lottery, an organization that was generally considered a hotbed of bribery and other corruption. He nevertheless accepted the position, for which he was paid handsomely, until the U.S. Congress banned the lottery in 1891. Beauregard died at home, in his bed, of heart trouble, in 1893.

For his part in the Shiloh attack, Beauregard's chief of staff Col. Thomas Jordan, who had devised the battle plans, was made General Thomas Jordan. After Beauregard was relieved, Jordan served as chief of staff for Braxton Bragg, but when Beauregard went to Charleston Jordan accompanied him. After the war he had a somewhat colorful career, becoming editor in chief of the *Memphis Appeal* and writing a popular book titled *The Campaigns of Lieutenant-General Forrest*. In 1868 he became a soldier of fortune, throwing his lot with the Cuban Liberation Army, of which he became general in chief. He resigned in 1870 and returned to New York City, where he became an editor and wrote about the Civil War. He died there in 1895 at the age of 76.

For two years after Beauregard's departure Braxton Bragg retained command of the Army of Tennessee, as it was known, operating mostly in middle Tennessee and then Chattanooga, from where he constantly sought to regain Nashville and Kentucky. Bragg was a harsh commander disliked by both his men and his officers, but he fought some tremendously tough and bloody battles for the Confederacy, such as Stones River, Perryville, and Chickamauga—winning the last, only to let the Federals slip from his grasp and later drive him from the state. After that, he stepped down and became a military adviser to Jefferson Davis, one of the few people in Richmond he could get along with. After the war he held several engineering positions, quarreling with everyone, in Texas, Louisiana, and Mobile, Alabama, where, in 1876, he was buried in the Magnolia Cemetery following a fatal heart attack.

Bishop-General Leonidas Polk never accomplished anything much more notable on the battlefield than getting himself blown nearly in two by a cannonball during the Atlanta Campaign. But he was adored by his men as a brave, industrious, and able commander at Shiloh and afterward. At Pine Mountain, Georgia, on June 14, 1864, while studying an enemy position in company with the army commander Joseph E. Johnston and another corps commander, William Hardee, the group was spotted by Sherman, no less, through his spyglasses. Sherman quickly ordered a nearby artillery battery to fire on these conspicuous Rebel officers, and the somewhat portly Polk was slow in finding cover; the third shot tore through his torso, killing him instantly. His principal legacy is having founded the University of the South at Sewanee, Tennessee, for which he laid the cornerstone in 1860, right before the war broke out.

William J. Hardee remained a competent but uninspired corps commander, nicknamed "Old Reliable" by his troops. He could not abide Bragg and was instrumental in having him relieved after the Battle of Chattanooga. After the war, Hardee decided to become a planter in Alabama where, in 1873, he died, and is buried in Selma.

John Cabell Breckinridge continued to serve in the Rebel army but like so many others he developed an intense distaste for Bragg, who returned the favor by accusing the 14th Vice President of the United States of being a drunkard. Ultimately Breckinridge got himself assigned to the eastern theater and performed creditably for Lee's army before resigning his commission in early 1865 to become Confederate secretary of war. After the surrender Breckinridge fled the country, first to Cuba, then England, and then to Canada, until the talk of hanging important Confederate officials died down, when he returned to Lexington, Kentucky, and resumed his law practice, resisting efforts by others to have him again run for office. He vehemently opposed the Ku Klux Klan and became president of a railroad before his end came, in 1875, from cirrhosis of the liver.

The Irish general Pat Cleburne went on after Shiloh to become known as the "Stonewall of the West," commanding a division through all of the heavy fighting. In 1864, however, he provoked the animosity of many in the high command by circulating a paper recommending that slaves be made into Confederate soldiers in exchange for their freedom. Cleburne had calculated that unless this was done the South would simply run out of manpower by 1864 or 1865. The suggestion proved so outrageous that it prompted the Rebel general Robert Toombs of Georgia, who had been the Confederacy's first secretary of state, to declare indignantly, "If slaves can be made into soldiers, then our whole *theory* of slavery is wrong."

In the final year of the war, Jefferson Davis at last came around to Cleburne's way of thinking and slaves were offered positions in the Confederate army. When Toombs raised his objection again, Davis countered with his own declaration, stating, "If the Confederacy dies, then its tombstone should read: 'Died of a Theory.' "

Many think that Cleburne's impolitic slavery proposal was responsible for his rising no higher than division commander instead of being given a corps, or even an army. It may also have been his death warrant, since corps and army commanders are not nearly so exposed to fire as generals commanding divisions and brigades.

Not long after the Battle of Atlanta Cleburne found himself riding north in middle Tennessee toward a rendezvous with the Yankee army at the terrible Battle of Franklin. When they passed by Ashwood, near Columbia, ancestral home of Leonidas Polk's family, Cleburne noticed a lovely ivy-covered brick Episcopal chapel on the property and remarked to one of his staff that "The church is so beautiful that to be buried there would almost be worth dying for." Next afternoon Cleburne, along with four other Rebel generals, were slain on the field at Franklin, and soon enough Pat Cleburne got his wish of being laid to rest in the cemetery of the lovely brick chapel at Ashwood, Tennessee.*

Nathan Bedford Forrest survived the war but no one knows how. One of his staff remarked that he fights "as if he courts death." He soon gained his own large cavalry command in the West and outfoxed his Yankee opposition at almost every turn, causing Jefferson Davis in his memoirs to lament that he did not realize just how great a general Forrest was until nearly the end of the war. His reputation was tarnished, however, by the infamous slaughter by his troops of black soldiers during the Battle of Fort Pillow on the Tennessee River in April 1864.

At war's end, Forrest dismissed his command with a brief farewell speech in which he told them, "You have been good soldiers,

---

* Ashwood is better known as Mount Pleasant, Tennessee. After the war Cleburne's remains were removed to his adopted state of Arkansas.

you can be good citizens." In the first year after the war, however, Forrest joined the newly organized Ku Klux Klan, rising to its leadership until the Klan's activities became so obnoxious to him that in 1869 he issued an order for the society to disband itself, which it did.* He became a Presbyterian, returned to farming, and died peacefully in his bed in 1877 at the age of 56.

Colonel David Stuart, whose Illinoisans held so bravely on the Union left at Shiloh, could never escape the adultery scandal that embroiled him in Chicago. He went on with Grant to fight at Vicksburg and on Grant's personal recommendation was nominated to brigadier general by President Lincoln, which at least to Stuart's mind would have vindicated him. But Chicago politics and vengeful social connections had a long political reach, and his nomination was denied by Congress, prompting Stuart to resign from the army in 1863. Grant, furious, lambasted the politicians who were responsible, but to no avail. Unable to fulfill his promise of taking his brigade to get drunk in New Orleans, Stuart instead opened a law practice in Detroit, where he died in 1868 at the age of 52.

Six months after Shiloh, William Camm of the 14th Illinois, whom we first met at Fort Donelson over the body of the beautiful dead Confederate boy, returned to Winchester, Illinois, and married his hometown sweetheart, Miss Kitty Mason, who produced a child that died in infancy, followed by her own death in 1864.

---

* In the early 1920s a second Klan arose and was active throughout the South and the Midwest. After World War II a third incarnation of the Klan surfaced during the civil rights movement.

Afterward Camm became a kind of Renaissance man, teaching, writing, painting—at which he was accomplished*—and dabbling in the quasi-socialist philosophy of Henry George, the "single-tax" man. In 1865 he remarried, fathered five children, and died in 1906 at the age of 69.

Of our correspondents in the front lines, Private Henry Morton Stanley, after his capture by the Yankees, was consigned to the dismal Camp Douglas near Chicago, where dead Confederate prisoners were carted off daily by the wagonload, and himself nearly died of disease, before talking his way out by enlisting in the U.S. Navy, from which he deserted as soon as possible. Stanley made his way back to his native Wales, only to have his mother disown him at the doorstep. Without resources, he managed to make a career as an explorer during the age of the great African explorations and began a lucrative business enterprise by selling accounts of his exploits to newspapers. In 1869 James Gordon Bennett, Jr., of the *New York Herald* employed him exclusively to find the Scottish missionary David Livingstone, who had gone to Africa in 1866 and not been heard from since. Stanley found him in 1871, living happily in what is now Tanzania, which, almost overnight, made Stanley a world hero. In 1899 he was knighted in London, where he died five years later, one of the most prominent, and most controversial,† of the 19th-century explorers.

---

* Among his work is an 1858 oil portrait of Abraham Lincoln, which was painted from actual sittings by the future President.

† He was said to shoot natives with the same cavalier abandon that he shot monkeys.

Ambrose Bierce fought the war to the end and was discharged with the rank of major. He settled afterward in San Francisco, where he became one of America's most prominent (and cynical) authors. His most distinguished works had roots in his experiences in the Civil War, including the story "An Occurrence at Owl Creek Bridge," whose title, at least, probably comes from the Shiloh battle. Some of his books still remain popular in print, including the acerbic *Devil's Dictionary*. In December 1913 Bierce disappeared into the chaos of the Mexican revolution and was never heard from again.

Another who gained notoriety as a journalist was 16-year-old musician fourth class John A. Cockerill, who after the war established himself prominently at midwestern newspapers before becoming editor in chief of Joseph Pulitzer's sensational *New York World*. Other diarists or memoirists attained rank; Pvt. Robert H. Fleming, for instance, who was wounded and found his way to the hospital boat only to discover his dying brother was aboard, became a captain before the war ended. (His older brother died in his arms while the Monday battle raged, and even in the confusion Fleming somehow persuaded the boat's carpenter to cobble together a rude coffin, in which he buried his brother in a proper grave that he dug himself atop the bluff instead of in the common pit where the Union slain were laid.)

***

Almost immediately word began to filter back north, far from the gunfire and the madding crowd at Shiloh, that a great battle was in progress along the Tennessee River. It reached Bowling Green, Kentucky, and 21-year-old Josie Underwood's family on April 6, while the first day's slaughter was still in progress, but details were sparse until the following week, when the fuller picture was drawn. On that Sunday, April 6, Josie wrote in her diary, "We are horribly uneasy. There were rumors today of a big battle. If there was, all we love on both sides must be in it. God have mercy and stop this cruel war—I pray—"

By April 15 there was definite confirmation: "The rumor is true!" Josie wrote. "Oh, the horror of it! Every soul I know on either side was in that battle!"

Josie's 15-year-old brother Warner had received a bad gunshot wound in his arm while wearing Yankee blue. He staggered home still in uniform, the right coat sleeve split in two and wrapped in bandages that had been applied on the battlefield. Josie tried to dress his gash, she said, but "When I unwound the dirty bandages—*maggots* fell out, and the wound itself was full of them and stunk so—it nearly knocked me down." It was hard, she said, to keep from fainting, and all Warner would say was, "God pity the poor fellows who are wounded so much worse and can't come home."

As more reports of the battle came in Josie's mother, who at the first hint of trouble had imprudently gone on a steamboat to Pittsburg Landing to look for Warner, told of "much indignation against Gen. Grant. Instead of being on the field or wherever [he] should have been, he was on a boat *drunk*—and but for Buell's army reaching there by forced marches, the result of the battle would have been a terrible defeat for Union army." These were the first impressions of Josie's mother upon arriving at Pittsburg Landing.

"The feeling between the rebel and Union people gets bitterer, and bitterer as the war goes on," Josie lamented. "Lizzy Wright sits on her front porch across the street and I on ours and merely the coldest bows and never a visit now."

A few days later came news that Josie's favorite cousin, Jack Henry, had been killed at Shiloh fighting as a captain with the Memphis Grays. His brother Gus got there in time to have him die in his arms. Jack Henry had been a close friend and law partner of Tom Grafton and was the one who had arranged the little charade on Josie's last night in Memphis so that she and Grafton could say goodbye alone. "A nobler, sweet soul never entered Heaven," Josie told her diary, "no matter how wrong the cause for which he died, he believed in it—to him it was sacred. Oh! The *crime* of the men on both sides. Fanatics North and South who brought about this cruel war."

More friends turned up wounded but at least springtime took hold. Numerous homes and buildings in Bowling Green had been turned into hospitals, and the city continued to be garrisoned by Union soldiers. Josie resumed her late afternoon rides over the fields of Mount Air, surrounding the charred remains of the plantation house. "I haven't heard a word from Tom Grafton since the Confederates left Bowling Green," she wrote on May 9, 1862, a month after the battle. "At first I thought it well, since by other means I could not find it in my heart to forbid his writing. Today I would give anything for one of his letters."

Summer came. Josie's father and his friend Congressman Grider managed to see that brother Warner received an appointment to West Point, which ensured that he would be out of the war for at least the foreseeable future. Josie worried about the family finances. "Pa's law practice is all broken up," she said, and the slaves at Mount Air "hardly make enough for their own living."

Then, for a change, fortune seemed to smile on the Underwoods. Despite his fierce opposition to Lincoln's election, Josie's father was appointed as U.S. consul to Glasgow, Scotland. They would leave for Washington at once, and Josie was going along as well. Lincoln, through the Kentucky politicians Henry Grider and John Crittenden, had been made aware of the Underwoods' misfortune, and the President told Josie's father that he had serious concerns about the warships the Scots were building for the Confederate navy on the river Clyde. He said that for the U.S. consul he "wanted a good lawyer—a *strong Presbyterian and* a Southern Union man, and that Pa fit the bill," Josie wrote.

While they were in the capital city Josie met and mixed with the crème de la crème of Washington society. On the first day, she was introduced to the Vice President, Hannibal Hamlin, and Lincoln's future judge advocate general of the army Joseph Holt, and there were senators, congressmen, and generals galore. On the second day she even met President Lincoln himself, by accident, when he was out riding near the White House. "He was on a long-tailed black pony (the horse looked so small) galloping along—a high silk hat on his head—black cloth suit on, the long coat tails flying behind him."

Lincoln stopped as Josie's father pulled up the carriage they were riding in. (Her father had known Lincoln previously in Congress.) The President "leaned over, shook hands with us," Josie said, "then slouched down on one side of the saddle, as any old farmer would do, and talked for about ten or 15 minutes with us." Josie thought the President was "a very common-looking man . . . but I must confess there was a kindliness in his face."

The rest of her visit was like a tale from a storybook. Josie met a prince and a princess, was nearly mixed up in a duel, and became the object of (an unsuccessful) seduction by an infamous ladies' man. By the end of July she was home again, awaiting her father's confirmation as U.S. consul. "All my life," she wrote in her diary, " I have longed to go to Europe. Now, Oh! How I hate to go so far away."

She and her mother again got into difficulty with the authorities for bringing food to prisoners—only this time it was with Union authorities over Confederate prisoners captured at Shiloh. Josie and her mother felt sorry for them, and had brought them some pies and cakes, when "a little upstart of an officer came up to me with a smirk," Josie said, and warned her to "be careful giving aid and comfort to rebels"—to which she "replied in a flash—when I wish advice I will seek it from *my friends*."

The summer of 1862 slipped away. Her cousin Winston was wounded serving with Stonewall Jackson in Virginia; her sister had a baby and the good news was sent through Union lines to her brother-in-law William Western, who was commanding a cavalry battalion with Bedford Forrest. Then on September 3 a letter came.

"Tom Grafton dead! Killed!" She fairly shrieked it out.

"At [the Battle of] Fair Oaks, near Richmond. A bursting shell—Oh! It is too horrible! 'No one in the world to grieve if I should die,' he said. Ah! Tom Grafton—how mistaken you were."

A week later Josie packed her diary in the trunk that would carry it to Scotland. "All our friends have been coming here to-day to say good bye. Who knows when or how we will meet again." The family sailed for Great Britain a few days later but Josie never resumed her journal.

When the war ended they returned to Bowling Green but life was not kind. Union soldiers had carried off all the livestock at Mount Air and practically everything else, including a large and valuable storage of wood and 35,000 bricks from the burned home that Underwood had salvaged in contemplation of building a new house. He sold off portions of the land and tried to resume his law practice but suffered a stroke in 1868 and died four years later. Somehow the remainder of Mount Air was lost, and in 1870 Josie married a New Yorker named Charles Nazro who started a bank in Bowling Green that soon failed. They then moved to Ballston Spa, New York, near Saratoga Springs, where Nazro obtained a low-paying office job. Though they lived in rented properties and were always short of money, during the next ten years Josie bore four children—two boys and two girls—and in 1889 the family drifted west, first to Denver then to San Diego where, in 1898, her husband died.

Afterward, Josie returned to live out the rest of her years in Bowling Green, where she relied on the kindness of friends and relatives and became active in literary and community organizations. She doubtless visited Mount Air but left no record of it and died in 1923. Among her meager possessions was the journal she kept from 1860 to 1862, which she willed to her 18-year-old granddaughter in Texas. There were only a few notations in Josie's diary following the death of Tom Grafton in 1862, but at the very last is a verse of poetry, the entry undated, a stanza from "Adieu," by Thomas Carlyle, as follows:

> *The saddest tears must fall, must fall,*
> *The saddest tears must fall;*
> *In weal or woe, in this world below,*
> *I'll love thee ever and all,*
> *My dear,*
> *I will love thee ever and all.*

The casualties of the Civil War of course weren't limited to the battlefield. Everywhere, North and South, the conflict cast a long and tragic shadow. Millions were affected and scarcely a home was untouched. It has been estimated that Civil War casualties, if measured by a percentage of today's U.S. population, would exceed 50 million, with 10 million of that number dead. Yet the toll of accumulated human suffering by the Josie Underwoods of the era remains incalculable.

CHAPTER 17

AN EXALTED
DISTINCTION

—▸◆◂—

F OR WEEKS AFTER THE BATTLE, PITTSBURG LANDING
resembled a colossal slaughterhouse. People told of hospital
boats headed downriver leaving a trail of human limbs in their wake
as the surgeons plied their grisly trade and flung the results overboard. The day after the battle Beauregard sent a messenger asking
for a truce to bury his dead, but Grant refused him, saying he was
already having the Confederate bodies buried along with those of
Union soldiers. The weather was getting warm, Grant said; there was
no time for politesse. Beauregard had also asked Grant for permission for local families to enter the battlefield to look for sons killed
or wounded in the fight, but Grant denied this as well. He still considered it a battlefield, with all the grim implications of that term.

In many cases the original burial parties had not dug their pits
deep enough, so that arms, legs, and even heads sometimes pro-
truded above the ground. The hundreds of dead horses also posed

a serious problem; they tried burning them, but that did not work well. Burying a horse is hard, time-consuming work and there was concern of a cholera outbreak. Even after Halleck began creeping the army south toward Corinth, a sizable detachment had to remain at the landing to process the train of the supplies to the army, all of which came by boat and had to be moved along the roads where the fighting had taken place. As the spring weather warmed, the stench, they said, was sickening, and with it came a biblical-size plague of bluebottle flies.

On the Tuesday after the battle, nine-year-old Elsie Duncan's mother "was on the verge of despair." She had tried to get inside the Union lines to look for her sons, afraid that they were dead or wounded, but because of Grant's order "the sentinels would not let her through." Then the older son, Joe, appeared. "He was black with gunsmoke," Elsie said. "His hat and coat was gone. His pants were torn with bullets but his flesh was not touched. Mother saw him and ran to meet him. He said, 'Oh, mother,' and caught her in his arms."

She spoke of the burying parties and said that, contrary to the official version, "The Yankees did not bury the Confederate dead. They threw them into the gullies and ravines and covered them with leaves and left them for the hogs to root up and eat up." This, she said indignantly, "*I* know to be the *truth*. I could not understand anyone to be so heartless to leave a human being unburied even if they were a rebel—they were dead."

"After the battle, everything was peaceful for a short time," Elsie wrote. She remembered Grant as "good and kind and did not allow his people to mistreat anyone or anything that we had left." She and the other small children played with the Yankee soldiers who sometimes gave them small presents, and Elsie's mother nursed the soldiers through epidemics of diarrhea and other ailments. Times were hard. All of their livestock had vanished during the battle. They planted a small garden to get by through the winter. Elsie's mother "made us clothes out of shirts and other things we picked up on the battlefield." Her mother also started a small school at home for neighborhood children; as many as 20 attended. One day after Corinth had been taken, "We saw a long line of soldiers, we could hear the horses feet," Elsie said. Next day, all the army camps were deserted. The Union soldiers had gone and darker times fell on Shiloh because, as Elsie wrote, "When the Yankee army marched away we were left without any protection."

Partisan groups, with old scores to settle, cropped up all over the county. Initially acting under the guise of representing the Federal army, these guerrillas were hardly more than nightriders, robbing, hanging, and threatening to hang anyone they had it in for—including Elsie's father, Joseph, who not only had served with the Rebel army but owned land and had some degree of wealth, making him a target. He and his older sons were forced to hide out in the cave, or "hut," deep in the woods as the partisans searched Elsie's house for them and threatened to hang anyone who gave him assistance—including Elsie's mother. These riffraff tore up the Duncans' garden, then demanded a huge kettle to cook the vegetables in—and out of plain meanness they cooked Elsie's pet cat.

An era of lawlessness descended on Hardin County. Rival partisan groups composed of men who claimed to be Confederates were also organized, and they were just as bad as the others. Basically, it was an excuse for low-minded people to run rampant, steal, and terrorize.

Finally Joseph Duncan took the family away. He had relatives and friends all over Tennessee and they stayed gone through most of the war, and even afterward returned to Shiloh only to work the land. When Elsie turned 16, her father died; and in 1871, when she turned 18, she married 36-year-old Branch Tanner Hurt, Jr., of Petersburg, Virginia, who had been a major in Robert E. Lee's Army of Northern Virginia. The wedding was held at the fashionable Peabody hotel in Memphis.

Elsie's mother took her remaining children and returned to Shiloh, but "where the house had stood was a briar patch," Elsie said. As her mother sat looking at it a man came up and introduced himself as the son of a wounded Yankee soldier whom Elsie's father had given water to on the battlefield that terrible Sunday. He took in Elsie's family at his own place nearby until they could get a new house started. Her mother "planted out the old orchard that was shot all to pieces in the battle. Only one peach tree was left," Elsie wrote.

In time, and now with a 15-month-old child of her own—the first of ten she would bear over the years—Elsie paid a visit to Shiloh, "but I was sorry I went there," she said. "All of the things I had thought were so beautiful were all gone." When the visit was over, Elsie caught a steamboat to Shreveport where she met her new husband. They bought a wagon and a team and, like so many others in those times, headed for Texas, but it was not for them. The couple returned to Mississippi and settled at Courtland, near Oxford, about 60 miles south of Memphis, where Major Hurt opened a successful mercantile business.

Elsie's mother had built only a small house at Shiloh and there had been discussion in the family of making it a larger and more elaborate place. But by the 1880s word got around that the government wanted to turn the whole area of Pittsburg Landing into a large military park. This raised concerns that any improvements to the house would only be condemned by the authorities. By then the boys were grown and married and had children of their own, so they decided to wait.

In 1890 Major Hurt died, leaving Elsie a widow at the age of 37, and not long afterward Elsie's mother fell gravely ill. By then Elsie had moved to Memphis and she caught the first train to Shiloh just in time to bid her mother goodbye. It had been her mother's wish to be buried at sunset, and so she was, "in the old Shiloh graveyard," Elsie said, near where the little church used to be.

That church had a curious end. After the battle, when the wounded and the dead had been removed from the bullet-pocked meetinghouse, someone issued orders to rip up the floorboards for coffins; someone else ordered the rest of the building dismantled to use its logs to build roads for Halleck's march to Corinth. Before that could happen, though, Union soldiers began taking pieces of the bloodstained pew benches as souvenirs. Then, as word got out, crowds arrived, and soon they'd whittled the entire structure down to nothing, not even a foundation left, just to have a scrap of wood to say they'd been there.

———◆———

They had come to see the elephant, and for many it was so terrible that they ran and hid beneath the bluff. It was terrible for others, too, but they stood their ground and faced it down, or died trying. No one who went through Shiloh would ever be the same. Confederate private Sam Watkins of the First Tennessee, Cheatham's division, Polk's corps, summed it up this way in his odd countrified elegance: "I had been feeling mean all morning as if I had stolen a sheep. I had heard and read of battlefields, seen pictures of battlefields, of horses and men, of cannons and wagons, all jumbled together, while the ground was strewn with dead and dying and wounded, but I must confess I never realized the 'pomp and circumstance' of the thing called 'glorious war' until I saw this. Men were lying in every conceivable position; the dead were lying with their eyes wide open, the wounded begging piteously for help, and some waving their hats and shouting for us to go forward. It all seemed to me a dream."

Watkins had it at least half right. For those who endured it Shiloh was more than a dream; it was a living nightmare that no one could forget. The sheer magnitude of the butchery staggered the imagination. In one sense, the battle had settled nothing except to keep the coffin makers busy. For two days, a hundred thousand American boys created a giant corpse factory in the Tennessee backwoods, and when it was over what was left of the Southern boys marched back to where they came from, and what remained of the Northern boys still held their camps and their field—the Yankee army had reached the Deep South, and though it got whipped from time to time it never was expelled.

The significance of Shiloh was not so much that the Rebel army failed to subdue Grant, or that Grant resisted it, than it was to impress on the nation—both nations—that there was never going to be any neat and exquisite military maneuver that would end the war, or even come *close* to ending the war. It was as if at Shiloh they had unleashed some giant, murderous thing that was going to drench the country with blood, just as Sherman had predicted back in 1860 during his fiery sermon at the Louisiana Military Academy.

As if to emphasize this, not even three months after the battle a shocking clash in Virginia between George B. McClellan and Robert E. Lee eclipsed even the horrors of Shiloh for utter savagery. What became known as the Seven Days Battles around Richmond produced some 36,000 casualties, of which more than 5,200 were killed—more than half again the Shiloh slaughter. The difference of course was that the armies were larger and the fighting lasted longer. But in that instance, the Confederates won, and so the score with Shiloh was evened, at least for the time being.

Another lesson that Shiloh taught, or should have taught, was not thoroughly learned until the final years of the conflict—which is that modern weaponry called for dramatic changes in Napoleonic tactics. The 50-year-old maxims about massed infantry charging and overcoming fixed positions was now outmoded. Charging in ranks directly against the kind of artillery and quick-loading small arms fire such as they had at Shiloh was a suicidal business and unprofitable unless you had plenty of men to spare, which the South did not.

With modern infantry training techniques, positions such as the Hornet's Nest would be isolated, then bypassed through fire-and-maneuver tactics and left to wither in the rear. But such approaches were not understood at the time—everyone preached Napoleon's old dictum "rush to the place where the firing is loudest"—and it wasn't until the later years, after the fearful slaughter in the Peninsula, Antietam, Gettysburg, and the Forty Days, that it became clear, to the soldiers at least, the old ways were obsolete. Grant seemed to have learned something of this at Chattanooga, then forgot it again when he went east, but by then he had more than enough men to spare and against Lee he used his army as a bludgeon instead of a rapier, despite the awful costs. In the end, of course, he turned out to be the winner, the Republic was saved from dissolution, and his victory was hailed as brilliant throughout the land, except, of course, in the South.

———— ❖ ————

It is interesting to play the "what-if" game, which most trained historians scoff at as a nonhistorical pursuit, usually just before they indulge in it themselves. Before Shiloh, the war had been in its infancy, but there was really no way to stop it because Southern leaders insisted that they had already formed a new country and no longer wished to be a part of the United States. Their position on that aspect was nonnegotiable, and so was President Lincoln's. In Sherman's estimation, "the Southern leaders were mad," which, coming from him, took on extra meaning.

And yet if responsible people in the South had looked at Shiloh as a harbinger of the long, bloody road ahead, it might have caused them to reconsider the wisdom of secession, but it would have taken a mighty effort by the women of the South, whose sons' futures were reflected in the offal of Shiloh, to bring pressure on their husbands to change the course of history.

That, however, is the slenderest of what-if threads, for as appalled and revolted as southerners were over the slaughter at Shiloh, in the end—as it often does in such cases—the results of the battle seemed only to make them more intransigent, hostile, determined, frenzied even, like a disturbed bed of ants. In fact, one only has to look at the persistence of the South the following year, in 1863, even after the twin Union victories at Gettysburg and Vicksburg— on the same *day*, and that day, ironically enough, the Fourth of July, no less—and still the South was defiant and undeterred for nearly two more years. Grant had been unfortunately clairvoyant after Shiloh to predict that the war could not be won until the South was entirely conquered—or, in his words, "prostrated."

The other what-if is less iffy and concerns the effect on the military fortunes of the Union if Grant had been defeated at Shiloh— if, perhaps, Beauregard had not called off his army and made one last grand charge to wipe Grant's army from its last-ditch position at Pittsburg Landing and Grant had been forced to surrender.

Could it have been done? Maybe, but it is doubtful. Grant's final position in the fading light of that April Sunday was unquestionably his strongest of the day, stronger even than the Hornet's Nest. His army, what was left of it, was concentrated at last. Buell was not fully on the field but he was there. The Confederate units were scattered and exhausted after a long day's fighting, and their commander Beauregard was more than a mile from the battlefront. Grant had massed enough artillery to blow whole ranks of Rebels to rags, and by then whatever Yankee soldiers still manning the line were, by the very definition of their presence, men of proven field merit.

Even so, if Beauregard—or Bragg, for that matter—could have rounded up another brigade or two and hit the Union line hard, who can say what would have happened? The Rebels had driven them all day, and they needed to break the Union line in only one place. Or if the Confederates had not missed the opportunity on the Union left after Chalmers and Jackson routed Stuart's men, if they had then rushed the landing instead of wheeling left and joining the fray at the Hornet's Nest . . . again, who can say?

Which brings us to what I think is the most interesting what-if about Shiloh. If Beauregard had, in fact, driven Grant's army into

395

the river, or to surrender, then neither Grant nor Sherman would have been the stellar figures they became in the future battles of the war. Instead, they would have joined McDowell, McClellan, Pope, Burnside, and Hooker in the dustbin of U.S. military history—the failed Union generals. So the crucial question then becomes who Lincoln could have found to face Robert E. Lee in the East and Bragg and Joe Johnston in the West. The administration had such a sorry record picking commanding generals that there might have been an entirely different outcome.

By 1864 the war had become so bloody and prolonged, and the citizens of the North so discontented, that Lincoln himself was convinced he would not be reelected and said so in a private note to his cabinet. And Lincoln's opponent, George McClellan, was campaigning on a platform of calling for a truce and compromise with the South. One thing for certain is that it was unwise—no matter how many men you had—to make any kind of mistake when Robert Lee was in the neighborhood. Let us then suppose that such a mistake was made against whomever would have taken Grant's place, and that it led to Lincoln's being defeated in 1864. The notion is almost too breathtaking to contemplate.

Of course none of these things happened. In the modern vernacular 150 years later, Shiloh "is what it is," and what it might have been recedes into the blurry mists of historians' daydreams and nightmares. What Shiloh is today, in fact, is one of America's great national military parks.

———◆———

What Elsie Duncan Hurt's mother had heard as rumor came true in 1894, after Congress voted to consecrate nearly 4,000 acres at

Pittsburg Landing for the benefit of those who fought there, and those yet to come, to see and understand what had happened on this ground. It was a masterful undertaking that became a splendid example of historical conservation and interpretation. Unlike Gettysburg and some of the eastern battlefields that were bisected and crisscrossed by busy commercial thoroughfares, Shiloh remains fairly remote, pristine, and mostly undisturbed by modern intrusions.

By the 1890s more than a generation had passed since the war, and the pernicious national hatreds of the 1860s had begun to fade. A battlefield commission was formed consisting of former Union and Confederate officers. Old soldiers of both sides returned and trudged the ground around Pittsburg Landing to help locate and map their former fighting positions. None other than Colonel Camm of the 14th Illinois was selected as surveyor, and Maj. David W. Reed, of the 12th Iowa, who had been wounded at Shiloh, became its first secretary and historian. The only remaining building that dated from the time of the battle, a log cabin, was restored, and many of those erected afterward—presumably including Elsie's mother's new house—were demolished.

All of the main features and events of the battle are preserved, including the Sunken Road, Bloody Pond, Hornet's Nest, the notable roads and farm fields, as well as the remains of the trunk of a large tree beneath which it is said General Johnston breathed his last. The old Shiloh meetinghouse has been reconstructed. Daily tours are given by knowledgeable guides, or you can just drive or walk around as you please.

Shortly after the war ended, the bodies of Union soldiers were disinterred from their rude trench graves and removed to a new 22-acre military cemetery beside the river. Today the National

Cemetery at Shiloh contains the remains of 3,856 U.S. soldiers, including Union men who were killed in nearby battles later in the war and also some from other American wars. The bones of the Confederate dead are not counted among those in the cemetery but remain on the battlefield anyway, where they were originally cast into mass graves, one of these containing more than 700 bodies stacked seven deep. Their burial trenches are lined off by granite markers interspersed with cannonballs, as are many other important historical sites in the park.

In time, as the construction permitted, the states were invited to build commemorative monuments, which they did, beginning in the early 1900s, in granite, marble, and bronze—the most dramatic of which is a spectacular seven-story Greek column, topped by a huge bronze eagle, a tribute by the state of Iowa to its soldiers in the battle. As well, there are scores of smaller state, regimental, and other monuments at appropriate sites within the battle area—more than 400 in all.

Decades after the conflict ended the Southern states remained in financial straits from the effects of the war and Reconstruction and were unable to compete in monumental grandeur with their Northern brethren, who had thrived since the conflict; thus their memorials are noticeably fewer and smaller, though no less moving because of the pathos of their artistry. And though the original organizers of the park took great pains to emphasize that the wounds of war were healed, even today there hovers over the Shiloh battlefield the murky notion of defiant might-have-beens tinged with animosities of the past.

Consider, for example, the most prominent Southern monument, commissioned in 1916 by the United Daughters of the Confederacy: an elaborate 18-foot-tall granite and bronze tableau fraught with insubordination and veiled with more awful meaning than a Greek tragedy.*

The soldier on the right of the statue "represents the Confederate infantryman who has snatched up his flag in defiance of the Northern Army . . . The one on the left represents the officers of the Confederate Army—head bowed in submission to the order to cease firing, when it seemed a Confederate victory was imminent." In the center is a trio of weeping women, representing "Defeated Victory," with the figure in front, representing the South, surrendering the laurel wreath of victory to the other two, Death and Night. "Death came to the commander [Johnston], and Night brought reinforcements to the enemy and the battle was lost," or so says National Park Service Historical Handbook No. 10, published in 1951.

Not much in the way of reconciliation there, a half century after the battle, just a big "well, we ought to have won it" instead.

Perhaps even less conciliatory, right down the street stands the Illinois State Monument, a massive granite pedestal crowned with a substantial bronze figure of a woman seated on a chair with a laurel wreath of victory on her head and bearing a vague resemblance to Lady Justice. The same Park Service handbook interprets it this way: "In her right hand is a sheathed sword. The scabbard is held with a firm grasp as if in readiness for release of the blade and a renewal of the battle should the occasion arise. Her gaze is bent watchfully toward enemy territory to the south."

---

* One of the most prominent backers of the monument was Mrs. William M. Inge, of Corinth, who had washed and prepared the body of General Johnston after he was killed. She almost single-handedly raised the $500,000 for the Confederate statue.

For the statues, at least, it's not over by a long shot, and considering the artistic tensions that their makers and backers injected into these insolent figures, a lively imagination could conjure up some fine Galatean mischief for those ghostly midnights when the myths say lifeless statues come alive.

———◆———

And what of the boys and the men whose bones still molder beneath the fertile ground of Shiloh's dark woods, the ones who went to see the elephant? There comes to mind an incident that occurred years later, about the time that the United Daughters of the Confederacy were building their memorial to the slaughter at the Shiloh National Military Park.

Across the Atlantic another slaughter was then in progress—one of the greatest in the history of all mankind—at the Battle of the Somme, in France, during the second year of the First World War. There, on a single day, July 1, 1916 —and mostly in the first *hour* of battle—more than 21,000 British soldiers were slain. Losses were particularly heavy in the trench held by the Ninth Battalion of the Devonshire Regiment; in fact, for all practical purposes it was wiped out and, as at Shiloh, the dead were summarily entombed in their trench, which was then shoveled over with dirt. Afterward, someone placed a wooden sign over it that weathered the years and said: "The Devonshires Held This Trench. They Hold It Still."

One of their number was a 23-year-old lieutenant named William Noel Hodgson, who had been a promising poet, the son of a bishop of the Church of England. A day before the battle opened Hodgson wrote his final, and best-known, poem, entitled "Before Action," the last verse of which says, with terrible prescience:

I, that on my familiar hill
Saw with uncomprehending eyes
A hundred of thy sunsets spill
Their fresh and sanguine sacrifice,
Ere the sun swings his noonday sword
Must say good-bye to all of this;—
By all delights that I shall miss,
Help me to die, O Lord. *

It was as if he had said it for all of them—the dead of Shiloh, of Waterloo, of the fields of France and Flanders; whether they all died in vain or whether none of them did, they were soldiers. They were not the politicians, or the editors, or the agitators, or the angry mobs but pawns in a greater game, and it was necessary for them to die, which, in the end, is what war is about. The Civil War was part of the growing pains of this nation, and in the process it cast off the scourge of slavery. Slavery would have been cast off anyway at some point, but better sooner than later, as doubtless the dead of both sides would have agreed, all things considered.

Those of them who lived long enough witnessed the onset of extraordinary times. They rode automobiles into the age of skyscrapers, electric lights, movies, airplanes, and indoor plumbing, and they watched new wars arise on an almost unimaginable scale. When they were gone, the trust they passed along remained

---

* The title of the celebrated World War I memoir *Good-Bye to All That* by the British poet Robert Graves was apparently taken from Hodgson's line here.

exceptional in the American character, a willingness to fight, and to die if necessary, for ideas instead of conquest and territory, and for ideals rather than plunder and pillage—an exalted distinction by any measure.

Acknowledgments and
Notes on Sources

———◆———

THERE SHOULD BE A SPECIAL KEY TO HIT ON MY keyboard that automatically and profoundly thanks all of the dogged historians who preceded me in the subject at hand, whatever it is, because when it comes to acknowledgments those are the first people who come to mind. They help shape the way you think, point you in the right directions, and give you intellectual food for thought. My thanks to the chroniclers of the Civil War, and in particular the Battle of Shiloh, are heartfelt, and my debt of gratitude is large.

Regarding Shiloh, the primary source of information as always is the U.S. Government's *War of the Rebellion: A Compilation of the Official Records of the Union and Confederate Armies.* Known in brief as the Official Records, or OR, this 128-volume collection of reports, orders, letters, statistics, and just about any other practical scrap of paper produced by the Civil War armies and navies

must be the basis—in this case, mostly Volume 10—for any serious study of the subject. Likewise helpful is the *Battles and Leaders
of the Civil War* series (B&L), published by the Century Magazine
Company between 1884 and 1887. Here—specifically in Volume
1—are the voices of the leaders as they recall events during the war.
Other solid primary information can be found in such collections
as *Southern Historical Society Papers* (SHSP), a 52-volume set now
in possession of the Virginia Historical Society, which contains
fascinating personal accounts of the Confederate participants. Its
Northern counterpart is the Military Order of the Loyal Legion
of the United States—or MOLLUS—which flourished in every
Northern state after the war, and to which former Union officers
read or presented "papers" recounting their wartime experiences.

I have not in the past been a big fan of the Internet as a source of
historical information because one could not always be sure of getting the real goods. But in recent years—in recent months actually,
and it is ongoing—sites such as Google Books have made available
actual facsimiles of the MOLLUS documents held by the various
states. And not just that; they are making ready for downloading
many if not most regimental histories and other critical documents
of the Civil War, including diaries and memoirs.

It is absolutely astonishing to me that I can type the name of
a Civil War regiment or diarist into an Internet search engine and
with a few strokes of a key download it into my computer, press
the print button, and a couple of minutes later have the exact rep-
lica of a 150-year-old document sitting on my desk ready to be
ring-punched and put into a binder. It is something that otherwise would have taken weeks or months for a library to locate, and
often required a personal trip to distant state archives. Likewise,

the information age has made facsimiles of the OR, SHSP, and B&L available on discs at reasonable prices,* and although they are somewhat awkward to use you can simply insert the disc into your computer and there it is. One can only believe that all these new research tools will make historical inquires far less time consuming for future historians.

In particular I would like to thank Sam Hood, himself a close relation of the Confederate general John Bell Hood, and Jack Dickinson, bibliographer of the Rosanna Alexander Blake Library of Confederate History at the Marshall University Library, for combing through the entire 40 bound volumes of the *Confederate Veteran* magazine (published in the South between 1893 and 1932, and containing articles and letters by Civil War veterans, both North and South) for Shiloh Battle material. It was truly a labor of great friendship, never to be forgotten.

As for general works, Bruce Catton's and Shelby Foote's volumes together have painted a fascinating backdrop for the theater of the war in the West. There are some good and highly educational books about the battle of Shiloh itself, including Larry J. Daniel's *Shiloh: The Battle That Changed the Civil War,* Wiley Sword's *Shiloh: Bloody April,* Edward Cunningham's *Shiloh and the Western Campaign of 1862,* and James Lee McDonough's *Shiloh—In Hell Before Night.* An invaluable source is *The Battle of Shiloh and the Organizations Engaged* (1902) by David W. Reed, a veteran of the battle and the first historian of the Shiloh National Battlefield Park.

---

* These CDs are about $30 to $50. To purchase the entire OR, for instance, would cost anywhere between $1,500 and $5,000, and even then you'd have to find somewhere to put it.

Many of the major players—Grant, Sherman, Beauregard, Buell, and others—left their recollections in print for posterity, while the various diaries and memoirs of participants in the battle are located as described in the bibliography. It is regrettable that photographs or artist's portraits of the diarists Elsie Duncan Hurt and Josie Underwood cannot be found. In the Underwood case it is almost certain that a portrait of her was painted at some point, but it was likely destroyed by the fire that consumed her family home, Mount Air. In any case a thorough search has turned up empty. A special mention, however, must go to the University of Kentucky Press and Nancy Baird for publishing and editing Josie Underwood's Civil War diary. Much tedious, persevering, and obviously loving toil went into putting the manuscript into perspective by tracking down the backgrounds of all the players and painting an excellent picture of the setting.

Likewise, the discovery of the memoir of Elsie Duncan Hurt bears telling. Returning to Memphis after serving as Tennessee's attorney general, prominent Memphis lawyer Michael Cody bought an old home, and in researching its ownership found that it was built in 1901 by Elsie Duncan Hurt. He also discovered Elsie's obituary, which said that she had written a memoir of her life during the Civil War. Intrigued, Cody worked for more than a year tracking down a relative, who he finally found living in Birmingham and who still had a copy of the memoir. He gave a copy to Cody, who—serving on the foundation board of the Memphis Public Library—donated it for posterity.

While I have not written extensively about the Battle of Shiloh, all my previous Civil War histories concerned battles in the western theater, and in so doing I have chronicled the careers of some of the major characters—for example, Grant, Sherman, and Halleck. In this story I uncovered as much fresh and interesting material about them as possible and strove to write about them distinctly, but on occasion it became necessary to weave in some of my earlier depictions. In *Vicksburg, 1863,* for example, I wrote, "The remarkable thing about Grant, was that he was so *unremarkable.*" There is no better or even equal way to express this that I know of, and to my mind the reader deserves the best.

I ask forbearance from the American Historical Association and the MLA Style Sheet, for I have occasionally taken liberty with direct quotations by sometimes eliminating ellipsis marks when they seemed to impede the flow and sense of a sentence or paragraph; likewise I have on occasion fiddled with punctuation where I thought it would lead to confusion. My thinking is that people living 150 years ago spoke a somewhat different language than we do today, and sometimes it needs to be adjusted slightly to make it clear. But never in any instance have I deliberately changed the meaning or sense of any original author or speaker.

I would especially like to thank Len Riedel of the Blue & Gray Education Society for getting this ball rolling in the first place. As a member of the BGES I am proud to help the organization by authorizing a special leather-bound limited edition of this book. I am particularly grateful to Jeanette and Carl Christman; Janet and Bill Riedel; Jim Anderson; Laurie and Corky Lowe; Frank Roberts; Bob Gailbraith; Trish and David Dubose, and Benjamin Brand for their generous support in underwriting the printing of the special volume.

Len had obtained access to a huge amount of historic material on the Battle of Corinth from the collection of Corinth historian Van Hedges, and out of that discussion grew the idea of a new account of the Battle of Shiloh and his introduction of me to Lisa Thomas, the steady, able senior editor of National Geographic Books, for whose patience, kindness, and solid editorial advice I am profoundly grateful. Also deserving of many thanks at the NGS are Marshall Kiker, illustrations specialist, for locating the images; Carl Mehler, NGS's director of maps, who oversaw the mapmaking; and Judith Klein, production editor, whose eagle eye stanched errors. Line editor Andrew Carlson deserves a Distinguished Service Cross for unraveling my tongue-twisting prose, while copy editor Don Kennison is entitled at least to a Purple Heart for having his sensibilities constantly assaulted by my obnoxious punctuation and syntax. The readers will certainly thank you, and so do I.

My literary agent, Theron Raines, added his inestimable wisdom and wise counsel by reading and commenting on the entire manuscript. Last, but never least, my wife, Anne-Clinton, and her mother, Dr. Wren Murphy, have as usual expended great time and greater effort in dealing with photographs, permissions, logging in books, manuscripts, and other research materials as well as indexing, organizing, and performing every other task to make this project run smoothly from the beginning. My everlasting thanks to you all.

Bibliography

Abernethy, Byron R., ed. *Private Elisha Stockwell, Jr. Sees the Civil War.* Norman: University of Oklahoma Press, 1958.

Ambrose, D. Leib. *History of the Seventh Regiment. Illinois Volunteer Infantry: From Its First Muster into the U.S. Service, April 25, 1861, to Its Final Muster Out July 9, 1865.* Springfield: Illinois Journal Company, 1868.

Ammen, Col. Jacob. "Wanted to See the Elephant," *Confederate Veteran,* vol. xxv, no. 5 (May 1917).

Anders, Leslie. *The Eighteenth Missouri.* New York: Bobbs-Merrill, 1968.

Anderson, T. B. "A Boy's Impressions at Shiloh." *Confederate Veteran,* vol. xix, no. 2 (February 1911).

Anon. "Battle Pictures from Shiloh." 570–573.

Arnold, James R. *Shiloh 1862: The Death of Innocence.* Oxford, UK: Osprey Publishing Ltd., 1998.

Arnold, Matthew, with a Rejoinder by Mark Twain (1887). John Y. Simon, ed. *General Grant.* Kent, Ohio: Kent State University Press, 1995.

Ashe, Captain S. A. *A Southern View of the Invasion of the Southern States and the War of 1861–65.* Wendell, N.C.: Avera Press, 1938.

Ayers, Edward L., ed. *"A House Divided . . ." Century of Great Civil War Quotations.* New York: John Wiley and Sons, 1997.

Baird, Nancy Disher, ed. *Josie Underwood's Civil War Diary.* Lexington: University Press of Kentucky, 2009.

Bartlett, Napier. *A Soldier's Story of the War; including the Marches and Battles of the Washington Artillery, and of other Louisiana Troops.* New Orleans: Clark and Hofeline, 1874.

Basso, Hamilton. *Beauregard: The Great Creole.* New York: Charles Scribner's, 1933.

Battles and Leaders of the Civil War, vol. 1. New York: Century Company, 1887.

Bell, John T. *Tramps & Triumphs of the Second Iowa Infantry.* Des Moines: Gibson, Miller and Richardson, 1886.

Bergeron, Arthur W., Jr., ed. *Civil War Reminiscences of Major Silas T. Grisamore C.S.A.* Baton Rouge: Louisiana State University Press, 1993.

Betts, Vicki. "A Revelation of War: Civilians in Hardin County, Tennessee, Spring 1862." *Citizen's Companion* (Morristown, Tenn., nd).

Bierce, Ambrose. "What I Saw of Shiloh" (1881). *Civil War Stories.* New York: Dover Publications, 1994.

Brewer, James D. *Tom Worthington's Civil War: Shiloh, Sherman and the Search for Vindication.* Jefferson, N.C.: McFarland and Company, 2001.

Briant, C. C. *History of the 6th Regiment Indiana Volunteer Infantry, of Both the Three Months' and Three Years' Services.* W. B. Burford, 1891.

Brinton, John H. *Personal Memoirs of John H. Brinton, Civil War Surgeon 1861–1865.* New York: Neale Publishing Company, 1914.

Brown, Dee Alexander. *The Bold Cavaliers. Morgan's 2nd Kentucky Cavalry Raiders.* Philadelphia: J. B. Lippincott, 1959.

Buck, Irving A. and Thomas Robson Hay, eds. *Cleburne and His Command and Pat Cleburne, Stonewall Jackson of the West.* Jackson, Tenn.: McCowat-Mercer Press, 1959.

Buell, General Don Carlos. "Demoralization of Grant's Army at Shiloh." *Confederate Veteran,* vol. xxv, no. 5 (May 1917).

Burress, L. R. "Shiloh." *Confederate Veteran,* vol. xxiii, no. 4 (April 1915).

———. "Who Lost Shiloh to the Confederacy?" *Confederate Veteran,* vol. xxi, no. 9 (September 1913).

Caddo, Fencibles. "Reminiscences of the Battle of Shiloh." *Confederate Veteran,* vol. ix, no. 11 (November 1901).

Cannon, John, ed. *Eye Witness of the Civil War in the West: Shiloh to Vicksburg. 1862–1863.* New York: Gallery Books, 1990.

Carrington, Second Lt. George Dodd. *Authentic Civil War Diary. Companion to the U.S. Civil War Center Endorsed Historical Novel* Fame's Eternal Camping-Grounds. Fame's Eternal Books, LLC, 2006 (© Tammy L. Mate).

Carruth, E. B. "Vivid Recollections of Shiloh." *Confederate Veteran,* vol. ix, no. 4 (April 1901).

Catton, Bruce. *Grant Moves South.* Boston: Little, Brown, 1960.

———. *This Hallowed Ground: The Story of the Union Side of the Civil War.* Garden City, N.Y.: Doubleday, 1956.

Chance, Joseph E. *The Second Texas Infantry: From Shiloh to Vicksburg.* Austin, Tex.: Eakin Press, 1984.

Cherry, Mrs. W. H. "Grant at Shiloh." *Confederate Veteran,* vol. i, no. 2 (February 1893).

Chisolm, Col. Alex Robert. "Gen. Beauregard at Shiloh." *Confederate Veteran,* vol. x, no. 5 (May 1902).

Cobb, Capt. "Cobb's Battery Not Captured at Shiloh." *Confederate Veteran,* vol. xiii, no. 2 (February 1905).

Cockerill, John C. "A Boy at Shiloh." In *Sketches of War History 1861–1865.* A Compilation of Miscellaneous Papers Read before the Ohio Commandery of the Loyal Legion April 1912–April 1916. Cincinnati: Broadfoot Publishing, 1993.

Conger, Col. Arthur L. Introduction by Brooks D. Simpson. *The Rise of U. S. Grant.* New York: Century Company, 1931.

Connelly, Thomas Lawrence. *Army of the Heartland: The Army of Tennessee, 1861–1862.* Baton Rouge: Louisiana State University Press, 1967.

Crocker, Capt. Lucien B., Henry S. Nourse, and John G. Brown. *The Story of the 55th Regiment Illinois Volunteer Infantry in the Civil War, 1861–1865.* Clinton, Mass.: W. J. Coulter, 1887.

Crozier, Emmet. *Yankee Reporters 1861–65.* New York: Oxford University Press, 1956.

Crummer, Wilbur F. *With Grant at Fort Donelson, Shiloh and Vicksburg and an Appreciation of General U. S. Grant.* Oak Park, Ill.: E. C. Crummer, 1915.

Crump, G. K. "Still Another Young Confederate." *Confederate Veteran,* vol. xii, no. 11 (November 1904).

Cumming, Kate. Richard Barksdale Harwell, ed. *Kate: The Journal of a Confederate Nurse.* Baton Rouge: Louisiana State University Press, 1959.

Cunningham, Dr. John. "Reminiscence of Shiloh." *Confederate Veteran,* vol. xvi, no. 11 (November 1908).

Cunningham, O. Edward. Gary Joiner and Timothy Smith, eds. *Shiloh and the Western Campaign of 1862.* New York: Savas Beatie, 2007.

Daniel, Larry J. *Shiloh: The Battle That Changed the Civil War.* New York: Simon and Schuster, 1997.

———, with additional text by Stacy D. Allen. *The Battle of Shiloh.* National Park Service Civil War Series on the Battle of Shiloh. Fort Washington, Penn.: Eastern National, 1998.

Davidson, N. P. "Maj. John H. Miller, a Fighting Parson." *Confederate Veteran,* vol. xviii, no. 1 (January 1910).

Davis, Burke. *The Civil War: Strange and Fascinating Facts.* New York: Fairfax Press, 1982.

Davis, William C. *The Fighting Men of the Civil War.* Norman: University of Oklahoma Press, 1998.

Deupree, J. G. "Reminiscences of Service with the First Mississippi Calvary." *Mississippi Historical Society*, vol. 7 (Jackson, Miss., 1903).

Dillahunty, Albert. *Shiloh. National Military Park*, Tennessee National Park Service Historical Handbook, series 10 (Washington, D.C., 1951).

Duke, Gen. Basil W. "Morgan's Cavalry Was at Shiloh." *Confederate Veteran,* vol. xiii, no. 5 (May 1905).

Duke, John K. *History of the Fifty-third Regiment. Ohio Volunteer Infantry During the War of the Rebellion, 1861 to 1865: Together with More than Thirty Personal Sketches of Officers and Men.* Portsmouth, Ohio: Blade Printing Co., 1900.

Eicher, David J. *The Civil War in Books: An Analytical Bibliography.* Chicago: University of Illinois Press, 1997.

Eisenschiml, Otto. "The 55th Illinois at Shiloh." *Journal of the Illinois State Historical Society* (1908–1984), vol. 56, no. 2, Civil War Centennial (Summer 1963): 193–211.

———. *The Story of Shiloh.* The Civil War Roundtable Club of Chicago, April 1946.

——— and E. B. Long. *As Luck Would Have It.* New York: Bobbs-Merrill, 1948.

——— and Ralph Newman. Introduction by Bruce Catton. *Eyewitness the Civil War as We Lived It.* New York: Universal Library, Grosset & Dunlap, 1956.

Ellis, W. B. "Who Lost Shiloh to the Confederacy?" *Confederate Veteran,* vol. xxii, no. 7 (July 1914).

Emerson, John W. "Grant's Life in the West. General Introductory Estimates of Grant's Career & Character." *Midland Monthly Magazine,* vol. vi, no. 4 (Des Moines, October 1896): 318–20.

Ewing, Joseph H. *Sherman at War.* Dayton, Ohio: Morningside, 1992.

Fiftieth Anniversary of the Great Battle of Shiloh, held at Pittsburg Landing, Tenn., April 6, 1912, by the National Association of Survivors. Oration by Samuel M. Howard of Gettysburg, South Dakota.

Fisher, Horace Cecil. *A Staff Officer's Story. The Personal Experiences of Colonel Horace Newton Fisher in the Civil War.* Boston: Thomas Todd Co., 1960.

Fleming, Robert H. "The Battle of Shiloh as a Private Saw It." *Sketches of War History.* Military Order of Loyal Legion of the US (MOLLUS), Ohio, vol. 6 (Cincinnati: Monfort): 132–46, 1908.

Fletcher, William A. *Rebel Private: Front and Rear Memoirs of a Confederate Soldier.* Beaumont, Tex., 1908.

Folmar, John Kent, ed. *From the Terrible Field. Civil War Letters of James M. Williams. Twenty-first Alabama Infantry Volunteers.* Tuscaloosa: University of Alabama Press, 1981.

Foote, Shelby. *The Civil War: A Narrative–Fort Sumter to Perryville.* New York: Vintage, 1958.

Force, M. F. *From Fort Henry to Corinth.* New York: Charles Scribner's & Sons, 1881.

Frank, Joseph Allan, and George A. Reaves. *"Seeing the Elephant": Raw Recruits at the Battle of Shiloh.* Chicago: University of Illinois Press, 2003.

Fritz, Karen E. *Voices in the Storm: Confederate Rhetoric, 1861–1865.* Denton, Tex.: University of North Texas Press, 1999.

Fuller, J.F.C. *The Generalship of Ulysses S. Grant.* London: J. Murray, 1929.

Garrison, Web. *Curiosities of the Civil War: Strange Stories, Infamous Characters, and Bizarre Events.* Nashville: Thomas Nelson, 1994.

George, Col. Henry. "Two Men Sought Water at Shiloh." *Confederate Veteran,* vol. xix, no. 9 (September 1911).

Gleeson, Ed. *Illinois Rebels. A Civil War Unit History of G. Company 15th Tennessee Regiment Volunteer Infantry. The Story of the Confederacy's Southern Illinois Company Men from Marion and Carbondale.* Carmel, Ind.: Guild Press of Indiana, 1996.

Goodwin, William. "Governor Johnston at Shiloh." *Confederate Veteran,* vol. iv, no. 9 (September 1896).

Gott, Kendall D. *Where the South Lost the War: An Analysis of the Fort Henry Fort Donelson Campaign, February 1862.* Mechanicsburg, Penn.: Stackpole Books, 2003.

Grant, Ulysses S. *Personal Memoirs of U. S. Grant. Selected Letters, 1839–1865.* New York: Library of America, 1990.

Grimsley, Mark, and Steven E. Woodworth. *Shiloh: A Battlefield Guide.* Lincoln: University of Nebraska Press, 2006.

Groom, Winston. *Vicksburg 1863.* New York: Knopf, 2009.

Hamby, J. A. "Strange Plight of a Federal Prisoner." *Confederate Veteran,* vol. xviii, no. 6 (June 1910).

Hannaford, Ebenezer. *The Story of a Regiment: A History of the Campaigns and Associations in the Field of the Sixth Regiment, Ohio Volunteer Infantry.* Cincinnati, 1868.

———. "Coming Up at Shiloh." *Continental Monthly Magazine* (October 1864).

Haskell, Fritz, ed. "Diary of Colonel William Camm 1861–1865." *Journal of the Illinois State Historical Society,* vol. 18 (January 1926): 793–909.

Hazen, General W. B. *A Narrative of Military Service.* Boston: Ticknor, 1885.

Henry, H. W. "My First Experience with a Yankee Shell." *Confederate Veteran,* vol. xxii, no. 7 (July 1914).

Henry, Hon. Pat. "Regimental Losses." *Confederate Veteran,* vol. xxiii, no. 11 (November 1915).

Hickenlooper, Andrew. "The Battle of Shiloh: Part I. Personal Experiences in the Battle." *Sketches of War History* (MOLLUS), Ohio, vol. 5 (Cincinnati: Robert Clarke, 1903), 402–483.

Hillyer, W. S. "Hillyer on Grant at Shiloh." *Confederate Veteran,* vol. i, no. 10 (October 1893).

Hogan, Rev. H. D. The Twenty-fourth Tennessee Regiment" *Confederate Veteran,* vol. xxxiii, no. 3 (March 1925).

Horsley, A. S. " Reminiscences of Shiloh." *Confederate Veteran,* vol. ii, no. 1 (January 1894).

Hosea, Lewis M. "The Second Day at Shiloh." In *Sketches of War History 1861–1865.* Ohio Commandery of MOLLUS (1906), vol. 6 (Cincinnati: Monfort, 1908): 195–218.

Hughes, Nathaniel Chears, Jr. *General William J. Hardee: Old Reliable.* (Southern Biography series) Baton Rouge: Louisiana State University Press, 1965.

———, ed. *The Civil War Memoir of Philip Daingerfield Stephenson, D. D. Private, Company K. 13th Arkansas Volunteer Infantry Loader, Piece No. 4, 5th Company, Washington Artillery, Army of Tennessee, CSA.* Baton Rouge: Louisiana State University Press, 1995.

Hurt, Elsie Carolina Duncan. *The Diary of Elsie Carolina Duncan Hurt.* Document. Memphis Public Library.

Johnston, William Preston. *The Life of General Albert Sidney Johnston, Embracing His Services in the Armies of the United States, the Republic of Texas, and the Confederate States.* New York: D. Appleton, 1879.

Jones, Archer. *Confederate Strategy from Shiloh to Vicksburg.* Baton Rouge: Louisiana State University Press, 1961.

Jones, Frank J. "Personal Recollections and Experience of a Soldier During the War of the Rebellion." *Sketches of War History.* Compilation of Miscellaneous Papers Read before the Ohio Commandery of MOLLUS, vol. 6 (Cincinnati: Monfort, 1908).

Jones, Howard. *Union in Peril: The Crisis over British Intervention in the Civil War.* Chapel Hill: University of North Carolina Press, 1992.

Jones, James A. "About the Battle of Shiloh." *Confederate Veteran,* vol. vii, no. 12 (December 1899).

Jones, Katharine M. *Heroines of Dixie: Confederate Women Tell Their Story of the War.* New York: Bobbs-Merrill, 1955.

Jordan, General Thomas, and J. P. Pryor. Introduction by Albert Castel. *The Campaigns of General Nathan Bedford Forrest and of Forrest's Calvary.* New Orleans, 1868.

Kagan, Neil, ed. Text by Stephen G. Hyslop. *Atlas of the Civil War: A Comprehensive Guide to the Tactics and Terrain of Battle.* Washington, D.C.: National Geographic, 2009.

———. *Eyewitness to the Civil War: The Complete History from Secession to Reconstruction.* Washington, D.C.: National Geographic, 2009.

Kaufmann, Wilhelm. *The Germans in the American Civil War.* Carlisle, Penn.: John Kallmann, 1999.

Kelley, Col. D. C. "Mistakes Concerning Battle of Shiloh." *Confederate Veteran,* vol. ix, no. 12 (December 1901).

Kelsey, Jasper. "The Battle of Shiloh." *Confederate Veteran,* vol. xxv, no. 2 (February 1917).

Kirwan, A. D., ed. *Johnny Green of the Orphan Brigade: The Journal of a Confederate Soldier.* Lexington: University Press of Kentucky, 1956.

Lathrop, Barnes F., ed. "A Confederate Artilleryman at Shiloh." *Civil War History,* vol. 1, 8 (1962): 373–85.

Le Monnier, Dr. Y. R. "Who Lost Shiloh to the Confederacy?" *Confederate Veteran,* vol. xxi, no. 11 (November 1913).

———. "Who Lost Shiloh to the Confederacy?" *Confederate Veteran,* vol. xxii, no. 9 (September 1914).

Logsdon, David R. *Eyewitnesses at the Battle of Shiloh.* Nashville: Kettle Mills Press, 1994.

Maher, Sister Mary Denis. *To Bind Up the Wounds: Catholic Sister Nurses in the U.S. Civil War.* Baton Rouge: Louisiana State University Press, 1989.

Martin, David G. *The Shiloh Campaign, March–April 1862.* Revised edition. Conshohocken, Penn.: Combined Books, 1996.

McBride, George W. "My Recollections of Shiloh." *Blue and Gray, The Patriotic American Magazine,* vol. 3, no. 1 (January 1895): 8–12.

McClendon, J. R. "A Faithful Negro, Frederick Pouncey." *Confederate Veteran,* vol. xi, no. 3 (March 1903).

McDonough, James Lee. *Shiloh—In Hell Before Night.* Knoxville: University of Tennessee, 1977.

McKee, John Miller. *The Great Panic: Being Incidents Connected with Two Weeks in the War in Tennessee.* Nashville: Johnson and Whiting, 1862.

Meadows, A. J. "The Fourth Tennessee Infantry." *Confederate Veteran,* vol. xiv, no. 7 (July 1906).

Mecklin, Augustus H. *Augustus Henry Mecklin Papers*. Mississippi Department of Archives and History, Jackson, Miss. nd.

Metzler, William E. *Morgan and His Dixie Cavaliers: An Account of the Confederate Cavalryman's Most Famous Exploits*. A Biography of the Colorful Confederate General. (General John H. Morgan.) Published by the author, 1976.

Moore, Col. John C. "Shiloh Issues Again." *Confederate Veteran*, vol. x, no. 7 (July 1902).

———. "Some Confederate War Incidents." *Confederate Veteran*, vol. xii, no. 3 (March 1904).

Newberry, Dr. J. S. *U.S. Sanitary Commission in the Valley of the Mississippi During War of Rebellion*. Cleveland: Fairbanks, Benedict, 1871.

Newcomb, Mary A. *Four Years of Personal Reminiscences of the War*. Chicago: H. S. Mills, 1893.

North, Nancy. "The Three-Armed" Soldier." *Confederate Veteran*, vol. xxxii, no. 1 (January 1924).

Olney, Warren. *The Battle of Shiloh as Seen by A Private Soldier*. A Paper Read Before California Commandery of the Military Order of the Loyal Legion of the United States (MOLLUS). May 31, 1889. Printed by Wayne and Judy Dasher, Nashville, Georgia, 2009.

Palmer, Mrs. Ella. "Reminiscences of Her Service in Hospitals." *Confederate Veteran*, vol. xviii, no. 2 (February 1910).

Parks, (Captain). Senior first lieutenant of heavy artillery, Hoadley's Arkansas Battery. "Other Heroic Virginians." *Confederate Veteran*, vol. xi, no. 2 (February 1903).

Patrick, Jeffrey L., ed. *Three Years with Wallace's Zouaves. The Civil War Memoirs of Thomas Wise Durham*. Macon: Mercer University Press, 2003.

Patton, General Robert M. "Soldier Sons of Ex-Governor Patton." *Confederate Veteran*, vol. xvii, no. 7 (July 1909).

Putnam, Douglas, Jr. "Reminiscences of the Battle of Shiloh." *Sketches of War History*. Ohio MOLLUS. Transcribed by Larry Stevens (Cincinnati: Robert Clark, 1890).

Reed, David W. With a new introduction by Timothy B. Smith. *The Battle of Shiloh and the Organizations Engaged*. Knoxville: University of Tennessee, 2008.

Rerick, John H. *The Forty-fourth Indiana Volunteer Infantry, History of Its Services in the War of the Rebellion and a Personal Record of Its Members*. LaGrange, Indiana, 1880.

Rich, Joseph W. *The Battle of Shiloh*. Iowa City: State Historical Society of Iowa, 1911.

———. "The Battle of Shiloh." *Iowa Journal of History and Politics*, vol. 7, no. 4 (October 1909).

———. "General Lew Wallace at Shiloh." *Iowa Journal of History and Politics*, vol. 18, no. 2 (April 1920).

Richardson, Albert D. *A Personal History of Ulysses Grant*. Chicago: American Publishing Co., 1868.

Ridley, Bromfield L. *Battles and Sketches of the Army of Tennessee*. Mexico, Mo.: Missouri Printing and Publishing Co., 1906.

Roland, Charles Pierce. *Albert Sidney Johnston: Soldier of Three Republics*. Lexington: University Press of Kentucky, 2001.

———. *Jefferson Davis's Greatest General: Albert Sidney Johnston*. Abilene, Tex.: McWhiney Foundation Press, 2000.

Ruff, Joseph. "Civil War Experiences of a German Emigrant as Told by the Late Joseph Ruff of Albion." *Michigan History Magazine,* vol. xxvii (Lansing: Michigan Historical Commission, 1943).

S.W.H. "A Union Veteran Hurlbut's Division." *Confederate Veteran,* vol. iii, no. 11 (November 1895).

Saxon, Mrs. Elizabeth Lyle. *Southern Woman's War-Time Reminiscences*. Lightning Source, Inc., 2009. Originally published Memphis, Tenn.: Press of the Pilcher Printing Co., 1905.

Sherman, William Tecumseh. *Sherman. Memoirs of General W. T. Sherman*. Second edition. New York: 1885. Originally published New York: Appleton, 1875.

Simpson, Brooks. *Ulysses S. Grant: Triumph Over Adversity, 1822–1865*. New York: Houghton Mifflin, 2000.

Smith, Timothy B. "Battle of Shiloh: Shattering Myths." *America's Civil War*. June 12, 2006.

———. *This Great Battlefield of Shiloh: History, Memory and the Establishment of a Civil War National Military Park*. Knoxville: University of Tennessee Press, 2004.

———. "Shiloh's False Hero." *Civil War Times,* vol. 47, no. 6, December 5, 2008, 28–35.

———. *The Untold Story of Shiloh: The Battle and the Battlefield*. Knoxville: University of Tennessee Press, 2006.

Staff Ride Handbook for the Battle of Shiloh, 6–7 April 1862. Lt. Col. Jeffrey J. Gudmens and Staff Ride Team Combat Studies Institute, Fort Leavenworth, Kansas, 2005.

Stanley, Henry M., and Lady Dorothy Stanley. *The Autobiography of Sir Henry Morton Stanley* (1909). Memphis: General Books, 2010.

———, and Nathaniel Cheairs Hughes, Jr. *Sir Henry Morton Stanley, Confederate*. Baton Rouge: Louisiana State University Press, 2000.

Stevenson, William G. *Thirteen Months in the Rebel Army: A Northerner Forced into the Southern Army*. New York: A.S. Barnes, 1959.

Stillwell, Leander. "In the Ranks at Shiloh." *War Talks in Kansas*. A Series of Papers Read before the Kansas Commandery of MOLLUS. March 2, 1892. Kansas City, Mo.: Franklin Hudson, 1906.

_____. *The Story of a Common Soldier of Army Life in the Civil War, 1861–1865.* Kansas City, Mo.: Franklin Hudson, 1920.

Sutherland, Daniel, ed. *Reminiscences Private William E. Bevens of the First Arkansas Infantry C.S.A.* Fayetteville: University of Arkansas Press, 1992.

Sword, Wiley. *Shiloh: Bloody April.* New York: William Morrow, 1974.

Symonds, Craig L. *Stonewall of the West: Patrick Cleburne and the Civil War.* Lawrence: University Press of Kansas, 1997.

Taylor, F. Hay, ed. *Reluctant Rebel: The Secret Diary of Robert Patrick, 1861–1865.* Baton Rouge: Louisiana State University Press, 1959.

Taylor, John T. "Reminiscences of Services as an Aide-de-Camp with General William Tecumseh Sherman." A Paper Prepared and Read before the Kansas Commandery of the MOLLUS, April 6, 1892. Kansas City, Mo.: Franklin Hudson, 1906.

Thomas, Benjamin Franklin. *Soldier Life: A Narrative of the Civil War.* Iowa City: Camp Polk Book Shop, 1907.

Thompson, Ed Porter. *History of the Orphan Brigade*, vol. 1. Louisville, Ky.: Lewis N. Thompson, 1898.

Thompson, Illene D., and Wilbur E. Thompson. *The Seventeenth Alabama Infantry: A Regimental History and Roster.* Westminster, Md.: Heritage Books, 2009.

Thompson, J. N. "The Gallant Old Forty-fourth Mississippi." *Confederate Veteran,* vol. xxviii, no. 11 (November 1920).

Throne, Mildred. "Iowa and the Battle of Shiloh: Comments on the Hornet's Nest 1862 and 1887." *Iowa Journal of History,* vol. 55, no. 3 (July 1957): 249–74.

———, ed. "The Letters from Shiloh." *Iowa Journal of History,* vol. 52, no. 3 (July 1954): 235–80.

Thruston, General G. P. "Buried by his Classmates—The Enemy." *Confederate Veteran,* vol. xiii, no. 6 (June 1905).

Trimpi, Helen B. *Crimson Confederates: Harvard Men Who Fought for the South.* Knoxville: University of Tennessee Press, 2009.

Tunno, M. R. "About Beauregard's Order at Shiloh." *Confederate Veteran,* vol. x, no. 2 (February 1902).

Turner, Joe. "Incident at Shiloh." *Confederate Veteran,* vol. xvii, no. 2 (March 1909).

Van Winkle, Alexander. "Incidents & Inquiries about Shiloh." *Confederate Veteran,* vol. xvi, no. 3 (March 1908).

Victor, Orville. *Incidents and Anecdotes of the War with Narratives of the Great Battles, etc.* New York: J. D. Torrey, 1866.

Wallace, Harold Lew. "Lew Wallace's March to Shiloh Revisited." *Indiana Magazine of History,* vol. 59 (1963): 19–31.

Wallace, Isabel. *Life and Letters of Gen. W.H.L. Wallace.* Chicago: R. R. Donnelley & Sons, 1909.

Wallace, Lew. *An Autobiography,* vol. II. New York: Harper & Brothers,1906.

War of the Rebellion. A Compilation of the Official Records of the Union and the Confederate Armies. Prepared Under the Direction of the Secretary of War, by BVT Lieut. Col. Robert N. Scott, Third U.S. Artillery, and Published Pursuant to Act of Congress Approved July 16, 1880. Series I, vol. X, in Two Parts. Part II: Correspondence, etc. Washington, D.C.: Government Printing Office, 1884.

Warner, Ezra J. *Generals in Blue: Lives of the Union Commanders.* Baton Rouge: Louisiana State University Press, 1981.

———. *Generals in Gray: Lives of the Confederate Commanders.* Baton Rouge: Louisiana State University Press, 1959.

Watkins, Samuel R. *Company Aytch, or a Side Show of the Big Show.* Edited and introduced by M. Thomas Inge. New York: Penguin Putnam, 1999.

Wheeler, J. A. "Cleburne's Brigade at Shiloh." *Confederate Veteran,* vol. ii, no. 1 (January 1894).

Wigle, Fred B. *The Drummer Boy of Shiloh: A New Military Allegory in Five Acts and Accompanying Tableaux.* Cleveland, 1897.

Wiley, Bell I. "Johnny Reb and Billy Yank at Shiloh." Address delivered at Shiloh Church, on the Shiloh Battlefield, April 8, 1972, at an observance of the 110th Anniversary of the engagement, sponsored by the *West Tennessee Historical Society,* vol. 26 (1972): 5–12.

Williams, J. M. "Faithful in His Devotion." *Confederate Veteran,* vol. xxii, no. 8 (August 1914).

Williams, Kenneth P. *Grant Rises in the West: The First Year, 1861–1862.* Lincoln: University of Nebraska Press, 1952.

Williams, T. Harry. *P.G.T. Beauregard: Napoleon in Gray.* Baton Rouge: Louisiana State University Press, 1955.

Willis, James. *Arkansas Confederates in the Western Theater.* Dayton, Ohio: Morningside House, 1998.

Wilson, Peter. *Many Must Fall: The Civil War Letters of Peter Wilson and His Companions.* Iowa City: Camp Polk Book Shop, 2008.

Woodworth, Steven E. *Jefferson Davis and His Generals: The Failure of Confederate Command in the West.* Lawrence: University Press of Kansas, 1990.

Wright, Charles. *A Corporal's Story: Experiences in the Ranks of Company C, 81st Ohio Vol. Infantry, During the War for the Maintenance of the Union, 1861–1864.* Philadelphia, 1887.

Wright, Henry H. *A History of the Sixth Iowa Infantry.* Iowa City: State Historical Society of Iowa, 1923.

Wyeth, John Allan. *That Devil Forrest: Life of General Nathan Bedford Forrest.* New York: Harper and Bros., 1987. Originally published 1899.

Young, Jesse Bowman, and Frank Beard. *What a Boy Saw in the Army: A Story of Sight Seeing and Adventure in the War for the Union.* New York: Hunt and Eaton, 1923.

The Battle of Shiloh and the Organizations Engaged

ORGANIZATION OF THE UNION ARMY
AT THE BATTLE OF SHILOH, TENNESSEE,
APRIL 6-7, 1862

ARMY OF THE TENNESSEE
Maj. Gen. U. S. GRANT, Commanding

FIRST DIVISION
Maj. Gen. JOHN A. McCLERNAND
First Brigade
Col. ABRAHAM M. HARE (wounded), 11th Iowa
Col. MARCELLUS M. CROCKER, 13th Iowa
8th Illinois:
Capt. James M. Ashmore (wounded)
Capt. William H. Harvey (killed)
Capt. Robert H. Sturgess
18th Illinois:
Maj. Samuel Eaton (wounded)
Capt. Daniel H. Brush (wounded)
Capt. William J. Dillion (killed)
Capt. Jabez J. Anderson
11th Iowa:
Lieut. Col. William Hall (wounded)
13th Iowa:
Col. Marcellus M. Crocker
Second Brigade
Col. C. CARROLL MARSH, 20th Illinois
11th Illinois:
Lieut. Col. Thomas E. G. Ransom (wounded)
Maj. Garrett Nevins (wounded)
Capt. Lloyd D. Waddell
Maj. Garrett Nevins
20th Illinois:

Lieut. Col. Evan Richards (wounded)
Capt. Orton Frisbie
45th Illinois:
Col. John E. Smith
48th Illinois:
Col. Isham N. Hayniea
Maj. Manning Mayfield
Third Brigade
Col. JULIUS RAITH (mortally wounded),
43d Illinois
Lieut. Col. ENOS P. WOOD, 17th Illinois
17th Illinois:
Lieut. Col. Enos P. Wood
Maj. Francis M. Smith
29th Illinois:
Lieut. Col. Charles M. Ferrell
43d Illinois:
Lieut. Col. Adolph Endelmann
49th Illinois:
Lieut. Col. Phineas Pease (wounded)
Unattached
Dresser's Battery (D), 2d Illinois Light Artillery,
Capt. James P. Timony
McAllister's Battery (D), 1st Illinois Light Artillery,
Capt. Edward McAllister (wounded)
Schwartz's Battery (E), 2d Illinois Light Artillery,
Lieut. George L. Nispel
Burrows' Battery, 14th Ohio Light Artillery,
Capt. Jerome B. Burrows (wounded)
1st Battalion, 4th Illinois Light Cavalry,
Lieut. Col. William McCullough
Carmichael's Company Illinois Cavalry,
Capt. Eagleton Carmichael
Stewart's Company Illinois Cavalry, Lieut. Ezra King

SECOND DIVISION
Brig. Gen. WILLIAM H. L. WALLACE
(mortally wounded)
Col. JAMES M. TUTTLE, 2d Iowa
First Brigade
Col. JAMES M. TUTTLE
2d Iowa:
Lt. Col. James Baker
7th Iowa:
Lt. Col. James C. Parrott
12th Iowa:
Col. Joseph J. Woods (wounded and captured)
Capt. Samuel R. Edgington (captured)
14th Iowa:
Col. Wm. T. Shaw (captured)
Second Brigade
Brig. Gen. JOHN McARTHUR (wounded)
Col. THOMAS MORTON, 81st Ohio
9th Illinois:
Col. August Mersy
12th Illinois:
Lieut. Col. Augustus L. Chetlain
Capt. James R. Hugunin
13th Missouri:
Col. Crafts J. Wright
14th Missouri:
Col. B. S. Compton
81st Ohio:
Col. Thomas Morton
Third Brigade
Col. THOMAS W. SWEENY (wounded), 52D Illinois
Col. SILAS D. BALDWIN, 57th Illinois
8th Iowa:
Col. James L. Geddes (wounded and captured)
7th Illinois:
Maj. Richard Rowett
50th Illinois:
Col. Moses M. Bane (wounded)
52d Illinois:
Maj. Henry Stark
Capt. Edwin A. Bowen
57th Illinois:
Col. Silas D. Baldwin
Capt. Gustav A. Busse
58th Illinois:
Col. Wm. F. Lynch (captured)
Artillery
Willard's Battery (A), 1st Illinois Light Artillery,
Lieut. Peter P. Wood
Maj. J. S. Cavender's Battalion Missouri Artillery:
Richardson's Battery (D), 1st Missouri Light Artillery,
Capt. Henry Richardson
Welker's Battery (H), 1st Missouri Light Artillery,
Capt. Frederick Welker
Stone's Battery (K), 1st Missouri Light Artillery,
Capt. George H. Stone
Cavalry
Company A, 2d Illinois Cavalry, Capt. John R. Hotaling
Company B, 2d Illinois Cavalry, Capt. Thomas J. Larison
Company C, 2d United States Cavalry, Lieut. James Powell
Company I, 4th United States Cavalry, Lieut. James Powell

THIRD DIVISION
Maj. Gen. LEW WALLACE
First Brigade
Col. MORGAN L. SMITH, 8th Missouri
11th Indiana:
Col. George F. McGinnis

24th Indiana:
Col. Alvin P. Hovey
8th Missouri:
Lieut. Col. James Peckham
Second Brigade
Col. JOHN M. THAYER, 1st Nebraska
23d Indiana:
Col. William L. Sanderson
1st Nebraska:
Lieut. Col. William D. McCord
58th Ohio:
Col. Valentine Bausenwein
68th Ohio:
(not engaged at Shiloh; remained at Crump's Landing)
Col. Samuel H. Steadman
Third Brigade
Col. CHARLES WHITTLESEY, 20th Ohio
20th Ohio:
Lieut. Col. Manning F. Force
56th Ohio:
(not engaged at Shiloh; remained at Crump's Landing)
Col. Peter Kinney
76th Ohio:
Col. Charles R. Woods
78th Ohio:
Col. Mortimer D. Leggett
Artillery
Thompson's Battery, 9th Indiana Light Artillery,
Lieut. George R. Brown
Buel's Battery (I), 1st Missouri Light Artillery,
Lieut. Charles H. Thurber
Cavalry
3d Battalion, 11th Illinois Cavalry, Maj. James F. Johnson
(not engaged at Shiloh; remained at Crump's Landing)
3d Battalion, 5th Ohio Cavalry, Maj. Charles S. Hayes
(not engaged at Shiloh; remained at Crump's Landing)

FOURTH DIVISION
Brig. Gen. STEPHEN A. HURLBUT
First Brigade
Col. NELSON G. WILLIAMS (wounded), 3d Iowa
Col. ISAAC C. PUGH, 41st Illinois
28th Illinois:
Col. Amory K. Johnson
32d Illinois:
Col. John Logan (wounded)
41st Illinois:
Col. Isaac C. Pugh
Lieut. Col. Ansel Tupper (killed)
Maj. John Warner
Capt. John H. Nale
3d Iowa:
Maj. William M. Stone (captured)
Lieut. George W. Crosley
Second Brigade
Col. JAMES C. VEATCH, 25th Indiana
14th Illinois:
Col. Cyrus Hall
15th Illinois:
Lieut. Col. Edward F. W. Ellis (killed)
Capt. Louis D. Kelley
Lieut. Col. William Cam, 14th Illinois
46th Illinois:
Col. John A. Davis (wounded)
Lieut. Col. John J. Jones
25th Indiana:
Lieut. Col. William H. Morgan (wounded)
Maj. John W. Foster

Third Brigade
Brig. Gen. JACOB G. LAUMAN
31st Indiana:
Col. Charles Cruft (wounded)
Lieut. Col. John Osborn
44th Indiana:
Col. Hugh B. Reed
17th Kentucky:
Col. John H. McHenry, Jr.
25th Kentucky:
Lieut. Col. Benjamin H. Bristow
Maj. William B. Wall (wounded)
Capt. B. T. Underwood
Col. John H. McHenry, Jr., 17th Kentucky
Artillery
Ross's Battery, 2d Michigan Light Artillery,
Lieut. Cuthbert W. Laing
Mann's Battery (C), 1st Missouri Light Artillery,
Lieut. Edward Brotzmann
Myers's Battery, 13th Ohio Light Artillery,
Capt. John B. Myers
Cavalry
1st and 2d Battalions 5th Ohio Cavalry,
Col. William H. H. Taylor

FIFTH DIVISION
Brig. Gen. WILLIAM T. SHERMAN (wounded)
First Brigade
Col. JOHN A. McDOWELL (disabled), 6th Iowa
40th Illinois:
Col. Stephan G. Hicks (wounded)
Lieut. Col. James W. Boothe
6th Iowa:
Capt. John Williams (wounded)
Capt. Madison M. Walden
46th Ohio:
Col. Thomas Worthington
Second Brigade
Col. DAVID STUART (wounded), 55th Illinois
Lieut. Col. OSCAR MALMBORG, 55th Illinois
Col. T. KILBY SMITH, 54th Ohio
55th Illinois:
Lieut. Col. Oscar Malmborg
54th Ohio:
Col. T. Kilby Smith
Lieut. Col. James A. Farden
71st Ohio:
Col. Rodney Mason
Third Brigade
Col. JESSE HILDEBRAND, 77th Ohio
53d Ohio:
Col. Jesse J. Appler
Lieut. Col. Robert A. Fulton
57th Ohio:
Lieut. Col. Americus V. Rice
77th Ohio:
Lieut. Col. Willis De Hass
Maj. Benjamin D. Fearing
Fourth Brigade
Col. RALPH P. BUCKLAND, 72d Ohio
48th Ohio:
Col. Peter J. Sullivan (wounded)
Lieut. Col. Job R. Parker
70th Ohio:
Col. Joseph R. Cockerill
72d Ohio:
Lieut. Col. Herman Canfield (killed)
Col. Ralph P. Buckland

Artillery
Maj. EZRA TAYLOR, Chief of Artillery
Taylor's Battery (B), 1st Illinois Light Artillery,
Capt. Samuel E. Barrett
Waterhouse's Battery (E), 1st Illinois Light Artillery:
Capt. Allen C. Waterhouse (wounded)
Lieut. Abial R Abbott (wounded)
Lieut. John A. Fitch
Morton Battery, 6th Indiana Light Artillery,
Capt. Frederick Behr (killed)
Cavalry
2d and 3d Battalions 4th Illinois Cavalry,
Col. T. Lyle Dickey
Thielemann's two companies Illinois Cavalry,
Capt. Christian Thielemann

SIXTH DIVISION
Brig. Gen. BENJAMIN M. PRENTISS (captured)
First Brigade
Col. EVERETT PEABODY (killed), 25th Missouri
12th Michigan:
Col. Francis Quinn
21st Missouri:
Col. David Moore (wounded)
Lieut. Col. H. M. Woodyard
25th Missouri:
Lieut. Col. Robert T. Van Horn
16th Wisconsin:
Col. Benjamin Allen (wounded)
Second Brigade
Col. MADISON MILLER (captured), 18th Missouri
61st Illinois:
Col. Jacob Fry
18th Missouri:
Lieut. Col. Isaac V. Pratt (captured)
18th Wisconsin:
Col. James S. Alban (killed)
Not Brigaded
16th Iowa:
(15th and 16th Iowa were on right in an independent command)
Col. Alexander Chambers (wounded)
Lieut. Col. Addison H. Sanders
15th Iowa:
(15th and 16th Iowa were on right in an independent command)
Col. Hugh T. Reid (wounded)
23d Missouri:
(arrived on field about 9 o'clock April 6)
Col. Jacob T. Tindall (killed)
Lieut. Col. Quin Morton (captured)
Artillery
Hickenlooper's Battery, 5th Ohio Light Artillery,
Capt. Andrew Hickenlooper
Munch's Battery, 1st Minnesota Light Artillery,
Capt. Emil Munch (wounded)
Lieut. William Pfaender
Cavalry
1st and 2d Battalions, 11th Illinois Cavalry,
Col. Robert G. Ingersoll
Unassigned Troops
15th Michigan:
(temporarily attached Monday to Fourth Brigade, Army of the Ohio)
Col. John M. Oliver
14th Wisconsin:
(temporarily attached Monday to Fourteenth Brigade, Army of the Ohio)

Col. David E. Wood
Battery H, 1st Illinois Light Artillery,
Capt. Axel Silfversparre
Battery I, 1st Illinois Light Artillery, Capt. Edward Bouton
Battery B, 2d Illinois Artillery, siege guns, Capt. Relly Madison
Battery F, 2d Illinois Light Artillery, Capt. John W. Powell
(wounded)
8th Battery, Ohio Light Artillery, Capt. Louis Markgraf

ARMY OF THE OHIO
Maj. Gen. DON CARLOS BUELL, Commanding

SECOND DIVISION
Brig, Gen. ALEXANDER McD. McCOOK
Fourth Brigade
Brig. Gen. LOVELL H. ROUSSEAU
6th Indiana:
Col. Thomas T. Crittenden
5th Kentucky:
Col. Harvey M. Buckley
1st Ohio:
Col. Benjamin F. Smith
1st Battalion, 15th United States:
Capt. Peter T. Swain, Maj. John H. King
1st Battalion, 16th United States:
Capt. Edwin F. Townsend, Maj. John H. King
1st Battalion, 19th United States:
Maj. Stephen D. Carpenter, Maj. John H. King
Fifth Brigade
Col. EDWARD N. KIRK (wounded), 34th Illinois
34th Illinois:
Maj. Charles N. Levanway (killed)
Capt. Hiram W. Bristol
29th Indiana:
Lieut. Col. David M. Dunn
30th Indiana:
Col. Sion S. Bass (mortally wounded)
Lieut. Col. Joseph B. Dodge
77th Pennsylvania:
Col. Frederick S. Stumbaugh
Sixth Brigade
Col. WILLIAM H. GIBSON, 40th Ohio
32d Indiana:
Col. August Willich
39th Indiana:
Col. Thomas J. Harrison
15th Ohio:
Maj. William Wallace
49th Ohio:
Lieut. Col. Albert M. Blackman
Artillery
Terrill's Battery (H), 5th United States Artillery,
Capt. William R. Terrill

FOURTH DIVISION
Brig. Gen. WILLIAM NELSON
Tenth Brigade
Col. JACOB AMMEN, 24th Ohio
36th Indiana:
Col. William Grose
6th Ohio:
Lieut. Col. Nicholas L. Anderson
24th Ohio:
Lieut. Col. Frederick C. Jones
Nineteenth Brigade
Col. WILLIAM B. HAZEN, 41st Ohio

9th Indiana:
Col. Gideon C. Moody
6th Kentucky:
Col. Walter C. Whitaker
41st Ohio:
Lieut. Col. George S. Mygatt
Twenty-second Brigade
Col. SANDERS D. BRUCE, 20th Kentucky
1st Kentucky:
Col. David A. Enyart
2d Kentucky:
Col. Thomas D. Sedgewick
20th Kentucky:
Lieut. Col. Charles S. Hanson

FIFTH DIVISION
Brig. Gen. THOMAS L. CRITTENDEN
Eleventh Brigade
Brig. Gen. JEREMIAH T. BOYLE
9th Kentucky, Col. Benjamin C. Grider
13th Kentucky, Col. Edward H. Hobson
19th Ohio, Col. Samuel Beatty
59th Ohio, Col. James P. Fyffe
Fourteenth Brigade
Col. WILLIAM SOOY SMITH, 13th Ohio
11th Kentucky:
Col. Pierce B. Hawkins
26th Kentucky:
Lieut. Col. Cicero Maxwell
13th Ohio:
Lieut. Col. Joseph G. Hawkins
Artillery
Bartlett's Battery (G), 1st Ohio Light Artillery,
Capt. Joseph Bartlett
Mendenhall's Batteries (H and M), 4th United States
Artillery, Capt. John Mendenhall

SIXTH DIVISION
Brig. Gen. THOMAS J. WOOD
(This division arrived upon the field about 2 o'clock on
Monday. Wagner's brigade reached the front and became
engaged, the 57th Indiana losing four men wounded.)
Twentieth Brigade
Brig. Gen. JAMES A. GARFIELD
13th Michigan:
Col. Michael Shoemaker
64th Ohio:
Col. John Ferguson
65th Ohio:
Col. Charles G. Harker
Twenty-first Brigade
Col. GEORGE D. WAGNER, 15th Indiana
15th Indiana:
Lieut. Col. Gustavus A. Wood
40th Indiana:
Col. John W. Blake
57th Indiana:
Col. Cyrus C. Hines
24th Kentucky:
Col. Lewis B. Grigsby

**ORGANIZATION OF THE CONFEDERATE
ARMY AT THE BATTLE OF SHILOH,
TENNESSEE, APRIL 6-7, 1862**

ARMY OF THE MISSISSIPPI
Gen. ALBERT SIDNEY JOHNSTON (killed)
Gen. G. T. BEAUREGARD

FIRST ARMY CORPS
Maj. Gen. LEONIDAS POLK

FIRST DIVISION
Brig. Gen. CHARLES CLARK (wounded)
Brig. Gen. ALEXANDER P. STEWART
First Brigade
Col. ROBERT M. RUSSELL, 12th Tennessee
11th Louisiana:
Col. Samuel F. Marks (wounded)
Lieut. Col. Robert H. Barrow
12th Tennessee:
Lieut. Col. Tyree H. Bell
Maj. Robert P. Caldwell
13th Tennessee:
Col. Alfred J. Vaughan, Jr.
22d Tennessee:
Col. Thomas J. Freeman (wounded)
Tennessee Battery, Capt. Smith P. Bankhead
Second Brigade
Brig. Gen. ALEXANDER P. STEWART
13th Arkansas:
Lieut. Col. A. D. Grayson (killed)
Maj. James A. McNeely (wounded)
Col. James C. Tappan
4th Tennessee:
Col. Rufus P. Neely
Lieut. Col. Otho F. Strahl
5th Tennessee:
Lieut. Col. Calvin D. Venable
33d Tennessee:
Col. Alexander W. Campbell (wounded)
Mississippi Battery, Capt. Thomas J. Stanford

SECOND DIVISION
Maj. Gen. BENJAMIN F. CHEATHAM (wounded)
First Brigade
Brig. Gen. BUSHROD R. JOHNSON (wounded)
Col. PRESTON SMITH, 154th Tennessee (wounded)
Blythe's Mississippi:
Col. A. K. Blythe (killed)
Lieut. Col. David L. Herron (killed)
Maj. James Moore
2d Tennessee:
Col. J. Knox Walker
15th Tennessee:
Lieut. Col. Robert C. Tyler (wounded)
Maj. John F. Hearn
154th Tennessee (senior):
Col. Preston Smith
Lieut. Col. Marcus J. Wright (wounded)
Tennessee Battery, Capt. Marshall T. Polk (wounded)
Second Brigade
Col. WILLIAM H. STEPHENS, 6th Tennessee
Col. GEORGE MANEY, 1st Tennessee
7th Kentucky:
Col. Charles Wickliffe (mortally wounded)
Lieut. Col. William D. Lannom
1st Tennessee (Battalion):
Col. George Maney
Maj. Hume R. Field
6th Tennessee:
Lieut. Col. Timothy P. Jones
9th Tennessee:
Col. Henry L. Douglass
Mississippi Battery, Capt. Melancthon Smith
Cavalry
1st Mississippi, Col. Andrew J. Lindsay

Mississippi and Alabama Battalion,
Lieut. Col. Richard H. Brewer
Unattached
47th Tennessee, Col. Munson R. Hill
(arrived on field April 7)

SECOND ARMY CORPS
Maj. Gen. BRAXTON BRAGG
Escort
Company Alabama Cavalry, Capt. Robert W. Smith

FIRST DIVISION
Brig. Gen. DANIEL RUGGLES
First Brigade
Col. RANDALL L. GIBSON, 13th Louisiana
1st Arkansas, Col. James F. Fagan
4th Louisiana:
Col. Henry W. Allen (wounded)
Lieut. Col. Samuel E. Hunter
13th Louisiana:
Maj. Anatole P. Avegno (mortally wounded)
Capt. Stephen O'Leary (wounded)
Capt. Edgar M. Dubroca
19th Louisiana:
Col. Benjamin L. Hodge
Lieut. Col. James M. Hollingsworth
Vaiden, or Bain's, Mississippi Battery,
Capt. S. C. Bain
Second Brigade
Brig. Gen. PATTON ANDERSON
1st Florida Battalion:
Maj. Thaddeus A. McDonell (wounded)
Capt. W. G. Poole
Capt. W. Capers Bird
17th Louisiana:
Lieut. Col. Charles Jones (wounded)
20th Louisiana:
Col. August Reichard
Confederate Guards Response Battalion,
Maj. Franklin H. Clack
9th Texas:
Col. Wright A. Stanley
Washington (Louisiana) Artillery, Fifth Company,
Capt. W. Irving Hodgson
Third Brigade
Col. PRESTON POND, Jr., 16th Louisiana
16th Louisiana:
Maj. Daniel Gober
18th Louisiana:
Col. Alfred Mouton (wounded)
Lieut. Col. Alfred Roman.
Crescent (Louisiana) Regiment:
Col. Marshall J. Smith
Orleans Guard (Louisiana) Battalion:
Maj. Leon Querouze (wounded)
38th Tennessee:
Col. Robert F. Looney
Ketchum's Alabama Battery, Capt. William H. Ketchum
Cavalry
Alabama Battalion (5 companies—Jenkins, Cox, Robins,
Tomlinson, and Smith)
Capt. Thomas F. Jenkins

SECOND DIVISION
Brig. Gen. JONES M. WITHERS
First Brigade
Brig. Gen. ADLEY H. GLADDEN (mortally wounded)
Col. DANIEL W. ADAMS (wounded), 22d Alabama

21st Alabama:
Lieut. Col. Stewart W. Cayce
Maj. Frederick Stewart
22d Alabama:
Col. Zach C. Deas
Lieut. Col. John C. Marrast
25th Alabama:
Col. John Q. Loomis (wounded)
Maj. George D. Johnston
26th Alabama:
Lieut. Col. John G. Coltart (wounded)
Lieut. Col. William D. Chadick
1st Louisiana:
Col. Daniel W. Adams
Maj. Fred H. Farrar, jr.
Robertson's, Alabama, Battery, Capt. Felix H. Robertson
Second Brigade
Brig. Gen. JAMES R. CHALMERS
5th Mississippi:
Col. Albert E. Fant
7th Mississippi:
Lieut. Col. Hamilton Mayson
9th Mississippi:
Lieut. Col. William A. Rankin (mortally wounded)
10th Mississippi:
Col. Robert A. Smith
52d Tennessee:
Col. Benjamin J. Lea
Gage's Alabama Battery, Capt. Charles P. Gage
Third Brigade
Brig. Gen. JOHN K. JACKSON
17th Alabama:
Lieut. Col. Robert C. Fariss
18th Alabama:
Col. Eli S. Shorter
19th Alabama:
Col. Joseph Wheeler
2d Texas:
Col. John C. Moore
Lieut. Col. William P. Rogers
Maj. Hal G. Runnels
Girardey's Georgia Battery, Capt. Isadore P. Girardey
Cavalry
Clanton's Alabama Regiment, Col. James H. Clanton
(wounded)

THIRD ARMY CORPS
Maj. Gen. WILLIAM J. HARDEE (wounded)
First Brigade
Brig. Gen. THOMAS C. HINDMAN (disabled),
commanding his own and Third Brigade
Col. R. G. SHAVER, 7th Arkansas (disabled)
2d Arkansas:
Col. Daniel C. Govan
Maj. Reuben F. Harvey
6th Arkansas:
Col. Alexander T. Hawthorn
7th Arkansas:
Lieut. Col. John M. Dean (killed)
Maj. James T. Martin
3d Confederate:
Col. John S. Marmaduke
Warren Light Artillery, or Swett's Mississippi Battery,
Capt. Charles Swett
Pillow's Flying Artillery, or Miller's Tennessee Battery,
Capt. —— Miller
Second Brigade
Brig. Gen. PATRICK R. CLEBURNE

15th Arkansas:
Lieut. Col. Archibald K. Patton (killed)
6th Mississippi:
Col. John J. Thornton (wounded)
Lieut. Col. W. A. Harper
2d Tennessee:
Col. William B. Bate (wounded)
Lieut. Col. David L. Goodall
5th (35th) Tennessee:
Col. Benjamin J. Hill
23d Tennessee:
Lieut. Col. James F. Neill (wounded)
Maj. Robert Cantrell
24th Tennessee:
Lieut. Col. Thomas H. Peebles
Shoup's Battalion
Trigg's (Austin) Arkansas Battery, Capt. John T. Trigg
Calvert's (Helena) Arkansas Battery, Capt. J. H. Calvert
Hubbard's Arkansas Battery, Capt. George T. Hubbard
Third Brigade
Brig. Gen. STERLING A. M. WOOD (disabled)
Col. WILLIAM K. PATTERSON, 8th Arkansas,
temporarily
16th Alabama:
Lieut. Col. John W. Harris
8th Arkansas:
Col. William K. Patterson
9th (14th) Arkansas (battalion):
Maj. John H. Kelly
3d Mississippi Battalion:
Maj. Aaron B. Hardcastle
27th Tennessee:
Col. Christopher H. Williams (killed)
Maj. Samuel T. Love (killed)
44th Tennessee:
Col. Coleman A. McDaniel
55th Tennessee:
Col. James L. McKoin
Harper's (Jefferson, Mississippi) Battery:
Capt. William L. Harper (wounded)
Lieut. Put Darden
Georgia Dragoons, Capt. Isaac W. Avery

RESERVE CORPS
Brig. Gen. JOHN C. BRECKINRIDGE
First Brigade
Col. ROBERT P. TRABUE, 4th Kentucky
(Clifton's) 4th Alabama Battalion:
Maj. James M. Clifton
31st Alabama:
Lieut. Col. Montgomery Gilbreath
3d Kentucky:
Lieut. Col. Benjamin Anderson (wounded)
4th Kentucky:
Lieut. Col. Andrew R. Hynes (wounded)
5th Kentucky:
Lieut. Col. Thomas H. Hunt
6th Kentucky:
Col. Joseph H. Lewis
Crew's Tennessee Battalion:
Lieut. Col. James M. Crews
Lyon's (Cobb's) Kentucky Battery, Capt. Robert Cobb
Byrne's Mississippi Battery, Capt. Edward P. Byrne
Morgan's Squadron, Kentucky Cavalry,
Capt. John H. Morgan
Second Brigade
Brig. Gen. JOHN S. BOWEN (wounded)
Col. JOHN D. MARTIN

9th Arkansas:
Col. Isaac L. Dunlop
10th Arkansas:
Col. Thomas H. Merrick
2d Confederate:
Col. John D. Martin
Maj. Thomas H. Mangum
1st Missouri:
Col. Lucius L. Rich
Pettus Flying Artillery, or Hudson's Mississippi Battery,
Capt. Alfred Hudson
Watson's Louisiana, Battery, ———.
Thompson's Company, Kentucky Cavalry,
Capt. Phil. B. Thompson
Third Brigade
Col. WINFIELD S. STATHAM, 15th Mississippi
15th Mississippi
22d Mississippi
19th Tennessee:
Col. David H. Cummings
20th Tennessee:
Col. Joel A. Battle (captured)
28th Tennessee
45th Tennessee:
Lieut. Col. Ephraim F. Lytle
Rutledge's Tennessee, Battery, Capt. Arthur M. Rutledge
Forrest's Regiment Tennessee Cavalry,
Col. Nathan B. Forrest (wounded)
Unattached
Wharton's Texas Regiment Cavalry, Col. John A. Warton (wounded)
Wirt Adams's Mississippi Regiment Cavalry,
Col. Wirt Adams
McClung's, Tennessee, Battery, Capt. Hugh L. W. McClung
Roberts Arkansas Battery

Commanding and Staff Officers
DEPARTMENT OF MISSISSIPPI
Maj. Gen. H. W. Halleck, commanding
Brig. Gen. Geo. W. Cullum, Chief of Staff
Capt. N. H. McLean, assistant adjutant-general
Capt. J. C. Kelton, assistant adjutant-general
Capt. P. M. Preston, assistant adjutant-general
Col. Richard D. Cutts, aid-de-camp
Capt. C. B. Throckmorton, aid-de-camp
Lieut. J. T. Price, aid-de-camp
Lieut. D. C. Wagner, aid-de-camp
Lieut. A. Backer, aid-de-camp
Brig. Gen. A. J. Smith, Chief of Cavalry
Col. J. V. D. Du Bois, Chief of Artillery
Col. George Thom, Chief of Engineers
Lieut. Col. J. B. McPherson, assistant chief of engineers
Col. J. C. McKibbin, Judge-Advocate
Maj. Robert Allen, Chief Quartermaster
Maj. T. J. Haines, Chief Commissary of Subsistence
Surg. J. J. B. Wright, Medical Director
Brig. Gen. W. Scott Ketchum, Inspector-General

ARMY OF THE TENNESSEE
Maj. Gen. U. S. Grant, commanding
Col. J. D. Webster, Chief of Staff
Capt. J. A. Rawlins, assistant adjutant general
Capt. W. S. Hillyer, aid-de-camp
Capt. W. R. Rowley, aid-de-camp
Capt. C. B. Lagow, aid-de-camp
Lieut. Col. J. B. McPherson, Chief of Engineers
Lieut. W. L. B. Jenney, assistant chief of engineers

Lieur. Wm. Kossak, assistant chief of engineers
Capt. J. P. Hawkins, Chief Commissary of Subsistence
Surg. Henry S. Hewitt, Medical Director
Col. G. G. Pride, volunteer aid

FIRST DIVISION
Maj. Gen John A. McClernand, commanding
Maj. Adolph Schwartz, (wounded) 2d Illinois Artillery, Chief of Staff
Maj. M. Brayman, acting assistant adjutant-general
Capt. Warren Stewart, (wounded) Illinois cavalry, aid-de-camp
Lieut. Henry C. Freeman, (wounded) aid-de-camp
Lieut. Jos. E. Hitt, 4th Illinois Cavalry, aid-de-camp
Lieut. A. B. Hall, 4th Illinois Cavalry, aid-de-camp
Lieut. S. R. Tresilian, assistant engineer
Lieut. Erastus S. Jones, ordnance officer
First Brigade
Col. Abraham M. Hare, (wounded) 11th Iowa, commanding
Lieut. and Adjt. Cornelius Cadle, Jr. 11th Iowa, acting assistant adjutant-general
Lieut. Samuel Caldwell, 8th Illinois, volunteer aid
Second Brigade
Col. C. C. Marsh, 20th Illinois, commanding
Lieut. E. P. Boas, acting assistant adjutant-general
Adjt. J. E. Thompson, (killed) 20th Illinois aid-de-camp
Capt. G. W. Kennard, acting assistant quartermaster
Surg. Christopher Goodbrake, brigade surgeon
Third Brigade
Col. Julius Raith, 43d Illinois, commanding
Lieut. Abraham H. Ryan, acting assistant adjutant-general

SECOND DIVISON
Brig. Gen. W. H. L. Wallace (killed) commanding
Capt. Wm. McMichael, (captured) assistant adjutant-general
Capt. T. J. Newham, aid-de-camp
Lieut. Cyrus E. Dickey, aid-de-camp
Lieut. Guyton I. Davis, 11th Illinois, aid-de-camp
Lieut. I. P. Rumsey, Taylor's Battery, aid-de-camp
First Brigade
Col. James M. Tuttle, 2d Iowa, commanding
Lieut. Jas. P. Sample, 7th Iowa, acting assistant adjutant-general
Second Brigade
Brig. Gen. John McArthur, (wounded) commanding
Lieut. Geo. L. Paddock, acting assistant adjutant-general
Lieut. George Mason, 12th Illinois, aid-de-camp
Third Brigade
Col. Thos. W. Sweeny, 52d Illinois, commanding
Lieutenant and Adjutant ——— Allen, 52d Illinois, acting assistant adjutant-general
Lieut. Wm. McCullough, 8th Iowa, aid-de-camp

THIRD DIVISION
Maj. Gen. Lewis Wallace, commanding
Capt. Frederick Knefler, assistant adjutant-general
Lieut. Addison W. Ware, aid-de-camp
Capt. E. T. Wallace, 11th Indiana, aid-de-camp
Lieut. John W. Ross, aid-de-camp
First Brigade
Col. Morgan L. Smith, 8th Missouri, commanding
Lieut. D. C. Coleman, acting assistant adjutant-general
Second Brigade
Col. John M. Thayer, 1st Nebraska, commanding
Lieut. S. A. Strickland, acting assistant adjutant-general
Capt. Allen Blacker, aid-de-camp
Lieut. William S. Whittin, aid-de-camp

Lieut. Col. Robt. K. Scott, 68th Ohio, volunteer aid
Capt. Lewis Y. Richards, 68th Ohio, volunteer aid
Mr. Geo. E. Spencer, volunteer aid
Third Brigade
Col. Charles Whittlesey, 20th Ohio, commanding
E. N. Owens, acting assistant adjutant-general

FOURTH DIVISION
Brig. Gen. Stephen A. Hurlbut, commanding
Capt. Smith D. Atkins, acting assistant adjutant-general
Lieut. J. C. Long, 9th U.S. Infantry, aid-de-camp
Capt. S. Simmons, acting commissary of subsistence
Surg. A. G. Keenan, Medical Director
Lieut. W. H. Dorchester, volunteer aid
First Brigade
Col. N. G. Williams, (wounded) 3d Iowa, commanding
Lieut. F. Sessions, acting assistant adjutant-general
Second Brigade
Col. James C. Veatch, 25th Indiana, commanding
Capt. F. W. Fox, 14th Illinois,
acting assistant adjutant-general
Lieutenant ——— Brunner, 25th Indiana, aid-de-camp
Surg. John T. Walker, brigade surgeon
Third Brigade
Brig. Gen. Jacob C. Veatch, 25th Indiana, commanding
Lieut. H. Scofield, (wounded)
acting assistant adjutant-general
Lieut. T. N. Barnes, aid-de-camp

FIFTH DIVISION
Brig. Gen. Wm. T. Sherman, (wounded) commanding
Capt. J. H. Hammond, assistant adjutant-general
Maj. W. D. Sanger, volunteer aid
Lieut. John Taylor, 5th Ohio, aid-de-camp
Lieut. W. D. Strong, assistant quartermaster
Lieut. J. C. McCoy, 54th Ohio, aid-de-camp
Maj. Ezra Taylor, chief of artillery
Capt. C. A. Morton, 32d Illinois,
acting commissary of subsistence
Surg. D. W. Hartshorn, Medical Director
Asst. Surg. Saml. L'Hommedieu, assistant medical director
Lieut. Wm. Kossak, engineer
First Brigade
Col. J. A. McDowell, 6th Iowa, commanding
Lieut. Byron K. Cowles, 6th Iowa, acting assistant
adjutant-general (absent)
Capt. Willard H. Harland, 6th Iowa, aid-de-camp
Second Brigade
Col. David Stuart, (wounded) 55th Illinois, commanding
Adjt. Charles Loomis, aid-de-camp
Third Brigade
Col. Jesse Hildebrand, 77th Ohio, commanding
Lieut. S. S. McNaughton, acting assistant adjutant-general
Fourth Brigade
Col. Ralph P. Buckland, 72d Ohio, commanding
Lieut. Eugene A. Rawson, 72d Ohio,
acting assistant adjutant-general
John B. Rice, surgeon
Lieut. D. M. Harkness, 72d Ohio, quartermaster

SIXTH DIVISION
Brig. Gen. Benj. M. Prentiss, (captured) commanding
Capt. Henry Binmore, assistant adjutant-general
Lieut. Edwin Moore, aid-de-camp
Surg. S. W. Everett, division surgeon
First Brigade
Col. Everett Peabody, (killed) 25th Missouri, commanding
Capt. Geo. K. Donnelly, assistant adjutant-general

Second Brigade
Col. Madison Miller, (captured) 18th Missouri,
commanding

ARMY OF THE OHIO
Maj. Gen. Don Carlos Buell, commanding
Col. James B. Fry, Chief of Staff
Capt. J. M. Wright, assistant adjutant-general
Lieut. A. F. Rockwell, aid-de-camp
Lieut. C. L. Fitzhugh, 4th U.S. Artillery. aid-de-camp
Lieut. T. J. Bush, 24th Kentucky, aid-de-camp
Capt. J. H. Gilmore, 19th U.S., Inspector of Artillery
Capt. E. Gay, 16th U. S., Inspector of Cavalry
Capt. H. C. Bankhead, 5th U.S., Inspector of Infantry
Capt., Nathaniel Michler, engineer
Surg. Robt. Murray, U.S.A., Medical Director

SECOND DIVISION
Brig. Gen. Alex. McD. McCook, commanding
Capt. Daniel McCook, assistant adjutant-general
Lieut. S. W. Davies, aid-de-camp
Lieut. W. T. Hoblitzell, aid-de-camp
Lieut. W. F. Staub, aid-de-camp
Capt. Orris Blake, provost-marshal
Capt. J. D. Williams, acting commissary of subsistence
Lieut. J. A. Campbell, ordnance officer
Surg. A. P. Meylert, Medical Director
Fourth Brigade
Brig. Gen. Lovell H. Rousseau, commanding
Lieut. D. Armstrong, acting assistant adjutant-general
Lieut. David Q. Rousseau, aid-de-camp
Lieut. John D. Wicklife, 2d Kentucky Cavalry, aid-de-camp
Capt. W. M. Carpenter, assistant quartermaster
Mr. E. F. Jewett, volunteer aid
Fifth Brigade
Col Edward N. Kirk, (wounded) 34th Illinois,
commanding
Capt. S. T. Davis, 77th Pennsylvania, acting assistant
adjutant-general
Capt. Abraham Beehler, 34th Illinois, aid-de-camp
Lieut. S. B. Dexter, 34th Illinois, aid-de-camp
Sixth Brigade
Col. W. H. Gibson, 49th Ohio, commanding
Capt. Henry Clay, assistant adjutant-general
Lieut. Wm. C. Turner, aid-de-camp
Lieut. E. A. Otis, aid-de-camp
Surg. S. W. Gross, brigade surgeon

FOURTH DIVISON
Brig. Gen. William Nelson, commanding
Capt. J. Mills Kendrick, U.S. Volunteers, assistant
adjutant-general
Lieut. Wm. P. Anderson, 6th Ohio, aid-de-camp
Lieut. Richard Southgate, 6th Ohio, aid-de-camp
W. Preston Graves, volunteer aid
Horace N. Fisher, volunteer aid
Capt. J. G. Chandler, U.S. Army, assistant quartermaster
Lieut. C. C. Peck, 6th Ohio, acting commissary of
subsistence
Lieut. Chas. C. Horton, 24th Ohio, ordnance of
subsistence
Capt. and Assr. Surg. B. J. D. Irwin, U.S. Army,
Medical Director
Tenth Brigade
Col. Jacob Ammen, 24th Ohio, commanding
Lieut. R. F. Wheeler, aid-de-camp

Nineteenth Brigade
Col. Wm. B. Hazen, 41st Ohio, commanding
Lieut. Robt. L. Kimberly, acting assistant adjutant-general
Lieut. Chas. D. Gaylord, aid-de-camp
Lieut. Wm. M. Beebe, Jr., aid-de-camp
Twenty-second Brigade
Col. Sanders D. Bruce, 20th Kentucky, commanding
Lieut. S. T. Corn, acting assistant adjutant-general
Lieut. Wickliffe Cooper, aid-de-camp

FIFTH DIVISION
Brig. Gen. Thos. L. Crittenden, commanding
Capt. Lyne Starling, assistant adjutant-general
Lieut. Louis M. Buford, aid-de-camp
Surg. Middleton Goldsmith, Medical Director
Eleventh Brigade
Brig. Gen. J. T. Boyle, commanding
Capt. John Boyle, assistant adjutant-general
Lieut. H. Q. Hughes, aid-de-camp
Lieut. H. T. Liggett, aid-de-camp
Lieut. John T. Farris, acting assistant quartermaster
Fourteenth Brigade
Col. Wm. Sooy Smith, 13th Ohio, commanding
Lieut. Frank J. Jones, 13th Ohio, acting assistant
adjutant-general
Lieut. R. E. Hackett, 26th Kentucky, aid-de-camp

SIXTH DIVISION
Brig. Gen. Thos. J. Wood, commanding
Capt. Wm. H. Schalter, assistant adjutant-general
Capt. Geo. W. Lennard, 36th Indiana, aid-de-camp
Capt. Fred A. Clark, 29th Indiana, aid-de-camp
Lieut. Col. Isaac Gass, 64th Ohio, inspector-general
Lieut. Clark S. Gregg, 65th Ohio, acting commissary
of subsistence
Lieut. Frank B. Hunt, 65th Ohio, ordnance officer
Lieut. John C. Martin, 21st Ohio, signal officer
Surg. Francis B. Mussy, Medical Director
Twentieth Brigade
Brig. Gen. James A. Garfield, commanding
Twenty-first Brigade
Col. Geo. D. Wagner, 15th Indiana, commanding

CONFEDERATE ARMY
Gen. Albert Sidney Johnston, (killed) commanding
Maj. Gen. Braxton Bragg, Chief of Staff
Capt. H. P. Brewster, assistant adjutant-general
Capt. N. Wickliffe, assistant adjutant-general
Lieut. George Baylor, aid-de-camp
Lieut. Thomas M. Jack, aid-de-camp
Governor Isham G. Harris, volunteer aid
Col. Wm. Preston, volunteer aid
Maj. D. M. Hayden, volunteer aid
Dr. E. W. Munford, volunteer aid
Calhoun Benham, volunteer aid
Capt. Theodore O'Hara, assistant inspector-general
Maj. Albert J. Smith, assistant quartermaster
Capt. W. L. Wickham, assistant quartermaster
Col. J. F. Gilmer, (wounded) Chief Engineer
Surg D. W. Yandell, Medical Director
Gen. G. T. BEAUREGARD, second in command,
commanding, Monday
Col. Thomas Jordan, assistant adjutant-general
Lieut. John W. Otey, assistant adjutant-general
Lieut. Col. S. W. Ferguson, aid-de-camp
Brig. Gen. James Trudeau, volunteer aid
Capt. W. W. Porter, volunteer aid
Maj. Geo. W. Brent, assistant inspector-general

Col. R. B. Lee, Chief of Subsistence
Capt. Clifton H. Smith, assistant adjutant-general
Col. Jacob Thompson, volunteer aid
Maj. Numa Augustine, volunteer aid
Maj. H. E. Peyton, volunteer aid
Capt. Albert Ferry, volunteer aid
Capt. B. B. Waddell, volunteer aid
Capt. E. H. Cummins, Signal Officer

FIRST CORPS
Maj. Gen. Leonidas Polk, commanding
Maj. Geo. Williamson, (wounded)
assistant adjutant-general
Lieut. W. B. Richmond, aid-de-camp
Lieut. A. H. Polk, aid-de-camp
Lieut. P. B. Spence, aid-de-camp
Lieut. John Rawle, aid-de-camp
Lieut. John S. Lanier, aid-de-camp
Lieut. Col. E. D. Blake, assistant inspector-general
Maj. Smith P. Bankhead, Chief of Artillery
Capt. J. T. Champney, Chief of Ordnance
Maj. Thomas Peters, assistant quartermaster
Surg W. D. Lyles, Medical Director
Lieut. W. M. Porter, volunteer aid

FIRST DIVISION
Brig. Gen. Charles Clark, (wounded) commanding
Capt. W. H. McCardle, assistant adjutant-general
Lieut. Wm. Yerger, Jr., aid-de-camp
Maj. W. H. Haynes, (wounded) acting commissary of
subsistence
James E. McClure, assistant quartermaster
Maj. Howell Hinds, assistant adjutant-general, Army of
Potomac, volunteer aid
Maj. W. M. Inge, assistant adjutant-general, Army of
Potomac, volunteer aid
Capt. John A. Buckner, 8th Kentucky, volunteer aid
First Brigade
Col. R. M. Russell, 12th Tennessee, commanding
Second Brigade
Brig. Gen. A. P. Stewart, commanding
Capt. Thomas W. Preston, (killed) assistant adjutant-general
Lieut. N. Green, Jr., aid-de-camp
Col. W. B. Ross, volunteer aid
Mr. Joseph D. Cross, volunteer aid

SECOND DIVISION
Maj. Gen. B. F. Cheatham, (wounded) commanding
Maj. James D. Porter, assistant adjutant-general
Capt. F. H. McNairy, aid-de-camp
Capt. T. F. Henry, aid-de-camp
A. L. Robertson, aid-de-camp
John Campbell, (killed) aid-de-camp
Judge Archibald Wright, volunteer aid
Col. Edward Pickett, Jr., 21st Tennessee, volunteer aid
Capt. Wm. Roundtree, volunteer aid
First Brigade
Brig. Gen. B. R. Johnson, (wounded) commanding
Maj. G. G. Rogers, assistant adjutant-general
Capt. Wm. T. Blakemore, aid-de-camp
Capt. D. L. Moore, volunteer aid
Capt. John H. Anderson, (wounded) 10th Tennessee,
volunteer aid
Second Brigade
Col. Wm. H. Stephens, 6th Tennessee, commanding
Lieut. Isaac M. Jackson, (mortally wounded)
assistant adjutant-general

Wm. D. Stephens, (wounded) aid-de-camp
Thos. A. Henderson, (wounded) aid-de-camp
Capt. A. L. Swingley, volunteer aid

SECOND ARMY CORPS

Maj. Gen. Braxton Bragg, commanding
Maj. George G. Garner, assistant adjutant-general
Capt. H. W. Walter, assistant adjutant-general
Capt. G. B. Cooke, assistant adjutant-general
Lieut. Towson Ellis, aid-de-camp
Lieut. F. S. Parker, aid-de-camp
Lieut. Col. F. Gardner, C. S. Army, assistant inspector-general
Lieut. Col. W. K. Beard, (wounded) Florida Volunteers, assisant inspector-general
Capt. S. H. Lockett, Chief Engineer
Maj. J. H. Hallonquist, Chief of Artillery
Capt. W. O. Williams, assistant chief of artillery
Capt. H. Oladowski, Chief of Ordnance
Maj. J. J. Walker, Chief of Subsistence
Maj. L. F. Johnston, Chief Quartermaster
Maj. O. P. Chaffee, assistant quartermaster
Surg. A. J. Foard, Medical Director
Surg. J. C. Nott, Medical Inspector
Lieut. Col. David Urquhart, volunteer aid

FIRST DIVISION

Brig. Gen. Daniel Ruggles, commanding
Capt. Roy M. Hooe, assistant adjutant-general
Lieut. M. B. Ruggles, aid-de-camp
Maj. E. S. Ruggles, (wounded) volunteer aid
Capt. G. M. Beck, volunteer aid
Col. S. S. Heard, 17th Louisiana, volunteer aid
Maj. J. H. Hallonquist, Chief of Artillery
Maj. John Claiborne, Chief Quartermaster
Lieut. L. D. Sandidge, assistant inspector-general
Surg. F. M. Hereford, (wounded) Medical Director
Dr. S. S. Sandidge, volunteer surgeon
First Brigade
Col. Randall L. Gibson, 13th Louisiana, commanding
Lieut. Benjamin King, (killed) aid-de-camp
Lieut. H. H. Bein, acting assistant adjutant-general
Mr. Robert Pugh, aid-de-camp
Second Brigade
Brig. Gen. Patton Anderson, commanding
Capt. William G. Barth, assistant adjutant-general
Lieut. Wm. M. Davidson, aid-de-camp
Lieut. John W. James, 5th Georgia, aid-de-camp
Capt. Henry D. Bulkley, acting commissary of subsistence
Capt. John T. Sibley, assistant quartermaster
Surg. C. B. Gamble, Medical Director
Lieut. Wm. McR. Jordan, (wounded) 1st Florida, aid-de-camp
Third Brigade
Col. Preston Pond, Jr. commanding
Lieut. O. O. Cobb, assistant adjutant-general

SECOND DIVISION

Brig. Gen. Jones M. Withers, commanding
Capt. D. E. Huger, assistant adjutant-general
Lieut. D. F. Withers, aid-de-camp
Lieut. B. M. Thomas, assistant inspector-general
R. W. Withers, volunteer aid
S. B. Howe, volunteer aid
Wm. Williamson, volunteer aid
L. E. Smith, volunteer aid
First Brigade
Brig. Gen. A. H. Gladden, (mortally wounded) commanding
Maj. C. D. Anderson, acting assistant adjutant-general

Adjt. Adolph Kent, 1st Louisiana, aid-de-camp
Adjt. John Stout, 25th Alabama, aid-de-camp
Adjt. Elias F. Travis, 22d Alabama, aid-de-camp
Sergt. Maj. ——— Nott, 22d Alabama, aid-de-camp
Second Brigade
Brig. Gen. James R. Chalmers, commanding
Capt. Henry Craft, assistant adjutant-general
Lieut. Geo. T. Banks, aid-de-camp
Lieut. W. T. Stricklin, 3d Mississippi, assistant inspector-general
Capt. R. S. Crumps, acting commissary of subsistence
Lieut. M. M. Shelley, volunteer aid
Mr. James Barr, volunteer aid
Third Brigade
Brig. Gen. John K. Jackson, commanding
Capt. J. B. Cummings, assistant adjutant-general

THIRD ARMY CORPS

Maj. Gen. Wm. J. Hardee, (wounded) commanding
Maj. W. D. Pickett, assistant adjutant-general
Lieut. Thomas W. Hunt, (wounded) aid-de-camp
Capt. William Clare, (wounded) aid-de-camp
Lieut. ——— Wilson, aid-de-camp
Capt. A. W. Clarkson, aid-de-camp
Maj. F. A. Shoup, Chief of Artillery
Lieut. Wm. Kearney, assistant inspector-general
Maj. L. O. Bridewell, Chief Quartermaster
Maj. W. E. Moore, Chief Commissary
Surg. G. W. Lawrence, Medical Director
Col. S. H. Perkins, volunteer aid
First Brigade
Col. R. G. SHAVER, 7th Arkansas, commanding
Second Brigade
Brig. Gen. P. R. Cleburne, commanding
Maj. J. K. Dixon, assistant adjutant and inspector-general
Third Brigade
Brig. Gen. S. A. M. Wood, (wounded) commanding
Lieut. Linus A. McClung, assistant adjutant-general
Lieut. H. C. Wood, aid-de-camp
Capt. Wm. Clare, (wounded) volunteer aid
Capt. Joshua Sledge, (wounded) volunteer aid
Capt. J. H. Coleman, volunteer aid
Mr. Frank Foster, volunteer aid
Lieut. S. Church, acting commissary of subsistence

RESERVE CORPS

Brig. Gen. John C. Breckinridge, commanding
First Brigade
Col. Robt. P. Trabue, 4th Kentucky, commanding
Joseph L. Robertson, assistant adjutant-general
Capt. Samuel Gray, volunteer aid
John Hooe, volunteer aid
Thomas B. Darragh, volunteer aid
Robt. W. McKee, volunteer aid
Charlton Morgan, (wounded) volunteer aid
Charles J. Maston, volunteer aid
Second Brigade
Brig. Gen. John S. Bowen, (wounded) commanding
Third Brigade
Col. Winfield S. Statham, 15th Mississippi, commanding.

Source: 1913 Report of the Shiloh National Military Park Commission

Index

Winston Groom is the author of 15 previous books, including *Vicksburg, 1863; Kearny's March; Patriotic Fire; Shrouds of Glory; Forrest Gump;* and *Conversations with the Enemy* (with Duncan Spencer), which was a Pulitzer Prize finalist. He lives with his wife and daughter in Point Clear, Alabama.

Map Sources

Western Theater of Operations, January–December, 1862

Interior Department, National Park Service. *The Civil War at a Glance.* U.S. Government Printing Office, 1995. Available online at http://nationalatlas.gov/articles/history/a_civilwar.html.

General sources

Daniel, Larry J. Shiloh: *The Battle That Changed the Civil War.* London: Touchstone, 1998.

Department of Military Art and Engineering, United States Military Academy, Brigadier General Vincent J. Esposito, comps. and eds. *The West Point Atlas of American Wars, Volume 1, 1689–1900.* New York: Frederick A. Praeger, 1959, 26–38.

National Park Service. History E-Library. Civil War Series: The Battle of Shiloh. Available online at http://www.nps.gov/history/history/online_books/civil_war_series/22/sec1.htm. Accessed December 2011.

Sneden, Robert Knox. Map, Battle of Pittsburg Landing or Shiloh: April 6th and 7th 1862. Available online at http://hdl.loc.gov/loc.ndlpcoop/gvhs01.vhs00314. Accessed December 2011.

———. Map showing position of Union Army at Pittsburg Landing before and after the battle 6th and 7th April 1862. Available online at http://hdl.loc.gov/loc.ndlpcoop/gvhs01.vhs00086. Accessed December 2011.

Consultant: Stacy D. Allen, Chief Park Ranger, Shiloh National Military Park

Illustrations Credits

1, Library of Congress, 3a07066; 2 (UP), National Archives and Records Administration, 200-S-CA-038; 2 (LO LE), Library of Congress, 06956; 2 (LO RT), Library of Congress, 19301; 3 (UP LE), National Archives and Records Administration, 111-B-4326;3 (UP RT), Library of Congress, 06577; 3 (LO LE), MOLLUS-MASS/USAMHI; 3 (LO RT), Library of Congress, 07370; 4 (UP LE), Library of Congress, 06378; 4 (UP RT), Library of Congress, 00934; 4 (LO LE), Library of Congress, 05688; 4 (LO RT), Abraham Lincoln Presidential Library & Museum; 5 (UP), Library of Congress, 04023; 5 (LO LE), Library of Congress, 23852; 5 (LO RT), National Archives and Records Administration, 111-B-1233; 6 (UP LE), Library of Congress, 3g07972; 6 (UP RT), Library of Congress, 06714; 6 (LO LE), Library of Congress, 3g07984; 6 (LO RT), Library of Congress, 04775; 7 (UP), Corbis; 7 (LO LE), Library of Congress, 3c28709; 7 (LO RT), Library of Congress, 02078; 8 (UP), From *The Photographic History of the Civil War* by Francis Trevelyan Miller, Volume 1, The Review of Reviews Co., New York, 1911; 8 (LO), Library of Congress, 3a09479; 9 (UP), Everett Collection/SuperStock; 9 (LO), From The Photographic History of the Civil War by Francis Trevelyan Miller, Volume 2, The Review of Reviews Co., New York, 1911; 10 (UP), Courtesy of the Smithsonian Institution Libraries, Washington, D.C.; 10 (LO), Library of Congress, 3b07180; 11 (UP LE), From History of the Swedes of Illinois by Ernst W. Olson, Part 1, The Engberg-Holmberg Publishing Company, Chicago, 1908; 11 (UP RT), Chicago Historical Society; 11 (LO LE), Prints and Photographs in the Clifton Waller Barrett Library of American Literature (Barrett Prints), Clifton Waller Barrett Library of American Literature, Special Collections, University of Virginia; 11 (LO CTR), Library of Congress, 3a47095; 11 (LO RT), Abraham Lincoln Presidential Library & Museum; 12 (UP), Library of Congress, 3b07177 and 3b07178; 12 (LO), Library of Congress, 04037; 13 (UP RT), Library of Congress, 3b47601; 13 (UP LE), Library of Congress, 04008; 13 (LO), Chicago Historical Society; 14 (UP LE), Library of Congress, 06191; 14 (UP RT), Library of Congress, 00082; 14 (LO), Shiloh National Military Park; 15, From *The Photographic History of the Civil War* by Francis Trevelyan Miller, Volume 1, The Review of Reviews Co., New York, 1911; 16 (UP), Shiloh National Military Park; 16 (LO), Shiloh National Military Park.